ARISTOTLE
III

LCL 400

ARISTOTLE

ON SOPHISTICAL REFUTATIONS
ON COMING-TO-BE AND PASSING-AWAY

TRANSLATED BY

E. S. FORSTER

ON THE COSMOS

TRANSLATED BY

D. J. FURLEY

HARVARD UNIVERSITY PRESS
CAMBRIDGE, MASSACHUSETTS
LONDON, ENGLAND

First published 1955
Reprinted 1965, 1978, 1992

ISBN 0-674-99441-8

*Printed in Great Britain by St Edmundsbury Press Ltd,
Bury St Edmunds, Suffolk, on acid-free paper.
Bound by Hunter & Foulis Ltd, Edinburgh, Scotland.*

CONTENTS

PREFATORY NOTE

PROFESSOR E. S. Forster completed his versions of *De Sophisticis Elenchis* and *De Generatione et Corruptione* before he died.   I have checked the proofs and added a brief index.

D. J. FURLEY

LONDON
January 1955

THE TRADITIONAL ORDER of the works of Aristotle as they appear since the edition of Immanuel Bekker (Berlin, 1831), and their division into volumes in this edition

THE TRADITIONAL ORDER

THE TRADITIONAL ORDER

THE TRADITIONAL ORDER

xii

DE SOPHISTICIS
ELENCHIS

INTRODUCTION

I. THE PLACE OF THE *TOPICA*
IN THE *ORGANON*

BOTH the *Topica* and the *De Sophisticis Elenchis* have always been regarded as genuine works of Aristotle. The two treatises are closely connected; the *De Sophisticis Elenchis* is an appendix to the *Topica* and its final section forms an epilogue to both treatises; indeed Aristotle himself seems sometimes to regard the two as forming a single work, since he twice quotes the *De Sophisticis Elenchis* under the title of the *Topica*.

It is generally admitted that what we call logic and Aristotle himself calls analytic was an early pre-occupation of the philosopher and a direct outcome of discussions on scientific method held in the Platonic Academy. Plato himself, however, never attempted a formal treatment of the subject and the theories put forward, for example, in the *Theaetetus*, *Sophist*, *Parmenides* and *Politicus* were never developed into a regular system. But while Aristotle's systematic treatment of the process of inference and, above all, his discovery of the syllogism owe little to Plato, it has been generally recognized that the Platonic dialogues contain some of the germs from which the Aristotelian system was afterwards developed; for

example, in the *Theaetetus* the doctrine of the categories is already implicit in the recognition of the abstract notions of substance, quality, quantity, relation, activity and passivity.

Of the logical treatises of Aristotle, which since about A.D. 200 have passed under the title of the *Organon* or ' instrument ' of science, the most important are (1) the *Prior Analytics*, in which he sets forth the doctrine of the syllogism in its formal aspect without reference to the subject-matter with which it deals, (2) the *Posterior Analytics*, in which he discusses the characteristics which reasoning must necessarily possess in order to be truly scientific, (3) the *Topica*, in which he treats of the modes of reasoning, which, while syllogistically correct, fall short of the conditions of scientific accuracy. The *Categories* and the *De Interpretatione* are subsidiary treatises dealing, in the main, with the term and the proposition.

A great deal of time and ingenuity has been expended, particularly by German scholars, in an attempt to fix the exact order in which the various treatises which constitute the *Organon* were composed. The problem is complicated by the fact that the treatises, in the form in which they have come down to us, seem to consist of rough notes, which were evidently subjected to a certain amount of revision due to the modification and development of his original doctrines. This process has naturally given rise to minor inconsistencies such as would naturally occur if corrections were made or additions inserted which were not completely adapted to the context in which they were placed.

It has been generally recognized that the whole

3

of the *Topica* does not belong to the same date. H. Maier [a] holds that the oldest portion consists of Books II-VII. 2 and that it was written under the direct influence of the Academy and belongs to the same period as the Aristotelian *Dialogues*, which have survived only in fragments ; in particular, he points out that the term συλλογισμός is not used in the technical sense which it afterwards acquired (or, if it is used in that sense, *e.g.*, in 130 a 7, it is a late insertion), whereas in the second half of Book VII the term is used in its well-known Aristotelian sense, and that, consequently, Books II-VII. 2 were composed before the philosopher made his greatest contribution to logic. He holds that Books I and VIII belong to the same period as Book VII. 4-5, and form an introduction and conclusion to the treatise written after the discovery of the syllogism and that the *De Sophisticis Elenchis* was a subsequent addition to the *Topica*. On the other hand, F. Solmsen [a] and P. Gohlke [a] hold that Books I-VII form the earlier portion of the work and that Book VIII and the *De Sophisticis Elenchis* were added subsequently.

As regards the relation of the *Topica* to the rest of the *Organon*, Maier considers the *Topica* as a whole to be earlier than the *Analytics* ; Solmsen suggests that the order was (1) *Topica* I-VII, (2) *Posterior Analytics* I, (3) *Topica* VIII and *De Sophisticis Elenchis*, (4) *Posterior Analytics* II, (5) *Prior Analytics* ; Gohlke holds that the traditional order of the two *Analytics* is correct, and that the *Topica* and *De Sophisticis Elenchis* presuppose the *Analytics*.

In short, there is general agreement that the bulk of the *Topica* embodies Aristotle's earliest contribu-

[a] See Bibliography.

tion to the systematic study of logic and that it was written in part before his discovery of the syllogism.

II. THE CONTENT OF THE *TOPICA*

The purpose of the *Topica* is, in the words of its author (100 a 18 ff.), ' to discover a method by which we shall be able to reason from generally accepted opinions about any problem set before us and shall ourselves, when sustaining an argument, avoid saying anything self-contradictory ' ; that is to say, it aims at enabling the two participants, the ' questioner ' and the ' answerer,' to sustain their parts in a dialectical discussion. The subject, then, of the treatise may be described as the dialectical syllogism based on premises which are merely probable as contrasted with the demonstrative, or scientific, syllogism, which is the subject of the *Posterior Analytics* and is based on premises which are true and immediate. The probable premises which make up the dialectical syllogism are described (100 b 21 f.) as ' those which commend themselves to all or to the majority or to the wise.' The uses of dialectic are, we are told, three in number, (1) for mental training, (2) for general conversation, and (3) for application to the sciences, because (*a*) if we can argue a question *pro* and *con*, we shall be in a better position to recognize truth and falsehood, and (*b*) since the first principles of the sciences cannot be scientifically demonstrated, the approach to them must be through the study of the opinions generally held about them.

After the general introduction in Book I, Aristotle, in Books II-VII. 3, gives a collection of the τόποι which

give their name to the treatise. The term τόποι is somewhat difficult to define. They may be described as ' commonplaces ' of argument or as general principles of probability which stand in the same relation to the dialectical syllogism as axioms stand to the demonstrative syllogism ; in other words, they are ' the pigeon-holes from which dialectical reasoning is to draw its arguments.' [a]

Books II and III deal with the problems of accident ; Books IV and V with those of genus and property ; Books VI and VII. 1-3 with those of definition. Books VII. 4-5 and Book VIII, after giving some additional notes, conclude the treatise by describing the practice of dialectical reasoning.

III. THE *DE SOPHISTICIS ELENCHIS*

Just as Aristotle treats of the demonstrative and the dialectical syllogism in the *Posterior Analytics* and the *Topica*, respectively, so in this treatise, which forms a kind of appendix to the *Topica*, he deals with the sophistical syllogism. A knowledge of this is part of the necessary equipment of the arguer, not in order that he may himself make use of it but that he may avoid it, and that the unwary may not be ensnared in the toils of sophistical argument ; in fact, Aristotle is carrying on the Socratic and early-Platonic tradition by attacking the Sophists, who taught the use of logical fallacy in order to make the worse cause appear the better.

The term ἔλεγχος is strictly applied to the confutation of an actual adversary, but it is also used more

[a] W. D. Ross, *Aristotle*, p. 59.

widely of the confutation of an imaginary opponent. The treatise is, in fact, a study of fallacies in general, which are classified under various headings and fall into two main classes, those which depend on the language employed and those which do not. Some of these fallacies would hardly deceive the most simple minds ; others, which Aristotle seems to have been the first person to expose and define, are capable not only of deceiving the innocent but also of escaping the notice of arguers who are employing them.

After two introductory chapters the work naturally falls into two parts, chapters 3-15, the refutation of fallacies, and chapters 16-33, the solution of fallacies, while chapter 34 forms an epilogue to the work.

IV. The Manuscripts

The chief manuscripts for the *Topica* and *De Sophisticis Elenchis* are :

A	Urbinas 35	saec. ix-x ineunt.
B	Marcianus 201	an. 955
C	Coislinianus 330	saec. xi
D	Coislinianus 170	saec. xiv
u	Basileensis F. 11.21	saec. xi-xii
C	Vaticanus 1024	' satis vetustus '
P	Vaticanus 207	' non recens '
f	Marcianus App. IV. 5	saec. xiv
q	Ambrosianus M. 71	saec. xv
N	Laurentianus 72. 18	saec. xv
i	Laurentianus 72. 15	saec. xiv
T	Laurentianus 72. 12	saec. xiii
O	Marcianus 204	saec. xiv

Of these A and B are in a class by themselves.

Bekker preferred A, Waitz B ; the Teubner Editors give a slight preference to B, the readings of which are sometimes supported by papyrus fragments. C sometimes preserves the true reading.

V. SELECT BIBLIOGRAPHY

EDITIONS

J. T. Buhle, Text, Latin Translation and Notes, Biponti, 1792.

I. Bekker, Text, Berlin, 1831, Oxford, 1837.

T. Waitz, Text and Notes, Leipzig, 1844–1846.

Y. Strache and M. Wallies, Teubner Text, Leipzig, 1923.

E. Poste (*De Sophisticis Elenchis* only), Text, Paraphrase and Notes, London, 1866.

TRANSLATIONS

T. Taylor, London, 1812.

O. F. Owen (Bohn's Classical Library), London, 1902.

W. A. Pickard-Cambridge (Oxford Translation), Oxford, 1928.

In French :

J. B. Saint-Hilaire, Paris, 1837.

In German :

J. H. von Kirchmann, Heidelberg, 1877.

E. Rolfes, Leipzig, 1922.

ARTICLES AND DISSERTATIONS

P. Gohlke, *Die Entstehung der aristotelischen Logik*, Berlin, 1936.

ON SOPHISTICAL REFUTATIONS

H. Maier, *Die Syllogistik des Aristoteles*, Tübingen, 1900.

F. Solmsen, *Die Entwicklung der aristotelischen Logik und Rhetorik*, Leipzig, 1929.

J. L. Stocks, ' The Composition of Aristotle's Logical Works,' *Classical Quarterly*, 1933, pp. 115-124.

In translating the *Topica* and *De Sophisticis Elenchis* I have used the text of Bekker in the Berlin Edition, and when I translate any other reading this is noted at the foot of the page. I have constantly referred to the Teubner text of Strache-Wallies, which does not, however, seem to me to mark any considerable advance on that of Bekker. I have found Waitz's edition of the *Organon* of great use, and the Latin version of Pacius is often helpful. I have frequently consulted the Oxford translation by W. A. Pickard-Cambridge. For the *De Sophisticis Elenchis* the notes and paraphrase in Poste's edition are often enlightening, though I cannot always agree with his interpretation.

My aim in translating has been to represent Aristotle's meaning as closely and faithfully as I can in simple English without resorting to paraphrase or trying to express it in modern terminology.

I have to thank my friend and former colleague Professor W. S. Maguinness, of King's College, London, for reading through my version and giving me the benefit of his fine scholarship and accuracy. He has suggested several improvements in the text which I have been glad to adopt.

9

ΑΡΙΣΤΟΤΕΛΟΥΣ ΠΕΡΙ
ΣΟΦΙΣΤΙΚΩΝ ΕΛΕΓΧΩΝ

I. Περὶ δὲ τῶν σοφιστικῶν ἐλέγχων καὶ τῶν
φαινομένων μὲν ἐλέγχων ὄντων δὲ παραλογισμῶν
ἀλλ᾽ οὐκ ἐλέγχων λέγωμεν, ἀρξάμενοι κατὰ φύσιν
ἀπὸ τῶν πρώτων.

Ὅτι μὲν οὖν οἱ μὲν εἰσὶ συλλογισμοί, οἱ δ᾽ οὐκ
ὄντες δοκοῦσι, φανερόν. ὥσπερ γὰρ καὶ ἐπὶ τῶν
25 ἄλλων τοῦτο γίνεται διά τινος ὁμοιότητος, καὶ
ἐπὶ τῶν λόγων ὡσαύτως ἔχει. καὶ γὰρ τὴν ἕξιν
οἱ μὲν ἔχουσιν εὖ, οἱ δὲ φαίνονται, φυλετικῶς
164 b 20 φυσήσαντες καὶ ἐπισκευάσαντες αὑτούς, καὶ καλοὶ
οἱ μὲν διὰ κάλλος, οἱ δὲ φαίνονται, κομμώσαντες
αὑτούς. ἐπί τε τῶν ἀψύχων ὡσαύτως· καὶ γὰρ
τούτων τὰ μὲν ἄργυρος τὰ δὲ χρυσός ἐστιν ἀληθῶς,
τὰ δ᾽ ἔστι μὲν οὔ, φαίνεται δὲ κατὰ τὴν αἴσθησιν,
οἷον τὰ μὲν λιθαργύρινα καὶ τὰ καττιτέρινα ἀργυρᾶ,
25 τὰ δὲ χολοβάφινα χρυσᾶ. τὸν αὐτὸν δὲ τρόπον
καὶ συλλογισμὸς καὶ ἔλεγχος ὁ μὲν ἔστιν, ὁ δ᾽ οὐκ

---

^a The reference appears to be provision of members of the
tribal choruses at Athens for choral competitions (see Xen.
Mem. iii. 4, 5).

ARISTOTLE ON
SOPHISTICAL REFUTATIONS

I. LET us now treat of sophistical refutations, that is, arguments which appear to be refutations but are really fallacies and not refutations, beginning, as is natural, with those which come first.

That some reasonings are really reasonings, but that others seem to be, but are not really, reasonings, is obvious. For, as this happens in other spheres from a similarity between the true and the false, so it happens also in arguments. For some people possess good physical condition, while others have merely the appearance of it, by blowing themselves out and dressing themselves up like the tribal choruses *a* ; again, some people are beautiful because of their beauty, while others have the appearance of beauty because they trick themselves out. So too with inanimate things ; for some of these are really silver and some gold, while others are not but only appear to our senses to be so ; for example, objects made of litharge *b* or tin appear to be silver, and yellow-coloured objects appear to be gold. In the same way also reasoning and refutation are sometimes real and sometimes not, but appear to be real

INTRO-
DUCTION
(chs. i-ii).
The dis-
tinction
between
reasonings
and refuta-
tions which
are genuine
and those
which are
only appar-
ent, *i.e.*
sophistical.

b Protoxide of lead, a by-product in the separation of silver from lead.

164 b

ἔστι μέν, φαίνεται δὲ διὰ τὴν ἀπειρίαν· οἱ γὰρ
ἄπειροι ὥσπερ ἂν ἀπέχοντες πόρρωθεν θεωροῦσιν.
165 a ὁ μὲν γὰρ συλλογισμὸς ἐκ τινῶν ἐστι τεθέντων
ὥστε λέγειν ἕτερόν τι ἐξ ἀνάγκης τῶν κειμένων
διὰ τῶν κειμένων, ἔλεγχος δὲ συλλογισμὸς μετ᾽
ἀντιφάσεως τοῦ συμπεράσματος. οἱ δὲ τοῦτο
ποιοῦσι μὲν οὔ, δοκοῦσι δὲ διὰ πολλὰς αἰτίας, ὧν
5 εἷς τόπος εὐφυέστατός ἐστι καὶ δημοσιώτατος ὁ
διὰ τῶν ὀνομάτων. ἐπεὶ γὰρ οὐκ ἔστιν αὐτὰ τὰ
πράγματα διαλέγεσθαι φέροντας, ἀλλὰ τοῖς ὀνόμασιν ἀντὶ τῶν πραγμάτων χρώμεθα συμβόλοις,
τὸ συμβαῖνον ἐπὶ τῶν ὀνομάτων καὶ ἐπὶ τῶν πραγμάτων ἡγούμεθα συμβαίνειν, καθάπερ ἐπὶ τῶν
10 ψήφων τοῖς λογιζομένοις. τὸ δ᾽ οὐκ ἔστιν ὅμοιον.
τὰ μὲν γὰρ ὀνόματα πεπέρανται καὶ τὸ τῶν λόγων
πλῆθος, τὰ δὲ πράγματα τὸν ἀριθμὸν ἄπειρά ἐστιν.
ἀναγκαῖον οὖν πλείω τὸν αὐτὸν λόγον καὶ τοὔνομα
τὸ ἓν σημαίνειν. ὥσπερ οὖν κἀκεῖ οἱ μὴ δεινοὶ
15 τὰς ψήφους φέρειν ὑπὸ τῶν ἐπιστημόνων παρα-
κρούονται, τὸν αὐτὸν τρόπον καὶ ἐπὶ τῶν λόγων οἱ
τῶν ὀνομάτων τῆς δυνάμεως ἄπειροι παραλογίζονται καὶ αὐτοὶ διαλεγόμενοι καὶ ἄλλων ἀκούοντες.
διὰ μὲν οὖν ταύτην τὴν αἰτίαν καὶ τὰς λεχθησο-
μένας ἔστι καὶ συλλογισμὸς καὶ ἔλεγχος φαινόμενος
20 μὲν οὐκ ὢν δέ. ἐπεὶ δ᾽ ἐστί τισι μᾶλλον πρὸ ἔργου
τὸ δοκεῖν εἶναι σοφοῖς ἢ τὸ εἶναι καὶ μὴ δοκεῖν
(ἔστι γὰρ ἡ σοφιστικὴ φαινομένη σοφία οὖσα δ᾽ οὔ,

12

owing to men's inexperience ; for the inexperienced are like those who view things from a distance. Reasoning is based on certain statements made in such a way as necessarily to cause the assertion of things other than those statements and as a result of those statements ; refutation, on the other hand, is reasoning accompanied by a contradiction of the conclusion. Some refutations do not affect their object but only appear to do so ; this may be due to several causes, of which the most fertile and widespread division is the argument which depends on names. For, since it is impossible to argue by introducing the actual things under discussion, but we use names as symbols in the place of the things, we think that what happens in the case of the names happens also in the case of the things, just as people who are counting think in the case of their counters. But the cases are not really similar ; for names and a quantity of terms are finite, whereas things are infinite in number ; and so the same expression and the single name must necessarily signify a number of things. As, therefore, in the above illustration, those who are not clever at managing the counters are deceived by the experts, in the same way in arguments also those who are unacquainted with the power of names are the victims of false reasoning, both when they are themselves arguing and when they are listening to others. For this reason, therefore, and for others which will be mentioned hereafter, there exist both reasoning and refutation which appear to be genuine but are not really so. But since in the eyes of some people it is more profitable to seem to be wise than to be wise without seeming to be so (for the sophistic art consists in apparent and

καὶ ὁ σοφιστὴς χρηματιστὴς ἀπὸ φαινομένης
σοφίας ἀλλ' οὐκ οὔσης), δῆλον ὅτι ἀναγκαῖον τούτοις καὶ τὸ τοῦ σοφοῦ ἔργον δοκεῖν ποιεῖν μᾶλλον
25 ἢ ποιεῖν καὶ μὴ δοκεῖν. ἔστι δ' ὡς ἐν πρὸς ἐν
εἰπεῖν ἔργον περὶ ἕκαστον τοῦ εἰδότος ἀψευδεῖν μὲν
αὐτὸν περὶ ὧν οἶδε, τὸν δὲ ψευδόμενον ἐμφανίζειν
δύνασθαι. ταῦτα δ' ἐστὶ τὸ μὲν ἐν τῷ δύνασθαι
δοῦναι λόγον, τὸ δ' ἐν τῷ λαβεῖν. ἀνάγκη οὖν
30 τοὺς βουλομένους σοφιστεύειν τὸ τῶν εἰρημένων
λόγων γένος ζητεῖν· πρὸ ἔργου γάρ ἐστιν· ἡ γὰρ
τοιαύτη δύναμις ποιήσει φαίνεσθαι σοφόν, οὗ τυγχάνουσι τὴν προαίρεσιν ἔχοντες.

Ὅτι μὲν οὖν ἔστι τι τοιοῦτον λόγων γένος, καὶ
ὅτι τοιαύτης ἐφίενται δυνάμεως οὓς καλοῦμεν σο-
φιστάς, δῆλον. πόσα δ' ἐστὶν εἴδη τῶν λόγων τῶν
35 σοφιστικῶν, καὶ ἐκ πόσων τὸν ἀριθμὸν ἡ δύναμις αὕτη συνέστηκε, καὶ πόσα μέρη τυγχάνει τῆς
πραγματείας ὄντα, καὶ περὶ τῶν ἄλλων τῶν συντε-
λούντων εἰς τὴν τέχνην ταύτην ἤδη λέγωμεν.

II. Ἔστι δὴ τῶν ἐν τῷ διαλέγεσθαι λόγων τέτταρα γένη, διδασκαλικοὶ καὶ διαλεκτικοὶ καὶ πειρα-
165 b στικοὶ καὶ ἐριστικοί, διδασκαλικοὶ μὲν οἱ ἐκ τῶν
οἰκείων ἀρχῶν ἑκάστου μαθήματος καὶ οὐκ ἐκ
τῶν τοῦ ἀποκρινομένου δοξῶν συλλογιζόμενοι (δεῖ
γὰρ πιστεύειν τὸν μανθάνοντα), διαλεκτικοὶ δ' οἱ
ἐκ τῶν ἐνδόξων συλλογιστικοὶ ἀντιφάσεως, πειρα-

not real wisdom, and the sophist is one who makes money from apparent and not real wisdom), it is clear that for these people it is essential to seem to perform the function of a wise man rather than actually to perform it without seeming to do so. To take a single point of comparison, it is the task of the man who has knowledge of a particular subject himself to refrain from fallacious arguments about the subjects of his knowledge and to be able to expose him who uses them. Of these functions the first consists in being able to give a reason, the second in being able to exact one. It is essential, therefore, for those who wish to play the sophist to seek out the kind of argument which we have mentioned ; for it is well worth his while, since the possession of such a faculty will cause him to appear to be wise, and this is the real purpose which sophists have in view.

It is clear, then, that a class of arguments of this kind exists, and that those whom we call sophists aim at this kind of faculty. Let us next discuss what are the various kinds of sophistical arguments and what are the various component parts of this faculty, and into what different divisions the treatment of the subject falls, and all the other elements which contribute to this art.

II. Of arguments used in discussion there are four kinds, Didactic, Dialectical, Examination-arguments and Contentious arguments. Didactic arguments are those which reason from the principles appropriate to each branch of learning and not from the opinions of the answerer (for he who is learning must take things on trust). Dialectical arguments are those which, starting from generally accepted opinions, reason to establish a contradiction. Examination-arguments

Four kinds of argument used in discussion :
(1) Didactic.
(2) Dialectical.
(3) Examination.

15

165 b

5 στικοὶ δ᾽ οἱ ἐκ τῶν δοκούντων τῷ ἀποκρινομένῳ
καὶ ἀναγκαίων εἰδέναι τῷ προσποιουμένῳ ἔχειν
τὴν ἐπιστήμην (ὃν τρόπον δέ, διώρισται ἐν ἑτέροις),
ἐριστικοὶ δ᾽ οἱ ἐκ τῶν φαινομένων ἐνδόξων μὴ
ὄντων δὲ συλλογιστικοὶ ἢ φαινόμενοι συλλογιστι-
κοί. περὶ μὲν οὖν τῶν ἀποδεικτικῶν ἐν τοῖς Ἀνα-
10 λυτικοῖς εἴρηται, περὶ δὲ τῶν διαλεκτικῶν καὶ
πειραστικῶν ἐν τοῖς ἄλλοις· περὶ δὲ τῶν ἀγωνιστικῶν καὶ ἐριστικῶν νῦν λέγωμεν.

III. Πρῶτον δὴ ληπτέον πόσων στοχάζονται οἱ
ἐν τοῖς λόγοις ἀγωνιζόμενοι καὶ διαφιλονεικοῦντες.
ἔστι δὲ πέντε ταῦτα τὸν ἀριθμόν, ἔλεγχος καὶ
15 ψεῦδος καὶ παράδοξον καὶ σολοικισμὸς καὶ πέμπτον
τὸ ποιῆσαι ἀδολεσχῆσαι τὸν προσδιαλεγόμενον·
τοῦτο δ᾽ ἐστὶ τὸ πολλάκις ἀναγκάζεσθαι ταὐτὸ
λέγειν· ἢ τὸ μὴ ὄν, ἀλλὰ τὸ φαινόμενον ἕκαστον
εἶναι τούτων. μάλιστα μὲν γὰρ προαιροῦνται
φαίνεσθαι ἐλέγχοντες, δεύτερον δὲ ψευδόμενόν τι
20 δεικνύναι, τρίτον εἰς παράδοξον ἄγειν, τέταρτον
δὲ σολοικίζειν ποιεῖν· τοῦτο δ᾽ ἐστὶ τὸ ποιῆσαι
τῇ λέξει βαρβαρίζειν ἐκ τοῦ λόγου τὸν ἀποκρινό-
μενον· τελευταῖον δὲ τὸ πλεονάκις ταὐτὸ λέγειν.

IV. Τρόποι δ᾽ εἰσὶ τοῦ μὲν ἐλέγχειν δύο· οἱ μὲν
γάρ εἰσι παρὰ τὴν λέξιν, οἱ δ᾽ ἔξω τῆς λέξεως.
25 ἔστι δὲ τὰ μὲν παρὰ τὴν λέξιν ἐμποιοῦντα τὴν
φαντασίαν ἓξ τὸν ἀριθμόν· ταῦτα δ᾽ ἐστὶν ὁμωνυμία,
ἀμφιβολία, σύνθεσις, διαίρεσις, προσῳδία, σχῆμα
λέξεως. τούτου δὲ πίστις ἥ τε διὰ τῆς ἐπαγωγῆς
καὶ συλλογισμός, ἄν τε ληφθῇ τις ἄλλος, καὶ ὅτι

---

a Topics 159 a 25 ff.
b Topics i-viii.

16

are those which are based on opinions held by the answerer and necessarily known to one who claims knowledge of the subject involved (in what manner, has been described elsewhere [a]). Contentious arguments are those which reason or seem to reason from opinions which appear to be, but are not really, generally accepted. Demonstrative arguments have been treated in the *Analytics*, and dialectical arguments and examinations have been dealt with elsewhere.[b] Let us now deal with competitive and contentious arguments.

(4) Contentious.

III. We must first of all comprehend the various objects at which those aim who compete and contend in argument. They number five : refutation, fallacy, paradox, solecism, and, fifthly, the reduction of one's opponent to a state of babbling, that is, making him to say the same thing over and over again ; or, if not the reality, at any rate the appearance of each of these things. Their first choice is a plain refutation, their second to show that their opponent is lying, their third to lead him on to a paradox, their fourth to make him commit a solecism (that is, to make the answerer, as a result of the argument, speak ungrammatically), and, lastly, to make him say the same thing over and over again.

THE PERPETRATION OF FALLACIES (chs. iii-xv). The aims of contentious argument are five in number.

IV. There are two modes of refutations ; one has to do with the language used, the other is unconnected with the language. The methods of producing a false illusion in connexion with language are six in number : equivocation, ambiguity, combination, division, accent and form of expression. The truth of this can be verified by induction and by syllogistic proof based on this (though some other assumption is also possible), that this is the number of ways in

(A) REFUTATION (chs. iv-xi). (a) Refutation by fallacies which depend on diction, which are six in number, being due to :

165 b

τοσαυταχῶς ἂν τοῖς αὐτοῖς ὀνόμασι καὶ λόγοις μὴ
30 ταὐτὸ δηλώσαιμεν. εἰσὶ δὲ παρὰ μὲν τὴν ὁμωνυμίαν οἱ τοιοίδε τῶν λόγων, οἷον ὅτι μανθάνουσιν
οἱ ἐπιστάμενοι· τὰ γὰρ ἀποστοματιζόμενα μανθάνουσιν οἱ γραμματικοί. τὸ γὰρ μανθάνειν ὁμώνυμον, τό τε ξυνιέναι χρώμενον τῇ ἐπιστήμῃ καὶ
τὸ λαμβάνειν ἐπιστήμην. καὶ πάλιν ὅτι τὰ κακὰ
35 ἀγαθά· τὰ γὰρ δέοντα ἀγαθά, τὰ δὲ κακὰ δέοντα.
διττὸν γὰρ τὸ δέον, τό τ' ἀναγκαῖον, ὃ συμβαίνει
πολλάκις καὶ ἐπὶ τῶν κακῶν (ἔστι γὰρ κακόν τι
ἀναγκαῖον), καὶ τἀγαθὰ δὲ δέοντά φαμεν εἶναι.
ἔτι τὸν αὐτὸν καθῆσθαι καὶ ἑστάναι, καὶ κάμνειν
καὶ ὑγιαίνειν. ὅσπερ γὰρ ἀνίστατο, ἕστηκεν, καὶ
166 a ὅσπερ ὑγιάζετο, ὑγιαίνει· ἀνίστατο δ' ὁ καθήμενος
καὶ ὑγιάζετο ὁ κάμνων. τὸ γὰρ τὸν κάμνοντα
ὁτιοῦν ποιεῖν ἢ πάσχειν οὐχ ἓν σημαίνει, ἀλλ' ὁτὲ
μὲν ὅτι ὁ νῦν κάμνων,[1] ὁτὲ δ' ὃς ἔκαμνε πρότερον.
5 πλὴν ὑγιάζετο μὲν καὶ κάμνων καὶ ὁ κάμνων·
ὑγιαίνει δ' οὐ κάμνων, ἀλλ' ὁ κάμνων, οὐ νῦν, ἀλλ'
ὁ πρότερον. παρὰ δὲ τὴν ἀμφιβολίαν οἱ τοιοίδε,
τὸ βούλεσθαι λαβεῖν με τοὺς πολεμίους. καὶ ἆρ'
ὅ τις γινώσκει, τοῦτο γινώσκει; καὶ γὰρ τὸν γινώ-
σκοντα καὶ τὸ γινωσκόμενον ἐνδέχεται ὡς γινώ-
σκοντα σημῆναι τούτῳ τῷ λόγῳ. καὶ ἆρα ὃ ὁρᾷ

---

[1] Deleting ἢ καθήμενος after κάμνων with Wallies.

[a] i.e. can write or spell.
[b] i.e. ' ought to be.'

18

which we can fail to indicate the same thing by the same terms or expressions. Arguments such as the following are based on equivocation : ' Those who know, learn ; for it is those who know the use of letters that learn [a] what is dictated to them.' Here ' learn ' is equivocal, meaning ' understand by using knowledge ' and ' acquire knowledge.' Or again, ' Evils are good, for what must exist is good, and evil must exist.' Here ' must exist ' is used in two senses ; it means ' what is necessary,' which is often true of evils (for some evil is necessary), and we also say that good things ' must exist.' [b] Or again, ' the same man is seated and standing and is a sick man and restored to health ; for it is the man who stood up that is standing, and it is he who was recovering his health that is restored to health, but it was the man who was seated that stood up and the man who was sick that was recovering.' For that ' the sick man ' does such and such a thing or has such and such a thing done to him, has not one meaning only but at one time means ' the man who is now sick,' and at another time ' the man who was formerly sick.' But it was the sick man who began to recover his health when he was actually sick, but he is in good health when he is not sick and is not the sick man now but the man who was formerly sick. The following examples are connected with ambiguity : ' To wish me the enemy to capture,' and ' when a man knows something, surely there is knowledge of this ' ; for it is possible by this expression to signify both the knower and the thing known as knowing.[c] And ' what a man sees, surely that

[c] *i.e.* ' knowledge of this ' can mean either knowledge on the part of the knower or knowledge of the thing known.

19

10 τις, τοῦτο ὁρᾷ; ὁρᾷ δὲ τὸν κίονα, ὥστε ὁρᾷ ὁ
κίων. καὶ ἆρα ὃ σὺ φὴς εἶναι, τοῦτο σὺ φὴς εἶναι;
φὴς δὲ λίθον εἶναι, σὺ ἄρα φὴς λίθος εἶναι. καὶ
ἆρ᾽ ἔστι σιγῶντα λέγειν; διττὸν γὰρ καὶ τὸ σιγῶντα λέγειν, τό τε τὸν λέγοντα σιγᾶν καὶ τὸ τὰ
λεγόμενα. εἰσὶ δὲ τρεῖς τρόποι τῶν παρὰ τὴν
15 ὁμωνυμίαν καὶ τὴν ἀμφιβολίαν, εἷς μὲν ὅταν ἢ ὁ
λόγος ἢ τοὔνομα κυρίως σημαίνῃ πλείω, οἷον ἀετὸς
καὶ κύων· εἷς δὲ ὅταν εἰωθότες ὦμεν οὕτω λέγειν·
τρίτος δὲ ὅταν τὸ συντεθὲν πλείω σημαίνῃ, κεχωρισμένον δὲ ἁπλῶς, οἷον τὸ ἐπίσταται γράμματα.
ἑκάτερον μὲν γάρ, εἰ ἔτυχεν, ἕν τι σημαίνει, τὸ
20 ἐπίσταται καὶ τὰ γράμματα· ἄμφω δὲ πλείω, ἢ τὸ
τὰ γράμματα αὐτὰ ἐπιστήμην ἔχειν ἢ τῶν γραμμάτων ἄλλον.

Ἡ μὲν οὖν ἀμφιβολία καὶ ὁμωνυμία παρὰ τούτους τοὺς τρόπους ἐστίν, παρὰ δὲ τὴν σύνθεσιν τὰ
τοιάδε, οἷον τὸ δύνασθαι καθήμενον βαδίζειν καὶ
25 μὴ γράφοντα γράφειν. οὐ γὰρ ταὐτὸ σημαίνει,
ἂν διελών τις εἴπῃ καὶ συνθείς, ὡς δυνατὸν τὸ¹
καθήμενον βαδίζειν²· καὶ τοῦθ᾽ ὡσαύτως ἄν τις
συνθῇ, τὸ μὴ γράφοντα γράφειν· σημαίνει γὰρ ὡς
ἔχει δύναμιν τοῦ μὴ γράφοντα γράφειν. ἐὰν δὲ
30 μὴ συνθῇ, ὅτι ἔχει δύναμιν, ὅτε οὐ γράφει, τοῦ

---

¹ Reading τὸ for τόν.
² Deleting καὶ μὴ γράφοντα γράφειν after βαδίζειν with
Wallies.

ᵃ The personal pronoun not being expressed in Greek,
τοῦτο, being neuter, can be either the subject or object of the
verb ὁρᾷ.　　　　　　　　ᵇ ' eagle ' or ' pediment.'

ᶜ ' Dog,' ' dogstar ' or ' Cynic philosopher.'

ᵈ In which case the meaning is that a man, while sitting,
has the power to walk (if he wishes to do so).

(he) [a] sees : a man a pillar sees, therefore the pillar sees.' Again, ' Surely you insist on being what you insist on being. You insist on a stone being : therefore, you insist on being a stone.' Again ' Surely speaking is possible of the silent.' 'Speaking of the silent ' can also be taken in two ways, either that the speaker is silent or the things spoken of are silent. There are three modes connected with equivocation and ambiguity : (1) when the expression or name properly signifies more than one thing, such as ἀετός [b] and κύων, [c] (2) when we customarily use a word in more than one sense, (3) when a word has more than one meaning in combination with another word, though by itself it has only one meaning, for example, ' knowing letters '; for it may so happen that taken separately ' knowing ' and ' letters ' have only one meaning, but taken together they have more than one meaning, namely, either that the letters themselves have knowledge or that someone else has knowledge of the letters.

Ambiguity and equivocation then take these forms. The following examples are connected with the combination of words, for instance, ' A man can walk when sitting and write when not writing.' The significance is not the same if one utters the words separately [d] as it is if one combines them, namely, ' a man can walk-while-sitting,' [e] and, similarly, in the other example, if one combines the words and says ' a man can write-when-not-writing,' for it means that he can write and not write at the same time ; whereas if one does not combine the words it means that, when he is not writing, he has the power to

(3) Combination of words.

---

[e] In which case the meaning is that it is possible for a man to walk and sit at the same time.

166 a

γράφειν. καί, μανθάνει νῦν γράμματα, εἴπερ ἐμάν-
θανεν ἃ ἐπίσταται. ἔτι τὸ ἓν μόνον δυνάμενον
φέρειν πολλὰ δύνασθαι φέρειν.

Παρὰ δὲ τὴν διαίρεσιν, ὅτι τὰ πέντ' ἐστὶ δύο
καὶ τρία, καὶ περιττὰ καὶ ἄρτια, καὶ τὸ μεῖζον ἴσον·
35 τοσοῦτον γὰρ καὶ ἔτι πρός. ὁ γὰρ αὐτὸς λόγος
διῃρημένος καὶ συγκείμενος οὐκ ἀεὶ ταὐτὸ σημαίνειν ἂν δόξειεν, οἷον " ἐγώ σ' ἔθηκα δοῦλον ὄντ'
ἐλεύθερον " καὶ τὸ " πεντήκοντ' ἀνδρῶν ἑκατὸν
λίπε δῖος Ἀχιλλεύς."

166 b

Παρὰ δὲ τὴν προσῳδίαν ἐν μὲν τοῖς ἄνευ γραφῆς
διαλεκτικοῖς οὐ ῥᾴδιον ποιῆσαι λόγον, ἐν δὲ τοῖς
γεγραμμένοις καὶ ποιήμασι μᾶλλον, οἷον καὶ τὸν
Ὅμηρον ἔνιοι διορθοῦνται πρὸς τοὺς ἐλέγχοντας
5 ὡς ἀτόπως εἰρηκότα " τὸ μὲν οὗ καταπύθεται
ὄμβρῳ." λύουσι γὰρ αὐτὸ τῇ προσῳδίᾳ, λέγοντες
τὸ οὗ ὀξύτερον. καὶ τὸ περὶ τὸ ἐνύπνιον τοῦ
Ἀγαμέμνονος, ὅτι οὐκ αὐτὸς ὁ Ζεὺς εἶπεν " δίδομεν δέ οἱ εὖχος ἀρέσθαι," ἀλλὰ τῷ ἐνυπνίῳ ἐνε-
τέλλετο διδόναι. τὰ μὲν οὖν τοιαῦτα παρὰ τὴν
προσῳδίαν ἐστίν.

10 Οἱ δὲ παρὰ τὸ σχῆμα τῆς λέξεως συμβαίνουσιν,

---

^a With a different combination of words this can mean,
' He understands now what he knows because he has understood letters.'

^b This can also be taken to mean, ' Being able to carry
many things, you can carry one single thing only.'

^c If 5 = 2 and 3, 5 = 2 and 5 = 3, and so 5 is both odd and
even : again, if 5 = 2 and 5 = 3, then 3 = 2, *i.e.* the greater =
the less, since 3 is also 2 + 1.

^d From an unknown source in Greek comedy imitated by
Terence, *Andria* 37.

write. Again, ' He now understands letters, since he has understood what he knows ' [a] ; and further, ' One single thing being able to carry, many things you can carry.' [b]

The following propositions are connected with division : ' 5 is 2 and 3,' ' 5 is odd and even,' ' the greater is equal to the less,' for it is so much and something more. [c] For the same sentence divided would not always seem to have the same meaning as when taken as a whole, for example, ' Free I made thee a slave ' [d] and ' goodly Achilles left a hundred (and) fifty men.' [e] *(4) Division of words.*

It is not easy to construct an argument relating to accent in discussions which are not written down, but it is easier in written matter and poetry. For example, some people emend Homer to meet the objection of critics that his phrase ' τὸ μὲν οὗ καταπύθεται ὄμβρῳ ' is a strange one. [f] For they solve the difficulty by a change of accent, pronouncing the ου more sharply. [g] Also in the passage about Agamemnon's dream [h] they say that Zeus himself did not say, ' But we grant [i] him to secure the fulfilment of his prayer ' but bade the dream to grant it. [j] Such examples, then, depend on accentuation. *(5) Accent.*

Refutations which depend on the form of expres- *(6) Form of expression.*

[e] Probably quoted from some Cyclic poem. The words can mean either ' left 150 men ' or ' left a hundred men fifty.'

[f] *Il.* xxiii. 328 : ' part of which decays in the rain.'

[g] *i.e.* substituting οὐ, ' not,' for οὗ : ' and it does not decay in the rain.'

[h] *Il.* ii. 1-35 ; but the actual words quoted occur in *Il.* xxi. 297 and are spoken by Poseidon. For this and the following example see *Poet.* 1461 a 22-23.

[i] *i.e.* δίδομεν.

[j] *i.e.* δίδομεν = διδόναι, the infinitive being used as an imperative.

ὅταν τὸ μὴ ταὐτὸ ὡσαύτως ἑρμηνεύηται, οἷον τὸ
ἄρρεν θῆλυ ἢ τὸ θῆλυ ἄρρεν, ἢ τὸ μεταξὺ θάτερον
τούτων, ἢ πάλιν τὸ ποιὸν ποσὸν ἢ τὸ ποσὸν ποιόν,
ἢ τὸ ποιοῦν πάσχον ἢ τὸ διακείμενον ποιεῖν, καὶ
15 τἆλλα δ', ὡς διῄρηται πρότερον. ἔστι γὰρ τὸ μὴ
τῶν ποιεῖν ὂν ὡς τῶν ποιεῖν τι τῇ λέξει σημαίνειν.
οἷον τὸ ὑγιαίνειν ὁμοίως τῷ σχήματι τῆς λέξεως
λέγεται τῷ τέμνειν ἢ οἰκοδομεῖν· καίτοι τὸ μὲν
ποιόν τι καὶ διακείμενόν πως δηλοῖ, τὸ δὲ ποιεῖν
τι. τὸν αὐτὸν δὲ τρόπον καὶ ἐπὶ τῶν ἄλλων.

20 Οἱ μὲν οὖν παρὰ τὴν λέξιν ἔλεγχοι ἐκ τούτων
τῶν τόπων εἰσίν· τῶν δ' ἔξω τῆς λέξεως παραλογισμῶν εἴδη ἐστὶν ἑπτά, ἓν μὲν παρὰ τὸ συμβεβηκός, δεύτερον δὲ τὸ ἁπλῶς ἢ μὴ ἁπλῶς ἀλλὰ
πῇ ἢ ποῦ ἢ ποτὲ ἢ πρός τι λέγεσθαι, τρίτον δὲ τὸ
παρὰ τὴν τοῦ ἐλέγχου ἄγνοιαν, τέταρτον δὲ τὸ
25 παρὰ τὸ ἑπόμενον, πέμπτον δὲ τὸ παρὰ ⟨τὸ⟩ τὸ ἐν
ἀρχῇ λαμβάνειν,[1] ἕκτον δὲ τὸ μὴ αἴτιον ὡς αἴτιον
τιθέναι, ἕβδομον δὲ τὸ τὰ πλείω ἐρωτήματα ἓν
ποιεῖν.

V. Οἱ μὲν οὖν παρὰ τὸ συμβεβηκὸς παραλογισμοί εἰσιν, ὅταν ὁμοίως ὁτιοῦν ἀξιωθῇ τῷ πράγ-
30 ματι καὶ τῷ συμβεβηκότι ὑπάρχειν. ἐπεὶ γὰρ τῷ
αὐτῷ πολλὰ συμβέβηκεν, οὐκ ἀνάγκη πᾶσι τοῖς
κατηγορουμένοις, καὶ καθ' οὗ κατηγορεῖται, ταὐτὰ[2]
πάντα ὑπάρχειν. οἷον εἰ ὁ Κορίσκος ἕτερον ἀν-

---

[1] Reading παρὰ ⟨τὸ⟩ τὸ ἐν ἀρχῇ λαμβάνειν with Strache.
[2] Reading ταὐτὰ with Casaubon.

24

sion occur when what is not the same is expressed in the same form ; for example, when the masculine is expressed by the feminine or *vice versa*, or the neuter by the masculine or feminine ; or again when a quality is expressed by a quantity or *vice versa*, or the active by a passive or a state by the active, and so forth according to the distinctions previously made.[a] For it is possible for something which is *not* of the nature of an action to signify by the language used something which is of the nature of an action ; for example, to ' flourish ' is a form of expression like to ' cut ' or to ' build ' ; yet the former denotes a quality and a certain disposition, the latter an action. So too with the other possible examples.

Refutations, then, connected with language are based on these commonplaces. Of fallacies unconnected with language there are seven kinds : (1) those connected with Accident ; (2) those in which an expression is used absolutely, or not absolutely but qualified as to manner or place or time or relation ; (3) those connected with ignorance of the nature of refutation ; (4) those connected with the consequent ; (5) those connected with the assumption of the original point to be proved ; (6) those which assert that what is not a cause is a cause ; (7) the making of several questions into one. *(b) By fallacies which are not dependent on diction. These are seven in number, depending on :*

V. Fallacies connected with Accident occur when it is claimed that some attribute belongs similarly to the thing and to its accident ; for since the same thing has many accidents, it does not necessarily follow that all the same attributes belong to all the predicates of a thing and to that of which they are predicated. For example, ' If Coriscus is different *(1) Accident.*

[a] *Topics* 103 b 20 ff.

θρώπου, αὐτὸς αὑτοῦ ἕτερος· ἔστι γὰρ ἄνθρωπος.
ἢ εἰ Σωκράτους ἕτερος, ὁ δὲ Σωκράτης ἄνθρωπος,
35 ἕτερον ἀνθρώπου φασὶν ὡμολογηκέναι διὰ τὸ συμ-
βεβηκέναι, οὗ ἔφησεν ἕτερον εἶναι, τοῦτον εἶναι
ἄνθρωπον.

Οἱ δὲ παρὰ τὸ ἁπλῶς τόδε ἢ πῇ λέγεσθαι καὶ μὴ
κυρίως, ὅταν τὸ ἐν μέρει λεγόμενον ὡς ἁπλῶς
167 a εἰρημένον ληφθῇ, οἷον εἰ τὸ μὴ ὄν ἐστι δοξαστόν,
ὅτι τὸ μὴ ὄν ἐστιν· οὐ γὰρ ταὐτὸν εἶναί τέ τι καὶ
εἶναι ἁπλῶς. ἢ πάλιν ὅτι τὸ ὂν οὐκ ἔστιν ὄν, εἰ
τῶν ὄντων τι μή ἐστιν, οἷον εἰ μὴ ἄνθρωπος. οὐ
5 γὰρ ταὐτὸ μὴ εἶναί τι καὶ ἁπλῶς μὴ εἶναι· φαίνεται
δὲ διὰ τὸ πάρεγγυς τῆς λέξεως καὶ μικρὸν διαφέρειν τὸ εἶναί τι τοῦ εἶναι καὶ τὸ μὴ εἶναί τι τοῦ μὴ
εἶναι. ὁμοίως δὲ καὶ τὸ παρὰ τὸ πῇ καὶ τὸ ἁπλῶς.
οἷον εἰ ὁ Ἰνδὸς ὅλος μέλας ὢν λευκός ἐστι τοὺς
ὀδόντας· λευκὸς ἄρα καὶ οὐ λευκός ἐστιν. ἢ εἰ
10 ἄμφω πῇ, ὅτι ἅμα τὰ ἐναντία ὑπάρχει. τὸ δὲ
τοιοῦτον ἐπ᾽ ἐνίων μὲν παντὶ θεωρῆσαι ῥᾴδιον, οἷον
εἰ λαβὼν τὸν Αἰθίοπα εἶναι μέλανα τοὺς ὀδόντας
ἔροιτ᾽ εἰ λευκός· εἰ οὖν ταύτῃ λευκός, ὅτι μέλας
καὶ οὐ μέλας, οἴοιτο διειλέχθαι συλλογιστικῶς
τελειώσας τὴν ἐρώτησιν. ἐπ᾽ ἐνίων δὲ λανθάνει

from " man," he is different from himself, for he is a
man ' ; or ' if he is different from Socrates, and
Socrates is a man,' they say that it has been admitted
that Coriscus is different from a man, because it is
an accident that the person from which he said that
Coriscus is different is a man.

Fallacies connected with the use of some particular (2) The
expression absolutely or in a certain respect and not use of words
in its proper sense, occur when that which is pre- or with
dicated in part only is taken as though it was predi- some quali-
cated absolutely. For example, ' If that-which-is-not fication.
is an object of opinion, then that-which-is-not is ' ;
for it is not the same thing ' to be something ' and
' to be ' absolutely. Or again, ' That-which-is is not,
if it is not one of the things which are, *e.g.* if it is not
a man.' For it is not the same thing ' not to be something ' and ' not to be ' absolutely ; but, owing to
the similarity of the language, ' to be something '
appears to differ only a little from ' to be,' and ' not
to be something ' from ' not to be.' In like manner
when something is predicated in a certain respect
and absolutely ; for example, ' If an Indian, being
black all over, is white in respect of his teeth, then
he is white and not white.' Or if both attributes
belong in a certain respect, they say that the contrary
attributes belong simultaneously. In some cases this
sort of fallacy can be easily perceived by anyone ;
if, for example, after securing an admission that the
Ethiopian is black, one were to ask whether he is
white in respect of his teeth, and then, if he be white
in this respect, were to think that he had finished
the interrogation and had proved dialectically that
he was both black and not black. In some cases, on
the other hand, the fallacy escapes detection, namely,

15 πολλάκις, ἐφ' ὅσων, ὅταν πῇ λέγηται, κἂν τὸ
ἁπλῶς δόξειεν ἀκολουθεῖν, καὶ ἐν ὅσοις μὴ ῥᾴδιον
θεωρῆσαι πότερον αὐτῶν κυρίως ἀποδοτέον. γίνεται δὲ τὸ τοιοῦτον ἐν οἷς ὁμοίως ὑπάρχει τὰ ἀντι-
κείμενα· δοκεῖ γὰρ ἢ ἄμφω ἢ μηδέτερον δοτέον
ἁπλῶς εἶναι κατηγορεῖν, οἷον εἰ τὸ μὲν ἥμισυ
20 λευκὸν τὸ δ' ἥμισυ μέλαν, πότερον λευκὸν ἢ
μέλαν;

Οἱ δὲ παρὰ τὸ μὴ διωρίσθαι τί ἐστι συλλογισμὸς
ἢ τί ἔλεγχος, ἀλλὰ παρὰ τὴν ἔλλειψιν γίνονται τοῦ
λόγου· ἔλεγχος μὲν γὰρ ἀντίφασις τοῦ αὐτοῦ καὶ
ἑνός, μὴ ὀνόματος ἀλλὰ πράγματος, καὶ ὀνόματος
25 μὴ συνωνύμου ἀλλὰ τοῦ αὐτοῦ, ἐκ τῶν δοθέντων,
ἐξ ἀνάγκης, μὴ συναριθμουμένου τοῦ ἐν ἀρχῇ,
κατὰ ταὐτὸ καὶ πρὸς ταὐτὸ καὶ ὡσαύτως καὶ ἐν
τῷ αὐτῷ χρόνῳ. τὸν αὐτὸν δὲ τρόπον καὶ τὸ
ψεύσασθαι περί τινος. ἔνιοι δὲ ἀπολιπόντες τι
τῶν λεχθέντων φαίνονται ἐλέγχειν, οἷον ὅτι ταὐτὸ
30 διπλάσιον καὶ οὐ διπλάσιον· τὰ γὰρ δύο τοῦ μὲν
ἑνὸς διπλάσια, τῶν δὲ τριῶν οὐ διπλάσια. ἢ εἰ τὸ
αὐτὸ τοῦ αὐτοῦ διπλάσιον καὶ οὐ διπλάσιον, ἀλλ'
οὐ κατὰ ταὐτό· κατὰ μὲν γὰρ τὸ μῆκος διπλάσιον,
κατὰ δὲ τὸ πλάτος οὐ διπλάσιον. ἢ εἰ τοῦ αὐτοῦ
καὶ κατὰ ταὐτὸ καὶ ὡσαύτως, ἀλλ' οὐχ ἅμα· διόπερ
35 ἐστὶ φαινόμενος ἔλεγχος. ἕλκοι δ' ἄν τις τοῦτον
καὶ εἰς τοὺς παρὰ τὴν λέξιν.

Οἱ δὲ παρὰ τὸ ἐν ἀρχῇ λαμβάνειν γίνονται μὲν

where, when an attribute is ascribed in some respect only, an absolute attribution would also seem to follow, and where it is not easy to see which of the attributes can be properly assigned. An instance of this occurs when both the opposite attributes belong similarly ; for then it is generally held that it must be conceded that either both or neither can be predicated absolutely ; for example, if something is half white and half black, is it white or black ?

Other fallacies arise because no definition has been given of what a syllogism is and what a refutation, and there is some defect in their definition. For a refutation is a contradiction of one and the same predicate, not of a name but of a thing, and not of a synonymous name but of an identical name, based on the given premisses and following necessarily from them (the original point at issue not being included) in the same respect, relation, manner and time. A false statement about something also occurs in the same manner. Some people, however, appear to refute, omitting some of the above-named points, showing, for example, that the same thing is double and not double, because two is the double of one but not the double of three. Or, they show that if the same thing is double and not double of the same thing, yet it is not double in the same respect ; for it is double in length but not double in breadth. Or, if it is double and not double of the same thing and in the same respect and manner, yet it is not so at the same time ; and so there is only an apparent refutation. One might, indeed, force this fallacy also into the category of those connected with language.

Fallacies connected with the assumption of the

(3) Ignoratio elenchi.

(4) Petitio principii.

29

167 a

οὕτως καὶ τοσαυταχῶς ὁσαχῶς ἐνδέχεται τὸ ἐξ
ἀρχῆς αἰτεῖσθαι, φαίνονται δ' ἐλέγχειν διὰ τὸ μὴ
δύνασθαι συνορᾶν τὸ ταὐτὸν καὶ τὸ ἕτερον.

167 b Ὁ δὲ παρὰ τὸ ἑπόμενον ἔλεγχος διὰ τὸ οἴεσθαι
ἀντιστρέφειν τὴν ἀκολούθησιν. ὅταν γὰρ τοῦδε
ὄντος ἐξ ἀνάγκης τοδὶ ᾖ, καὶ τοῦδε ὄντος οἴονται
καὶ θάτερον εἶναι ἐξ ἀνάγκης. ὅθεν καὶ αἱ περὶ
5 τὴν δόξαν ἐκ τῆς αἰσθήσεως ἀπάται γίνονται.
πολλάκις γὰρ τὴν χολὴν μέλι ὑπέλαβον διὰ τὸ ἕπε-
σθαι τὸ ξανθὸν χρῶμα τῷ μέλιτι· καὶ ἐπεὶ συμβαίνει τὴν γῆν ὕσαντος γίνεσθαι διάβροχον, κἂν
ᾖ διάβροχος, ὑπολαμβάνομεν ὗσαι. τὸ δ' οὐκ
ἀναγκαῖον. ἔν τε τοῖς ῥητορικοῖς αἱ κατὰ τὸ σημεῖον ἀποδείξεις ἐκ τῶν ἑπομένων εἰσίν. βουλό-
10 μενοι γὰρ δεῖξαι ὅτι μοιχός, τὸ ἑπόμενον ἔλαβον,
ὅτι καλλωπιστὴς ἢ ὅτι νύκτωρ ὁρᾶται πλανώμενος.
πολλοῖς δὲ ταῦτα μὲν ὑπάρχει, τὸ δὲ κατηγορούμενον οὐχ ὑπάρχει. ὁμοίως δὲ καὶ ἐν τοῖς συλλο-
γιστικοῖς, οἷον ὁ Μελίσσου λόγος ὅτι ἄπειρον τὸ
ἅπαν, λαβὼν τὸ μὲν ἅπαν ἀγένητον (ἐκ γὰρ μὴ
15 ὄντος οὐδὲν ἂν γενέσθαι), τὸ δὲ γενόμενον ἐξ ἀρχῆς
γενέσθαι. εἰ μὴ οὖν γέγονεν, ἀρχὴν οὐκ ἔχει τὸ
πᾶν, ὥστ' ἄπειρον. οὐκ ἀνάγκη δὲ τοῦτο συμ-
βαίνειν· οὐ γὰρ εἰ τὸ γενόμενον ἅπαν ἀρχὴν ἔχει,
καὶ εἴ τι ἀρχὴν ἔχει, γέγονεν, ὥσπερ οὐδ' εἰ ὁ
20 πυρέττων θερμός, καὶ τὸν θερμὸν ἀνάγκη πυρέττειν.

30

original point to be proved arise in the same manner and in the same number of ways as it is possible to beg the original point ; they have an appearance of achieving a refutation because men fail to perceive at the same time what is the same and what is different.

The refutation connected with the consequent is (5) The due to the idea that consequence is convertible. For consequent. whenever, if A is, B necessarily is, men also fancy that, if B is, A necessarily is. It is from this source that deceptions connected with opinion based on sense-perception arise. For men often take gall for honey because a yellow colour accompanies honey ; and since it happens that the earth becomes drenched when it has rained, if it is drenched, we think that it has rained, though this is not necessarily true. In rhetorical arguments proofs from signs are founded on consequences ; for, when men wish to prove that a man is an adulterer, they seize upon the consequence of that character, namely, that the man dresses himself elaborately or is seen wandering abroad at night —facts that are true of many people, while the accusation is not true. So, too, in dialectical reasonings ; for example, the argument of Melissus that the universe is infinite assumes that the universe has not come into being (for nothing could come into being from what does not exist) and that everything which has come into being has come from a beginning; if, therefore, the universe has not come into being, it has no beginning and therefore is infinite. But this does not necessarily follow ; for even if what has come into being always has a beginning, anything that has a beginning need not have come to be, any more than it follows that a man who is hot must be in a fever because a man who is in a fever is hot.

Ὁ δὲ παρὰ τὸ μὴ αἴτιον ὡς αἴτιον, ὅταν προσ-
ληφθῇ τὸ ἀναίτιον ὡς παρ' ἐκεῖνο γινομένου τοῦ
ἐλέγχου. συμβαίνει δὲ τὸ τοιοῦτον ἐν τοῖς εἰς τὸ
ἀδύνατον συλλογισμοῖς· ἐν τούτοις γὰρ ἀναγκαῖον
25 ἀναιρεῖν τι τῶν κειμένων. ἐὰν οὖν ἐγκαταριθμηθῇ
ἐν τοῖς ἀναγκαίοις ἐρωτήμασι πρὸς τὸ συμβαῖνον
ἀδύνατον, δόξει παρὰ τοῦτο γίνεσθαι πολλάκις ὁ
ἔλεγχος, οἷον ὅτι οὐκ ἔστι ψυχὴ καὶ ζωὴ ταὐτόν·
εἰ γὰρ φθορᾷ γένεσις ἐναντίον, καὶ τῇ τινὶ φθορᾷ
ἔσται τις γένεσις ἐναντίον· ὁ δὲ θάνατος φθορά τις
30 καὶ ἐναντίον ζωῇ, ὥστε γένεσις ἡ ζωὴ καὶ τὸ ζῆν
γίνεσθαι· τοῦτο δ' ἀδύνατον· οὐκ ἄρα ταὐτὸν ἡ
ψυχὴ καὶ ἡ ζωή. οὐ δὴ συλλελόγισται· συμβαίνει
γάρ, κἂν μή τις ταὐτὸ φῇ τὴν ζωὴν τῇ ψυχῇ, τὸ
ἀδύνατον, ἀλλὰ μόνον ἐναντίον ζωὴν μὲν θανάτῳ
ὄντι φθορᾷ, φθορᾷ δὲ γένεσιν. ἀσυλλόγιστοι μὲν
35 οὖν ἁπλῶς οὐκ εἰσὶν οἱ τοιοῦτοι λόγοι, πρὸς δὲ τὸ
προκείμενον ἀσυλλόγιστοι. καὶ λανθάνει πολλάκις
οὐχ ἧττον αὐτοὺς τοὺς ἐρωτῶντας τὸ τοιοῦτον.

Οἱ μὲν οὖν παρὰ τὸ ἑπόμενον καὶ παρὰ τὸ μὴ
αἴτιον λόγοι τοιοῦτοί εἰσιν· οἱ δὲ παρὰ τὸ τὰ δύο
ἐρωτήματα ἓν ποιεῖν, ὅταν λανθάνῃ πλείω ὄντα καὶ
168 a ὡς ἑνὸς ὄντος ἀποδοθῇ ἀπόκρισις μία. ἐπ' ἐνίων
μὲν οὖν ῥᾴδιον ἰδεῖν ὅτι πλείω καὶ ὅτι οὐ δοτέον

32

The refutation connected with taking as a cause (6) Mis-
what is not a cause, occurs when that which is not taken cause.
a cause is foisted into the argument as though the
refutation were due to it. Such a case occurs in
reasonings leading up to an impossibility; for in
these one is bound to destroy one of the premisses.
If, therefore, what is not a cause is enumerated among
the questions which are necessary for the production
of the resultant impossibility, the refutation will
often seem to come about as the result of it; for
example, in the argument that ' soul ' and ' life ' are
not identical. For if coming-into-being is contrary
to perishing, then a particular kind of coming-into-
being will be contrary to a particular kind of perishing;
now death is a particular kind of perishing and contrary to life; life, therefore, is a coming-into-being
and to live is to come-into-being. But this is impossible; and so the soul and life are not identical.
But this conclusion is not the result of reasoning;
for the impossibility occurs even if one does not
assert that life is identical with the soul but merely
says that life is contrary to death, which is a perishing,
and that coming-into-being is contrary to perishing.
Such arguments are not absolutely inconclusive but
only inconclusive as regards the point at issue, and
the questioners themselves are often equally uncon-
scious of such a state of affairs.

Such, then, are the arguments connected with the (7) Plur-
consequent and the falsely imputed cause. Those ality of
which are connected with the union of two questions questions.
in one occur, when it is not noticed that they are
more than one and one answer is given as though
there was only one question. Sometimes it is easy
to see that there is more than one question and

ἀπόκρισιν, οἷον πότερον ἡ γῆ θάλαττά ἐστιν ἢ ὁ
οὐρανός; ἐπ' ἐνίων δ' ἧττον, καὶ ὡς ἑνὸς ὄντος
ἢ ὁμολογοῦσι τῷ μὴ ἀποκρίνεσθαι τὸ ἐρωτώμενον,
5 ἢ ἐλέγχεσθαι φαίνονται, οἷον ἆρ' οὗτος καὶ οὗτός
ἐστιν ἄνθρωπος; ὥστ' ἄν τις τύπτῃ τοῦτον καὶ
τοῦτον, ἄνθρωπον ἀλλ' οὐκ ἀνθρώπους τυπτήσει.
ἢ πάλιν, ὧν τὰ μέν ἐστιν ἀγαθὰ τὰ δ' οὐκ ἀγαθά,
πάντα ἀγαθὰ ἢ οὐκ ἀγαθά; ὁπότερον γὰρ ἂν φῇ,
10 ἔστι μὲν ὡς ἔλεγχον ἢ ψεῦδος φαινόμενον δόξειεν
ἂν ποιεῖν· τὸ γὰρ φάναι τῶν μὴ ἀγαθῶν τι εἶναι
ἀγαθὸν ἢ τῶν ἀγαθῶν μὴ ἀγαθὸν ψεῦδος. ὁτὲ δὲ
προσληφθέντων τινῶν κἂν ἔλεγχος γίνοιτο ἀληθινός,
οἷον εἴ τις δοίη ὁμοίως ἓν καὶ πολλὰ λέγεσθαι
λευκὰ καὶ γυμνὰ καὶ τυφλά. εἰ γὰρ τυφλὸν τὸ
μὴ ἔχον ὄψιν πεφυκὸς δ' ἔχειν, καὶ τυφλὰ ἔσται
15 τὰ μὴ ἔχοντα ὄψιν πεφυκότα δ' ἔχειν. ὅταν οὖν
τὸ μὲν ἔχῃ τὸ δὲ μὴ ἔχῃ, τὰ ἄμφω ἔσται ἢ ὁρῶντα
ἢ τυφλά· ὅπερ ἀδύνατον.

VI. Ἢ δὴ οὕτως διαιρετέον τοὺς φαινομένους
συλλογισμοὺς καὶ ἐλέγχους, ἢ πάντας ἀνακτέον
εἰς τὴν τοῦ ἐλέγχου ἄγνοιαν, ἀρχὴν ταύτην ποιη-
20 σαμένους· ἔστι γὰρ ἅπαντας ἀναλῦσαι τοὺς λεχθέν-
τας τρόπους εἰς τὸν τοῦ ἐλέγχου διορισμόν. πρῶτον
μὲν εἰ ἀσυλλόγιστοι· δεῖ γὰρ ἐκ τῶν κειμένων
συμβαίνειν τὸ συμπέρασμα, ὥστε λέγειν ἐξ ἀνάγκης
ἀλλὰ μὴ φαίνεσθαι. ἔπειτα καὶ κατὰ τὰ μέρη τοῦ

that an answer should not be given, for example, when it is asked ' Is the earth sea, or is the sky ? ' Sometimes, however, it is less easy, and thinking that there is only one question, people either give in by not answering the question or suffer an apparent refutation. For example, ' Is A and is B a man ? ' ' If so, if a man strikes A and B, he will strike a man, not men ? ' Or again, ' Where part is good and part evil, is the whole good or evil ? ' Either answer might possibly seem to involve an apparent refutation or false statement ; for to say that something is good when it is not good or not good when it is good is a false statement. Sometimes, however, if certain premisses are added, there might be a genuine refutation. For example, if one agrees that a single thing and a number of things are alike called ' white ' or ' naked ' or ' blind.' For if ' blind ' is used of something which does not possess sight though it is its nature to possess it, it will also describe a number of things which do not possess sight though it is their nature to possess it. When, therefore, one thing has sight while another has not, they will either both be able to see or both be blind ; which is impossible.

VI. We must either divide apparent reasonings and refutations in the manner just described or else refer them all to a false conception of refutation, making this our basis ; for it is possible to resolve all the kinds of fallacy which we have mentioned into violations of the definition of refutation. Firstly, we must see if they are inconclusive ; for the conclusion ought to follow from the premisses laid down, so that we state it of necessity and do not merely appear to do so. Next, we ought to see if they accord with the

[Note (a). The above fallacies can all be repre- sented as forms of a single fal- lacy, i.e. *ignoratio elenchi*.]

διορισμοῦ. τῶν μὲν γὰρ ἐν τῇ λέξει οἱ μέν εἰσι
25 παρὰ τὸ διττόν, οἷον ἥ τε ὁμωνυμία καὶ ὁ λόγος
καὶ ἡ ὁμοιοσχημοσύνη (σύνηθες γὰρ τὸ πάντα ὡς
τόδε τι σημαίνειν), ἡ δὲ σύνθεσις καὶ διαίρεσις καὶ
προσῳδία τῷ μὴ τὸν αὐτὸν εἶναι τὸν λόγον ἢ
τοὔνομα διαφέρον. ἔδει δὲ καὶ τοῦτο, καθάπερ
καὶ τὸ πρᾶγμα, ταὐτόν, εἰ μέλλει ἔλεγχος ἢ συλ-
30 λογισμὸς ἔσεσθαι, οἷον εἰ λώπιον, μὴ ἱμάτιον συλλογίσασθαι ἀλλὰ λώπιον. ἀληθὲς μὲν γὰρ κἀκεῖνο,
ἀλλ᾿ οὐ συλλελόγισται, ἀλλ᾿ ἔτι ἐρωτήματος δεῖ,
ὅτι ταὐτὸν σημαίνει, πρὸς τὸν ζητοῦντα τὸ διὰ τί.

Οἱ δὲ παρὰ τὸ συμβεβηκὸς ὁρισθέντος τοῦ συλ-
35 λογισμοῦ φανεροὶ γίνονται. τὸν αὐτὸν γὰρ ὁρισμὸν
δεῖ καὶ τοῦ ἐλέγχου γίνεσθαι, πλὴν προσκεῖσθαι
τὴν ἀντίφασιν· ὁ γὰρ ἔλεγχος συλλογισμὸς ἀντιφάσεως. εἰ οὖν μή ἐστι συλλογισμὸς τοῦ συμβεβηκότος, οὐ γίνεται ἔλεγχος. οὐ γὰρ εἰ τούτων
ὄντων ἀνάγκη τόδ᾿ εἶναι, τοῦτο δ᾿ ἐστὶ λευκόν,
40 ἀνάγκη λευκὸν εἶναι διὰ τὸν συλλογισμόν. οὐδ᾿
168 b εἰ τὸ τρίγωνον δυοῖν ὀρθαῖν ἴσας ἔχει, συμβέβηκε
δ᾿ αὐτῷ σχήματι εἶναι ἢ πρώτῳ ἢ ἀρχῇ, ὅτι
σχῆμα ἢ ἀρχὴ ἢ πρῶτον τοῦτο. οὐ γὰρ ᾗ σχῆμα
οὐδ᾿ ᾗ πρῶτον, ἀλλ᾿ ᾗ τρίγωνον, ἡ ἀπόδειξις.
ὁμοίως δὲ καὶ ἐπὶ τῶν ἄλλων. ὥστ᾿ εἰ ὁ ἔλεγχος
5 συλλογισμός τις, οὐκ ἂν εἴη ὁ κατὰ συμβεβηκὸς
ἔλεγχος. ἀλλὰ παρὰ τοῦτο καὶ οἱ τεχνῖται καὶ

remaining parts of the definition. For of the fallacies connected with language, some are due to a double meaning, for example equivocation and ambiguous phraseology and similarity of formation (for it is customary to indicate everything as a particular substance), whereas composition, division and accentuation are due to the phrase not being the same or the name different. For the name also, like the thing signified, ought to be the same, if refutation or reasoning is to result. For example, if the subject is a mantle, you should come to a conclusion about a mantle, not about a cloak; for the latter conclusion is also a true one, but the reasoning is not complete, and a further question must be asked to prove that words mean the same thing, if the answerer asks how you have refuted him.

Fallacies connected with Accident become obvious when ' proof ' has been defined. For the same definition ought to be true also of refutation, except that ' the contradictory ' is added; for refutation is a proof of the contradictory. If, therefore, there is no proof of the accident, no refutation takes place. For if, when A and B are, C is, and C is white, it does not necessarily follow that it is white because of the syllogism. And again, if the triangle has its angles equal to two right angles, and it happens to be a figure, element or principle, it does not necessarily follow that because it is a figure, element or principle it has this character; for the demonstration is concerned with it not *qua* figure or *qua* element but *qua* triangle. And so likewise with the other instances. Thus, if refutation is a kind of proof, an argument depending on an accident could not be a refutation. Yet it is along these lines that specialists and men of

37

ὅλως οἱ ἐπιστήμονες ὑπὸ τῶν ἀνεπιστημόνων
ἐλέγχονται· κατὰ συμβεβηκὸς γὰρ ποιοῦνται τοὺς
συλλογισμοὺς πρὸς τοὺς εἰδότας. οἱ δ' οὐ δυνά-
μενοι διαιρεῖν ἢ ἐρωτώμενοι διδόασιν ἢ οὐ δόντες
10 οἴονται δεδωκέναι.

Οἱ δὲ παρὰ τὸ πῆ καὶ ἁπλῶς, ὅτι οὐ τοῦ αὐτοῦ
ἡ κατάφασις καὶ ἡ ἀπόφασις. τοῦ γὰρ πῆ λευκοῦ
τὸ πῆ οὐ λευκόν, τοῦ δ' ἁπλῶς λευκοῦ τὸ ἁπλῶς
οὐ λευκὸν ἀπόφασις. εἰ οὖν δόντος πῆ εἶναι λευκὸν
15 ὡς ἁπλῶς εἰρημένου λαμβάνει, οὐ ποιεῖ ἔλεγχον,
φαίνεται δὲ διὰ τὴν ἄγνοιαν τοῦ τί ἐστιν ἔλεγχος.

Φανερώτατοι δὲ πάντων οἱ πρότερον λεχθέντες
παρὰ τὸν τοῦ ἐλέγχου διορισμόν· διὸ καὶ προσ-
ηγορεύθησαν οὕτως· παρὰ γὰρ τοῦ λόγου τὴν
20 ἔλλειψιν ἡ φαντασία γίνεται, καὶ διαιρουμένοις
οὕτως κοινὸν ἐπὶ πᾶσι τούτοις θετέον τὴν τοῦ
λόγου ἔλλειψιν.

Οἵ τε παρὰ τὸ λαμβάνειν τὸ ἐν ἀρχῇ καὶ τὸ ἀναίτιον ὡς αἴτιον τιθέναι δῆλοι διὰ τοῦ ὁρισμοῦ. δεῖ
γὰρ τὸ συμπέρασμα τῷ ταῦτ' εἶναι[1] συμβαίνειν,
25 ὅπερ οὐκ ἦν ἐν τοῖς ἀναιτίοις· καὶ πάλιν μὴ ἀριθ-
μουμένου τοῦ ἐξ ἀρχῆς, ὅπερ οὐκ ἔχουσιν οἱ παρὰ
τὴν αἴτησιν τοῦ ἐν ἀρχῇ.

Οἱ δὲ παρὰ τὸ ἑπόμενον μέρος εἰσὶ τοῦ συμβε-
βηκότος· τὸ γὰρ ἑπόμενον συμβέβηκε, διαφέρει δὲ

---

[1] Omitting αἴτια τοῦ after εἶναι with ABC.

[a] 167 a 21 ff.
[b] παραλογισμοί from παρά and λόγος in the sense of ' definition.'

science in general are refuted by the unscientific; for they argue with the men of science with reasonings based on accident, and the latter, being incapable of making distinctions, either give in when questioned, or think that they have done so when they have not.

Fallacies which depend on whether a statement is made in a limited sense or absolutely occur because the affirmation and denial are not of the same thing. For 'not partly white' is the negation of 'partly white,' and 'not absolutely white' of 'absolutely white.' If, then, one takes the admission that something is partially white to mean that it is absolutely white, he does not cause a refutation but only seems to do so owing to ignorance of what a refutation is.

(3) The confusion of absolute and qualified statements.

The clearest fallacies of all are those already mentioned [a] as connected with the definition of refutation (hence also their name) [b]; for the semblance of a refutation is due to the defect in the definition, and, if we distinguish fallacies in this way, we must put down 'defect of definition' as common to all these cases.

(4) Defective definition.

Fallacies due to assuming the original point and stating as a cause what is not a cause are clearly exposed by means of the definition. For the conclusion ought to follow because this and that is so, which is not the case when the alleged cause is not the cause; and, again, the conclusion should follow without the original point being included, which is not true of arguments based on the begging of the original point.

(5) Petitio principii.

Fallacies connected with the consequent form part of those due to accident; for the consequent is an accident but differs from the accident because the

(6) The consequent.

τοῦ συμβεβηκότος, ὅτι τὸ μὲν συμβεβηκὸς ἔστιν
30 ἐφ' ἑνὸς μόνου λαβεῖν, οἷον ταὐτὸ εἶναι τὸ ξανθὸν
καὶ μέλι καὶ τὸ λευκὸν καὶ κύκνον, τὸ δὲ παρεπό-
μενον ἀεὶ ἐν πλείοσιν· τὰ γὰρ ἑνὶ ταὐτῷ ταὐτὰ
καὶ ἀλλήλοις ἀξιοῦμεν εἶναι ταὐτά· διὸ γίνεται
παρὰ τὸ ἑπόμενον ἔλεγχος. ἔστι δ' οὐ πάντως
ἀληθές, οἷον ἂν ᾖ λευκὸν κατὰ συμβεβηκός· καὶ
35 γὰρ ἡ χιὼν καὶ ὁ κύκνος τῷ λευκῷ ταὐτόν. ἢ
πάλιν, ὡς ἐν τῷ Μελίσσου λόγῳ, τὸ αὐτὸ εἶναι
λαμβάνει τὸ γεγονέναι καὶ ἀρχὴν ἔχειν, ἢ τὸ ἴσα[1]
γίνεσθαι καὶ ταὐτὸ μέγεθος λαμβάνειν. ὅτι γὰρ
τὸ γεγονὸς ἔχει ἀρχήν, καὶ τὸ ἔχον ἀρχὴν γεγονέναι
ἀξιοῖ, ὡς ἄμφω ταὐτὰ ὄντα τῷ ἀρχὴν ἔχειν, τό
40 τε γεγονὸς καὶ τὸ πεπερασμένον.[2] ὁμοίως δὲ καὶ
169 a ἐπὶ τῶν ἴσων γινομένων εἰ τὰ τὸ αὐτὸ μέγεθος
καὶ ἓν λαμβάνοντα ἴσα γίνεται, καὶ τὰ ἴσα γινόμενα
ἓν μέγεθος λαμβάνει. ὥστε τὸ ἑπόμενον λαμβάνει.
ἐπεὶ οὖν ὁ παρὰ τὸ συμβεβηκὸς ἔλεγχος ἐν τῇ
ἀγνοίᾳ τοῦ ἐλέγχου, φανερὸν ὅτι καὶ ὁ παρὰ τὸ
5 ἑπόμενον. ἐπισκεπτέον δὲ τοῦτο καὶ ἄλλως.

Οἱ δὲ παρὰ τὸ τὰ πλείω ἐρωτήματα ἓν ποιεῖν ἐν
τῷ μὴ διαρθροῦν ἡμᾶς ἢ μὴ διαιρεῖν τὸν τῆς προτάσεως λόγον. ἡ γὰρ πρότασίς ἐστιν ἓν καθ' ἑνός.

---

[1] Reading ἴσα for ἴσοις.
[2] Bekker misprints πεπερασμένον as πεπερασμένων.

---

[a] But it does not follow that because snow is white and
swan is white, therefore snow is swan.
[b] Cf. 167 b 13 f.
[c] Cf. 179 a 26 ff., 181 a 22 ff.

accident can be secured in the case of a single thing by itself, for example, a yellow thing and honey are identical, and so is a white thing and a swan, whereas the consequent always exists in more than one thing; for we claim that things which are the same as one and the same thing are the same as one another; and this is how refutation proceeds when the consequent is involved. It is not, however, always true, for example, in the case of accidental whiteness; for both 'snow' and 'swan' are the same in respect of whiteness.[a] Or again, as in the argument of Melissus,[b] someone takes 'to have come into being' and 'to have a beginning' as the same thing, and 'to become equal' as the same thing as 'to take on the same magnitude.' For because what has come into being has a beginning, he claims also that what has a beginning has come into being, on the ground that 'having come into being' and 'being finite' are both the same thing, because both have a beginning. Similarly, too, in the case of things which become equal, he assumes that, if things which take on one and the same magnitude become equal, then also things which become equal take on the same magnitude. In doing so he is assuming the consequent. Since, then, the refutation where accident is concerned depends on ignorance of the nature of refutation, so also, it is clear, does the refutation where the consequent is concerned. But we must examine this question from other points of view also.[c]

Fallacies connected with the union of several questions in one are due to our failure to differentiate or distinguish the definition of the term 'proposition.' For a proposition is a single predication about a single subject. For the same definition applies

(7) The union of several questions in one.

169 a

ὁ γὰρ αὐτὸς ὅρος ἑνὸς μόνου καὶ ἁπλῶς τοῦ πράγ-
10 ματος, οἷον ἀνθρώπου καὶ ἑνὸς μόνου ἀνθρώπου·
ὁμοίως δὲ καὶ ἐπὶ τῶν ἄλλων. εἰ οὖν μία πρότασις
ἡ ἓν καθ᾽ ἑνὸς ἀξιοῦσα, καὶ ἁπλῶς ἔσται πρότασις
ἡ τοιαύτη ἐρώτησις. ἐπεὶ δ᾽ ὁ συλλογισμὸς ἐκ
προτάσεων, ὁ δ᾽ ἔλεγχος συλλογισμός, καὶ ὁ ἔλεγχος ἔσται ἐκ προτάσεων. εἰ οὖν ἡ πρότασις ἓν
15 καθ᾽ ἑνός, φανερὸν ὅτι καὶ οὗτος ἐν τῇ τοῦ ἐλέγχου
ἀγνοίᾳ· φαίνεται γὰρ εἶναι πρότασις ἡ οὐκ οὖσα
πρότασις. εἰ μὲν οὖν δέδωκεν ἀπόκρισιν ὡς πρὸς
μίαν ἐρώτησιν, ἔσται ἔλεγχος, εἰ δὲ μὴ δέδωκεν
ἀλλὰ φαίνεται, φαινόμενος ἔλεγχος. ὥστε πάντες
οἱ τρόποι¹ πίπτουσιν εἰς τὴν τοῦ ἐλέγχου ἄγνοιαν,
20 οἱ μὲν οὖν παρὰ τὴν λέξιν, ὅτι φαινομένη ἡ²
ἀντίφασις, ὅπερ ἦν ἴδιον τοῦ ἐλέγχου, οἱ δ᾽ ἄλλοι
παρὰ τὸν τοῦ συλλογισμοῦ ὅρον.

VII. Ἡ δ᾽ ἀπάτη γίνεται τῶν μὲν παρὰ τὴν
ὁμωνυμίαν καὶ τὸν λόγον τῷ μὴ δύνασθαι διαιρεῖν
τὸ πολλαχῶς λεγόμενον (ἔνια γὰρ οὐκ εὔπορον
25 διελεῖν, οἷον τὸ ἓν καὶ τὸ ὂν καὶ τὸ ταὐτόν), τῶν
δὲ παρὰ σύνθεσιν καὶ διαίρεσιν τῷ μηδὲν οἴεσθαι
διαφέρειν συντιθέμενον ἢ διαιρούμενον τὸν λόγον,
καθάπερ ἐπὶ τῶν πλείστων. ὁμοίως δὲ καὶ τῶν
παρὰ τὴν προσῳδίαν· οὐ γὰρ ἄλλο δοκεῖ σημαίνειν
ἀνιέμενος καὶ ἐπιτεινόμενος ὁ λόγος, ἐπ᾽ οὐδενὸς

---

¹ Reading τρόποι for τόποι with Michael Ephesius.
² Adding ἡ with Wallies.

to ' one single thing ' and to ' the thing ' simply ;
the definition, for example, of ' man ' and of ' one
single man ' is the same, and so, too, with the other
instances. If, therefore, a ' single proposition ' is
one which claims a single predicate for a single subject, a ' proposition,' simply, will also be a question
of this kind. And since reasoning is based on propositions, and refutation is a process of reasoning,
refutation will also be based on propositions. If,
therefore, a proposition is a single predication about
a single thing, clearly this fallacy also depends on
ignorance of the nature of refutation ; for what is
not a proposition appears to be one. If, therefore,
a man has given an answer as though to a single
question, there will be a refutation, but if he has not
given it but only appears to have done so, there will
be only an apparent refutation. Thus all the kinds
of fallacy fall under the heading of ignorance of the
nature of refutation—those connected with language
because the contradiction, which is a particular characteristic of refutation, is only apparent, and the
rest because of the definition of reasoning.

VII. In fallacies connected with verbal equivocation and ambiguous phrases the deception arises from
the inability to distinguish the various meanings of a
term (for there are some which it is not easy to distinguish, for example, the meanings of ' unity,' ' being '
and ' identity '). In fallacies connected with combination and disjunction the deception is due to the supposition that it makes no difference whether the term is
combined or disjoined, as indeed is generally the case.
So, too, in those connected with accentuation ; for
it does not seem ever, or seems very seldom, to alter
the significance of the word whether it is pronounced

[Note (β).
All the
above fal-
lacies arise
from con-
fused think-
ing and the
inability to
make dis-
tinctions.]

169 a

30 ἢ οὐκ ἐπὶ πολλῶν. τῶν δὲ παρὰ τὸ σχῆμα διὰ
τὴν ὁμοιότητα τῆς λέξεως. χαλεπὸν γὰρ διελεῖν
ποῖα ὡσαύτως καὶ ποῖα ὡς ἑτέρως λέγεται· σχεδὸν
γὰρ ὁ τοῦτο δυνάμενος ποιεῖν ἐγγύς ἐστι τοῦ
θεωρεῖν τἀληθές. μάλιστα δ' ἐπισπᾶται[1] συνεπι-
νεύειν, ὅτι πᾶν τὸ κατηγορούμενόν τινος ὑπο-
35 λαμβάνομεν τόδε τι καὶ ὡς ἓν ὑπακούομεν· τῷ γὰρ
ἑνὶ καὶ τῇ οὐσίᾳ μάλιστα δοκεῖ παρέπεσθαι τὸ
τόδε τι καὶ τὸ ὄν. διὸ καὶ τῶν παρὰ τὴν λέξιν
οὗτος ὁ τρόπος θετέος, πρῶτον μὲν ὅτι μᾶλλον ἡ
ἀπάτη γίνεται μετ' ἄλλων σκοπουμένοις ἢ καθ'
αὑτούς (ἡ μὲν γὰρ μετ' ἄλλου σκέψις διὰ λόγων,
40 ἡ δὲ καθ' αὑτὸν οὐχ ἧττον δι' αὐτοῦ τοῦ πράγ-
169 b ματος), εἶτα καὶ καθ' αὑτὸν ἀπατᾶσθαι συμβαίνει,
ὅταν ἐπὶ τοῦ λόγου ποιῆται τὴν σκέψιν· ἔτι ἡ μὲν
ἀπάτη ἐκ τῆς ὁμοιότητος, ἡ δ' ὁμοιότης ἐκ τῆς
λέξεως. τῶν δὲ παρὰ τὸ συμβεβηκὸς διὰ τὸ μὴ
δύνασθαι διακρίνειν τὸ ταὐτὸν καὶ τὸ ἕτερον καὶ
5 ἓν καὶ πολλά, μηδὲ τοῖς ποίοις τῶν κατηγορημάτων
πάντα ταὐτὰ καὶ τῷ πράγματι συμβέβηκεν. ὁμοίως
δὲ καὶ τῶν παρὰ τὸ ἑπόμενον· μέρος γάρ τι τοῦ
συμβεβηκότος τὸ ἑπόμενον. ἔτι καὶ ἐπὶ πολλῶν
φαίνεται καὶ ἀξιοῦται οὕτως, εἰ τόδε ἀπὸ τοῦδε
μὴ χωρίζεται, μηδ' ἀπὸ θατέρου χωρίζεσθαι θά-
10 τερον. τῶν δὲ παρὰ τὴν ἔλλειψιν τοῦ λόγου καὶ

---

[1] Reading with Poste ἐπισπᾶται for ἐπίσταται.

with a lower or a higher pitch. In fallacies connected with the form of expression the deception is due to similarity of language ; for it is difficult to distinguish what sort of things belong to the same and what to different categories ; for he who can do this very nearly approaches a vision of the truth. What in particular seduces us into giving our assent to the fallacy is the fact that we suppose that every predicate of something is an individual thing and it presents itself to our ears as a single thing ; for it is to the one and to substance that ' individuality ' and ' being ' are generally held most truly to be attached. On this account also this kind of fallacy must be classed among those connected with language ; firstly, because the deception occurs more commonly when we are inquiring with others than by ourselves (for an inquiry with someone else is carried on by means of words, whereas in our own minds it is carried on quite as much by means of the thing itself) ; secondly, because, even in solitary inquiry, a man is apt to be deceived when he carries on his inquiry by means of words ; and, thirdly, the deception arises from the similarity, and the similarity arises from the language. In fallacies connected with accident the deception is due to inability to distinguish the identical and the different, the one and the many, and what kinds of predicates have all the same accidents as their subject. So, too, in fallacies connected with the consequent ; for the consequent is a branch of the accident. Furthermore, in many cases it appears to be true and is treated as axiomatic that, if A is inseparable from B, then also B is inseparable from A. In fallacies connected with the defect in the definition of refutation and with the distinction

45

τῶν παρὰ τὸ πῇ καὶ ἁπλῶς ἐν τῷ παρὰ μικρὸν ἡ
ἀπάτη· ὡς γὰρ οὐδὲν προσσημαῖνον τὸ τί ἢ πῇ ἢ
πῶς ἢ τὸ νῦν καθόλου συγχωροῦμεν. ὁμοίως δὲ
καὶ ἐπὶ τῶν τὸ ἐν ἀρχῇ λαμβανόντων καὶ τῶν
ἀναιτίων, καὶ ὅσοι τὰ πλείω ἐρωτήματα ὡς ἓν
15 ποιοῦσιν· ἐν ἅπασι γὰρ ἡ ἀπάτη διὰ τὸ παρὰ
μικρόν· οὐ γὰρ διακριβοῦμεν οὔτε τῆς προτάσεως
οὔτε τοῦ συλλογισμοῦ τὸν ὅρον διὰ τὴν εἰρημένην
αἰτίαν.

VIII. Ἐπεὶ δ᾽ ἔχομεν παρ᾽ ὅσα γίνονται οἱ φαινόμενοι συλλογισμοί, ἔχομεν καὶ παρ᾽ ὁπόσα οἱ
20 σοφιστικοὶ γένοιντ᾽ ἂν συλλογισμοὶ καὶ ἔλεγχοι.
λέγω δὲ σοφιστικὸν ἔλεγχον καὶ συλλογισμὸν οὐ
μόνον τὸν φαινόμενον συλλογισμὸν ἢ ἔλεγχον, μὴ
ὄντα δέ, ἀλλὰ καὶ τὸν ὄντα μέν, φαινόμενον δὲ
οἰκεῖον τοῦ πράγματος. εἰσὶ δ᾽ οὗτοι οἱ μὴ κατὰ
τὸ πρᾶγμα ἐλέγχοντες καὶ δεικνύντες ἀγνοοῦντας,
25 ὅπερ ἦν τῆς πειραστικῆς. ἔστι δ᾽ ἡ πειραστικὴ
μέρος τῆς διαλεκτικῆς· αὕτη δὲ δύναται συλλογίζεσθαι ψεῦδος δι᾽ ἄγνοιαν τοῦ διδόντος τὸν λόγον.
οἱ δὲ σοφιστικοὶ ἔλεγχοι, ἂν καὶ συλλογίζωνται τὴν
ἀντίφασιν, οὐ ποιοῦσι δῆλον εἰ ἀγνοεῖ· καὶ γὰρ τὸν
εἰδότα ἐμποδίζουσι τούτοις τοῖς λόγοις.

30 Ὅτι δ᾽ ἔχομεν αὐτοὺς τῇ αὐτῇ μεθόδῳ, δῆλον·
παρ᾽ ὅσα γὰρ φαίνεται τοῖς ἀκούουσιν ὡς ἠρωτημένα συλλελογίσθαι, παρὰ ταῦτα κἂν τῷ ἀποκρινομένῳ δόξειεν, ὥστ᾽ ἔσονται συλλογισμοὶ ψευδεῖς
διὰ τούτων ἢ πάντων ἢ ἐνίων· ὁ γὰρ μὴ ἐρωτηθεὶς

between a qualified and an absolute statement the deception is due to the minuteness of the difference ; for we regard the qualification of a particular case or respect or manner or time as having no extra significance and concede the universality of the proposition. So, too, when people assume the original point and when the wrong cause is assigned and when several questions are united in one ; for in all these cases the deception is due to the minuteness of the difference ; for we fail accurately to carry out the definition of ' proposition ' and ' reasoning ' from the above-mentioned cause.

VIII. Since we know the various sources from which apparent reasonings arise, we also know those from which sophistical reasonings and refutations would arise. By sophistical refutation and reasoning I mean not only the seeming but unreal reasoning or refutation but also one which, though real, only seems to be, but is not really, germane to the subject in hand. These are those which fail to refute and show up ignorance within the sphere of the subject in hand, and this is the function of examination. Now this is a department of dialectic, but it may reach a false conclusion owing to the ignorance of the person under examination. But sophistical refutations, even if they prove the contradictory of his view, do not make clear whether he is ignorant ; for men try to entrap even the man of scientific knowledge by these arguments.

(c) By refutations which, though valid, only appear to be germane to the subject under discussion.

That we know them by the same method is clear ; for the same reasons which make the hearers think that a conclusion has been reached as a result of questions, would make the answerer think so too, so that there will be false proofs as a result of all or some of these causes ; for what a man thinks he has

[Note (a). Sophistical refutations proceed on the same lines as apparent proof.]

35 οἴεται δεδωκέναι, κἂν ἐρωτηθεὶς θείη. πλὴν ἐπί
γέ τινων ἅμα συμβαίνει προσερωτᾶν τὸ ἐνδεὲς καὶ
τὸ ψεῦδος ἐμφανίζειν, οἷον ἐν τοῖς παρὰ τὴν λέξιν
καὶ τὸν σολοικισμόν. εἰ οὖν οἱ παραλογισμοὶ τῆς
ἀντιφάσεως παρὰ τὸν φαινόμενον ἔλεγχόν εἰσι, δῆλον ὅτι παρὰ τοσαῦτα ἂν καὶ τῶν ψευδῶν εἴησαν
40 συλλογισμοὶ παρ' ὅσα καὶ ὁ φαινόμενος ἔλεγχος.
170 a ὁ δὲ φαινόμενος παρὰ τὰ μόρια τοῦ ἀληθινοῦ· ἑκάστου γὰρ ἐκλείποντος φανείη ἂν ἔλεγχος, οἷον ὁ
παρὰ τὸ μὴ συμβαῖνον διὰ τὸν λόγον, ὁ εἰς τὸ
ἀδύνατον καὶ ὁ τὰς δύο ἐρωτήσεις μίαν ποιῶν παρὰ
τὴν πρότασιν, καὶ ἀντὶ τοῦ καθ' αὑτὸ ὁ παρὰ τὸ
5 συμβεβηκός, καὶ τὸ τούτου μόριον, ὁ παρὰ τὸ
ἑπόμενον· ἔτι τὸ μὴ ἐπὶ τοῦ πράγματος ἀλλ' ἐπὶ
τοῦ λόγου συμβαίνειν· εἶτ' ἀντὶ τοῦ καθόλου τὴν
ἀντίφασιν καὶ κατὰ ταὐτὸ καὶ πρὸς ταὐτὸ καὶ
ὡσαύτως παρά τε τὸ ἐπί τι ἢ παρ' ἕκαστον τούτων·
ἔτι παρὰ τὸ μὴ ἐναριθμουμένου τοῦ ἐν ἀρχῇ τὸ ἐν
10 ἀρχῇ λαμβάνειν. ὥστ' ἔχοιμεν ἂν παρ' ὅσα γίνονται
οἱ παραλογισμοί· παρὰ πλείω μὲν γὰρ οὐκ ἂν εἶεν,
παρὰ δὲ τὰ εἰρημένα ἔσονται πάντες.

Ἔστι δ' ὁ σοφιστικὸς ἔλεγχος οὐχ ἁπλῶς ἔλεγχος, ἀλλὰ πρός τινα· καὶ ὁ συλλογισμὸς ὡσαύτως.

conceded without being questioned, he would grant if he were to be questioned. But of course it sometimes happens that, as soon as we ask the requisite question, we make the falsehood obvious, as happens in verbal fallacies and those due to solecism. If, therefore, false proofs of the contradictory depend on the apparent refutation, it is clear that proofs of false conclusions must be also due to the same number of causes as the apparent refutation. Now the apparent refutation depends on the elements which compose a genuine one; for, if any one of these is lacking, there would only be an apparent refutation, for example, that which is due to the conclusion not resulting from the argument (the reduction to an impossibility), and that which unites two questions in one and is due to a fault in the proposition, and that which is due to the substitution of an accident for the essence of a thing, and—a subdivision of the last mentioned—that which is due to the consequent; moreover, there is the case where the result follows in word only and not in reality, and also where, instead of the contradiction being universal and in the same respect, relation and manner, there is a restriction in extent or in connexion with another of these qualifications; and then again there is the case of the assumption of the original point due to a disregard of the principle of not reckoning it in. Thus we should know the various conditions under which false proofs occur, for there are no further conditions under which they could occur, but they will always result from the above causes.

A sophistical refutation is not an absolute refutation but is relative to some person, and so likewise is a sophistical proof. For unless the refutation which

[Note (δ). A sophistical refutation is not

ἂν μὲν γὰρ μὴ λάβῃ ὅ τε παρὰ τὸ ὁμώνυμον ἓν
15 σημαίνειν καὶ ὁ παρὰ τὴν ὁμοιοσχημοσύνην τὸ
μόνον τόδε καὶ οἱ ἄλλοι ὡσαύτως, οὔτ᾽ ἔλεγχοι
οὔτε συλλογισμοὶ ἔσονται, οὔθ᾽ ἁπλῶς οὔτε πρὸς
τὸν ἐρωτώμενον· ἐὰν δὲ λάβωσι, πρὸς μὲν τὸν
ἐρωτώμενον ἔσονται, ἁπλῶς δ᾽ οὐκ ἔσονται· οὐ γὰρ
ἓν σημαῖνον εἰλήφασιν, ἀλλὰ φαινόμενον, καὶ παρὰ
τοῦδε.

20 IX. Παρὰ πόσα δ᾽ ἐλέγχονται οἱ ἐλεγχόμενοι,
οὐ δεῖ πειρᾶσθαι λαμβάνειν ἄνευ τῆς τῶν ὄντων
ἐπιστήμης ἁπάντων. τοῦτο δ᾽ οὐδεμιᾶς ἐστὶ τέχ-
νης· ἄπειροι γὰρ ἴσως αἱ ἐπιστῆμαι, ὥστε δῆλον
ὅτι καὶ αἱ ἀποδείξεις. ἔλεγχοι δ᾽ εἰσὶ καὶ ἀληθεῖς·
ὅσα γὰρ ἔστιν ἀποδεῖξαι, ἔστι καὶ ἐλέγξαι τὸν
25 θέμενον τὴν ἀντίφασιν τοῦ ἀληθοῦς, οἷον εἰ σύμ-
μετρον τὴν διάμετρον ἔθηκεν, ἐλέγξειεν ἄν τις τῇ
ἀποδείξει ὅτι ἀσύμμετρος. ὥστε πάντων δεήσει
ἐπιστήμονας εἶναι· οἱ μὲν γὰρ ἔσονται παρὰ τὰς
ἐν γεωμετρίᾳ ἀρχὰς καὶ τὰ τούτων συμπεράσματα,
οἱ δὲ παρὰ τὰς ἐν ἰατρικῇ, οἱ δὲ παρὰ τὰς τῶν
30 ἄλλων ἐπιστημῶν. ἀλλὰ μὴν καὶ οἱ ψευδεῖς ἔλεγχοι
ὁμοίως ἐν ἀπείροις· καθ᾽ ἑκάστην γὰρ τέχνην ἐστὶ
ψευδὴς συλλογισμός, οἷον κατὰ γεωμετρίαν ὁ γεω-
μετρικὸς καὶ κατὰ ἰατρικὴν ὁ ἰατρικός. λέγω δὲ
τὸ κατὰ τὴν τέχνην τὸ κατὰ τὰς ἐκείνης ἀρχάς.
35 δῆλον οὖν ὅτι οὐ πάντων τῶν ἐλέγχων ἀλλὰ τῶν

depends on equivocation assumes that the equivocal term has only a single meaning, and unless that which depends on similarity of termination assumes that there is only substance, and so on, neither refutation nor proof will be possible, either absolutely or relatively, to the answerer ; whereas, if they do make these assumptions, they will be possible relatively to the answerer, but not absolutely ; for they have not secured a statement which has a single meaning but only one which appears to be such, and only from a particular person. [absolute but is relative to the answerer.]

IX. Without a knowledge of everything which exists we ought not to try and grasp the various ways in which the refutation of those who are refuted is brought about. This, however, is not the function of any art ; for the sciences are possibly infinite, and so clearly demonstrations are also infinite. Now there are true as well as false refutations ; for wherever demonstration is possible, it is possible also to refute him who maintains the contradictory of the truth ; for example, if a man maintains that the diagonal of a square is commensurate with its sides, one should refute him by proving that it is incommensurate. So we shall need to have scientific knowledge of everything ; for some refutations will depend on the principles of geometry and their conclusions, others on those of medicine, and others on those of the other sciences. Moreover, false refutations also are among things which are infinite ; for every art has a false proof peculiar to it, geometry a geometrical proof and medicine a medical proof. By ' peculiar to an art ' I mean ' in accordance with the principles of that art.' It is clear, then, that we need not grasp the commonplaces of all refutations [Note (γ). A complete grasp of all refutations is impossible, because they are infinite in number.]

51

170 a

παρὰ τὴν διαλεκτικὴν ληπτέον τοὺς τόπους· οὗτοι
γὰρ κοινοὶ πρὸς ἅπασαν τέχνην καὶ δύναμιν. καὶ
τὸν μὲν καθ' ἑκάστην ἐπιστήμην ἔλεγχον τοῦ ἐπι-
στήμονός ἐστι θεωρεῖν, εἴτε μὴ ὢν φαίνεται εἴ τ'
ἔστι, διὰ τί ἔστι· τὸν δ' ἐκ τῶν κοινῶν καὶ ὑπὸ
40 μηδεμίαν τέχνην τῶν διαλεκτικῶν. εἰ γὰρ ἔχομεν
ἐξ ὧν οἱ ἔνδοξοι συλλογισμοὶ περὶ ὁτιοῦν, ἔχομεν
170 b ἐξ ὧν οἱ ἔλεγχοι· ὁ γὰρ ἔλεγχός ἐστιν ἀντιφάσεως
συλλογισμός, ὥστ' ἢ εἷς ἢ δύο συλλογισμοὶ ἀντιφάσεως ἔλεγχός ἐστιν. ἔχομεν ἄρα παρ' ὁπόσα
πάντες εἰσὶν οἱ τοιοῦτοι. εἰ δὲ τοῦτ' ἔχομεν, καὶ
5 τὰς λύσεις ἔχομεν· αἱ γὰρ τούτων ἐνστάσεις λύσεις
εἰσίν. ἔχομεν δέ, παρ' ὁπόσα γίνονται, καὶ τοὺς
φαινομένους, φαινομένους δὲ οὐχ ὁτῳοῦν ἀλλὰ τοῖς
τοιοῖσδε· ἀόριστα γάρ ἐστιν, ἐάν τις σκοπῇ παρ'
ὁπόσα φαίνονται τοῖς τυχοῦσιν. ὥστε φανερὸν
ὅτι τοῦ διαλεκτικοῦ ἐστὶ τὸ δύνασθαι λαβεῖν παρ'
ὅσα γίνεται διὰ τῶν κοινῶν ἢ ὢν ἔλεγχος ἢ φαινό-
10 μενος ἔλεγχος, καὶ ἢ διαλεκτικὸς ἢ φαινόμενος
διαλεκτικὸς ἢ πειραστικός.

X. Οὐκ ἔστι δὲ διαφορὰ τῶν λόγων ἣν λέγουσί
τινες, τὸ εἶναι τοὺς μὲν πρὸς τοὔνομα λόγους,
ἑτέρους δὲ πρὸς τὴν διάνοιαν· ἄτοπον γὰρ τὸ ὑπο-
15 λαμβάνειν ἄλλους μὲν εἶναι πρὸς τοὔνομα λόγους,
ἑτέρους δὲ πρὸς τὴν διάνοιαν, ἀλλ' οὐ τοὺς αὐτούς.
τί γάρ ἐστι τὸ μὴ πρὸς τὴν διάνοιαν ἀλλ' ἢ ὅταν
μὴ χρῆται τῷ ὀνόματι, ἐφ' ᾧ οἰόμενος ἐρωτᾶσθαι,[1]

---

[1] Reading with Poste ἐφ' ᾧ οἰόμενος ἐρωτᾶσθαι for οἰόμενος
ἐρωτᾶσθαι ἐφ' ᾧ of the mss.

but only those which concern dialectic ; for these are common to every art and faculty. And it is the function of the scientific man to examine the refutation which is peculiar to each science and see whether it is apparent only and not real, or, if it is real, why it is so ; whereas it is the function of dialecticians to examine a refutation which depends on common principles which do not fall under any one art. For if we know the sources of generally accepted proofs about any particular subject, we know also the sources of the refutations ; for a refutation is a proof of a contradictory, and so one or two proofs of a contradictory make up a refutation. We know, then, the various sources of all such proofs, and, knowing these, we also know their solutions ; for the objections to these are the solutions. We also know the various sources of apparent refutations—apparent, that is, not to everyone but only to a certain kind of mind ; for it would be an endless task to examine the various ways in which they are apparent to the man in the street. It is, therefore, clear that it is the function of the dialectician to be able to grasp the various ways in which, on the basis of common principles, a real or apparent refutation, that is, dialectical or apparently dialectical or part of an examination, is brought about.

X. No real distinction, such as some people propose, exists between arguments used against the word and those used against the thought ; for it is absurd to suppose that some arguments are used against the word and others against the thought, and not the same in both cases. For what is failure to use the argument against the thought except what happens when a man does not apply the term in the meaning about which the man questioned thought that he

[Note (δ). The functions of the dialectician and the scientist distinguished.]

[Note (ε). Various distinctions.]
(a) Arguments against the word x those against the thought.

53

ὁ ἐρωτώμενος ἔδωκεν; τὸ δ' αὐτὸ τοῦτό ἐστι καὶ
πρὸς τοὔνομα. τὸ δὲ πρὸς τὴν διάνοιαν, ὅταν ἐφ'
20 ᾧ ἔδωκεν διανοηθείς. εἰ δὴ¹ πλείω σημαίνοντος
τοῦ ὀνόματος οἴοιτο ἓν σημαίνειν καὶ ὁ ἐρωτῶν
καὶ ὁ ἐρωτώμενος, οἷον ἴσως τὸ ὂν ἢ τὸ ἓν πολλὰ
σημαίνει, ἀλλὰ καὶ ὁ ἀποκρινόμενος καὶ ὁ ἐρωτῶν²
ἓν οἰόμενος εἶναι ἠρώτησε, καὶ ἔστιν ὁ λόγος ὅτι
ἓν πάντα, οὗτος πρὸς τοὔνομα ἔσται ἢ πρὸς τὴν
25 διάνοιαν τοῦ ἐρωτωμένου διειλεγμένος; εἰ δέ γέ
τις πολλὰ οἴεται σημαίνειν, δῆλον ὅτι οὐ πρὸς τὴν
διάνοιαν. πρῶτον μὲν γὰρ περὶ τοὺς τοιούτους
ἐστὶ λόγους τὸ πρὸς τοὔνομα καὶ πρὸς τὴν διάνοιαν
ὅσοι πλείω σημαίνουσιν, εἶτα περὶ ὁντινοῦν ἐστίν·
οὐ γὰρ ἐν τῷ λόγῳ ἐστὶ τὸ πρὸς τὴν διάνοιαν εἶναι,
30 ἀλλ' ἐν τῷ τὸν ἀποκρινόμενον ἔχειν πως πρὸς τὰ
δεδομένα. εἶτα πρὸς τοὔνομα πάντας ἐνδέχεται
αὐτοὺς εἶναι. τὸ γὰρ πρὸς τοὔνομα τὸ μὴ πρὸς
τὴν διάνοιαν εἶναί ἐστιν ἐνταῦθα. εἰ γὰρ μὴ πάντες,
ἔσονταί τινες ἕτεροι οὔτε πρὸς τοὔνομα οὔτε πρὸς
τὴν διάνοιαν· οἱ δέ φασι πάντας, καὶ διαιροῦνται
35 ἢ πρὸς τοὔνομα ἢ πρὸς τὴν διάνοιαν εἶναι πάντας,
ἄλλους δ' οὔ. ἀλλὰ μὴν ὅσοι συλλογισμοί εἰσι
παρὰ τὸ πλεοναχῶς, τούτων εἰσί τινες οἱ παρὰ

---

¹ Omitting τις after εἰ δή.
² Omitting Ζήνων after ἐρωτῶν as a gloss.

was being questioned when he made the concession ?
And this is equivalent to using it against the word ;
whereas to use it against the thought is to apply it
to the sense about which the man was thinking when
he made the concession. If, then, when the word has
more than one meaning, both the questioner and
the man questioned were to think that it had only
one meaning—as, for example, ' unity ' and ' being '
have several meanings but both the answerer answers
and the questioner puts his question on the supposition that there is only one meaning and that the
argument is that all things are one—will the argument have been directed against the word and not
rather against the thought of the man questioned ?
If, on the contrary, one of them thinks that the word
has several meanings, obviously the argument is not
directed against the thought. For application to
the word and application to the thought belong
primarily to arguments which signify several things
ambiguously, but, secondarily, to any argument whatsoever ; for the application to the thought does not
depend on the argument but on a certain attitude
of mind in the answerer towards what has been conceded. Next, it is possible for all arguments to be
applied to the word ; for in the case under discussion ' to be applied to the word ' means ' not to
be applied to the thought.' For if all are not applied
to the word or the thought, there will be a third class
not applied to either ; but they declare that the
classification is exhaustive and divide them into those
applied to the word and those applied to the thought,
and there is no other class. But, as a matter of fact,
reasonings dependent on the word are amongst those
dependent on a multiplicity of meanings. For it is an

τοὔνομα. ἀτόπως μὲν γὰρ καὶ εἴρηται τὸ παρὰ
τοὔνομα φάναι πάντας τοὺς παρὰ τὴν λέξιν· ἀλλ'
οὖν εἰσί τινες παραλογισμοὶ οὐ τῷ τὸν ἀποκρινόμενον πρὸς τούτους ἔχειν πως, ἀλλὰ τῷ τοιονδὶ
40 ἐρώτημα τὸν λόγον αὐτὸν ἔχειν, ὃ πλείω σημαίνει.

"Ὅλως τε ἄτοπον τὸ περὶ ἐλέγχου διαλέγεσθαι,
ἀλλὰ μὴ πρότερον περὶ συλλογισμοῦ· ὁ γὰρ ἔλεγχος
συλλογισμός ἐστιν, ὥστε χρὴ καὶ περὶ συλλογισμοῦ
πρότερον ἢ περὶ ψευδοῦς ἐλέγχου· ἔστι γὰρ ὁ τοιοῦ-
5 τος ἔλεγχος φαινόμενος συλλογισμὸς ἀντιφάσεως.
διὸ ἢ ἐν τῷ συλλογισμῷ ἔσται τὸ αἴτιον ἢ ἐν τῇ
ἀντιφάσει (προσκεῖσθαι γὰρ δεῖ τὴν ἀντίφασιν),
ὁτὲ δ' ἐν ἀμφοῖν, ἂν ᾖ φαινόμενος ἔλεγχος. ἔστι
δὲ ὁ μὲν τοῦ σιγῶντα λέγειν ἐν τῇ ἀντιφάσει, οὐκ
ἐν τῷ συλλογισμῷ, ὁ δέ, ἃ μὴ ἔχοι τις, δοῦναι, ἐν
10 ἀμφοῖν, ὁ δὲ ὅτι ἡ Ὁμήρου ποίησις σχῆμα διὰ τοῦ
κύκλου ἐν τῷ συλλογισμῷ. ὁ δ' ἐν μηδετέρῳ
ἀληθὴς συλλογισμός.

Ἀλλὰ δὴ ὅθεν ὁ λόγος ἦλθε, πότερον οἱ ἐν τοῖς
μαθήμασι λόγοι πρὸς τὴν διάνοιάν εἰσιν ἢ οὔ; καὶ
εἴ τινι δοκεῖ πολλὰ σημαίνειν τὸ τρίγωνον, καὶ
15 ἔδωκε μὴ ὡς τοῦτο τὸ σχῆμα ἐφ' οὗ συνεπεράνατο
ὅτι δύο ὀρθαί, πότερον πρὸς τὴν διάνοιαν οὗτος
διείλεκται τὴν ἐκείνου ἢ οὔ;

Ἔτι εἰ πολλὰ μὲν σημαίνει τοὔνομα, ὁ δὲ μὴ νοεῖ

absurd statement that 'dependent on the name' describes all arguments connected with language. The truth is that there are some false arguments which do not depend on a particular attitude of mind on the part of the answerer towards them but are due to the fact that the argument itself involves the kind of question which can bear more than one meaning.

It is quite absurd to discuss refutation without previously discussing proof ; for refutation is a proof, and so we ought to discuss proof before discussing false refutation ; for such refutation is an apparent proof of a contradiction. Therefore the cause of falsity will lie either in the proof or in the contradiction (for the contradiction must be added), but sometimes in both, if there be a merely apparent refutation. In the argument that ' the silent speaks,' the refutation lies in the contradiction, not in the proof ; in the argument that ' a man can give away what he has not got,' it lies in both ; in the argument that ' Homer's poetry is a figure ' because it forms a ' cycle,' it lies in the proof. The argument that errs in neither respect is a true proof. *(Refutation and Proof.)*

But to resume from the point whence the argument digressed,[a] Are mathematical arguments always applied to the thought or not ? If anyone thinks that the term ' triangle ' has several meanings and has granted it in a sense other than a figure which he has proved to contain two right angles, has the questioner reasoned against the answerer's thought or not ?

Further, if the name has several meanings but the answerer does not think or imagine that this is so,

[a] 170 b 40.

171 a

μηδ' οἴεται, πῶς οὗτος οὐ πρὸς τὴν διάνοιαν διείλεκται; ἢ πῶς δεῖ ἐρωτᾶν πλὴν διδόναι διαίρεσιν,
20 εἶτ' ἐρωτήσει¹ τις εἰ ἔστι σιγῶντα λέγειν ἢ οὔ, ἢ
ἔστι μὲν ὡς οὔ, ἔστι δ' ὡς ναί; εἰ δή τις δοίη
μηδαμῶς, ὁ δὲ διαλεχθείη, ἆρ' οὐ πρὸς τὴν διάνοιαν
διείλεκται; καίτοι ὁ λόγος δοκεῖ τῶν παρὰ τοὔνομα εἶναι. οὐκ ἄρα ἐστὶ γένος τι λόγων τὸ πρὸς
τὴν διάνοιαν. ἀλλ' οἱ μὲν πρὸς τοὔνομά εἰσι· καὶ
25 τοιοῦτοι οὐ πάντες, οὐχ ὅτι οἱ ἔλεγχοι, ἀλλ' οὐδ'
οἱ φαινόμενοι ἔλεγχοι. εἰσὶ γὰρ καὶ μὴ παρὰ τὴν
λέξιν φαινόμενοι ἔλεγχοι, οἷον οἱ παρὰ τὸ συμβεβηκὸς καὶ ἕτεροι.

Εἰ δέ τις ἀξιοῖ διαιρεῖν, ὅτι λέγω δὲ σιγῶντα
λέγειν τὰ μὲν ὡδὶ τὰ δ' ὡδί, ἀλλὰ τοῦτό γ' ἐστὶ
30 πρῶτον μὲν ἄτοπον, τὸ ἀξιοῦν (ἐνίοτε γὰρ οὐ δοκεῖ
τὸ ἐρωτώμενον πολλαχῶς ἔχειν, ἀδύνατον δὲ
διαιρεῖν ὃ μὴ οἴεται)· ἔπειτα τὸ διδάσκειν τί ἄλλο
ἔσται; φανερὸν γὰρ ποιήσει ὡς ἔχει τῷ μήτ'
ἐσκεμμένῳ μήτ' εἰδότι μήθ' ὑπολαμβάνοντι ὅτι ἄλλως λέγεται. ἐπεὶ καὶ ἐν τοῖς μὴ διπλοῖς τί κωλύει
35 τοῦτο παθεῖν; ἆρα ἴσαι αἱ μονάδες ταῖς δυάσιν ἐν
τοῖς τέτταρσιν; εἰσὶ δὲ δυάδες αἱ μὲν ὡδὶ ἐνοῦσαι
αἱ δὲ ὡδί. καὶ ἆρα τῶν ἐναντίων μία ἐπιστήμη ἢ
οὔ; ἔστι δ' ἐναντία τὰ μὲν γνωστὰ τὰ δ' ἄγνωστα.

¹ Reading εἶτ' ἐρωτήσει for εἶτ' ἐρωτήσειε.

has not the questioner reasoned against his thought ?
Or how else must the question be asked except by
offering a distinction ? In which case one will ask,
' Is it or is it not possible for a man to speak when
silent, or is the answer in one sense " No," in another
" Yes " ? ' But if the answerer were to refuse to
grant the possibility in any sense and the questioner
were to argue that it is possible, has he not argued
against the thought of his opponent ? Yet the argument is generally regarded as among those connected
with the name ; there is not, therefore, any class
of argument which is directed against the thought.
Some arguments are directed against the name, and
such arguments are not all of them even apparent
refutations, still less true refutations. For there are
also apparent refutations which are not connected
with language, for example, amongst others, those
connected with accident.

  But if one claims to make distinctions, saying,
' By " the silent speaking " I mean sometimes one
thing and sometimes another,' this claim is, in the
first place, absurd (for sometimes the question does
not seem to involve any ambiguity, and it is impossible to make a distinction where no ambiguity is
suspected) ; and, secondly, what else will didactic
argument be but this ? For it will make clear the
position to one who neither has considered nor knows
nor conceives that a second meaning is possible.
For why should not the same process be used where
there is no double meaning ? ' Are the units in four
equal to the twos ? Bear in mind that the twos are
contained in one sense in one way and in another
sense in another way.' Again, ' Is the knowledge
of contraries one or not ? Notice that some contraries

171 b ὥστ' ἔοικεν ἀγνοεῖν ὁ τοῦτο ἀξιῶν ὅτι ἕτερον τὸ διδάσκειν τοῦ διαλέγεσθαι, καὶ ὅτι δεῖ τὸν μὲν διδάσκοντα μὴ ἐρωτᾶν ἀλλ' αὐτὸν δῆλα ποιεῖν, τὸν δ' ἐρωτᾶν.

XI. Ἔτι τὸ φάναι ἢ ἀποφάναι ἀξιοῦν οὐ δεικνύντος ἐστίν, ἀλλὰ πεῖραν λαμβάνοντος. ἡ γὰρ
5 πειραστικὴ ἐστι διαλεκτική τις καὶ θεωρεῖ οὐ τὸν εἰδότα ἀλλὰ τὸν ἀγνοοῦντα καὶ προσποιούμενον. ὁ μὲν οὖν κατὰ τὸ πρᾶγμα θεωρῶν τὰ κοινὰ διαλεκτικός, ὁ δὲ τοῦτο φαινομένως ποιῶν σοφιστικός. καὶ συλλογισμὸς ἐριστικὸς καὶ σοφιστικός ἐστιν εἷς μὲν ὁ φαινόμενος συλλογισμός, περὶ ὧν ἡ δια-
10 λεκτικὴ πειραστική ἐστι, κἂν ἀληθὲς τὸ συμπέρασμα ᾖ· τοῦ γὰρ διὰ τί ἀπατητικός ἐστι· καὶ ὅσοι μὴ ὄντες κατὰ τὴν ἑκάστου μέθοδον παραλογισμοὶ δοκοῦσιν εἶναι κατὰ τὴν τέχνην. τὰ γὰρ ψευδογραφήματα οὐκ ἐριστικά (κατὰ γὰρ τὰ ὑπὸ τὴν τέχνην οἱ παραλογισμοί), οὐδέ γ' εἴ τί ἐστι ψευδογράφημα
15 περὶ ἀληθές, οἷον τὸ Ἱπποκράτους ἢ ὁ τετραγωνισμὸς ὁ διὰ τῶν μηνίσκων. ἀλλ' ὡς Βρύσων ἐτετραγώνιζε τὸν κύκλον, εἰ καὶ τετραγωνίζεται ὁ κύκλος, ἀλλ' ὅτι οὐ κατὰ τὸ πρᾶγμα, διὰ τοῦτο σοφιστικός. ὥστε ὅ τε περὶ τῶνδε φαινόμενος συλλογισμὸς ἐριστικὸς λόγος, καὶ ὁ κατὰ τὸ πρᾶγμα

---

[a] On the method of squaring the circle by means of lunules and those employed by Hippocrates and Bryson see Ivor Thomas, *Greek Mathematical Works* (Loeb Classical Library), vol. I, pp. 234-253, 310-313 (Hippocrates); 314-317 (Bryson); and E. Poste, *Soph. El.* pp. 245 ff.

are knowable, others are not.' Thus the man who makes this claim seems not to know that didactic is one thing and dialectic another, and that the man who employs didactic should not ask questions but himself make things clear, while the dialectician asks questions.

XI. Further, to demand that the answerer should either affirm or deny is not the function of one who is displaying something but of one who is making an examination. For the art of examination is a kind of dialectic and has in view not the man who knows but the man who is ignorant and pretends to know. The man, then, who views general principles in the light of the particular case is a dialectician, while he who only apparently does this is a sophist. Now one form of contentious and sophistic reasoning is reasoning which is only apparent, with which dialectic deals as a method of examination, even though the conclusion be true ; for it is deceptive in the matter of cause. Then there are those false reasonings which do not accord with the method of inquiry peculiar to the subject yet seem to accord with the art concerned. For false geometrical figures are not contentious (for the resultant fallacies accord with the subject-matter of the art), and the same is the case with any false figure illustrating something which is true, for example, Hippocrates' figure or the squaring of the circle by means of lunules.[a] On the other hand, Bryson's method of squaring the circle, even though this be successful, is nevertheless sophistical, because it does not accord with the subject-matter concerned. And so any merely apparent reasoning on these topics is a contentious argument, and any reasoning which merely appears to accord

20 φαινόμενος συλλογισμός, κἂν ᾖ συλλογισμός, ἐριστικὸς λόγος· φαινόμενος γάρ ἐστι κατὰ τὸ πρᾶγμα,
ὥστ᾽ ἀπατητικὸς καὶ ἄδικος. ὥσπερ γὰρ ἡ ἐν
ἀγῶνι ἀδικία εἶδός τι ἔχει καὶ ἔστιν ἀδικομαχία
τις, οὕτως ἐν ἀντιλογίᾳ ἀδικομαχία ἡ ἐριστική
ἐστιν· ἐκεῖ τε γὰρ οἱ πάντως νικᾶν προαιρούμενοι
25 πάντων ἅπτονται καὶ ἐνταῦθα οἱ ἐριστικοί. οἱ μὲν
οὖν τῆς νίκης αὐτῆς χάριν τοιοῦτοι ἐριστικοὶ ἄνθρωποι καὶ φιλέριδες δοκοῦσιν εἶναι, οἱ δὲ δόξης
χάριν τῆς εἰς χρηματισμὸν σοφιστικοί· ἡ γὰρ
σοφιστική ἐστιν, ὥσπερ εἴπομεν, χρηματιστική
τις ἀπὸ σοφίας φαινομένης, διὸ φαινομένης ἀπο-
30 δείξεως ἐφίενται. καὶ τῶν λόγων τῶν αὐτῶν μέν
εἰσιν οἱ φιλέριδες καὶ σοφισταί, ἀλλ᾽ οὐ τῶν αὐτῶν
ἕνεκεν. καὶ λόγος ὁ αὐτὸς μὲν ἔσται σοφιστικὸς
καὶ ἐριστικός, ἀλλ᾽ οὐ κατὰ ταὐτόν, ἀλλ᾽ ᾗ μὲν
νίκης φαινομένης, ἐριστικός, ᾗ δὲ σοφίας, σοφισ-
τικός· καὶ γὰρ ἡ σοφιστική ἐστι φαινομένη σοφία
35 τις ἀλλ᾽ οὐκ οὖσα. ὁ δ᾽ ἐριστικός ἐστί πως οὕτως
ἔχων πρὸς τὸν διαλεκτικὸν ὡς ὁ ψευδογράφος πρὸς
τὸν γεωμετρικόν· ἐκ γὰρ τῶν αὐτῶν τῷ διαλεκτικῷ[1]
παραλογίζεται καὶ ὁ ψευδογράφος τῷ γεωμέτρῃ.[2]
ἀλλ᾽ ὁ μὲν οὐκ ἐριστικός, ὅτι ἐκ τῶν ἀρχῶν καὶ
172 a συμπερασμάτων τῶν ὑπὸ τὴν τέχνην ψευδογράφει·
ὁ δ᾽ ὑπὸ τὴν διαλεκτικὴν περὶ μὲν τἆλλα ὅτι ἐρι-

---

[1] Reading τῷ διαλεκτικῷ with Wallies for διαλεκτικῇ.
[2] Reading τῷ γεωμέτρῃ with Poste for τὸν γεωμέτρην.

[a] 165 a 22.

with the subject-matter, even though it be genuine
reasoning, is contentious argument ; for it only
apparently accords with the subject-matter and so
is deceptive and unfair. For just as unfairness in an
athletic contest takes a definite form and is an unfair
kind of fighting, so contentious reasoning is an unfair kind of fighting in argument ; for in the former
case those who are bent on victory at all costs stick
at nothing, so too in the latter case do contentious
arguers. Those, then, who behave like this merely (d) Con-
to win a victory, are generally regarded as contentious tentious x
and quarrelsome, while those who do so to win a sophistical
reputation which will help them to make money are argument.
regarded as sophistical. For, as we have said,[a] the
art of the sophist is a money-making art which trades
on apparent wisdom, and so sophists aim at apparent
proof. Quarrelsome people and sophists use the same
arguments, but not for the same reasons ; and the
same argument will be sophistical and contentious
but not from the same point of view. If the semblance
of victory is the motive, it is contentious ; if the
semblance of wisdom, it is sophistical : for sophistry
is an appearance of wisdom without the reality. The (e) Further
contentious arguer bears much the same relation to comparisons
between
the dialectician as the drawer of false geometrical contentious
figures bears to the geometrician ; for he reasons and dia-
falsely on the same basis as the dialectician, while lectical
the drawer of false figures argues on the same basis argument.
as the true geometrician. But the latter is not a
contentious reasoner, because he constructs his false
figure on the principles and conclusions which
come under the art of geometry, whereas the former,
arguing on principles which come under dialectic,
will clearly be contentious on the other subjects.

στικός ἔσται δῆλον. οἷον ὁ τετραγωνισμὸς ὁ μὲν
διὰ τῶν μηνίσκων οὐκ ἐριστικός, ὁ δὲ Βρύσωνος
ἐριστικός· καὶ τὸν μὲν οὐκ ἔστι μετενεγκεῖν ἀλλ'
5 ἢ πρὸς γεωμετρίαν μόνον διὰ τὸ ἐκ τῶν ἰδίων
εἶναι ἀρχῶν, τὸν δὲ πρὸς πολλούς, ὅσοι μὴ ἴσασι
τὸ δυνατὸν ἐν ἑκάστῳ καὶ τὸ ἀδύνατον· ἁρμόσει
γάρ. ἢ ὡς Ἀντιφῶν ἐτετραγώνιζεν. ἢ εἴ τις μὴ
φαίη βέλτιον εἶναι ἀπὸ δείπνου περιπατεῖν διὰ τὸν
Ζήνωνος λόγον, οὐκ ἰατρικός· κοινὸς γάρ. εἰ μὲν
10 οὖν πάντῃ ὁμοίως εἶχεν ὁ ἐριστικὸς πρὸς τὸν διαλεκτικὸν τῷ ψευδογράφῳ πρὸς τὸν γεωμέτρην, οὐκ
ἂν ἦν περὶ ἐκείνων ἐριστικός. νῦν δ' οὐκ ἔστιν ὁ
διαλεκτικὸς περὶ γένος τι ὡρισμένον, οὐδὲ δεικ-
τικὸς οὐδενός, οὐδὲ τοιοῦτος οἷος ὁ καθόλου. οὔτε
γάρ ἐστιν ἅπαντα ἐν ἑνί τινι γένει, οὔτε εἰ εἴη, οἷόν
15 τε ὑπὸ τὰς αὐτὰς ἀρχὰς εἶναι τὰ ὄντα. ὥστ' οὐδεμία τέχνη τῶν δεικνυουσῶν τινὰ φύσιν ἐρωτητική ἐστιν· οὐ γὰρ ἔξεστιν ὁποτερονοῦν τῶν μορίων
δοῦναι· συλλογισμὸς γὰρ οὐ γίνεται ἐξ ἀμφοῖν. ἡ
δὲ διαλεκτικὴ ἐρωτητική ἐστιν. εἰ δ' ἐδείκνυεν,
20 εἰ καὶ μὴ πάντα, ἀλλὰ τά γε πρῶτα καὶ τὰς οἰκείας
ἀρχὰς οὐκ ἂν ἠρώτα. μὴ διδόντος[1] γὰρ οὐκ ἂν ἔτι
εἶχεν ἐξ ὧν ἔτι διαλέξεται πρὸς τὴν ἔνστασιν. ἡ

---

[1] Bekker's διδόντας is a misprint for διδόντος.

---

[a] See *Phys.* 185 a 17 ; Ivor Thomas, *op. cit.* pp. 310-317.
[b] That motion is impossible ; see *Phys.* 239 b 10 ff.

For example, the squaring of the circle by means of lunules is not contentious, whereas Bryson's method *is* contentious. It is impossible to transfer the former outside the sphere of geometry because it is based on principles which are peculiar to geometry, whereas the latter can be used against many disputants, namely, all those who do not know what is possible and what impossible in any particular case ; for it will always be applicable. And the same is true of the way in which Antiphon used to square the circle.[a] Or, again, if someone were to deny that it is better to take a walk after dinner because of Zeno's argument,[b] it would not be a medical argument ; for it is of a general application. Accordingly, if the contentious argument stood in every respect in the same relation to the dialectical as the constructor of false figures stands to the geometrician, there would be no contentious argument on those topics. But, as it is, dialectical argument has no definite sphere, nor does it demonstrate anything in particular, nor is it of the nature of the universal. For there is no genus which includes all things, and, if there were, it would not be possible for them to come under the same principles. So no art which aims at showing the nature of anything proceeds by interrogation ; for it is impossible to grant either one of two portions of the question ; for a proof cannot result from both of them. Dialectic, however, does proceed by interrogation, whereas, if it aimed at showing something, it would refrain from questions, if not about everything, at any rate about primary things and particular principles ; for if the opponent refused to grant these, dialectic would no longer have any basis on which to argue against the

δ' αὐτὴ καὶ πειραστική. οὐδὲ γὰρ ἡ πειραστικὴ
τοιαύτη ἐστὶν οἷα ἡ γεωμετρία, ἀλλ' ἣν ἂν ἔχοι
καὶ μὴ εἰδώς τις. ἔξεστι γὰρ πεῖραν λαβεῖν καὶ
τὸν μὴ εἰδότα τὸ πρᾶγμα τοῦ μὴ εἰδότος, εἴπερ
25 καὶ δίδωσιν οὐκ ἐξ ὧν οἶδεν οὐδ' ἐκ τῶν ἰδίων,
ἀλλ' ἐκ τῶν ἑπομένων, ὅσα τοιαῦτά ἐστιν ἃ εἰδότα
μὲν οὐδὲν κωλύει μὴ εἰδέναι τὴν τέχνην, μὴ εἰδότα
δ' ἀνάγκη ἀγνοεῖν. ὥστε φανερὸν ὅτι οὐδενὸς
ὡρισμένου ἡ πειραστικὴ ἐπιστήμη ἐστίν. διὸ καὶ
περὶ πάντων ἐστί· πᾶσαι γὰρ αἱ τέχναι χρῶνται
30 καὶ κοινοῖς τισίν. διὸ πάντες καὶ οἱ ἰδιῶται τρόπον
τινὰ χρῶνται τῇ διαλεκτικῇ καὶ πειραστικῇ· πάντες
γὰρ μέχρι τινὸς ἐγχειροῦσιν ἀνακρίνειν τοὺς ἐπαγ-
γελλομένους. ταῦτα δ' ἐστὶ τὰ κοινά· ταῦτα γὰρ
οὐδὲν ἧττον ἴσασιν αὐτοί, κἂν δοκῶσι λίαν ἔξω
λέγειν. ἐλέγχουσιν οὖν ἅπαντες· ἀτέχνως γὰρ
35 μετέχουσι τούτου οὗ ἐντέχνως ἡ διαλεκτική ἐστι,
καὶ ὁ τέχνῃ συλλογιστικῇ πειραστικὸς διαλεκτικός.
ἐπεὶ δ' ἐστὶ πολλὰ μὲν ταὐτὰ[1] κατὰ πάντων, οὐ
τοιαῦτα δ' ὥστε φύσιν τινὰ εἶναι καὶ γένος, ἀλλ'
οἷον αἱ ἀποφάσεις, τὰ δ' οὐ τοιαῦτα ἀλλὰ ἴδια,
ἔστιν ἐκ τούτων περὶ ἁπάντων πεῖραν λαμβάνειν,

---

[1] Reading ταὐτὰ for ταῦτα with BC and omitting καὶ with AB.

objection. Dialectic is at the same time an art of examination ; for neither is the art of examination of the same nature as geometry but it is an art which a man could possess even without any scientific knowledge. For even a man without knowledge of the subject can examine another who is without knowledge, if the latter makes concessions based not on what he knows nor on the special principles of the subject but on the consequential facts, which are such that, though to know them does not prevent him from being ignorant of the art in question, yet not to know them necessarily involves ignorance of it. Clearly, therefore, the art of examination is not knowledge of any definite subject, and it therefore follows that it deals with every subject ; for all the arts employ also certain common principles. Accordingly, everyone, including the unscientific, makes some kind of use of dialectic and the art of examination ; for all, up to a certain point, attempt to test those who profess knowledge. Now this is where the common principles come in ; for they know these of themselves just as well as the scientists, even though their expression of them seems to be very inaccurate. Thus they all practise refutation ; for they perform unmethodically the task which dialectic performs methodically, and the man who carries out an examination by means of an art of reasoning is a dialectician. Now there are many identical principles in every sphere, but these are not such as to have a particular nature and form a particular class— resembling, in this respect, negations—while others are not of this kind but limited to special spheres ; it is, therefore, possible by means of these to hold examinations on every subject, and that there can be an

172 b καὶ εἶναι τέχνην τινά, καὶ μὴ τοιαύτην εἶναι οἷαι
αἱ δεικνύουσαι. διόπερ ὁ ἐριστικὸς οὐκ ἔστιν
οὕτως ἔχων πάντη ὡς ὁ ψευδογράφος· οὐ γὰρ ἔσται
παραλογιστικὸς ἐξ ὡρισμένου τινὸς γένους ἀρχῶν,
ἀλλὰ περὶ πᾶν γένος ἔσται ὁ ἐριστικός.

5 Τρόποι μὲν οὖν εἰσὶν οὗτοι τῶν σοφιστικῶν ἐλέγ-
χων· ὅτι δ᾽ ἐστὶ τοῦ διαλεκτικοῦ τὸ θεωρῆσαι περὶ
τούτων καὶ δύνασθαι ταῦτα ποιεῖν, οὐ χαλεπὸν
ἰδεῖν· ἡ γὰρ περὶ τὰς προτάσεις μέθοδος ἅπασαν
ἔχει ταύτην τὴν θεωρίαν.

XII. Καὶ περὶ μὲν τῶν ἐλέγχων εἴρηται τῶν
10 φαινομένων· περὶ δὲ τοῦ ψευδόμενόν τι δεῖξαι καὶ
τὸν λόγον εἰς ἄδοξον ἀγαγεῖν (τοῦτο γὰρ ἦν δεύτερον τῆς σοφιστικῆς προαιρέσεως) πρῶτον μὲν οὖν
ἐκ τοῦ πυνθάνεσθαί πως καὶ διὰ τῆς ἐρωτήσεως
συμβαίνει μάλιστα. τὸ γὰρ πρὸς μηδὲν ὁρίσαντα
κείμενον ἐρωτᾶν θηρευτικόν ἐστι τούτων· εἰκῇ γὰρ
15 λέγοντες ἁμαρτάνουσι μᾶλλον· εἰκῇ δὲ λέγουσιν,
ὅταν μηδὲν ἔχωσι προκείμενον. τό τε ἐρωτᾶν
πολλά, κἂν ὡρισμένον ᾖ πρὸς ὃ διαλέγεται, καὶ τὸ
τὰ δοκοῦντα λέγειν ἀξιοῦν ποιεῖ τιν᾽ εὐπορίαν τοῦ
εἰς ἄδοξον ἀγαγεῖν ἢ ψεῦδος· ἐάν τε ἐρωτώμενος
φῇ ἢ ἀποφῇ τούτων τι, ἄγειν πρὸς ἃ ἐπιχειρήματος
20 εὐπορεῖ. δυνατὸν δὲ νῦν ἧττον κακουργεῖν διὰ
τούτων ἢ πρότερον· ἀπαιτοῦνται γὰρ τί τοῦτο πρὸς
τὸ ἐν ἀρχῇ. στοιχεῖον δὲ τοῦ τυχεῖν ἢ ψεύδους
τινὸς ἢ ἀδόξου τὸ μηδεμίαν εὐθὺς ἐρωτᾶν θέσιν,

art of doing this, though not of the same kind as the demonstrative arts. For this reason the contentious arguer is not in all respects in the same position as the constructor of a false geometrical figure ; for the contentious arguer will not reason falsely on principles of a definite class but will deal with every kind.

These, then, are the modes of sophistical refutations. It is easy to see that to investigate them and to be able to apply them is the task of the dialectician ; for the method of dealing with propositions constitutes the whole of this study.

XII. We have now dealt with apparent refutations. As for showing that the answerer is stating a fallacy and leading the argument towards a paradox—for this was the second aim of the sophist—this is, in the first place, best achieved by some kind of inquiry and by questioning. For to ask a question without defining it in relation to a subject laid down is a good method of hunting out things of this sort ; for people are more likely to fall into error when they speak at random, and they speak at random when they have no definite subject set before them. Also to ask a number of questions, even though the point against which one is arguing is defined, and to demand that the answerer should say what he thinks, gives ample opportunity of leading a man into a paradox or fallacy, and also, if, when asked, he says ' yes ' or ' no ' to any of the questions, of leading him to topics on which one has abundant material for attacking him. This unfair method, however, is much less practicable than formerly ; for people demand, ' What has this to do with the original question ? ' An elementary rule for obtaining a fallacious or paradoxical statement is not to put any thesis directly but to pretend that

(B) FAL-LACY AND (C) PARA-DOX.
How these are to be caused :

(a) By ask-ing vague questions.

(b) By ask-ing numer-ous ques-tions.

172 b

ἀλλὰ φάσκειν ἐρωτᾶν μαθεῖν βουλόμενον· χώραν
γὰρ ἐπιχειρήματος ἡ σκέψις ποιεῖ.

25 Πρὸς δὲ τὸ ψευδόμενον δεῖξαι ἴδιος τόπος ὁ σοφιστικός, τὸ ἄγειν πρὸς τοιαῦτα πρὸς ἃ εὐπορεῖ
λόγων· ἔσται δὲ καὶ καλῶς καὶ μὴ καλῶς τοῦτο
ποιεῖν, καθάπερ ἐλέχθη πρότερον.

Πάλιν πρὸς τὸ παράδοξα λέγειν σκοπεῖν ἐκ τίνος
30 γένους ὁ διαλεγόμενος, εἶτ' ἐπερωτᾶν ὃ τοῖς πολλοῖς οὗτοι λέγουσι παράδοξον· ἔστι γὰρ ἑκάστοις
τι τοιοῦτον. στοιχεῖον δὲ τούτων τὸ τὰς ἑκάστων
εἰληφέναι θέσεις ἐν ταῖς προτάσεσιν. λύσις δὲ καὶ
τούτων ἡ προσήκουσα φέρεται τὸ ἐμφανίζειν ὅτι
οὐ διὰ τὸν λόγον συμβαίνει τὸ ἄδοξον· ἀεὶ δὲ τοῦτο
35 καὶ βούλεται ὁ ἀγωνιζόμενος.

Ἔτι δ' ἐκ τῶν βουλήσεων καὶ τῶν φανερῶν
δοξῶν. οὐ γὰρ ταὐτὰ βούλονταί τε καὶ φασίν,
ἀλλὰ λέγουσι μὲν τοὺς εὐσχημονεστάτους τῶν λόγων, βούλονται δὲ τὰ φαινόμενα λυσιτελεῖν, οἷον

173 a τεθνάναι καλῶς μᾶλλον ἢ ζῆν ἡδέως φασὶ δεῖν καὶ
πένεσθαι δικαίως μᾶλλον ἢ πλουτεῖν αἰσχρῶς, βούλονται δὲ τἀναντία. τὸν μὲν οὖν λέγοντα κατὰ τὰς
βουλήσεις εἰς τὰς φανερὰς δόξας ἀκτέον, τὸν δὲ
κατὰ ταύτας εἰς τὰς ἀποκεκρυμμένας· ἀμφοτέρως
5 γὰρ ἀναγκαῖον παράδοξα λέγειν· ἢ γὰρ πρὸς τὰς
φανερὰς ἢ πρὸς τὰς ἀφανεῖς δόξας ἐροῦσιν ἐναντία.

ᵃ *Topics* 111 b 32 ff.

one is asking from a desire to learn ; for this method of inquiry gives an opening for attack.

A special method of showing up a fallacy is the sophistical method, namely, to lead one's opponent to the kind of statements against which one has plenty of arguments ; it will be possible to do this in a right and in a wrong way, as has already been said.[a]

Again, to elicit a paradox, you should see to what school the person who is discussing with you belongs, and then question him on some pronouncement of that school which most people regard as paradoxical ; for every school has some tenet of this kind. An elementary rule in this connexion is to have a ready-made collection of the theses of the different schools among your propositions. The proper solution here too is to make it clear that the paradox does not result because of the argument ; now your opponent always desires that this should be so.

Furthermore, you should seek for paradoxes in men's wishes and professed opinions. For they do not wish the same things as they declare that they wish, but they give utterance to the most becoming sentiments, whereas they desire what they think is to their interest. They declare, for example, that a noble death ought to be preferred to a pleasurable life and honourable poverty to discreditable wealth ; but their wishes are the opposite of their words. He, therefore, whose statements agree with his wishes must be led to express the opinions usually professed, and he whose statements agree with the latter must be led to state the opinions usually hidden ; for in both cases they must necessarily fall into paradox, for they will contradict either their professed or their secret opinions.

(c) By inducing one's opponent to make statements which can be easily refuted.

(d) By questioning him on the tenets of the philosophical school to which he belongs, or his views in general.

71

Πλεῖστος δὲ τόπος ἐστὶ τοῦ ποιεῖν παράδοξα
λέγειν, ὥσπερ καὶ ὁ Καλλικλῆς ἐν τῷ Γοργίᾳ γέγραπται λέγων, καὶ οἱ ἀρχαῖοι δὲ πάντες ᾤοντο
10 συμβαίνειν, παρὰ τὸ κατὰ φύσιν καὶ κατὰ τὸν
νόμον· ἐναντία γὰρ εἶναι φύσιν καὶ νόμον, καὶ τὴν
δικαιοσύνην κατὰ νόμον μὲν εἶναι καλὸν κατὰ φύσιν δ' οὐ καλόν. δεῖν οὖν πρὸς μὲν τὸν εἰπόντα
κατὰ φύσιν κατὰ νόμον ἀπαντᾶν, πρὸς δὲ τὸν κατὰ
νόμον ἐπὶ τὴν φύσιν ἄγειν· ἀμφοτέρως γὰρ ἔσται[1]
15 λέγειν παράδοξα. ἦν δὲ τὸ μὲν κατὰ φύσιν
αὐτοῖς τὸ ἀληθές, τὸ δὲ κατὰ νόμον τὸ τοῖς πολλοῖς
δοκοῦν. ὥστε δῆλον ὅτι κἀκεῖνοι, καθάπερ καὶ οἱ
νῦν, ἢ ἐλέγξαι ἢ παράδοξα λέγειν τὸν ἀποκρινόμενον ἐπεχείρουν ποιεῖν.

Ἔνια δὲ τῶν ἐρωτημάτων ἔχει ἀμφοτέρως ἄδοξον
20 εἶναι τὴν ἀπόκρισιν, οἷον πότερον τοῖς σοφοῖς ἢ τῷ
πατρὶ δεῖ πείθεσθαι, καὶ τὰ συμφέροντα πράττειν
ἢ τὰ δίκαια, καὶ ἀδικεῖσθαι αἱρετώτερον ἢ βλάπτειν.
δεῖ δ' ἄγειν εἰς τὰ τοῖς πολλοῖς καὶ τοῖς σοφοῖς
ἐναντία, ἐὰν μὲν λέγῃ τις ὡς οἱ περὶ τοὺς λόγους,
25 εἰς τὰ τοῖς πολλοῖς, ἐὰν δ' ὡς οἱ πολλοί, ἐπὶ τὰ
τοῖς ἐν λόγῳ. φασὶ γὰρ οἱ μὲν ἐξ ἀνάγκης τὸν
εὐδαίμονα δίκαιον εἶναι· τοῖς δὲ πολλοῖς ἄδοξον τὸ
βασιλέα μὴ εὐδαιμονεῖν. ἔστι δὲ τὸ εἰς τὰ οὕτως
ἄδοξα συνάγειν τὸ αὐτὸ τῷ εἰς τὴν κατὰ φύσιν καὶ
κατὰ νόμον ὑπεναντίωσιν ἄγειν· ὁ μὲν γὰρ νόμος
30 δόξα τῶν πολλῶν, οἱ δὲ σοφοὶ κατὰ φύσιν καὶ κατ'
ἀλήθειαν λέγουσιν.

---

[1] Reading ἔσται for εἶναι.

[a] Plato, *Gorgias* 482 E.

A commonplace rule which makes men utter paradoxes in abundance is the application of the standards of nature and law, which Callicles is represented as applying in the *Gorgias* [a] and which all the ancients regarded as valid ; for according to them Nature and Law are opposites, and justice is a good thing according to law but not according to nature. Therefore, to a man who speaks in terms of nature you must reply in terms of law, and when he speaks in terms of law you must lead the argument to terms of nature ; for in both cases the result will be that he utters paradoxes. In the view of the ancients what accorded with nature was the truth, while what accorded with law was the general opinion of mankind. It is, therefore, clear that they also, like the men of to-day, tried to refute the answerer or to make him utter paradoxes.

Some questions involve a paradox whichever way they are answered ; for example, ' Ought one to obey the wise or one's father ? ' and, ' Ought one to do what is expedient or what is just ? ' and ' Is it preferable to suffer or to inflict a wrong ? ' You ought to lead men to opinions opposed to those of the majority and of the wise—if a man speaks as trained arguers do, you should lead him to opinions opposed to the majority ; if he speaks as do the majority, to opinions opposed to expert reasoners. For some say that the happy man is necessarily just, but in the view of the majority it is paradoxical that a king should not be happy. To lead a man to paradoxes of this kind is the same thing as to bring him into opposition to the standards of nature and law ; for law is the opinion of the majority, but the utterances of the wise accord with the standards of nature and truth.

(*e*) By asking questions, the answers to which must be paradoxical.

XIII. Καὶ τὰ μὲν παράδοξα ἐκ τούτων δεῖ ζητεῖν
τῶν τόπων· περὶ δὲ τοῦ ποιῆσαι ἀδολεσχεῖν, ὃ μὲν
λέγομεν τὸ ἀδολεσχεῖν, εἰρήκαμεν ἤδη. πάντες δὲ
οἱ τοιοίδε λόγοι τοῦτο βούλονται ποιεῖν· εἰ μηδὲν
35 διαφέρει τὸ ὄνομα ἢ τὸν λόγον εἰπεῖν, διπλάσιον
δὲ καὶ διπλάσιον ἡμίσεος ταὐτό, εἰ ἄρα ἐστὶν ἡμίσεος διπλάσιον, ἔσται ἡμίσεος ἡμίσεος διπλάσιον.
καὶ πάλιν ἂν ἀντὶ τοῦ διπλάσιον διπλάσιον ἡμίσεος
τεθῇ, τρὶς ἔσται εἰρημένον, ἡμίσεος ἡμίσεος ἡμίσεος
διπλάσιον. καὶ ἆρά ἐστιν ἡ ἐπιθυμία ἡδέος; τοῦτο
40 δ᾽ ἐστὶν ὄρεξις ἡδέος· ἔστιν ἄρα ἡ ἐπιθυμία ὄρεξις
ἡδέος ἡδέος.

173 b Εἰσὶ δὲ πάντες οἱ τοιοῦτοι τῶν λόγων ἔν τε τοῖς
πρός τι, ὅσα μὴ μόνον τὰ γένη ἀλλὰ καὶ αὐτὰ πρός
τι λέγεται, καὶ πρὸς τὸ αὐτὸ καὶ ἓν ἀποδίδοται (οἷον
ἥ τε ὄρεξις τινὸς ὄρεξις καὶ ἡ ἐπιθυμία τινὸς ἐπι-
5 θυμία, καὶ τὸ διπλάσιον τινὸς διπλάσιον καὶ διπλάσιον ἡμίσεος)· καὶ ὅσων ἡ οὐσία οὐκ ὄντων
πρός τι ὅλως, ὧν εἰσὶν ἕξεις ἢ πάθη ἤ τι τοιοῦτον,
ἐν τῷ λόγῳ αὐτῶν προσδηλοῦται κατηγορουμένων
ἐπὶ τούτοις. οἷον τὸ περιττὸν ἀριθμὸς μέσον ἔχων·
ἔστι δ᾽ ἀριθμὸς περιττός· ἔστιν ἄρα ἀριθμὸς μέσον
10 ἔχων ἀριθμός. καὶ εἰ τὸ σιμὸν κοιλότης ῥινός
ἐστιν, ἔστι δὲ ῥὶς σιμή, ἔστιν ἄρα ῥὶς ῥὶς κοίλη.

Φαίνονται δὲ ποιεῖν οὐ ποιοῦντες ἐνίοτε διὰ τὸ μὴ
προσπυνθάνεσθαι εἰ σημαίνει τι καθ᾽ αὑτὸ λεχθὲν

ᵃ 165 b 16.

XIII. It is, then, by these commonplace rules that you should seek to obtain paradoxes. Next, as to making people babble, we have already said what we mean by this term.[a] Arguments of the following kind all have this end in view ; ' If it makes no difference whether one uses the term or the definition of it, and " double " and " double of half " are the same thing, then if " double " is " double of half," it will be " double of half of half " ; and if " double of half " be substituted again for " double," there will be a triple repetition, " double of half of half of half." ' Again, ' Is not " desire " " desire of pleasure ? " Now " desire is an appetite for pleasure " : therefore " desire is an appetite for pleasure of pleasure." '

All arguments of this kind take place (a) when relative terms are used, where not only the genera but the terms themselves are relative and are rendered in relation to one and the same thing (for example, appetite is appetite for something, and desire is desire of something, and double is double of something, namely, double of half), and (b) where terms are used of which, though they are not relative at all, the substance (namely, the things of which they are states or affections or the like) is indicated in their definition, since they are predicated of these things. For example, ' odd ' is a ' number which has a middle unit,' and an ' odd number ' exists, therefore an ' odd number ' is ' number-that-has-a middle-unit number.' Again, if ' snubness ' is ' concavity of the nose,' and there is a ' snub nose,' then a ' snub nose ' is a ' concave-nose nose.'

Men sometimes appear to induce ' babbling ' when they do not really do so, because they do not further inquire whether ' double ' used by itself has a signifi-

τὸ διπλάσιον ἢ οὐδέν, καὶ εἴ τι σημαίνει, πότερον
15 τὸ αὐτὸ ἢ ἕτερον, ἀλλὰ τὸ συμπέρασμα λέγειν
εὐθύς. ἀλλὰ φαίνεται διὰ τὸ τὸ ὄνομα ταὐτὸ εἶναι
ταὐτὸ καὶ σημαίνειν.

XIV. Σολοικισμὸς δ' οἷον μέν ἐστιν εἴρηται πρότερον.[a] ἔστι δὲ τοῦτο καὶ ποιεῖν καὶ μὴ ποιοῦντα
φαίνεσθαι καὶ ποιοῦντα μὴ δοκεῖν, καθάπερ ὁ
20 Πρωταγόρας ἔλεγεν, εἰ ὁ μῆνις καὶ ὁ πήληξ ἄρρεν
ἐστίν· ὁ μὲν γὰρ λέγων οὐλομένην σολοικίζει μὲν
κατ' ἐκεῖνον, οὐ φαίνεται δὲ τοῖς ἄλλοις, ὁ δὲ οὐλόμενον φαίνεται μὲν ἀλλ' οὐ σολοικίζει. δῆλον οὖν
ὅτι κἂν τέχνῃ τις τοῦτο δύναιτο ποιεῖν· διὸ πολλοὶ
τῶν λόγων οὐ συλλογιζόμενοι σολοικισμὸν φαίνον-
25 ται συλλογίζεσθαι, καθάπερ ἐν τοῖς ἐλέγχοις.

Εἰσὶ δὲ πάντες σχεδὸν οἱ φαινόμενοι σολοικισμοὶ
παρὰ τὸ τόδε, καὶ ὅταν ἡ πτῶσις μήτε ἄρρεν μήτε
θῆλυ δηλοῖ ἀλλὰ τὸ μεταξύ. τὸ μὲν οὗτος ἄρρεν
σημαίνει, τὸ δ' αὕτη θῆλυ· τὸ δὲ τοῦτο θέλει μὲν τὸ
30 μεταξὺ σημαίνειν, πολλάκις δὲ σημαίνει κἀκείνων
ἑκάτερον, οἷον τί τοῦτο; Καλλιόπη, ξύλον, Κορίσκος. τοῦ μὲν οὖν ἄρρενος καὶ τοῦ θήλεος διαφέρουσιν αἱ πτώσεις ἅπασαι, τοῦ δὲ μεταξὺ αἱ μὲν
αἱ δ' οὔ. δοθέντος δὴ πολλάκις τοῦτο, συλλογί-
ζονται ὡς εἰρημένου τοῦτον· ὁμοίως δὲ καὶ ἄλλην
35 πτῶσιν ἀντ' ἄλλης. ὁ δὲ παραλογισμὸς γίνεται
διὰ τὸ κοινὸν εἶναι τὸ τοῦτο πλειόνων πτώσεων·[b]

ᵃ 165 b 20.   ᵇ Because it is in fact feminine.

cation or no, and, if it has, whether the same or a
different one, but they appear to draw the conclusion
immediately. It appears, however, to have the same
signification also because the word is the same.

XIV. What solecism is has already been stated.[a] (E) SOLE-
It is possible to commit it, and not to commit it, How this
yet to seem to do so, as well as to commit it, yet can be
seem not to do so. If, as Protagoras used to say, induced.
μῆνις (wrath) and πήληξ (helmet) are masculine,
according to him, he who calls wrath a 'destruc-
tress' (οὐλομένην) commits a solecism, though he
does not appear to anyone else to do so,[b] but he
who calls it a 'destructor' (οὐλόμενον) appears to
commit a solecism but does not do so. It is obvious,
therefore, that one might produce this effect by art
also; therefore many arguments appear to infer a
solecism, when they do not really do so, as happens
also with refutations.

Almost all apparent solecisms occur owing to the
word 'this' or 'it' (τόδε) and when the inflection
denotes neither the masculine nor the feminine but
the neuter. 'He' (οὗτος) denotes a masculine, 'she'
(αὕτη) a feminine, whereas 'this' or 'it' (τοῦτο),
though meaning to signify a neuter, often signifies
either a masculine or a feminine. For example,
'What is this (τοῦτο)?' 'It is Calliope,' or 'It is
a log' or 'It is Coriscus.' The case-forms of the
masculine and feminine are all different, but some
of those of the neuter are different and others not.
Often, therefore, when 'it' (τοῦτο) has been granted,
people argue as if 'him' (τοῦτον) had been used, and
they similarly use another case in place of some
other. The false reasoning arises because 'it' (τοῦτο)
is common to more than one case; for it signifies

173 b

τὸ γὰρ τοῦτο σημαίνει ὁτὲ μὲν οὗτος ὁτὲ δὲ τοῦτον.
δεῖ δ' ἐναλλὰξ σημαίνειν, μετὰ μὲν τοῦ ἔστι τὸ
οὗτος, μετὰ δὲ τοῦ εἶναι τὸ τοῦτον, οἷον ἔστι
Κορίσκος, εἶναι Κορίσκον. καὶ ἐπὶ τῶν θηλέων
40 ὀνομάτων ὡσαύτως, καὶ ἐπὶ τῶν λεγομένων μὲν
174 a σκευῶν ἐχόντων δὲ θηλείας ἢ ἄρρενος κλῆσιν. ὅσα
γὰρ εἰς τὸ ο καὶ τὸ ν τελευτᾷ, ταῦτα μόνα σκεύους
ἔχει κλῆσιν, οἷον ξύλον, σχοινίον, τὰ δὲ μὴ οὕτως
ἄρρενος ἢ θήλεος, ὧν ἔνια φέρομεν ἐπὶ τὰ σκεύη,
5 οἷον ἀσκὸς μὲν ἄρρεν τοὔνομα, κλίνη δὲ θῆλυ.
διόπερ καὶ ἐπὶ τῶν τοιούτων ὡσαύτως τὸ ἔστι καὶ
τὸ εἶναι διοίσει. καὶ τρόπον τινὰ ὅμοιός ἐστιν ὁ
σολοικισμὸς τοῖς παρὰ τὸ τὰ μὴ ὅμοια ὁμοίως
λεγομένοις ἐλέγχοις. ὥσπερ γὰρ ἐκείνοις ἐπὶ τῶν
πραγμάτων, τούτοις ἐπὶ τῶν ὀνομάτων συμπίπτει
σολοικίζειν· ἄνθρωπος γὰρ καὶ λευκὸν καὶ πρᾶγμα
καὶ ὄνομά ἐστιν.

10 Φανερὸν οὖν ὅτι τὸν σολοικισμὸν πειρατέον ἐκ
τῶν εἰρημένων πτώσεων συλλογίζεσθαι.

Εἴδη μὲν οὖν ταῦτα τῶν ἀγωνιστικῶν λόγων καὶ
μέρη τῶν εἰδῶν καὶ τρόποι οἱ εἰρημένοι. διαφέρει
δ' οὐ μικρόν, ἐὰν ταχθῇ πως τὰ περὶ τὴν ἐρώτησιν
15 πρὸς τὸ λανθάνειν, ὥσπερ ἐν τοῖς διαλεκτικοῖς.
ἐφεξῆς οὖν τοῖς εἰρημένοις ταῦτα πρῶτον λεκτέον.

XV. Ἔστι δὴ πρὸς τὸ ἐλέγχειν ἓν μὲν μῆκος·

---

[a] *i.e.* the fallacy from the figure of speech (*figura dictionis*).

sometimes ' he ' (οὗτος) and sometimes ' him ' (τοῦτον). It ought to signify them alternately ; with the indicative ' is ' (ἐστί) it ought to signify the nominative ' he ' (οὗτος) ; with the infinitive ' to be ' (εἶναι) it ought to signify ' him ' (τοῦτον), for example, ' It is Coriscus,' ' [I believe] it to be Coriscus.' So likewise with feminine nouns and with so-called articles of use, which can have either a masculine or a feminine designation ; for only those which end in -ον have the designation which belongs to an article of use, e.g., ξύλον (log), σχοινίον (rope). Those which do not take this form have a masculine or a feminine termination, and some of these we apply to articles of use ; for example, ἀσκός (wine-skin) is masculine and κλίνη (bed) is feminine. Therefore, in such cases there will be the same difference when the indicative ' is ' (ἐστί) is used and the infinitive ' to be ' (εἶναι). Also, in a way, solecism resembles the kind of refutation which is due to the use of similar terms for dissimilar things [a] ; for as in the one case it happens that we commit a solecism in the category of actual things, so in the other we commit it in that of names ; for ' man ' and ' white ' are both names and things.

Clearly, then, we must try and argue up to a solecism on the basis of the above-mentioned case-forms.

These are the branches of competitive arguments and their sub-divisions, and the above are the methods of employing them. Now it makes no small difference whether the accompaniments of the question are arranged in a certain way with a view to concealment, as in dialectics. Therefore, as a sequel to what has been said above, we must first treat of this subject.

XV. To effect a refutation one expedient is length ; How to ask

79

χαλεπὸν γὰρ ἅμα πολλὰ συνορᾶν. εἰς δὲ τὸ μῆκος
τοῖς προειρημένοις στοιχείοις χρηστέον. ἓν δὲ
20 τάχος· ὑστερίζοντες γὰρ ἧττον προορῶσιν. ἔτι δ'
ὀργὴ καὶ φιλονεικία· ταραττόμενοι γὰρ ἧττον δύνανται φυλάττεσθαι πάντες. στοιχεῖα δὲ τῆς ὀργῆς
τό τε φανερὸν ἑαυτὸν ποιεῖν βουλόμενον ἀδικεῖν
καὶ τὸ παράπαν ἀναισχυντεῖν. ἔτι τὸ ἐναλλὰξ τὰ
ἐρωτήματα τιθέναι, ἐάν τε πρὸς ταὐτὸ πλείους τις
25 ἔχῃ λόγους, ἐάν τε καὶ ὅτι οὕτως καὶ ὅτι οὐχ
οὕτως· ἅμα γὰρ συμβαίνει ἢ πρὸς πλείω ἢ πρὸς
τἀναντία ποιεῖσθαι τὴν φυλακήν. ὅλως δὲ πάντα
τὰ πρὸς τὴν κρύψιν λεχθέντα πρότερον χρήσιμα
καὶ πρὸς τοὺς ἀγωνιστικοὺς λόγους· ἡ γὰρ κρύψις
ἐστὶ τοῦ λαθεῖν χάριν, τὸ δὲ λαθεῖν τῆς ἀπάτης.
30 Πρὸς δὲ τοὺς ἀνανεύοντας ἅττ' ἂν οἰηθῶσιν
εἶναι πρὸς τὸν λόγον, ἐξ ἀποφάσεως ἐρωτητέον,
ὡς τοὐναντίον βουλόμενον, ἢ καὶ ἐξ ἴσου ποιοῦντα
τὴν ἐρώτησιν· ἀδήλου γὰρ ὄντος τοῦ τί βούλεται
λαβεῖν ἧττον δυσκολαίνουσιν. ὅταν τ' ἐπὶ τῶν
μερῶν διδῷ τις τὸ καθ' ἕκαστον, ἐπάγοντα τὸ
35 καθόλου πολλάκις οὐκ ἐρωτητέον, ἀλλ' ὡς δεδο-
μένῳ χρηστέον· ἐνίοτε γὰρ οἴονται καὶ αὐτοὶ δεδωκέναι καὶ τοῖς ἀκούουσι φαίνονται διὰ τὴν τῆς

---

^a *Topics* viii. 1.

for it is difficult to keep many things in view simultaneously. To produce length the above-mentioned elementary rules must be employed. One resource is speed ; for when people lag behind they see less far ahead. Further, there are anger and contentiousness ; for when people are agitated they are always less capable of being on their guard. Elementary rules for rousing anger are to make it plain that one wishes to act unfairly and to behave in an altogether shameless manner. Another device is to put one's questions alternately, whether one has several arguments leading up to the same point or whether one has arguments proving both that this is so and that this is not so ; for the result is that the answerer is on his guard at the same time against either several or contrary attacks. In a word, all the resources for concealment mentioned before [a] are also useful against competitive arguments ; for concealment is for the purpose of escaping detection, and escape from detection is for the purpose of deception.

When dealing with those who refuse to consent to anything which they think is in favour of your argument, you must put your question in a negative form, as though you wanted the opposite of what you really want, or, at any rate, as if you were asking your question with indifference ; for people are less troublesome when it is not clear what one wants to secure. Often, when in dealing with particulars a man grants the individual case, you ought not, in the process of induction, to make the universal the subject of your question but assume that it is granted and use it accordingly ; for sometimes people think that they have themselves granted it and appear to their hearers to have done so, because they recall

questions effectively : (1) By prolixity and rapidity.

(2) By alternating questions.

(3) By interrogation from negation.

(4) By assuming that the universal has been granted.

81

174 a

ἐπαγωγῆς μνείαν, ὡς οὐκ ἂν ἠρωτημένα μάτην.
ἐν οἷς τε μὴ ὀνόματι σημαίνεται τὸ καθόλου, ἀλλὰ
τῇ ὁμοιότητι χρηστέον πρὸς τὸ συμφέρον· λανθάνει
40 γὰρ ἡ ὁμοιότης πολλάκις. πρός τε τὸ λαβεῖν τὴν
174 b πρότασιν τοὐναντίον παραβάλλοντα χρὴ πυνθάνεσθαι. οἷον εἰ δέοι λαβεῖν ὅτι δεῖ πάντα τῷ πατρὶ
πείθεσθαι, πότερον ἅπαντα δεῖ πείθεσθαι τοῖς γο-
νεῦσιν ἢ πάντ' ἀπειθεῖν; καὶ τὸ πολλάκις πολλά,
5 πότερον πολλὰ συγχωρητέον ἢ ὀλίγα; μᾶλλον γάρ,
εἴπερ ἀνάγκη, δόξειεν ἂν εἶναι πολλά· παρατιθε-
μένων γὰρ ἐγγὺς τῶν ἐναντίων, καὶ μείζω καὶ
μεγάλα φαίνεται καὶ χείρω καὶ βελτίω τοῖς ἀνθρώποις.

Σφόδρα δὲ καὶ πολλάκις ποιεῖ δοκεῖν ἐληλέγχθαι
τὸ μάλιστα σοφιστικὸν συκοφάντημα τῶν ἐρωτών-
10 των, τὸ μηδὲν συλλογισαμένους μὴ ἐρώτημα ποιεῖν
τὸ τελευταῖον, ἀλλὰ συμπεραντικῶς εἰπεῖν, ὡς
συλλελογισμένους, οὐκ ἄρα τὸ καὶ τό.

Σοφιστικὸν δὲ καὶ τὸ κειμένου παραδόξου τὸ
φαινόμενον ἀξιοῦν ἀποκρίνεσθαι προκειμένου τοῦ
δοκοῦντος ἐξ ἀρχῆς, καὶ τὴν ἐρώτησιν τῶν τοιού-
15 των οὕτω ποιεῖσθαι, πότερόν σοι δοκεῖ; ἀνάγκη
γάρ, ἂν ᾖ τὸ ἐρώτημα ἐξ ὧν ὁ συλλογισμός, ἢ
ἔλεγχον ἢ παράδοξον γίνεσθαι, δόντος μὲν ἔλεγχον,

---

[a] Cf. *Topics* 156 b 10 ff.

the process of induction and think that the question would not have been asked without some object. Where there is no term to signify the universal, you should nevertheless use the resemblance of the particulars [a] for your advantage ; for the resemblance often passes unnoticed. Also, in order to secure your premiss, you should contrast it with its contrary in your question. For example, if you want to secure the premiss that one ought to obey one's father in all things, you should ask whether one should obey one's parents in all things or disobey them in all things. If you want to establish that the multiplication of a number many times over results in a large number, you should ask whether it should be conceded that it is a large or that it is a small number ; for, if pressed, one would rather that it should seem to be large. For the juxtaposition of contraries increases the quantity and quality of things, both relatively and absolutely, in the eyes of men.

(5) By assuming that a proposition is effected through comparison of the contrary.

Often the most sophistical of all frauds practised by questioners produces a striking appearance of refutation, when, though they have proved nothing, they do not put the final proposition in the form of a question but state conclusively, as though they had proved it, that ' such and such a thing, then, is not the case.'

(6) By substituting a statement for a question.

Another sophistical trick is, when the thesis is a paradox, to demand, when the generally accepted view is originally proposed, that the answerer should reply what he thinks about it, and to put one's question in some such form as ' Is that your opinion ? ' For, if the question is one of the premisses of the argument, either a refutation or a paradox must result. If he grants the premiss, there will be a

(7) By placing your opponent on the horns of a dilemma.

83

μὴ δόντος δὲ μηδὲ δοκεῖν φάσκοντος ἄδοξον, μὴ
δόντος δὲ δοκεῖν δ' ὁμολογοῦντος ἐλεγχοειδές.

Ἔτι καθάπερ καὶ ἐν τοῖς ῥητορικοῖς, καὶ ἐν τοῖς
20 ἐλεγκτικοῖς ὁμοίως τὰ ἐναντιώματα θεωρητέον ἢ
πρὸς τὰ ὑφ' ἑαυτοῦ λεγόμενα, ἢ πρὸς οὓς ὁμολογεῖ
καλῶς λέγειν ἢ πράττειν, ἔτι πρὸς τοὺς δοκοῦντας
τοιούτους ἢ πρὸς τοὺς ὁμοίους ἢ πρὸς τοὺς πλεί-
στους ἢ πρὸς πάντας. ὥσπερ τε καὶ ἀποκρινόμενοι
πολλάκις, ὅταν ἐλέγχωνται, ποιοῦσι διττόν, ἂν
25 μέλλῃ συμβαίνειν ἐλεγχθήσεσθαι, καὶ ἐρωτῶντας
χρηστέον ποτὲ τούτῳ πρὸς τοὺς ἐνισταμένους, ἂν
ὡδὶ μὲν συμβαίνῃ ὡδὶ δὲ μή, ὅτι οὕτως εἴληφεν,
οἷον ὁ Κλεοφῶν ποιεῖ ἐν τῷ Μανδροβούλῳ. δεῖ δὲ
καὶ ἀφισταμένους τοῦ λόγου τὰ λοιπὰ τῶν ἐπιχει-
ρημάτων ἐπιτέμνειν, καὶ τὸν ἀποκρινόμενον, ἂν
30 προαισθάνηται, προενίστασθαι καὶ προαγορεύειν.
ἐπιχειρητέον δ' ἐνίοτε καὶ πρὸς ἄλλα τοῦ εἰρημένου, ἐκεῖνο ἐκλαβόντας, ἐὰν μὴ πρὸς τὸ κείμενον
ἔχῃ τις ἐπιχειρεῖν· ὅπερ ὁ Λυκόφρων ἐποίησε προβληθέντος λύραν ἐγκωμιάζειν. πρὸς δὲ τοὺς ἀπ-
αιτοῦντας πρός τι ἐπιχειρεῖν, ἐπειδὴ δοκεῖ δεῖν
35 ἀποδιδόναι τὴν αἰτίαν, λεχθέντων δ' ἐνίων εὐφυ-
λακτότερον, τὸ καθόλου συμβαῖνον ἐν τοῖς ἐλέγχοις
λέγειν, τὴν ἀντίφασιν, ὅ τι ἔφησεν ἀποφῆσαι, ἢ ὃ

---

[a] It has been conjectured that the author of this dialogue
was Speusippus.

refutation ; if he refuses to grant it and even denies that it is the generally accepted view, he utters a paradox ; if he refuses to grant it but admits that it is the generally accepted view, there will be the appearance of a refutation.

Moreover, as in rhetorical arguments, so likewise also in refutations, you ought to look for contradictions between the answerer's views and either his own statements or the views of those whose words and actions he admits to be right, or of those who are generally held to bear a like character and to resemble them, or of the majority, or of all mankind. (8) By seeking contradictions between the views of your opponent and the school to which he belongs.

Also, just as answerers, when they are being refuted, often draw a distinction, if they are on the point of being refuted, so questioners also ought sometimes, when dealing with objectors, if the objection is valid against one sense of the word but not against another, to resort to the expedient of declaring that the opponent has taken it in such and such a sense, as Cleophon does in the *Mandrobulus*.ᵃ They ought also to withdraw from the argument and cut short their other attacks, while the answerer, if he perceives this move in time, should raise anticipatory objections and get his argument in first. One should also sometimes attack points other than the one mentioned, excluding it if one can make no attack on the position laid down, as Lycophron did when it was suggested that he should deliver an encomium on the lyre. To those who demand that one should take some definite point of attack (since it is generally held that one ought to assign the object of a question, whereas if certain statements are made the defence is easier), you should say that your aim is the usual result of refutation, namely, to deny what your opponent (9) By pleading that a term has a double sense.

(10) By withdrawal from your position to avoid attack.

(11) By attacking irrelevant points.

(12) By maintaining that your object is simply the contradiction of your opponent's thesis.

ἀπέφησε φῆσαι, ἀλλὰ μὴ ὅτι τῶν ἐναντίων ἡ αὐτὴ
ἐπιστήμη ἢ οὐχ ἡ αὐτή. οὐ δεῖ δὲ τὸ συμπέρασμα
προτατικῶς ἐρωτᾶν· ἔνια δ' οὐδ' ἐρωτητέον, ἀλλ'
40 ὡς ὁμολογουμένοις[1] χρηστέον.

175 a XVI. Ἐξ ὧν μὲν οὖν αἱ ἐρωτήσεις, καὶ πῶς
ἐρωτητέον ἐν ταῖς ἀγωνιστικαῖς διατριβαῖς, εἴρηται·
περὶ δὲ ἀποκρίσεως, καὶ πῶς χρὴ λύειν καὶ τί, καὶ
πρὸς τίνα χρῆσιν οἱ τοιοῦτοι τῶν λόγων ὠφέλιμοι,
μετὰ ταῦτα λεκτέον.

5 Χρήσιμοι μὲν οὖν εἰσὶ πρὸς μὲν φιλοσοφίαν διὰ
δύο. πρῶτον μὲν γὰρ ὡς ἐπὶ τὸ πολὺ γινόμενοι
παρὰ τὴν λέξιν ἄμεινον ἔχειν ποιοῦσι πρὸς τὸ
ποσαχῶς ἕκαστον λέγεται, καὶ ποῖα ὁμοίως καὶ
ποῖα ἑτέρως ἐπί τε τῶν πραγμάτων συμβαίνει καὶ
10 ἐπὶ τῶν ὀνομάτων. δεύτερον δὲ πρὸς τὰς καθ'
αὐτὸν ζητήσεις· ὁ γὰρ ὑφ' ἑτέρου ῥᾳδίως παραλογιζόμενος καὶ τοῦτο μὴ αἰσθανόμενος κἂν αὐτὸς
ὑφ' αὑτοῦ τοῦτο πάθοι πολλάκις. τρίτον δὲ καὶ
τὸ λοιπὸν ἔτι πρὸς δόξαν, τὸ περὶ πάντα γεγυμνάσθαι δοκεῖν καὶ μηδενὸς ἀπείρως ἔχειν· τὸ γὰρ
15 κοινωνοῦντα λόγων ψέγειν λόγους, μηδὲν ἔχοντα
διορίζειν περὶ τῆς φαυλότητος αὐτῶν, ὑποψίαν
δίδωσι τοῦ δοκεῖν δυσχεραίνειν οὐ διὰ τἀληθὲς
ἀλλὰ δι' ἀπειρίαν.

Ἀποκρινομένοις δὲ πῶς ἀπαντητέον πρὸς τοὺς
τοιούτους λόγους, φανερόν, εἴπερ ὀρθῶς εἰρήκαμεν
πρότερον ἐξ ὧν εἰσὶν οἱ παραλογισμοί, καὶ τὰς ἐν
20 τῷ πυνθάνεσθαι πλεονεξίας ἱκανῶς διείλομεν. οὐ
ταὐτὸν δ' ἐστὶ λαβόντα τε τὸν λόγον ἰδεῖν καὶ λῦσαι
τὴν μοχθηρίαν, καὶ ἐρωτώμενον ἀπαντᾶν δύνασθαι

---

[1] Reading ὁμολογουμένοις with Wallies for ὁμολογουμένῳ.

affirmed and affirm what he denied, and not to prove that the knowledge of contraries is the same or not the same. One should not ask the conclusion in the form of a proposition, and some propositions should not be asked at all but treated as admitted.

XVI. We have now dealt with the sources of questions and how they ought to be asked in competitive arguments. We must next treat of answering, and how solutions are brought about, and what are their subjects, and for what purpose such arguments are useful.

They are useful for philosophy for two reasons. In the first place, as they generally turn on language, they put us in a better position to appreciate the various meanings which a term can have and what similarities and differences attach to things and their names. Secondly, they are useful for the questions which arise in one's own mind ; for he who is easily led astray by another person into false reasoning and does not notice his error, might also often fall into this error in his own mind. A third and last reason is that they establish our reputation, by giving us the credit of having received a universal training and of having left nothing untried ; for that one who is taking part in an argument should find fault with arguments without being able to specify where their weakness lies, rouses a suspicion that his annoyance is apparently not in the interests of truth but due to inexperience.

How answerers should meet such arguments is obvious if we have adequately described above [a] the sources of false arguments and distinguished the fraudulent methods of questioning. To take an argument and see and disentangle the fault in it is not the same thing as to be able to meet it promptly when

THE SOLUTION OF FALLACIES (chs. xvi-xxxiii). General Remarks. The reasons for studying solutions.

The necessity for practice.

[a] 165 b 24 ff.

175 a

ταχέως. ὃ γὰρ ἴσμεν, πολλάκις μετατιθέμενον ἀγ-
νοοῦμεν. ἔτι δ᾽, ὥσπερ ἐν τοῖς ἄλλοις τὸ θᾶττον καὶ
τὸ βραδύτερον ἐκ τοῦ γεγυμνάσθαι γίνεται μᾶλλον,
25 οὕτω καὶ ἐπὶ τῶν λόγων ἔχει, ὥστε, ἂν δῆλον
μὲν ἡμῖν ᾖ, ἀμελέτητοι δ᾽ ὦμεν, ὑστεροῦμεν τῶν
καιρῶν πολλάκις. συμβαίνει δέ ποτε, καθάπερ ἐν
τοῖς διαγράμμασιν· καὶ γὰρ ἐκεῖ ἀναλύσαντες ἐνίοτε
συνθεῖναι πάλιν ἀδυνατοῦμεν· οὕτω καὶ ἐν τοῖς
30 ἐλέγχοις, εἰδότες παρ᾽ ὃ ὁ λόγος συμβαίνει συν-
εῖραι, διαλῦσαι τὸν λόγον ἀποροῦμεν.

XVII. Πρῶτον μὲν οὖν, ὥσπερ συλλογίζεσθαί
φαμεν ἐνδόξως ποτὲ μᾶλλον ἢ ἀληθῶς προαιρεῖσθαι
δεῖν, οὕτω καὶ λυτέον ποτὲ μᾶλλον ἐνδόξως ἢ κατὰ
τἀληθές. ὅλως γὰρ πρὸς τοὺς ἐριστικοὺς μαχε-
35 τέον οὐχ ὡς ἐλέγχοντας ἀλλ᾽ ὡς φαινομένους· οὐ
γάρ φαμεν συλλογίζεσθαί γε αὐτούς, ὥστε πρὸς
τὸ μὴ δοκεῖν διορθωτέον. εἰ γάρ ἐστιν ὁ ἔλεγχος
ἀντίφασις μὴ ὁμώνυμος ἔκ τινων, οὐδὲν ἂν δέοι
διαιρεῖσθαι πρὸς τἀμφίβολα καὶ τὴν ὁμωνυμίαν·
οὐ γὰρ ποιεῖ συλλογισμόν. ἀλλ᾽ οὐδενὸς ἄλλου
40 χάριν προσδιαιρετέον ἀλλ᾽ ἢ ὅτι τὸ συμπέρασμα
φαίνεται ἐλεγχοειδές. οὔκουν τὸ ἐλεγχθῆναι ἀλλὰ
τὸ δοκεῖν εὐλαβητέον, ἐπεὶ τό γ᾽ ἐρωτᾶν ἀμφίβολα
175 b καὶ τὰ παρὰ τὴν ὁμωνυμίαν, ὅσαι τ᾽ ἄλλαι τοιαῦται
παρακρούσεις, καὶ τὸν ἀληθινὸν ἔλεγχον ἀφανίζει
καὶ τὸν ἐλεγχόμενον καὶ μὴ ἐλεγχόμενον ἄδηλον
ποιεῖ. ἐπεὶ γὰρ ἔξεστιν ἐπὶ τέλει συμπερανομένου

one is asked a question. For we often fail to recognize something which we know when it is presented in a different form. Furthermore, as in other spheres a greater degree of speed or slowness is rather a question of training, so in argument also ; therefore, even though something may be clear to us, yet, if we lack practice, we often miss our opportunities. The same thing happens sometimes as with geometrical diagrams ; for there we sometimes analyse a figure but cannot reconstruct it ; so too in refutations we know how the argument is strung together, but we are at a loss how to take it to pieces.

XVII. In the first place, then, just as we say that we ought sometimes deliberately to argue plausibly rather than truthfully, so too we ought sometimes to solve questions plausibly rather than according to truth. For, generally speaking, when we have to fight against contentious arguers, we ought to regard them not as trying to refute us but as merely appearing to do so ; for we deny that they are arguing a case, so that they must be corrected so as not to appear to be doing so. For if refutation is unequivocal contradiction based on certain premises, there can be no necessity to make distinctions against ambiguity and equivocation ; for they do not make up the proof. But the only other reason for making further distinctions is because the conclusion looks like a refutation. One must, therefore, beware not of being refuted but of appearing to be so, since the asking of ambiguities and questions involving equivocation and all similar fraudulent artifices mask even a genuine refutation and make it uncertain who is refuted and who is not. For when it is possible in the end, when the conclusion is reached, to say that

Apparent solutions, rather than real, must sometimes be sought.

5 μὴ ὅπερ ἔφησεν ἀποφῆσαι λέγειν, ἀλλ' ὁμωνύμως,
εἰ καὶ ὅτι μάλιστ' ἔτυχεν ἐπὶ ταὐτὸν φέρων, ἄδηλον
εἰ ἐλήλεγκται· ἄδηλον γὰρ εἰ ἀληθῆ λέγει νῦν. εἰ
δὲ διελὼν ἤρετο τὸ ὁμώνυμον ἢ τὸ ἀμφίβολον,
οὐκ ἂν ἄδηλος ἦν ὁ ἔλεγχος. ὅ τ' ἐπιζητοῦσι νῦν
μὲν ἧττον πρότερον δὲ μᾶλλον οἱ ἐριστικοί, τὸ ἢ
10 ναί ἢ οὒ ἀποκρίνεσθαι τὸν ἐρωτώμενον, ἐγίνετ'
ἄν. νῦν δὲ διὰ τὸ μὴ καλῶς ἐρωτᾶν τοὺς πυνθανο-
μένους ἀνάγκη προσαποκρίνεσθαί τι τὸν ἐρωτώμενον, διορθοῦντα τὴν μοχθηρίαν τῆς προτάσεως,
ἐπεὶ διελομένου γε ἱκανῶς ἢ ναί ἢ οὒ ἀνάγκη λέγειν
τὸν ἀποκρινόμενον.

15 Εἰ δέ τις ὑπολήψεται τὸν κατὰ ὁμωνυμίαν ἔλεγχον
εἶναι, τρόπον τινὰ οὐκ ἔσται διαφυγεῖν τὸ ἐλέγχεσθαι τὸν ἀποκρινόμενον· ἐπὶ γὰρ τῶν ὁρατῶν
ἀναγκαῖον ὃ ἔφησεν ἀποφῆσαι ὄνομα, καὶ ὃ ἀπέφησε φῆσαι. ὡς γὰρ διορθοῦνταί τινες, οὐδὲν
20 ὄφελος. οὐ γὰρ Κορίσκον φασὶν εἶναι μουσικὸν
καὶ ἄμουσον, ἀλλὰ τοῦτον τὸν Κορίσκον μουσικὸν
καὶ τοῦτον τὸν Κορίσκον ἄμουσον. ὁ γὰρ αὐτὸς
ἔσται λόγος τὸ τοῦτον[1] τὸν Κορίσκον τῷ τοῦτον
τὸν Κορίσκον ἄμουσον εἶναι ἢ μουσικόν· ὅπερ ἅμα
φησί τε καὶ ἀπόφησιν. ἀλλ' ἴσως οὐ ταὐτὸ ση-
μαίνει· οὐδὲ γὰρ ἐκεῖ τοὔνομα. ὥστε τί διαφέρει;[2]

---

[1] τοῦτον added by Waitz.
[2] Poste reads τί for τι and adds the question mark.

one's opponent contradicted what he asserted only by means of an equivocation, however true it may be that he happened to be tending in the same direction, it is uncertain whether a refutation has taken place ; for it is uncertain whether he is speaking the truth now. If, however, one had made a distinction and questioned the equivocal or ambiguous term, the refutation would not have been uncertain. Also, the object of contentious arguers—though it is less their aim in these days than formerly—would have been carried out, namely, that the person questioned should answer ' Yes ' or ' No ' ; as it is, however, because the questioners put their questions improperly, the person questioned is obliged to add something in his answer by way of correcting the unfairness of the proposition, since, if the questioner makes adequate distinctions, the answerer must say either ' Yes ' or ' No.'

If anyone is going to imagine that an argument which rests on equivocal terms is a refutation, it will be impossible for the answerer to avoid being refuted in a certain sense ; for in dealing with visible things one must necessarily deny the term which he asserted and assert that which he denied. For the correction which some people suggest is useless. For they do not say that Coriscus is musical and unmusical, but that *this* Coriscus is musical and *this* Coriscus is unmusical. For it will be making use of the same expression to say that *this* Coriscus is unmusical (or musical) as to say that *this* Coriscus is so ; and one is affirming and denying this at the same time. But perhaps it does not mean the same thing ; for neither did the name in the former case ; so what is the difference ? But if he is going to assign to the

If one supposes that an argument which rests on equivocation is a refutation, the answerer cannot escape being in a sense refuted.

91

25 εἰ δὲ τῷ μὲν τὸ ἁπλῶς λέγειν Κορίσκον ἀποδώσει,
τῷ δὲ προσθήσει τὸ τινὰ ἢ τόνδε, ἄτοπον· οὐδὲν
γὰρ μᾶλλον θατέρῳ· ὁποτέρῳ γὰρ ἂν οὐδὲν διαφέρει.

Οὐ μὴν ἀλλ' ἐπειδὴ ἄδηλος μέν ἐστιν ὁ μὴ διορι-
σάμενος τὴν ἀμφιβολίαν πότερον ἐλήλεγκται ἢ οὐκ
30 ἐλήλεγκται, δέδοται δ' ἐν τοῖς λόγοις τὸ διελεῖν,
φανερὸν ὅτι τὸ μὴ διορίσαντα δοῦναι τὴν ἐρώτησιν
ἀλλ' ἁπλῶς ἁμάρτημά ἐστιν, ὥστε κἂν εἰ μὴ αὐτός,
ἀλλ' ὅ γε λόγος ἐληλεγμένῳ ὅμοιός ἐστιν. συμβαίνει μέντοι πολλάκις ὁρῶντας τὴν ἀμφιβολίαν
ὀκνεῖν διαιρεῖσθαι διὰ τὴν πυκνότητα τῶν τὰ τοι-
35 αῦτα προτεινόντων, ὅπως μὴ πρὸς ἅπαν δοκῶσι
δυσκολαίνειν· εἶτ' οὐκ ἂν οἰηθέντων παρὰ τοῦτο
γενέσθαι τὸν λόγον, πολλάκις ἀπήντησε παράδοξον.
ὥστ' ἐπειδὴ δέδοται διαιρεῖν, οὐκ ὀκνητέον, καθάπερ
ἐλέχθη πρότερον.

Εἰ δὲ τὰ δύο ἐρωτήματα μὴ ἓν ποιεῖ τις ἐρώτημα,
40 οὐδ' ἂν ὁ παρὰ τὴν ὁμωνυμίαν καὶ τὴν ἀμφιβολίαν
ἐγίνετο παραλογισμός, ἀλλ' ἢ ἔλεγχος ἢ οὔ. τί
176 a γὰρ διαφέρει ἐρωτῆσαι εἰ Καλλίας καὶ Θεμιστοκλῆς
μουσικοί εἰσιν ἢ εἰ ἀμφοτέροις ἓν ὄνομα ἦν ἑτέροις
οὖσιν; εἰ γὰρ πλείω δηλοῖ ἑνός, πλείω ἠρώτησεν.
εἰ οὖν μὴ ὀρθὸν πρὸς δύο ἐρωτήσεις μίαν ἀπόκρισιν
ἀξιοῦν λαμβάνειν ἁπλῶς, φανερὸν ὅτι οὐδενὶ προσ-
5 ήκει τῶν ὁμωνύμων ἀποκρίνεσθαι ἁπλῶς, οὐδ' εἰ

one person the simple appellation ' Coriscus,' while
to the other he adds ' a certain ' or ' that,' it is absurd ;
for the addition belongs no more to the one than to
the other ; for it makes no difference to whichever
of the two he adds it.

However, since, if one does not distinguish the
meanings of a doubtful term, it is not clear whether
he has been confuted or not, and since the right to
draw distinctions is conceded in arguments, it is
obvious that to grant the question simply, without
making distinctions, is a mistake ; so that, even if
the man himself does not appear to be refuted, yet
his argument certainly appears to be so. It frequently
happens, however, that, though people see the
ambiguity, they hesitate to make the distinction,
because of the numerous occasions on which people
propose subjects of this kind, in order to avoid seeming
to be acting perversely all the time. Then, again,
though people would never have thought that the
argument would hinge upon this point, they are often
confronted with a paradox. So, since the right to
draw a distinction is conceded, we must not hesitate
to use it, as was said before. The am-
biguity
must be
explained.

If one does not make two questions into one, the
fallacy which depends on equivocation and ambiguity
would not exist either, but either refutation or absence
of refutation. For what is the difference between asking whether Callias and Themistocles are musical and
asking the same question about two people both with
the same name ? For if one indicates more things
than one, one has asked more questions than one. If,
therefore, it is not correct to demand simply to
receive one answer to two questions, clearly it is not
proper to give a simple answer to any equivocal The ques-
tioner by
ambiguity
makes two
questions
into one.

κατὰ πάντων ἀληθές, ὥσπερ ἀξιοῦσί τινες. οὐδὲν
γὰρ τοῦτο διαφέρει ἢ εἰ ἤρετο, Κορίσκος καὶ
Καλλίας πότερον οἴκοι εἰσὶν ἢ οὐκ οἴκοι, εἴτε παρόν-
των ἀμφοῖν εἴτε μὴ παρόντων· ἀμφοτέρως γὰρ
πλείους αἱ προτάσεις· οὐ γὰρ εἰ ἀληθὲς εἶπεν,[1] διὰ
10 τοῦτο μία ἡ ἐρώτησις. ἐγχωρεῖ γὰρ καὶ μυρία
ἕτερα ἐρωτηθέντα ἐρωτήματα ἅπαντα ἢ ναὶ ἢ οὒ
ἀληθὲς εἶναι λέγειν· ἀλλ' ὅμως οὐκ ἀποκριτέον μιᾷ
ἀποκρίσει· ἀναιρεῖται γὰρ τὸ διαλέγεσθαι. τοῦτο
δ' ὅμοιον ὡς εἰ καὶ τὸ αὐτὸ ὄνομα τεθείη τοῖς
ἑτέροις. εἰ οὖν μὴ δεῖ πρὸς δύο ἐρωτήσεις μίαν
15 ἀπόκρισιν διδόναι, φανερὸν ὅτι οὐδ' ἐπὶ τῶν ὁμωνύμων τὸ ναὶ ἢ οὒ λεκτέον. οὐδὲ γὰρ ὁ εἰπὼν
ἀποκέκριται ἀλλ' εἴρηκεν. ἀλλ' ἀξιοῦταί[2] πως ἐν
τοῖς διαλεγομένοις διὰ τὸ λανθάνειν τὸ συμβαῖνον.

Ὥσπερ οὖν εἴπομεν, ἐπειδήπερ οὐδ' ἔλεγχοί
20 τινες ὄντες δοκοῦσιν εἶναι, κατὰ τὸν αὐτὸν τρόπον
καὶ λύσεις δόξουσιν εἶναί τινες οὐκ οὖσαι λύσεις·
ἃς δή φαμεν ἐνίοτε μᾶλλον δεῖν φέρειν ἢ τὰς ἀληθεῖς ἐν τοῖς ἀγωνιστικοῖς λόγοις καὶ τῇ πρὸς τὸ
διττὸν ἀπαντήσει. ἀποκριτέον δ' ἐπὶ μὲν τῶν
δοκούντων τὸ ἔστω λέγοντα· καὶ γὰρ οὕτως ἥκιστα
25 γίνοιτ' ἂν παρεξέλεγχος· ἂν δέ τι παράδοξον ἀναγ-
κάζηται λέγειν, ἐνταῦθα μάλιστα προσθετέον τὸ
δοκεῖν· οὕτω γὰρ ἂν οὔτ' ἔλεγχος οὔτε παράδοξον
γίνεσθαι δόξειεν. ἐπεὶ δὲ πῶς αἰτεῖται τὸ ἐν ἀρχῇ

---

[1] Reading εἶπεν for εἰπεῖν.
[2] Reading ἀξιοῦταί for ἀξιοῦνταί with Wallies.

question, even though the term is true of all the subjects, as some people claim that one ought. For this is just the same as asking ' Are Coriscus and Callias at home or not at home ?,' whether they are both at home or not there ; for in both cases the number of propositions is more than one. For if the answer is true, it does not follow that the question is a single one. For it is possible that it is true to say ' yes ' or ' no ' when asked a countless number of questions ; but, for all that, one ought not to answer them with a single reply, for that means the ruin of discussion. This resembles the case of the same name being applied to different things. If, therefore, one must not give one answer to two questions, it is obvious that neither should one say ' yes ' or ' no ' where equivocal terms are used ; for then the speaker has not given an answer but made a statement, but it is regarded in a way as an answer amongst those who argue, because they do not realize what is the result.

As we said, then, since there are some seeming refutations which are not really refutations, in like manner also there are some seeming solutions which are not really solutions. These we say that we ought sometimes to bring forward in preference to true refutations in competitive argument and in meeting ambiguity. In the case of statements which appear to be true one must answer with the phrase ' granted ' ; for then there is the least likelihood of any accessory refutation ; but if one is obliged to say something paradoxical, then in particular one must add that it seems so, for then there can be no appearance either of refutation or of paradox. Since it is clear what ' begging the original question ' means and since

How the reply is to be made.

95

176 a

δῆλον, οἴονται δὲ πάντες, ἂν[1] ᾖ σύνεγγυς, ἀναιρετέον καὶ μὴ συγχωρητέον εἶναι ἔνια ὡς τὸ ἐν ἀρχῇ
30 αἰτοῦντος, ὅταν τὸ[2] τοιοῦτον ἀξιοῖ τις ὃ ἀναγκαῖον
μὲν συμβαίνειν ἐκ τῆς θέσεως, ᾗ δὲ ψεῦδος ἢ ἄδοξον,
ταὐτὸ λεκτέον· τὰ γὰρ ἐξ ἀνάγκης συμβαίνοντα
τῆς αὐτῆς εἶναι δοκεῖ θέσεως. ἔτι ὅταν τὸ καθόλου
μὴ ὀνόματι ληφθῇ ἀλλὰ παραβολῇ, λεκτέον ὅτι οὐχ
35 ὡς ἐδόθη οὐδ' ὡς προὔτεινε λαμβάνει· καὶ γὰρ
παρὰ τοῦτο γίνεται πολλάκις ἔλεγχος.

Ἐξειργόμενον δὲ τούτων ἐπὶ τὸ μὴ καλῶς δε-
δεῖχθαι πορευτέον, ἀπαντῶντα κατὰ τὸν εἰρημένον
διορισμόν.

Ἐν μὲν οὖν τοῖς κυρίως λεγομένοις ὀνόμασιν
ἀνάγκη ἀποκρίνεσθαι ἢ ἁπλῶς ἢ διαιρούμενον. ἃ
40 δὲ συνυπονοοῦντες τίθεμεν, οἷον ὅσα μὴ σαφῶς
176 b ἀλλὰ κολοβῶς ἐρωτᾶται, παρὰ τοῦτο συμβαίνει
ὁ ἔλεγχος, οἷον ἆρ' ὃ ἂν ᾖ Ἀθηναίων, κτῆμά ἐστιν
Ἀθηναίων; ναί. ὁμοίως δὲ καὶ ἐπὶ τῶν ἄλλων.
ἀλλὰ μὴν ὁ ἄνθρωπός ἐστι τῶν ζῴων; ναί. κτῆμα
5 ἄρα ὁ ἄνθρωπος τῶν ζῴων. τὸν γὰρ ἄνθρωπον
τῶν ζῴων λέγομεν, ὅτι ζῷόν ἐστι, καὶ Λύσανδρον
τῶν Λακώνων, ὅτι Λάκων. δῆλον οὖν ὡς ἐν οἷς
ἀσαφὲς τὸ προτεινόμενον οὐ συγχωρητέον ἁπλῶς.

Ὅταν δὲ δυοῖν ὄντοιν θατέρου μὲν ὄντος ἐξ

---

[1] Reading ἂν for ἃν with Wallies.
[2] Reading τὸ for τε with Wallies.

---

[a] 168 a 17 ff.

people always consider that assumptions which lie near the conclusion must be demolished and that some of them must not be conceded on the ground that the opponent is begging the question, so when someone claims something of such a nature that it must necessarily follow from the thesis and it is false or paradoxical, we must use the same plea ; for the necessary consequences are generally regarded as part of the same thesis. Furthermore, when the universal which has been obtained has no name but is indicated by a comparison only, we must say that the questioner takes it not in the sense in which it was granted nor as he proposed it ; for a refutation often hinges on this point too.

When we are excluded from these expedients, we must have recourse to the plea that the argument has not been properly set forth, attacking it on the basis of the classification of fallacies given above.[a]

When terms are used in their proper senses, one must answer either simply or by making a distinction. It is when our statement implies our meaning without expressing it—for example, when a question is not asked clearly but in a shortened form—that refutation ensues. For instance, ' Is whatever belongs to the Athenians a property of the Athenians ?' ' Yes ; and this is likewise true of everything else.' ' Well, then, does man belong to the animals ?' ' Yes.' ' Then man is a property of the animals. For we say that man " belongs to " the animals because he is an animal, just as we say that Lysander " belongs to " the Laconians because he is a Laconian.' Obviously, therefore, when the premiss is not clear, it must not be conceded simply. *What is obscure in an argument must not be conceded.*

When it is generally held that, if one of two things *Other de-*

97

176 b

ἀνάγκης θάτερον εἶναι δοκῇ, θατέρου δὲ τοῦτο μὴ
10 ἐξ ἀνάγκης, ἐρωτώμενον πότερον¹ δεῖ τὸ ἔλαττον
διδόναι· χαλεπώτερον γὰρ συλλογίσασθαι ἐκ πλειόνων. ἐὰν δ' ἐπιχειρῇ ὅτι τῷ μέν ἐστιν ἐναντίον
τῷ δ' οὐκ ἔστιν, ἂν ὁ λόγος ἀληθὴς ᾖ, ἐναντίον
φάναι, ὄνομα δὲ μὴ κεῖσθαι τοῦ ἑτέρου.

'Επεὶ δ' ἔνια μὲν ὧν λέγουσιν οἱ πολλοὶ τὸν μὴ
15 συγχωροῦντα ψεύδεσθαι ἂν φαῖεν ἔνια δ' οὔ, οἷον
ὅσα ἀμφιδοξοῦσιν (πότερον γὰρ φθαρτὴ ἢ ἀθάνατος
ἡ ψυχὴ τῶν ζῴων, οὐ διώρισται τοῖς πολλοῖς), ἐν
οἷς οὖν ἄδηλον ποτέρως εἴωθε λέγεσθαι τὸ προτεινόμενον, πότερον ὡς αἱ γνῶμαι (καλοῦσι γὰρ
γνώμας καὶ τὰς ἀληθεῖς δόξας καὶ τὰς ὅλας ἀποφά-
20 σεις), ἢ ὡς ἡ διάμετρος ἀσύμμετρος, ἔτι τε² οὗ
τἀληθὲς ἀμφιδοξεῖται, μάλιστα μεταφέρων ἄν τις
λανθάνοι τὰ ὀνόματα περὶ τούτων. διὰ μὲν γὰρ τὸ
ἄδηλον εἶναι ποτέρως ἔχει τἀληθές, οὐ δόξει σοφί-
ζεσθαι, διὰ δὲ τὸ ἀμφιδοξεῖν οὐ δόξει ψεύδεσθαι·
25 ἡ γὰρ³ μεταφορὰ ποιήσει τὸν λόγον ἀνεξέλεγκτον.

"Ετι ὅσα ἄν τις προαισθάνηται τῶν ἐρωτημάτων,
προενστατέον καὶ προαγορευτέον· οὕτω γὰρ ἂν
μάλιστα τὸν πυνθανόμενον κωλύσειν.

¹ Reading πότερον for πρότερον.
² Inserting τε after ἔτι.
³ Reading γὰρ for δὲ with AB.

is true, then the other is necessarily true, but, if the second is true, the first is not necessarily true, when asked which is true, we ought to concede the less inclusive ; for the greater the number of premisses, the more difficult it is to draw a conclusion. If the disputant tries to establish that A has a contrary while B has not, if his contention is true, we ought to say that both have a contrary but that no name is laid down for one of the two.

vices to be employed.

Regarding some of the statements which they make, most people would declare that anyone who did not concede them was lying, while they would not say so about others, for example, about subjects on which people disagree (for instance, most people have no decided opinion whether the soul of living creatures is destructible or immortal). Therefore, when it is uncertain in which sense the suggested premiss is generally used, whether as maxims are employed (for people call both true opinions and general affirmations by the name of ' maxims ') or like the statement, ' the diagonal of a square is incommensurate with its sides,' and further, where the truth is a matter of uncertainty,—in these cases one has an excellent opportunity of changing the terms without being found out. For, because it is uncertain in which sense the premiss bears its true meaning, one will not be regarded as playing the sophist, and, because of the disagreement on the subject, one will not be regarded as lying ; for the change will make the argument proof against refutation.

Furthermore, whenever one foresees any question, one must be the first to make one's objection and say what one has to say, for thus one can best disconcert the questioner.

XVIII. Ἐπεὶ δ' ἐστὶν ἡ μὲν ὀρθὴ λύσις ἐμφά-
30 νισις ψευδοῦς συλλογισμοῦ, παρ' ὁποίαν ἐρώτησιν
συμβαίνει τὸ ψεῦδος, ὁ δὲ ψευδὴς συλλογισμὸς
λέγεται διχῶς (ἢ γὰρ εἰ συλλελόγισται ψεῦδος, ἢ
εἰ μὴ ὢν συλλογισμὸς δοκεῖ εἶναι συλλογισμός),
εἴη ἂν ἥ τε εἰρημένη νῦν λύσις καὶ ἡ τοῦ φαινο-
μένου συλλογισμοῦ παρὰ τί φαίνεται τῶν ἐρωτη-
35 μάτων διόρθωσις. ὥστε συμβαίνει τῶν λόγων τοὺς
μὲν συλλελογισμένους ἀνελόντα, τοὺς δὲ φαινομένους διελόντα λύειν. πάλιν δ' ἐπεὶ τῶν συλλε-
λογισμένων λόγων οἱ μὲν ἀληθὲς οἱ δὲ ψεῦδος
ἔχουσι τὸ συμπέρασμα, τοὺς μὲν κατὰ τὸ συμπέρασμα ψευδεῖς διχῶς ἐνδέχεται λύειν· καὶ γὰρ
40 τῷ ἀνελεῖν τι τῶν ἠρωτημένων, καὶ τῷ δεῖξαι τὸ
177 a συμπέρασμα ἔχον οὐχ οὕτως· τοὺς δὲ κατὰ τὰς
προτάσεις τῷ ἀνελεῖν τι μόνον· τὸ γὰρ συμπέρασμα
ἀληθές. ὥστε τοῖς βουλομένοις λύειν λόγον πρῶτον
μὲν σκεπτέον εἰ συλλελόγισται ἢ ἀσυλλόγιστος,
5 εἶτα πότερον ἀληθὲς τὸ συμπέρασμα ἢ ψεῦδος,
ὅπως ἢ διαιροῦντες ἢ ἀναιροῦντες λύωμεν, καὶ
ἀναιροῦντες ἢ ὧδε ἢ ὧδε, καθάπερ ἐλέχθη πρότερον.
διαφέρει δὲ πλεῖστον ἐρωτώμενόν τε καὶ μὴ λύειν
λόγον· τὸ μὲν γὰρ προϊδεῖν χαλεπόν, τὸ δὲ κατὰ
σχολὴν ἰδεῖν ῥᾷον.

XIX. Τῶν μὲν οὖν παρὰ τὴν ὁμωνυμίαν καὶ τὴν
10 ἀμφιβολίαν ἐλέγχων οἱ μὲν ἔχουσι τῶν ἐρωτημάτων
τι πλείω σημαῖνον, οἱ δὲ τὸ συμπέρασμα πολλαχῶς

XVIII. Since a correct solution is an exposure of false reasoning, indicating the nature of the question on which the fallacy hinges, and since ' false reasoning ' can mean one of two things (for it occurs either if a false conclusion has been reached or if what is not a proof appears to be such), there must be both the solution described just now,[a] and also the rectification of the apparent proof by showing on which of the questions it hinges. The result is that one solves the correctly reasoned arguments by demolishing them, the apparent reasonings by making distinctions. Again, since some correctly reasoned arguments are true, while others are false, in their conclusions, it is possible to solve those which are false in their conclusion in two ways, either by demolishing one of the questions or by showing that the conclusion is not as stated. Those arguments, on the other hand, which are false in their premisses can only be solved by the demolition of one of the premisses, since the conclusion is true. Those, therefore, who wish to solve an argument should observe, firstly, whether it has been correctly reasoned or is not reasoned, and, next, whether the conclusion is true or false, in order that we may achieve a solution either by making a distinction or by demolishing a premiss and doing so in one or other of the two ways just described.[b] There is a very wide difference between solving an argument when one is being questioned and when one is not ; for in the latter case it is difficult to see what is coming, but when one is at leisure it is easier to see one's way.

XIX. Of the refutations which hinge upon equivocation and ambiguity some involve a question which bears more than one sense, while others have

Genuine solution.

(A) The Solution of REFUTATIONS (chs. xix-xxxii).

λεγόμενον, οἷον ἐν μὲν τῷ σιγῶντα λέγειν τὸ συμπέρασμα διττόν, ἐν δὲ τῷ μὴ συνεπίστασθαι τὸν
ἐπιστάμενον ἓν τῶν ἐρωτημάτων ἀμφίβολον. καὶ
τὸ διττὸν ὁτὲ μὲν ἔστιν, ὁτὲ δ' οὐκ ἔστιν, ἀλλὰ
15 σημαίνει τὸ διττὸν τὸ μὲν ὂν τὸ δ' οὐκ ὄν.

Ὅσοις μὲν οὖν ἐν τῷ τέλει τὸ πολλαχῶς, ἂν μὴ
προλάβῃ[1] τὴν ἀντίφασιν, οὐ γίνεται ἔλεγχος, οἷον
ἐν τῷ τὸν τυφλὸν ὁρᾶν· ἄνευ γὰρ ἀντιφάσεως οὐκ
ἦν ἔλεγχος. ὅσοις δ' ἐν τοῖς ἐρωτήμασιν, οὐκ
20 ἀνάγκη προαποφῆσαι τὸ διττόν· οὐ γὰρ πρὸς τοῦτο
ἀλλὰ διὰ τοῦτο ὁ λόγος. ἐν ἀρχῇ μὲν οὖν τὸ
διπλοῦν καὶ ὄνομα καὶ λόγον οὕτως ἀποκριτέον,
ὅτι ἔστιν ὡς, ἔστι δ' ὡς οὔ, ὥσπερ τὸ σιγῶντα
λέγειν, ὅτι ἔστιν ὡς, ἔστι δ' ὡς οὔ. καὶ τὰ δέοντα
πρακτέον ἔστιν ἅ, ἔστι δ' ἃ οὔ· τὰ γὰρ δέοντα
25 λέγεται πολλαχῶς. ἐὰν δὲ λάθῃ, ἐπὶ τέλει προστι-
θέντα τῇ ἐρωτήσει διορθωτέον· ἆρ' ἔστι σιγῶντα
λέγειν; οὔ, ἀλλὰ τόνδε σιγῶντα. καὶ ἐν τοῖς
ἔχουσι δὲ τὸ πλεοναχῶς ἐν ταῖς προτάσεσιν ὁμοίως.
οὐκ ἄρα συνεπίστανται ὅ τι ἐπίστανται; ναί, ἀλλ'
οὐχ οἱ οὕτως ἐπιστάμενοι· οὐ γὰρ ταὐτόν ἐστιν ὅτι

---

[1] Reading προλάβῃ with B.

a conclusion which can bear several meanings ; for example, in the argument about ' the speech of the silent,' the conclusion has a double meaning, and in the argument that ' a man who knows is not conscious of what he knows,' one of the questions involves ambiguity. Also, that which has a double meaning is sometimes true and sometimes false, the term ' double ' signifying that which is partly true and partly untrue.

(a) Those dependent on diction: (chs. xix-xxiii). (1) Equivocation.

When the diversity of meaning occurs in the conclusion, no refutation takes place, unless the questioner secures a contradiction beforehand, as, for example, in the argument about the ' seeing of the blind ' ; for there never was refutation without contradiction. Where the diversity of meaning occurs in the questions, there is no need to deny the ambiguity beforehand ; for the argument is not directed towards it as a conclusion but carried on by means of it. At the beginning, therefore, one ought to reply to an ambiguous term or expression in the following manner, that ' in one sense it is so and in another it is not so ' ; for example ' the speaking of the silent ' is possible in one sense but not in another. Or again, ' what needs must is to be done sometimes and not at other times ' ; for the term ' what needs must ' can bear several meanings. If one does not notice the ambiguity, one should make a correction at the end by adding to the questioning : ' Is the speaking of the silent possible ? ' ' No, but speaking of this particular man when he is silent is possible.' So likewise also where the variety of meaning is contained in the premisses : ' Are not people conscious of what they know ? ' ' Yes, but not those who know in this particular way ' ; for it is not the same thing

(2) Ambiguity.

103

30 οὐκ ἔστι συνεπίστασθαι καὶ ὅτι τοὺς ὡδὶ ἐπιστα-
μένους οὐκ ἔστιν. ὅλως τε μαχετέον, ἂν καὶ
ἁπλῶς συλλογίζηται, ὅτι οὐχ ὃ ἔφησεν ἀπέφησε
πρᾶγμα, ἀλλ᾽ ὄνομα· ὥστ᾽ οὐκ ἔλεγχος.

XX. Φανερὸν δὲ καὶ τοὺς παρὰ τὴν διαίρεσιν
καὶ σύνθεσιν πῶς λυτέον· ἂν γὰρ διαιρούμενος καὶ
35 συντιθέμενος ὁ λόγος ἕτερον σημαίνῃ, συμπεραινομένου τοὐναντίον λεκτέον. εἰσὶ δὲ πάντες οἱ τοιοῦτοι λόγοι παρὰ τὴν σύνθεσιν ἢ διαίρεσιν. ἆρ᾽
ᾧ εἶδες σὺ τοῦτον τυπτόμενον, τούτῳ ἐτύπτετο
οὗτος; καὶ ᾧ ἐτύπτετο, τούτῳ σὺ εἶδες; ἔχει
177 b μὲν οὖν τι κἀκ τῶν ἀμφιβόλων ἐρωτημάτων, ἀλλ᾽
ἔστι παρὰ σύνθεσιν. οὐ γάρ ἐστι διττὸν τὸ παρὰ
τὴν διαίρεσιν (οὐ γὰρ ὁ αὐτὸς λόγος γίνεται διαιρούμενος), εἴπερ μὴ καὶ τὸ ὄρος καὶ ὄρος τῇ προσῳδίᾳ
λεχθὲν σημαίνει ἕτερον. (ἀλλ᾽ ἐν μὲν τοῖς γεγραμ-
5 μένοις ταὐτὸν ὄνομα, ὅταν ἐκ τῶν αὐτῶν στοιχείων
γεγραμμένον ᾖ καὶ ὡσαύτως, κἀκεῖ δ᾽ ἤδη παρά-
σημα ποιοῦνται, τὰ δὲ φθεγγόμενα οὐ ταὐτά.) ὥστ᾽
οὐ διττὸν τὸ παρὰ διαίρεσιν. φανερὸν δὲ καὶ ὅτι
οὐ πάντες οἱ ἔλεγχοι παρὰ τὸ διττόν, καθάπερ
τινές φασιν.

10 Διαιρετέον οὖν τῷ ἀποκρινομένῳ· οὐ γὰρ ταὐτὸν

---

a In both examples the meaning can be either ' with a
stick ' or ' with your eyes.'

b *i.e.* breathings and accents.

to say that it is not possible for those who know to be conscious of what they know and that those who know in a particular way cannot be conscious of their knowledge. Generally speaking, too, even though one's opponent argues in a straightforward manner, one must contend that what he has contradicted is not the actual fact which one affirmed but merely its name, and so there is no refutation.

XX. It is evident, too, how fallacies which turn on the division and combination of words should be solved ; for, if the expression signifies something different when it is divided and when it is combined, when the opponent is drawing his conclusion we must take the words in the contrary sense. All such expressions as the following turn upon the combination or division of words : ' Was so-and-so being beaten with that with which you saw him being beaten ? ' and ' Did you see him being beaten with that with which he was being beaten ? ' [a] The argument here has something of the fallacy due to ambiguous questions, but it actually turns on combination. For what turns on the division of words is not really ambiguous (for the expression when divided differently is not the same), unless indeed ὅρος and ὄρος, pronounced according to the breathing, constitute a single word with different meanings. (In written language a word is the same when it is written with the same letters and in the same manner, though people now put in additional signs,[b] but the words when spoken are not the same.) Therefore an expression whose meaning turns on division is not ambiguous, and it is clear also that all refutations do not turn upon ambiguity, as some people say.

It is for the answerer to make the division ; for

177 b

ἰδεῖν τοῖς ὀφθαλμοῖς τυπτόμενον καὶ τὸ φάναι ἰδεῖν
τοῖς ὀφθαλμοῖς τυπτόμενον. καὶ ὁ Εὐθυδήμου δὲ
λόγος, ἆρ' οἶδας σὺ νῦν οὔσας ἐν Πειραιεῖ τριήρεις
ἐν Σικελίᾳ ὤν; καὶ πάλιν, ἆρ' ἔστιν ἀγαθὸν ὄντα
15 σκυτέα μοχθηρὸν εἶναι; εἴη δ' ἄν τις ἀγαθὸς ὢν
σκυτεὺς μοχθηρός· ὥστ' ἔσται ἀγαθὸς σκυτεὺς
μοχθηρός. ἆρ' ὧν αἱ ἐπιστῆμαι σπουδαῖαι, σπου-
δαῖα τὰ μαθήματα; τοῦ δὲ κακοῦ σπουδαῖον τὸ
μάθημα· σπουδαῖον ἄρα μάθημα τὸ κακόν. ἀλλὰ
μὴν καὶ κακὸν καὶ μάθημα τὸ κακόν, ὥστε κακὸν
μάθημα τὸ κακόν. ἀλλ' ἐστὶ κακῶν σπουδαία ἐπι-
20 στήμη. ἆρ' ἀληθὲς εἰπεῖν νῦν ὅτι σὺ γέγονας;
γέγονας ἄρα νῦν. ἢ ἄλλο σημαίνει διαιρεθέν; ἀληθὲς γὰρ εἰπεῖν νῦν ὅτι σὺ γέγονας, ἀλλ' οὐ νῦν
γέγονας. ἆρ' ὡς δύνασαι καὶ ἃ δύνασαι, οὕτως
καὶ ταῦτα ποιήσαις ἄν; οὐ κιθαρίζων δ' ἔχεις
δύναμιν τοῦ κιθαρίζειν· κιθαρίσαις ἂν ἄρα οὐ κιθαρί-
25 ζων. ἢ οὐ τούτου ἔχει τὴν δύναμιν τοῦ οὐ κιθαρίζων κιθαρίζειν, ἀλλ' ὅτε οὐ ποιεῖ, τοῦ ποιεῖν;

Λύουσι δέ τινες τοῦτον καὶ ἄλλως. εἰ γὰρ ἔδωκεν
ὡς δύναται ποιεῖν, οὔ φασι συμβαίνειν μὴ κιθαρί-
ζοντα κιθαρίζειν· οὐ γὰρ πάντως ὡς δύναται ποιεῖν,
30 δεδόσθαι ποιήσειν· οὐ ταὐτὸν δ' εἶναι ὡς δύναται

---

^a See *Rhet.* 1401 a 27 and Cope and Sandys' note.

ON SOPHISTICAL REFUTATIONS, xx

' I-saw-a-man-being-beaten with my eyes ' is not
the same thing as to say ' I saw a man being-beaten-
with-my-eyes.'—Then there is Euthydemus' saying,
' Do you know now in Sicily that there are triremes
in Piraeus ? [a] '—And, again, ' Can a good man who
is a cobbler be bad ? ' ' No.' ' But a man who is
good can be a bad cobbler ; therefore he will be a
good-bad cobbler.'—Again, ' Things of which the
knowledge is good are good objects of learning, are
they not ? ' ' Yes.' ' But the knowledge of evil is
good ; therefore evil is a good object of learning.'
' But, further, evil is both evil and an object of
learning, so that evil is an evil object of learning ;
but it has already been seen that the knowledge of
evils is good.'—' Is it true to say at the present
moment you are born ? ' ' Yes.' ' Then you are born
at the present moment.' Does not a different division
of the words signify something different ? For it is
true to say-at-the-present-moment that you are
born, but not to say you are born-at-the-present-
moment.—Again, ' Can you do what you can and as
you can ? ' ' Yes.' ' And when you are not playing
the harp you have the power of playing the harp ;
and so you could play the harp when you are not
playing the harp.' In other words, he does not possess
the power of playing-when-he-is-not-playing, but he
possesses the power of doing it when he is not doing
it.

Some people solve this in another manner also.
If he has granted that a man can do what he can do,
they say that it does not follow that he can play the
harp when he is not playing it ; for it has not been
granted that he will do it in every way in which he
can,—for it is not the same thing to do it in the way

107

177 b

καὶ πάντως ὡς δύναται ποιεῖν. ἀλλὰ φανερὸν ὅτι
οὐ καλῶς λύουσιν· τῶν γὰρ παρὰ ταὐτὸν λόγων ἡ
αὐτὴ λύσις, αὕτη δ᾽ οὐχ ἁρμόσει ἐπὶ πάντας οὐδὲ
πάντως ἐρωτωμένους, ἀλλ᾽ ἔστι πρὸς τὸν ἐρωτῶντα,
οὐ πρὸς τὸν λόγον.

35 XXI. Παρὰ δὲ τὴν προσῳδίαν λόγοι μὲν οὐκ
εἰσίν, οὔτε τῶν γεγραμμένων οὔτε τῶν λεγομένων,
πλὴν εἴ τινες ὀλίγοι γένοιντ᾽ ἄν, οἷον οὗτος ὁ λόγος.
ἆρά γ᾽ ἐστὶ τὸ οὗ καταλύεις οἰκία; ναί. οὐκοῦν τὸ
178 a οὗ καταλύεις τοῦ καταλύεις ἀπόφασις; ναί. ἔφησας
δ᾽ εἶναι τὸ οὗ καταλύεις οἰκίαν· ἡ οἰκία ἄρα ἀπόφασις. ὡς δὴ λυτέον, δῆλον· οὐ γὰρ ταὐτὸ σημαίνει
ὀξύτερον τὸ δὲ βαρύτερον ῥηθέν.

XXII. Δῆλον δὲ καὶ τοῖς παρὰ τὸ ὡσαύτως λέ-
5 γεσθαι τὰ μὴ ταὐτὰ πῶς ἀπαντητέον, ἐπείπερ
ἔχομεν τὰ γένη τῶν κατηγοριῶν. ὁ μὲν γὰρ ἔδωκεν
ἐρωτηθεὶς μὴ ὑπάρχειν τι τούτων ὅσα τί ἐστι
σημαίνει· ὁ δ᾽ ἔδειξεν ὑπάρχον τι τῶν πρός τι ἢ
ποσῶν, δοκούντων δὲ τί ἐστι σημαίνειν διὰ τὴν
λέξιν, οἷον ἐν τῷδε τῷ λόγῳ. ἆρ᾽ ἐνδέχεται τὸ
10 αὐτὸ ἅμα ποιεῖν τε καὶ πεποιηκέναι; οὔ. ἀλλὰ
μὴν ὁρᾶν γέ τι ἅμα καὶ ἑωρακέναι τὸ αὐτὸ καὶ
κατὰ ταὐτὸ ἐνδέχεται. ἆρ᾽ ἐστί τι τῶν πάσχειν
ποιεῖν τι; οὔ. οὐκοῦν τὸ τέμνεται καίεται αἰσθά-
νεται ὁμοίως λέγεται, καὶ πάντα πάσχειν τι ση-

ᵃ The point here is the difference of breathing and the
presence or absence of the circumflex accent.

in which he can and in *every* way in which he can. But clearly this solution is not a good one ; for the solution of arguments which turn on an identical principle is identical, whereas this solution will not suit every argument nor every form of question into which it can be put, but is directed against the questioner, not against the argument.

XXI. Arguments do not arise owing to accentua- (5) Wrong tion either in written or in spoken language, though accents. a few might occur such as the following : A house is ' where you lodge ' (οὗ καταλύεις), isn't it ? Yes. Is not ' you do not lodge ' (οὐ καταλύεις) the negation of ' you lodge ' (καταλύεις) ? Yes. But you said that ' where you lodge ' (οὗ καταλύεις) was a house ; therefore a house is a negation. It is obvious how this must be solved ; for the spoken word is not the same with the acuter and with the graver accent.[a]

XXII. It is plain also how we must meet arguments (6) Similar that turn on the identical expression of things which expressions are not identical, seeing that we possess the various for different kinds of categories. Suppose that one man when things. questioned has granted that something which denotes a substance is not an attribute, and another man has shown that something is an attribute which is in the category of relation or quantity but generally held, because of its expression, to denote a substance, as for example in the following argument : Is it pos- Examples. sible to be doing and to have done the same thing at the same time ? No. But it is surely possible to be seeing and to have seen the same thing at the same time and under the same conditions. Or again, Is any form of passivity a form of activity ? No. Then ' he is cut,' ' he is burnt,' ' he is affected by a sensible object ' are similar kinds of expression and all denote

178 a

μαίνει· πάλιν δὲ τὸ λέγειν τρέχειν ὁρᾶν ὁμοίως
15 ἀλλήλοις λέγεται· ἀλλὰ μὴν τό γ᾽ ὁρᾶν αἰσθάνεσθαί
τί ἐστιν, ὥστε καὶ πάσχειν τι ἅμα καὶ ποιεῖν. εἰ
δέ τις ἐκεῖ δοὺς μὴ ἐνδέχεσθαι ἅμα ταὐτὸ ποιεῖν
καὶ πεποιηκέναι, τὸ ὁρᾶν καὶ ἑωρακέναι φαίη
ἐγχωρεῖν, οὔπω ἐλήλεγκται, εἰ μὴ λέγοι τὸ ὁρᾶν
ποιεῖν τι ἀλλὰ πάσχειν· προσδεῖ γὰρ τούτου τοῦ
20 ἐρωτήματος· ἀλλ᾽ ὑπὸ τοῦ ἀκούοντος ὑπολαμ-
βάνεται δεδωκέναι, ὅτε τὸ τέμνειν ποιεῖν τι καὶ τὸ
τετμηκέναι πεποιηκέναι ἔδωκε, καὶ ὅσα ἄλλα
ὁμοίως λέγεται. τὸ γὰρ λοιπὸν αὐτὸς προστίθησιν
ὁ ἀκούων ὡς ὁμοίως λεγόμενον· τὸ δὲ λέγεται μὲν
οὐχ ὁμοίως, φαίνεται δὲ διὰ τὴν λέξιν. τὸ αὐτὸ
25 δὲ συμβαίνει ὅπερ ἐν ταῖς ὁμωνυμίαις· οἴεται γὰρ
ἐν τοῖς ὁμωνύμοις ὁ ἀγνὼς τῶν λόγων ὃ ἔφησεν
ἀποφῆσαι πρᾶγμα, οὐκ ὄνομα· τὸ δὲ ἔτι προσδεῖ
ἐρωτήματος, εἰ ἐφ᾽ ἓν βλέπων λέγει τὸ ὁμώνυμον·
οὕτως γὰρ δόντος ἔσται ἔλεγχος.

Ὅμοιοι δὲ καὶ οἵδε οἱ λόγοι τούτοις, εἰ ὅ τις
30 ἔχων ὕστερον μὴ ἔχει ἀπέβαλεν· ὁ γὰρ ἕνα μόνον
ἀποβαλὼν ἀστράγαλον οὐχ ἕξει δέκα ἀστραγάλους.
ἢ ὃ μὲν μὴ ἔχει πρότερον ἔχων, ἀποβέβληκεν, ὅσον
δὲ μὴ ἔχει ἢ ὅσα, οὐκ ἀνάγκη τοσαῦτα ἀποβαλεῖν.

---

[a] Knucklebones were used as dice by the Greeks.

some form of passivity ; and, on the other hand, ' to say,' ' to run,' and ' to see ' are forms of expression similar to one another ; but ' to see ' is surely a way of being affected by a sensible object, so that passivity and activity occur at the same time. In the former case, if someone, after granting that it is impossible to be doing and to have done the same thing at the same time, were to say that it *is* possible to see a thing and to have seen it, he has not yet been refuted supposing that he declares that seeing is a form not of activity but of passivity. For this further question is necessary, though he is supposed by the hearer to have granted it when he granted that ' to cut ' is ' to be doing something ' and ' to have cut ' is ' to have done something,' and so with similar forms of expression. For the hearer himself adds the rest, on the supposition that the significance is similar, whereas it is not really similar but only appears so owing to the expression. The same thing occurs as in fallacies of ambiguity ; for in dealing with ambiguous terms the man who is not an expert in argument thinks that his opponent has denied the fact which he asserted, not the term, whereas yet another question needs to be asked, namely, whether he is using the ambiguous term with his eye upon one meaning only ; for if he grants this, a refutation will be achieved.

Similar to the above are also the following argu- ments : Has a man lost what he had and afterwards has not ? For he who has lost one die [a] only will no longer have ten dice. Is not what really happens that he has lost something which he had before but no longer has, but it does not follow that he has lost the whole amount or number which he no longer

Examples *(continued)*.

111

178 a

ἐρωτήσας οὖν ὃ ἔχει, συνάγει ἐπὶ τοῦ ὅσα· τὰ γὰρ

35 δέκα ποσά. εἰ οὖν ἤρετο ἐξ ἀρχῆς εἰ ὅσα τις μὴ

ἔχει πρότερον ἔχων, ἆρά γε ἀποβέβληκε τοσαῦτα,

οὐδεὶς ἂν ἔδωκεν, ἀλλ᾽ ἢ τοσαῦτα ἢ τούτων τι. καὶ

ὅτι δοίη ἄν τις ὃ μὴ ἔχει. οὐ γὰρ ἔχει ἕνα μόνον

ἀστράγαλον. ἢ οὐ δέδωκεν ὃ οὐκ εἶχεν, ἀλλ᾽ ὡς

οὐκ εἶχε, τὸν ἕνα; τὸ γὰρ μόνον οὐ τόδε σημαίνει

178 b οὐδὲ τοιόνδε οὐδὲ τοσόνδε, ἀλλ᾽ ὡς ἔχει πρός τι,

οἷον ὅτι οὐ μετ᾽ ἄλλου. ὥσπερ οὖν εἰ ἤρετο ἆρ᾽ ὃ

μή τις ἔχει δοίη ἄν, μὴ φάντος δὲ ἔροιτο εἰ δοίη

ἄν τίς τι ταχέως μὴ ἔχων ταχέως, φήσαντος δὲ

συλλογίζοιτο ὅτι δοίη ἄν τις ὃ μὴ ἔχει. καὶ

5 φανερὸν ὅτι οὐ συλλελόγισται· τὸ γὰρ ταχέως οὐ

τόδε διδόναι ἀλλ᾽ ὧδε διδόναι ἐστίν· ὡς δὲ μὴ ἔχει

τις, δοίη ἄν, οἷον ἡδέως ἔχων δοίη ἂν λυπηρῶς.

Ὅμοιοι δὲ καὶ οἱ τοιοίδε πάντες. ἆρ᾽ ᾗ μὴ ἔχει

χειρὶ τύπτοι ἄν; ἢ ᾧ μὴ ἔχει ὀφθαλμῷ ἴδοι ἄν;

10 οὐ γὰρ ἔχει ἕνα μόνον. λύουσι μὲν οὖν τινὲς λέ-

γοντες καὶ ὡς ἔχει ἕνα μόνον καὶ ὀφθαλμὸν καὶ

has ? In the question, therefore, he is dealing with that which he has, in the conclusion with the total number ; for the number was ten. If, therefore, he had asked in the first place whether a man who formerly possessed a number of objects which he no longer possesses, has lost the total number of them, no one would have granted this, but would have said that he had lost either the total number or one of the objects. Again, it is argued that a man could give what he had not got ; for what he has not got is one die only. Is not what really happens that he has not given that which he has not got but has given it in a manner in which he has not got it, namely, as a single unit ? For ' single unit ' does not denote either a particular kind of thing or a quality or a quantity but a certain relation to something else, namely, dissociation from anything else. It is, therefore, as though he had asked whether a man could give what he has not got, and on receiving the answer ' No,' were to ask whether a man could give something quickly when he had not got it quickly, and, on receiving the answer ' Yes,' were to infer that a man could give what he had not got. It is obvious that he has not drawn a correct inference ; for ' giving quickly ' does not denote giving a particular thing but giving in a particular manner, and a man could give something in a manner in which he did not get it ; for example, he could get it with pleasure and give it with pain.

Similar also are all the following arguments : Further examples. ' Could a man strike with a hand that he has not got or see with an eye that he has not got ? ' For he has not got only one eye. Some people, therefore, solve this by saying that the man who has more than one

113

ἀλλ' ὁτιοῦν ὁ πλείω ἔχων. οἱ δὲ καὶ ὡς ὃ ἔχει
ἔλαβεν· ἐδίδου γὰρ μίαν μόνον οὗτος ψῆφον· καὶ
οὗτός γ' ἔχει, φασί, μίαν μόνην παρὰ τούτου
ψῆφον. οἱ δ' εὐθὺς τὴν ἐρώτησιν ἀναιροῦντες, ὅτι
15 ἐνδέχεται ὃ μὴ ἔλαβεν ἔχειν, οἷον οἶνον λαβόντα
ἡδύν, διαφθαρέντος ἐν τῇ λήψει, ἔχειν ὀξύν. ἀλλ'
ὅπερ ἐλέχθη καὶ πρότερον, οὗτοι πάντες οὐ πρὸς
τὸν λόγον ἀλλὰ πρὸς τὸν ἄνθρωπον λύουσιν. εἰ
γὰρ ἦν αὕτη λύσις, δόντα τὸ ἀντικείμενον οὐχ οἷόν
τε λύειν, καθάπερ ἐπὶ τῶν ἄλλων· οἷον εἰ ἔστι μὲν
20 ὃ ἔστι δ' ὃ οὔ, ἡ λύσις, ἂν ἁπλῶς δῷ λέγεσθαι,
συμπεραίνεται· ἐὰν δὲ μὴ συμπεραίνηται, οὐκ ἂν
εἴη λύσις· ἐν δὲ τοῖς προειρημένοις πάντων διδο-
μένων οὐδέ φαμεν γίνεσθαι συλλογισμόν.

Ἔτι δὲ καὶ οἶδ' εἰσὶ τούτων τῶν λόγων. ἆρ'
25 ὃ γέγραπται, ἔγραφέ τις; γέγραπται δὲ νῦν ὅτι σὺ
κάθησαι, ψευδὴς λόγος· ἦν δ' ἀληθής, ὅτ' ἐγράφετο·
ἅμα ἄρα ἐγράφετο ψευδὴς καὶ ἀληθής. τὸ γὰρ
ψευδῆ ἢ ἀληθῆ λόγον ἢ δόξαν εἶναι οὐ τόδε ἀλλὰ
τοιόνδε σημαίνει· ὁ γὰρ αὐτὸς λόγος καὶ ἐπὶ τῆς
30 δόξης. καὶ ἆρ' ὃ μανθάνει ὁ μανθάνων, τοῦτ' ἐστὶν
ὃ μανθάνει; μανθάνει δέ τις τὸ βραδὺ ταχύ. οὐ
τοίνυν ὃ μανθάνει ἀλλ' ὡς μανθάνει εἴρηκεν. καὶ
ἆρ' ὃ βαδίζει τις πατεῖ; βαδίζει δὲ τὴν ἡμέραν

ᵃ It seems probable that a new argument is dealt with here,
cf. b 36 καὶ ὅτι κτλ. οἱ δὲ possibly introduced a second solution of the previous argument which has fallen out.
ᵇ But B may already possess other pebbles.
ᶜ 177 b 33.

114

eye (or whatever it is) has also only one. There is also [a] the argument of some people that ' what a man has, he has received ' : A only gave one pebble, and B has, they say, only one pebble from A.[b] Other people argue by directly demolishing the question raised, saying that one can have what one has not received ; for example, one can receive wine that is sound but have it in a sour condition if it has gone bad in the process of transfer. But, as was said before,[c] all these people direct their solutions not to the argument but to the man. For if this were a real solution, it would be impossible to achieve a solution by granting the opposite, as happens in all other cases ; for example, if ' it is partly so and partly not so ' is the solution, an admission that the expression is used without qualification makes the conclusion valid ; but if no conclusion is reached, there cannot be a solution. In the above examples, even though everything is conceded, yet we say that no proof has been effected.

Moreover, the following also belong to this class of arguments : ' If something is written, did someone write it ? ' It is written that ' you are sitting ' ; this is a false statement, but was true at the time when it was written ; therefore what was written is at the same time false and true. No, for the falsity or truth of a statement or opinion does not denote a substance but a quality ; for the same account applies to an opinion as to a statement. Again, ' Is what the learner learns that which he learns ? ' A man learns a slow march quick ; it is not then *what* he learns that is meant but *how* he learns it. Again, ' Does a man trample on that through which he walks ? ' But he walks through the whole day. Was not what

115

178 b

ὅλην. ἢ οὐχ ὃ βαδίζει ἀλλ' ὅτε βαδίζει εἴρηκεν·
οὐδ' ὅταν τὴν κύλικα πίνειν, ὃ πίνει ἀλλ' ἐξ οὗ.
35 καὶ ἆρ' ὅ τις οἶδεν ἢ μαθὼν ἢ εὑρὼν οἶδεν; ὧν δὲ
τὸ μὲν εὗρε τὸ δ' ἔμαθε, τὰ ἄμφω οὐδέτερον. ἢ ὃ
μὲν ἅπαν, ἃ δ' ⟨οὐχ⟩ ἅπαντα;[1] καὶ ὅτι ἔστι τις τρίτος ἄνθρωπος παρ' αὐτὸν καὶ τοὺς καθ' ἕκαστον. τὸ
γὰρ ἄνθρωπος καὶ ἅπαν τὸ κοινὸν οὐ τόδε τι, ἀλλὰ
τοιόνδε τι ἢ πρός τι ἢ πῶς ἢ τῶν τοιούτων τι ση-
179 a μαίνει. ὁμοίως δὲ καὶ ἐπὶ τοῦ Κορίσκος καὶ Κορίσκος μουσικός, πότερον ταὐτὸν ἢ ἕτερον; τὸ
μὲν γὰρ τόδε τι τὸ δὲ τοιόνδε σημαίνει, ὥστ' οὐκ
ἔστιν αὐτὸ ἐκθέσθαι· οὐ τὸ ἐκτίθεσθαι δὲ ποιεῖ τὸν
τρίτον ἄνθρωπον, ἀλλὰ τὸ ὅπερ τόδε τι εἶναι συγ-
5 χωρεῖν. οὐ γὰρ ἔσται τόδε τι εἶναι, ὅπερ Καλλίας,
καὶ ὅπερ ἄνθρωπός ἐστιν. οὐδ' εἴ τις τὸ ἐκτιθέ-
μενον μὴ ὅπερ τόδε τι εἶναι λέγοι ἀλλ' ὅπερ ποιόν,
οὐδὲν διοίσει· ἔσται γὰρ τὸ παρὰ τοὺς πολλοὺς ἕν
τι, οἷον ὁ ἄνθρωπος. φανερὸν οὖν ὅτι οὐ δοτέον
τόδε τι εἶναι τὸ κοινῇ κατηγορούμενον ἐπὶ πᾶσιν,
10 ἀλλ' ἤτοι ποιὸν ἢ πρός τι ἢ ποσὸν ἢ τῶν τοιούτων
τι σημαίνειν.

XXIII. Ὅλως δ' ἐν τοῖς παρὰ τὴν λέξιν λόγοις
ἀεὶ κατὰ τὸ ἀντικείμενον ἔσται ἡ λύσις ἢ παρ' ὅ

---

[1] Reading ἃ δ' ⟨οὐχ⟩ ἅπαντα with Pickard-Cambridge.

was meant not what he walks through but when he walks? Just as when we talk of a man drinking a cup, we refer not to what he drinks but to that out of which he drinks. Again, ' Is it not either by learning or by discovery that a man knows what he knows?' But, supposing that of two things he has discovered one and learnt the other, he has not either discovered or learnt the two taken together. Is it not true to say that what he knows is each single thing, but not all the things taken together? There is also the argument that there is a ' third man ' beside ' man ' and ' individual men.' This is not so, for ' man ' and every generic term denotes not an individual substance but a quality or relation or mode or something of the kind. So, too, with the question whether ' Coriscus ' and ' the musician Coriscus ' are the same thing or different. For the one term denotes an individual substance, the other a quality, so that it is impossible to isolate it; for it is not the process of isolation which produces the ' third man ' but the admission that there is an individual substance. For ' man ' will not be an individual substance as Callias is, nor will it make any difference if one were to say that what is isolated is not an individual substance but a quality; for there will still be a one as contrasted with the many, for instance ' man.' It is obvious, therefore, that it must not be granted that the term predicated universally of a class is an individual substance, but we must say that it denotes either a quality or a relation or a quantity or something of the kind.

XXIII. To sum up, in dealing with arguments which turn on language the solution will always depend on the opposite of that on which the argument

117

ἐστιν ὁ λόγος. οἷον εἰ παρὰ σύνθεσιν ὁ λόγος, ἡ
λύσις διελόντι, εἰ δὲ παρὰ διαίρεσιν, συνθέντι. πάλιν
15 εἰ παρὰ προσῳδίαν ὀξεῖαν, ἡ βαρεῖα προσῳδία
λύσις, εἰ δὲ παρὰ βαρεῖαν, ἡ ὀξεῖα. εἰ δὲ παρ᾽
ὁμωνυμίαν, ἔστι τὸ ἀντικείμενον ὄνομα εἰπόντα
λύειν, οἷον εἰ ἄψυχον¹ συμβαίνει λέγειν, ἀποφή-
σαντα μὴ εἶναι, δηλοῦν ὡς ἔστιν ἔμψυχον· εἰ δ᾽
ἄψυχον ἔφησεν, ὁ δ᾽ ἔμψυχον συνελογίσατο, λέγειν
20 ὡς ἔστιν ἄψυχον. ὁμοίως δὲ καὶ ἐπὶ τῆς ἀμφι-
βολίας. εἰ δὲ παρ᾽ ὁμοιότητα λέξεως, τὸ ἀντικείμενον ἔσται λύσις. ἆρ᾽ ὃ μὴ ἔχει, δοίη ἄν τις;
ἢ οὐχ ὃ μὴ ἔχει, ἀλλ᾽ ὡς οὐκ ἔχει, οἷον ἕνα μόνον
ἀστράγαλον. ἆρ᾽ ὃ ἐπίσταται, μαθὼν ἢ εὑρὼν
ἐπίσταται; ἀλλ᾽ οὐχ ἃ ἐπίσταται. καὶ² ὃ βαδίζει
25 πατεῖ, ἀλλ᾽ οὐχ ὅτε. ὁμοίως δὲ καὶ ἐπὶ τῶν
ἄλλων.

XXIV. Πρὸς δὲ τοὺς παρὰ τὸ συμβεβηκὸς μία
μὲν ἡ αὐτὴ λύσις πρὸς ἅπαντας. ἐπεὶ γὰρ ἀδι-
όριστόν ἐστι τὸ πότε λεκτέον ἐπὶ τοῦ πράγματος,
ὅταν ἐπὶ τοῦ συμβεβηκότος ὑπάρχῃ, καὶ ἐπ᾽ ἐνίων
30 μὲν δοκεῖ καὶ φασίν, ἐπ᾽ ἐνίων δ᾽ οὔ φασιν ἀναγκαῖον εἶναι, ῥητέον οὖν συμβιβασθέντος³ ὁμοίως
πρὸς ἅπαντας ὅτι οὐκ ἀναγκαῖον. ἔχειν δὲ δεῖ
προφέρειν τὸ οἷον. εἰσὶ δὲ πάντες οἱ τοιοίδε τῶν
λόγων παρὰ τὸ συμβεβηκός. ἆρ᾽ οἶδας ὃ μέλλω

---

¹ Reading ἄψυχον with Poste for ἔμψυχον.
² Omitting εἰ after καὶ.
³ Reading συμβιβασθέντος with A.

ᵃ See note on 178 a 31.　　ᵇ See 178 b 32-33.

turns ; for example, if the argument turns on com- which depend on diction. bination, the solution will be by division, if on division, by combination. Again, if it turns on acute accentuation, grave accentuation will be the solution, and *vice versa.* If it turns on equivocation, it can be solved by the use of the opposite term ; for example, if it so happens that one says something is inanimate after having denied that it is so, one must show that it is animate ; and, if one has said that it is inanimate and one's opponent has argued that it is animate, one must assert that it is inanimate. Similarly, too, in the case of ambiguity ; if the argument turns on similarity of language, the opposite will be the solution. 'Could one give what one has not got ? ' Surely not *what* he has not got but he could give it in *a way in which* he has not got it, for example, a single die *a* by itself. ' Does a man know the *thing* which he knows by learning or discovery ? ' Yes, but not ' the *thing*s which he knows.' Also a man tramples on the *thing* through which he walks, not on the *time* through which he walks.*b* And similarly, too, with the other instances.

XXIV. To meet arguments which turn upon acci- (b) Solutions not dependent on diction (chs. xxiv-xxx).
(1) Accident.
(a) By denying the consequence from the accident to the subject. dent one and the same solution is universally applicable. It is undetermined on what occasions the attribute should be applied to the subject where it belongs to the accident, and sometimes it is generally held and stated to belong and sometimes it is denied that it necessarily belongs. We must, therefore, when a conclusion has been reached, assert in every case alike that it does not necessarily belong. But we must have an example to bring forward. All such arguments as the following turn on accident : ' Do you know what I am about to ask you ? ' ' Do you know the man

179 a

σε ἐρωτᾶν; ἆρ' οἶδας τὸν προσιόντα ἢ τὸν ἐγ-
κεκαλυμμένον; ἆρ' ὁ ἀνδριὰς σόν ἐστιν ἔργον, ἢ
35 σὸς ὁ κύων πατήρ; ἆρα τὰ ὀλιγάκις ὀλίγα ὀλίγα;
φανερὸν γὰρ ἐν ἅπασι τούτοις ὅτι οὐκ ἀνάγκη τὸ
κατὰ τοῦ συμβεβηκότος καὶ κατὰ τοῦ πράγματος
ἀληθεύεσθαι· μόνοις γὰρ τοῖς κατὰ τὴν οὐσίαν
ἀδιαφόροις καὶ ἐν οὖσιν ἅπαντα δοκεῖ ταὐτὰ ὑπάρ-
179 b χειν· τῷ δ' ἀγαθῷ οὐ ταὐτόν ἐστιν ἀγαθῷ τ' εἶναι
καὶ μέλλοντι ἐρωτᾶσθαι, οὐδὲ τῷ προσιόντι ἢ ἐγ-
κεκαλυμμένῳ προσιόντι τε εἶναι καὶ Κορίσκῳ· ὥστ'
οὐκ εἰ οἶδα τὸν Κορίσκον, ἀγνοῶ δὲ τὸν προσιόντα,
τὸν αὐτὸν οἶδα καὶ ἀγνοῶ· οὐδ' εἰ τοῦτ' ἐστὶν ἐμόν,
5 ἔστι δ' ἔργον, ἐμόν ἐστιν ἔργον, ἀλλ' ἢ κτῆμα ἢ
πρᾶγμα ἢ ἄλλο τι. τὸν αὐτὸν δὲ τρόπον καὶ ἐπὶ
τῶν ἄλλων.

Λύουσι δέ τινες ἀναιροῦντες τὴν ἐρώτησιν· φασὶ
γὰρ ἐνδέχεσθαι ταὐτὸ πρᾶγμα εἰδέναι καὶ ἀγνοεῖν,
ἀλλὰ μὴ κατὰ ταὐτό· τὸν οὖν προσιόντα οὐκ εἰδότες,
10 τὸν δὲ Κορίσκον εἰδότες, ταὐτὸ μὲν εἰδέναι καὶ
ἀγνοεῖν φασίν, ἀλλ' οὐ κατὰ ταὐτό. καίτοι πρῶτον
μέν, καθάπερ ἤδη εἴπομεν, δεῖ τῶν παρὰ ταὐτὸ
λόγων τὴν αὐτὴν εἶναι διόρθωσιν· αὕτη δ' οὐκ
ἔσται, ἄν τις μὴ ἐπὶ τοῦ εἰδέναι ἀλλ' ἐπὶ τοῦ εἶναι
ἢ πῶς ἔχειν τὸ αὐτὸ ἀξίωμα λαμβάνῃ, οἷον εἰ ὅδε

---

[a] See 179 b 15. *Cf.* Plato, *Euthydemus* 298 E.

[b] The reference here is to the question (a 33) ' Do you
know what I am about to ask you ? ' The reply is ' no.'
' I am going to ask you about the good ; therefore, you do
not know about the good.'

[c] 177 b 31.

who is coming towards us ? ' or ' the man with his
face covered ? ' ' Is the statue your work ? ' or ' Is
the dog your father ? '[a] ' Is the result of multiplying
a small number by another small number itself a
small number ? ' It is obvious that in all these
instances it does not necessarily follow that the
attribute which is true of the accident is also true of
the subject. For it is only to things which are in-
distinguishable and one in essence that all the same
attributes are generally held to belong ; but in the
case of the good, it is not the same thing to be good
and to be about to be the subject of a question.[b] Nor
in the case of ' the man who is coming towards us '
(or ' with his face covered '), is ' to be coming towards
us ' the same thing as ' to be Coriscus ' ; so that,
if I know Coriscus but do not know the man who is
coming towards me, it does not follow that I know
and do not know the same man. And again, if this
is ' mine ' and if it is also ' a piece of work,' it is not
therefore ' a piece of my work ' but may be my
possession or chattel or something else. The other
instances can be treated in the same way.

Some people obtain a solution by demolishing the (β) By de-
thesis of the question ; for they say that it is possible the original
to know and not to know the same thing but not question.
in the same respect ; when, therefore, they do not
know the man who is coming towards them but know
Coriscus, they say that they know and do not know
the same thing but not in the same respect. Yet in
the first place, as we have already said,[c] the method
of correcting arguments which turn on the same
principle ought to be identical, yet this will not be so, if
one takes the same axiom to apply not to ' knowledge '
but to ' existence ' or ' being in a certain state ' ; for

15 ἐστὶ πατήρ, ἔστι δὲ σός· εἰ γὰρ ἐπ' ἐνίων τοῦτ'
ἐστὶν ἀληθὲς καὶ ἐνδέχεται ταὐτὸ εἰδέναι καὶ
ἀγνοεῖν, ἀλλ' ἐνταῦθα οὐδὲν κοινωνεῖ τὸ λεχθέν.
οὐδὲν δὲ κωλύει τὸν αὐτὸν λόγον πλείους μοχθηρίας
ἔχειν. ἀλλ' οὐχ ἡ πάσης ἁμαρτίας ἐμφάνισις λύσις
ἐστίν· ἐγχωρεῖ γὰρ ὅτι μὲν ψεῦδος συλλελόγισται
20 δεῖξαί τινα, παρ' ὃ δὲ μὴ δεῖξαι, οἷον τὸν Ζήνωνος
λόγον, ὅτι οὐκ ἔστι κινηθῆναι. ὥστε καὶ εἴ τις
ἐπιχειροίη συνάγειν ὡς ἀδύνατον, ἁμαρτάνει, κἂν
εἰ μυριάκις ᾖ συλλελογισμένος· οὐ γάρ ἐστιν αὕτη
λύσις. ἦν γὰρ ἡ λύσις ἐμφάνισις ψευδοῦς συλλογισμοῦ, παρ' ὃ ψευδής· εἰ οὖν μὴ συλλελόγισται ἢ
25 καὶ ἀληθὲς ἢ ψεῦδος ⟨ψευδῶς⟩[1] ἐπιχειρεῖ συνάγειν,
ἡ ἐκείνου δήλωσις λύσις ἐστίν. ἴσως δὲ καὶ τοῦτ'
ἐπ' ἐνίων οὐδὲν κωλύει συμβαίνειν· πλὴν ἐπί γε
τούτων οὐδὲ τοῦτο δόξειεν ἄν· καὶ γὰρ τὸν Κορίσκον ὅτι Κορίσκος οἶδε, καὶ τὸ προσιὸν ὅτι προσ-
ιόν. ἐνδέχεσθαι δὲ δοκεῖ τὸ αὐτὸ εἰδέναι καὶ μή,
30 οἷον ὅτι μὲν λευκὸν εἰδέναι, ὅτι δὲ μουσικὸν μὴ
γνωρίζειν· οὕτω γὰρ τὸ αὐτὸ οἶδε καὶ οὐκ οἶδεν,
ἀλλ' οὐ κατὰ ταὐτόν. τὸ δὲ προσιὸν καὶ Κορίσκον,
καὶ ὅτι προσιὸν καὶ ὅτι Κορίσκος, οἶδεν.

'Ομοίως δ' ἁμαρτάνουσι καὶ οἱ λύοντες, ὅτι ἅπας

---

[1] Reading with W. A. Pickard-Cambridge ψεῦδος ⟨ψευδῶς⟩.

[a] Cf. a 34 f., the false conclusion being, ' This dog is your
father.'

example, ' this dog is a father, this dog is yours.' [a]
Though it is sometimes true and it is possible to know
and not to know the same thing, yet the suggested
solution is quite inapplicable in the above instance.
But there is no reason why the same argument should
not contain several flaws, but it is not the exposure
of every fault that forms a solution ; for it is possible
for a man to show that a false conclusion has been
reached without showing on what point it turns, as,
for instance, in Zeno's argument that motion is impossible. Even, therefore, if one were to attempt
to infer the impossibility of this view, he is wrong,
even though he has given countless proofs ; for this
procedure does not constitute a solution, for a solution is, as we saw, an exposure of false reasoning,
showing on what the falsity depends. If, therefore,
he has not proved his case or else if he attempts to
draw an inference, whether true or false, by false
means, the unmasking of this procedure is a solution.
But perhaps, though in some cases there is nothing
to prevent this happening, yet it would not be generally admitted in the instances given above ; for he
knows that Coriscus is Coriscus and that what is
coming towards him is coming towards him. But
there are cases in which it is generally held to be
possible to know and not to know the same thing ;
for instance, one can know that someone is white
but be ignorant of the fact that he is musical, thus
knowing and not knowing the same thing but not
in the same respect ; but as to what is coming towards
him and Coriscus, he knows both that it is coming
towards him and that he is Coriscus.

An error similar to that made by those whom we (Erroneous
have mentioned is committed by those who solve methods of
solution.)

35 ἀριθμὸς ὀλίγος, ὥσπερ οὓς εἴπομεν· εἰ γὰρ μὴ
συμπεραινομένου, τοῦτο παραλιπόντες, ἀληθὲς συμ-
πεπεράνθαι φασί, πάντα γὰρ εἶναι καὶ πολὺν καὶ
ὀλίγον, ἁμαρτάνουσιν.

Ἔνιοι δὲ καὶ τῷ διττῷ λύουσι τοὺς συλλογισμούς,
οἷον ὅτι σός ἐστι πατὴρ ἢ υἱὸς ἢ δοῦλος. καίτοι
φανερὸν ὡς εἰ παρὰ τὸ πολλαχῶς λέγεσθαι φαίνεται
ὁ ἔλεγχος, δεῖ τοὔνομα ἢ τὸν λόγον κυρίως εἶναι
πλειόνων· τὸ δὲ τόνδ' εἶναι τοῦδε τέκνον οὐδεὶς
λέγει κυρίως, εἰ δεσπότης ἐστὶ τέκνου· ἀλλὰ παρὰ
5 τὸ συμβεβηκὸς ἡ σύνθεσίς ἐστιν. ἆρ' ἐστὶ τοῦτο
σόν; ναί. ἔστι δὲ τοῦτο τέκνον; σὸν ἄρα τοῦτο
τέκνον· ὅτι συμβέβηκεν εἶναι καὶ σὸν καὶ τέκνον,
ἀλλ' οὐ σὸν τέκνον.

Καὶ τὸ εἶναι τῶν κακῶν τι ἀγαθόν· ἡ γὰρ φρόνη-
σίς ἐστιν ἐπιστήμη τῶν κακῶν. τὸ δὲ τοῦτο τού-
10 των εἶναι οὐ λέγεται πολλαχῶς, ἀλλὰ κτῆμα. εἰ
δ' ἄρα πολλαχῶς (καὶ γὰρ τὸν ἄνθρωπον τῶν ζῴων
φαμὲν εἶναι, ἀλλ' οὔ τι κτῆμα) καὶ ἐάν τι πρὸς τὰ
κακὰ λέγηται ὡς τινός, διὰ τοῦτο τῶν κακῶν ἐστίν,
ἀλλ' οὐ τοῦτο τῶν κακῶν. παρὰ τὸ πῇ οὖν καὶ
ἁπλῶς φαίνεται. καίτοι ἐνδέχεται ἴσως ἀγαθὸν
15 εἶναί τι τῶν κακῶν διττῶς, ἀλλ' οὐκ ἐπὶ τοῦ λόγου
τούτου, ἀλλ' εἴ τι δοῦλον εἴη ἀγαθὸν μοχθηροῦ,
μᾶλλον. ἴσως δ' οὐδ' οὕτως· οὐ γὰρ εἰ ἀγαθὸν καὶ

---

the argument that every number is small; for if, when no conclusion has been reached, they pass over the fact and say that a conclusion has been reached and is true because every number is both large and small, they are committing an error.

Some people, too, solve these reasonings by the principle of ambiguity, saying, for example, that 'yours' means 'your father' or 'your son' or 'your slave.' Yet it is obvious that, if the refutation turns upon the possibility of several meanings, the term or expression ought to be used literally in several senses; but no one speaks of A as B's child in the literal sense if B is the child's master, but the combination is due to accident. 'Is A yours?' 'Yes.' 'Is A a child?' 'Yes.' 'Then A is your child,' for he happens to be both yours and a child; but for all that he is not 'your child.'

There is also the argument that 'something " of evils " is good; for wisdom is a knowledge " of evils."' But the statement that this is 'of so-and-so'[a] is not used with several meanings but denotes possession. Granting, however, that the genitive has more than one meaning (for we say that man is 'of the animals,' though not a possession of theirs), and if the relation of so-and-so to evils is expressed by the genitive, it is therefore a so-and-so 'of evils,' but so-and-so is not one of the evils. The difference seems to be due to whether the genitive is used in a particular sense or absolutely. Yet it is perhaps possible for the saying 'Something of evils is good' to be ambiguous, though not in the example given above, but rather in the phrase 'a slave is good of the wicked.' But perhaps this example is not to the point either; for if something is 'good' and 'of so-and-so,' it is not at

τούτου, ἀγαθὸν τούτου ἅμα. οὐδὲ τὸ τὸν ἄνθρωπον
φάναι τῶν ζῴων εἶναι οὐ λέγεται πολλαχῶς· οὐ
20 γὰρ εἴ ποτέ τι σημαίνομεν ἀφελόντες, τοῦτο λέγεται πολλαχῶς· καὶ γὰρ τὸ ἥμισυ εἰπόντες τοῦ
ἔπους δός μοι Ἰλιάδα σημαίνομεν, οἷον τὸ μῆνιν
ἄειδε θεά.

XXV. Τοὺς δὲ παρὰ τὸ κυρίως τόδε ἢ πῇ ἢ
ποῦ ἢ πῶς ἢ πρός τι λέγεσθαι καὶ μὴ ἁπλῶς,
25 λυτέον σκοποῦντι τὸ συμπέρασμα πρὸς τὴν ἀντίφασιν, εἰ ἐνδέχεται τούτων τι πεπονθέναι. τὰ γὰρ
ἐναντία καὶ τὰ ἀντικείμενα καὶ φάσιν καὶ ἀπόφασιν
ἁπλῶς μὲν ἀδύνατον ὑπάρχειν τῷ αὐτῷ, πῇ μέντοι
ἑκάτερον ἢ πρός τι ἢ πῶς, ἢ τὸ μὲν πῇ τὸ δ'
ἁπλῶς, οὐδὲν κωλύει. ὥστ' εἰ τόδε μὲν ἁπλῶς
30 τόδε δὲ πῇ, οὔπω ἔλεγχος. τοῦτο δ' ἐν τῷ συμ-
περάσματι θεωρητέον πρὸς τὴν ἀντίφασιν.

Εἰσὶ δὲ πάντες οἱ τοιοῦτοι λόγοι τοῦτ' ἔχοντες.
ἆρ' ἐνδέχεται τὸ μὴ ὂν εἶναι; ἀλλὰ μὴν ἔστι γέ
τι μὴ ὄν. ὁμοίως δὲ καὶ τὸ ὂν οὐκ ἔσται· οὐ γὰρ
35 ἔσται τι τῶν ὄντων. ἆρ' ἐνδέχεται τὸν αὐτὸν ἅμα
εὐορκεῖν καὶ ἐπιορκεῖν; ἆρ' ἐγχωρεῖ τὸν αὐτὸν
ἅμα τῷ αὐτῷ πείθεσθαι καὶ ἀπειθεῖν; ἢ οὔτε
τὸ εἶναί τι καὶ εἶναι ταὐτόν; τὸ δὲ μὴ ὄν, οὐκ εἰ
ἔστι τι, καὶ ἔστιν ἁπλῶς· οὔτ' εἰ εὐορκεῖ τόδε ἢ
126

the same time ' so and-so's good.' Nor is the statement that ' man is of the animals ' used with several meanings ; for a phrase does not acquire several senses every time we express its meaning in an elliptical form ; for we express, ' Give me the *Iliad* ' by quoting the half line ' Sing, goddess, the wrath.'

XXV. Arguments which turn upon the use of an expression not in its proper sense but with validity in respect only of a particular thing or in a particular respect or place or degree or relation and not absolutely, must be solved by examining the conclusion in the light of its contradictory, to see if it can possibly have been affected in any of these ways. For it is impossible for contraries and opposites and an affirmative and a negative to belong absolutely to the same subject ; on the other hand, there is no reason why each should not belong in a particular respect or relation or manner, or one in a particular respect and the other absolutely. Thus if one belongs absolutely and the other in a particular respect, no refutation has yet been reached. This point must be examined in the conclusion by comparison with its contradictory. *(2) The use of words with or without qualification.*

All the following arguments are of this kind : Is it possible for what is-not to be ? But surely it *is* something which is not. Similarly, too, Being will not be ; for it will *not be* any particular thing which is.—Is it possible for the same man at the same time to keep and to break his oath ?—Is it possible for the same man at the same time to obey and disobey the same order ? Is it not true, in the first place, that being something and Being are not the same thing ? On the other hand, Not-being, even if it is something, has not absolute being as well. Secondly, if a man keeps his oath on a particular occasion or in a par- *Examples.*

180 a

τῇδε, ἀνάγκη καὶ εὐορκεῖν, ὁ δ' ὀμόσας ἐπιορκήσειν
180 b εὐορκεῖ ἐπιορκῶν τοῦτο μόνον, εὐορκεῖ δὲ οὔ· οὐδ'
ὁ ἀπειθῶν πείθεται, ἀλλά τι πείθεται. ὅμοιος δ'
ὁ λόγος καὶ περὶ τοῦ ψεύδεσθαι τὸν αὐτὸν ἅμα καὶ
ἀληθεύειν· ἀλλὰ διὰ τὸ μὴ εἶναι εὐθεώρητον, ποτέρως ἄν τις ἀποδοίη τὸ ἁπλῶς ἀληθεύειν ἢ ψεύδε-
5 σθαι, δύσκολον φαίνεται. κωλύει δ' τὸν αὐτὸν¹ οὐδὲν
ἁπλῶς μὲν εἶναι ψευδῆ, πῇ δ' ἀληθῆ, ἢ τινὸς καὶ
εἶναι ἀληθῆ τινά, ἀληθῆ δὲ ⟨αὐτὸν⟩ μή.² ὁμοίως δὲ
καὶ ἐπὶ τῶν πρός τι καὶ ποῦ καὶ πότε· πάντες γὰρ
οἱ τοιοῦτοι λόγοι παρὰ τοῦτο συμβαίνουσιν. ἆρ'
ἡ ὑγίεια ἢ ὁ πλοῦτος ἀγαθόν; ἀλλὰ τῷ ἄφρονι
10 καὶ μὴ ὀρθῶς χρωμένῳ οὐκ ἀγαθόν· ἀγαθὸν ἄρα
καὶ οὐκ ἀγαθόν. ἆρα τὸ ὑγιαίνειν ἢ δύνασθαι ἐν
πόλει ἀγαθόν; ἀλλ' ἔστιν ὅτε οὐ βέλτιον· ταὐτὸν
ἄρα τῷ αὐτῷ ἀγαθὸν καὶ οὐκ ἀγαθόν. ἢ οὐδὲν
κωλύει ἁπλῶς ὂν ἀγαθὸν τῷδε μὴ εἶναι ἀγαθόν, ἢ
τῷδε μὲν ἀγαθόν, ἀλλ' οὐ νῦν ἢ οὐκ ἐνταῦθ' ἀγαθόν;
15 ἆρ' ὃ μὴ βούλοιτ' ἂν ὁ φρόνιμος, κακόν; ἀποβαλεῖν δ' οὐ βούλεται τἀγαθόν· κακὸν ἄρα τἀγαθόν.
οὐ γὰρ ταὐτὸν εἰπεῖν τἀγαθὸν εἶναι κακὸν καὶ τὸ
ἀποβαλεῖν τἀγαθόν. ὁμοίως δὲ καὶ ὁ τοῦ κλέπτου

¹ Reading τὸν αὐτὸν or τοῦτον for αὐτόν.

ticular respect, it does not necessarily follow that he is a keeper of oaths, but he who he has sworn that he will break his oath keeps his oath on this particular occasion only by foreswearing himself, but is not a keeper of oaths ; nor is he who disobeys obedient, except to a particular order. The argument is similar which deals with the question whether the same man can say what is at the same time both true and false ; but it presents apparent difficulties because it is not easy to see whether the qualification ' absolutely ' should be applied to ' true ' or to ' false.' But there is no reason why the same man should not be absolutely a liar yet tell the truth in some respects, or that some of a man's words should be true but he himself not be truthful. Similarly, too, if there are qualifications of relation or place or time. All the following arguments turn upon a point of this kind. Is health (or wealth) a good thing ? But to the fool who misuses it, it is not a good thing ; it is, therefore, a good thing and not a good thing.—Is health (or political power) a good thing ? But there are times when it is not better than other things ; therefore the same thing is both good and not good for the same man. Or is there no reason why a thing should not be absolutely good but not good for a particular person, or good for a particular person, but not good at the present moment or here ?—Is that which the wise man would not wish, an evil ? But he does not wish for the rejection of the good ; therefore, the good is an evil. This is not true ; for it is not the same thing to say that the good is an evil and that the rejection of the good is an evil. So likewise with the argument about the thief ; it does not follow,

---

[2] Reading ἀληθῆ δὲ ⟨αὑτὸν⟩ μή.

λόγος. οὐ γὰρ εἰ κακόν ἐστιν ὁ κλέπτης, καὶ τὸ
20 λαβεῖν ἐστι κακόν· οὔκουν τὸ κακὸν βούλεται, ἀλλὰ
τἀγαθόν· τὸ γὰρ λαβεῖν ἀγαθὸν ἀγαθόν. καὶ ἡ
νόσος κακόν ἐστιν, ἀλλ' οὐ τὸ ἀποβαλεῖν νόσον.
ἆρα τὸ δίκαιον τοῦ ἀδίκου καὶ τὸ δικαίως τοῦ
ἀδίκως αἱρετώτερον; ἀλλ' ἀποθανεῖν ἀδίκως αἱρετώτερον. ἆρα δίκαιόν ἐστι τὰ αὑτοῦ ἔχειν ἕκαστον;
25 ἃ δ' ἄν τις κρίνῃ κατὰ δόξαν τὴν αὑτοῦ, κἂν ᾖ
ψευδῆ, κύριά ἐστιν ἐκ τοῦ νόμου· τὸ αὐτὸ ἄρα
δίκαιον καὶ οὐ δίκαιον. καὶ πότερα δεῖ κρίνειν τὸν
τὰ δίκαια λέγοντα ἢ τὸν τὰ ἄδικα; ἀλλὰ μὴν καὶ
τὸν ἀδικούμενον δίκαιόν ἐστιν ἱκανῶς λέγειν ἃ
ἔπαθεν· ταῦτα δ' ἦν ἄδικα. οὐ γὰρ εἰ παθεῖν τι
ἀδίκως αἱρετόν, τὸ ἀδίκως αἱρετώτερον τοῦ δι-
30 καίως· ἀλλ' ἁπλῶς μὲν τὸ δικαίως, τοδὶ μέντοι
οὐδὲν κωλύει ἀδίκως ἢ δικαίως. καὶ τὸ ἔχειν τὰ
αὑτοῦ δίκαιον, τὸ δὲ τἀλλότρια οὐ δίκαιον· κρίσιν
μέντοι ταύτην δικαίαν εἶναι οὐδὲν κωλύει, οἷον ἂν
ᾖ κατὰ δόξαν τοῦ κρίναντος· οὐ γὰρ εἰ δίκαιον
τοδὶ ἢ ὡδί, καὶ ἁπλῶς δίκαιον. ὁμοίως δὲ καὶ
35 ἄδικα ὄντα οὐδὲν κωλύει λέγειν γε αὐτὰ δίκαιον
εἶναι· οὐ γὰρ εἰ λέγειν δίκαιον, ἀνάγκη δίκαια
εἶναι, ὥσπερ οὐδ' εἰ ὠφέλιμον λέγειν, ὠφέλιμα.
ὁμοίως δὲ καὶ ἐπὶ τῶν δικαίων. ὥστ' οὐκ εἰ

if the thief is an evil, that to acquire things is also an evil. The thief, therefore, does not wish for what is evil but for what is good ; for to acquire something good is good. Also disease is an evil, but to get rid of disease is not an evil.—Is what is just preferable to what is unjust and are just circumstances preferable to unjust ? But it is preferable to be put to death unjustly.—Is it just that each man should have his own ? But judgements which a man passes in accordance with his personal opinion, even if they are false, are valid in the eyes of the law ; the same thing, therefore, is just and not just.—Again, should judgement be given in favour of him who says what is just or of him who says what is unjust ? But it is just for the victim of injustice to state in full the things which he has suffered, and these things were unjust. For if to suffer something unjustly is an object of choice, it does not follow that unjust circumstances are preferable to just, but, absolutely, justice is preferable ; but this does not prevent unjust circumstances being preferable to just in a particular case. Again, it is just that a man should have his own, and it is not just that he should have what belongs to another ; but there is no reason why any judgement which is given in accordance with the judge's opinion should not be just ; for, if it is just in a particular case and in particular circumstances, it is not also absolutely just. Similarly, too, there is no reason why, though things are unjust, merely saying them should not be just. For if to say things is just, it does not follow that they are just, any more than, if it is expedient to say things, it follows that those things are expedient. Similarly, too, with things that are just. So that if what is said is unjust,

131

180 b

τὰ λεγόμενα ἄδικα, ὁ λέγων ἄδικα νικᾷ· λέγει
γὰρ ἃ λέγειν ἐστὶ δίκαια, ἁπλῶς δὲ καὶ παθεῖν
ἄδικα.

181 a   XXVI. Τοῖς δὲ παρὰ τὸν ὁρισμὸν γινομένοις τοῦ
ἐλέγχου, καθάπερ ὑπεγράφη πρότερον, ἀπαντητέον
σκοποῦσι τὸ συμπέρασμα πρὸς τὴν ἀντίφασιν, ὅπως
ἔσται τὸ αὐτὸ καὶ κατὰ τὸ αὐτὸ καὶ πρὸς τὸ αὐτὸ
5 καὶ ὡσαύτως καὶ ἐν τῷ αὐτῷ χρόνῳ. ἐὰν δ' ἐν
ἀρχῇ προσέρηται, οὐχ ὁμολογητέον ὡς ἀδύνατον
τὸ αὐτὸ εἶναι διπλάσιον καὶ μὴ διπλάσιον, ἀλλὰ
φατέον, μὴ μέντοι ὡδί, ὥς ποτ' ἦν τὸ ἐλέγχεσθαι
διωμολογημένον. εἰσὶ δὲ πάντες οἵδ' οἱ λόγοι
παρὰ τὸ τοιοῦτο. ἆρ' ὁ εἰδὼς ἕκαστον ὅτι ἕκαστον,
10 οἶδε τὸ πρᾶγμα; καὶ ὁ ἀγνοῶν ὡσαύτως; εἰδὼς
δέ τις τὸν Κορίσκον ὅτι Κορίσκος, ἀγνοοίη ἂν ὅτι
μουσικός, ὥστε ταὐτὸ ἐπίσταται καὶ ἀγνοεῖ. ἆρα
τὸ τετράπηχυ τοῦ τριπήχεος μεῖζον; γένοιτο δ'
ἂν ἐκ τριπήχους τετράπηχυ κατὰ τὸ μῆκος· τὸ δὲ
μεῖζον ἐλάττονος μεῖζον· αὐτὸ ἄρα αὑτοῦ μεῖζον
καὶ ἔλαττον.

15   XXVII. Τοὺς δὲ παρὰ τὸ αἰτεῖσθαι καὶ λαμβάνειν τὸ ἐν ἀρχῇ πυνθανομένῳ μέν, ἂν ᾖ δῆλον,
οὐ δοτέον, οὐδ' ἂν ἔνδοξον ᾖ, λέγοντα τἀληθές.
ἂν δὲ λάθῃ, τὴν ἄγνοιαν διὰ τὴν μοχθηρίαν τῶν

―――――――――
ᵃ 167 a 23.

it does not follow that it is a case of the man who uses unjust pleas winning his cause; for he is saying things which it is just for him to say but which are, absolutely, unjust for anyone to suffer.

XXVI. Refutations which are connected with the definition of the refutation must, as suggested above,[a] be met by examining the conclusion in the light of its contradictory and seeing how the same term shall be present in the same respect and in the same relation, manner and time. In putting this additional question at the beginning, you must not admit that it is impossible for the same thing to be both double and not double but must admit the possibility but not in the way that was once admitted to fulfil the conditions of a refutation. All the following arguments depend upon a point of this kind. ' Does he who knows that A is A, know the thing A ? ' And, similarly, ' Does he who does not know that A is A, not know the thing A ? ' But one who knows that Coriscus is Coriscus, might not know that he is musical, so that he both knows and is ignorant of the same thing.—Again, ' Is an object which is four cubits long greater than an object which is three cubits long ? ' But an object three cubits long might become four cubits long. Now the greater is greater than the less ; therefore the object is itself greater and less than itself.

XXVII. In refutations which are connected with the begging and assuming of the original point at issue, it should not be granted to a questioner, if his procedure is obvious, even though his view is generally accepted, but you should state the truth. If, on the other hand, his procedure is not detected, you should, owing to the badness of such arguments,

(3) Ignoratio elenchi.

(4) Petitio principii.

τοιούτων λόγων εἰς τὸν ἐρωτῶντα μεταστρεπτέον
ὡς οὐ διειλεγμένον· ὁ γὰρ ἔλεγχος ἄνευ τοῦ ἐξ
20 ἀρχῆς. εἶθ' ὅτι ἐδόθη οὐχ ὡς τούτῳ χρησομένου,
ἀλλ' ὡς πρὸς τοῦτο συλλογιουμένου τοὐναντίον ἢ
ἐπὶ τῶν παρεξελέγχων.

XXVIII. Καὶ τοὺς διὰ τοῦ παρεπομένου συμ-
βιβάζοντας ἐπ' αὐτοῦ τοῦ λόγου δεικτέον. ἔστι δὲ
διττὴ ἡ τῶν ἑπομένων ἀκολούθησις. ἢ γὰρ ὡς τῷ
25 ἐν μέρει τὸ καθόλου, οἷον ἀνθρώπῳ ζῷον· ἀξιοῦται
γάρ, εἰ τόδε μετὰ τοῦδε, καὶ τόδ' εἶναι μετὰ τοῦδε.
ἢ κατὰ τὰς ἀντιθέσεις· εἰ γὰρ τόδε τῷδε ἀκολουθεῖ,
τῷ ἀντικειμένῳ τὸ ἀντικείμενον. παρ' ὃ καὶ ὁ τοῦ
Μελίσσου λόγος· εἰ γὰρ τὸ γεγονὸς ἔχει ἀρχήν, τὸ
ἀγένητον ἀξιοῖ μὴ ἔχειν, ὥστ' εἰ ἀγένητος ὁ οὐρα-
30 νός, καὶ ἄπειρος. τὸ δ' οὐκ ἔστιν· ἀνάπαλιν γὰρ
ἡ ἀκολούθησις.

XXIX. Ὅσοι τε παρὰ τὸ προστιθέναι τι συλλο-
γίζονται, σκοπεῖν εἰ ἀφαιρουμένου συμβαίνει μηδὲν
ἧττον τὸ ἀδύνατον. κἄπειτα τοῦτο ἐμφανιστέον,
καὶ λεκτέον ὡς ἔδωκεν οὐχ ὡς δοκοῦν ἀλλ' ὡς
35 πρὸς τὸν λόγον, ὁ δὲ κέχρηται οὐδὲν πρὸς τὸν
λόγον.

XXX. Πρὸς δὲ τοὺς τὰ πλείω ἐρωτήματα ἓν
ποιοῦντας εὐθὺς ἐν ἀρχῇ διοριστέον. ἐρώτησις
γὰρ μία πρὸς ἣν μία ἀπόκρισίς ἐστιν, ὥστ' οὔτε

make your ignorance recoil on the head of the questioner, on the ground that he has not argued properly; for refutation must proceed without any assumption of the original point. Next, you must argue that the point was granted with the idea that he was going to use it not as a premiss but in order to argue the opposite view to it or for the purpose of refutations on side issues.

XXVIII. Again, those refutations which draw their conclusions through the consequent must be exposed in the argument itself. There are two ways in which consequences follow: Either as the universal follows from the particular, as 'animal' follows from 'man'; for it is claimed that, if A accompanies B, then B also accompanies A. Or else the process goes by opposites; for if A follows B, A's opposite will follow B's opposite. It is on this, too, that the argument of Melissus depends; for he claims that, if that which has come to be has a beginning, that which has not come to be has no beginning, and so, if the heaven has not come to be, it is also eternal. But this is not true; for the sequence is the reverse. (5) The consequent.

XXIX. In refutations which are argued by means of some addition, you must examine whether the impossibility occurs none the less when the addition has been withdrawn. If so, then the answerer should make this fact clear and should state that he granted the addition not because he believed in it but for the sake of the argument, but that his opponent has made no use of it at all for his argument. (6) Insertion of irrelevant matter.

XXX. In dealing with those who make several questions into one, you should draw a distinction immediately at the beginning. For a question is single to which there is only one answer, so that one (7) Multiplicity of questions.

181 a

πλείω καθ᾽ ἑνὸς οὔτε ἓν κατὰ πολλῶν, ἀλλ᾽ ἓν καθ᾽
181 b ἑνὸς φατέον ἢ ἀποφατέον. ὥσπερ δὲ ἐπὶ τῶν ὁμωνύμων ὁτὲ μὲν ἀμφοῖν ὁτὲ δ᾽ οὐδετέρῳ ὑπάρχει,
ὥστε μὴ ἁπλοῦ ὄντος τοῦ ἐρωτήματος ἁπλῶς ἀποκρινομένοις οὐδὲν συμβαίνει πάσχειν, ὁμοίως καὶ
ἐπὶ τούτων. ὅταν μὲν οὖν τὰ πλείω τῷ ἑνὶ ἢ τὸ
5 ἓν τοῖς πολλοῖς ὑπάρχῃ, τῷ ἁπλῶς δόντι καὶ ἁμαρ-
τόντι ταύτην τὴν ἁμαρτίαν οὐδὲν ὑπεναντίωμα
συμβαίνει· ὅταν δὲ τῷ μὲν τῷ δὲ μή, ἢ πλείω κατὰ
πλειόνων, καὶ ἔστιν ὡς ὑπάρχει ἀμφότερα ἀμφοτέροις, ἔστι δ᾽ ὡς οὐχ ὑπάρχει πάλιν, ὥστε τοῦτ᾽
εὐλαβητέον. οἷον ἐν τοῖσδε τοῖς λόγοις. εἰ τὸ μέν
10 ἐστιν ἀγαθὸν τὸ δὲ κακόν, ὅτι ταῦτα ἀληθὲς εἰπεῖν
ἀγαθὸν καὶ κακὸν καὶ πάλιν μήτ᾽ ἀγαθὸν μήτε
κακόν (οὐκ ἔστι γὰρ ἑκάτερον ἑκάτερον), ὥστε
ταὐτὸ ἀγαθὸν καὶ κακὸν καὶ οὔτ᾽ ἀγαθὸν οὔτε κακόν.
καὶ εἰ ἕκαστον αὐτὸ αὑτῷ ταὐτόν, καὶ ἄλλου ἕτερον,
ἐπειδὴ[1] οὐκ ἄλλοις ταὐτὰ ἀλλ᾽ αὑτοῖς, καὶ ἕτερα
15 αὑτῶν, ταὐτὰ ἑαυτοῖς ἕτερα καὶ ταὐτά. ἔτι εἰ τὸ
μὲν ἀγαθὸν κακὸν γίνεται, τὸ δὲ κακὸν ἀγαθὸν
ἐστιν, δύο γένοιτ᾽ ἄν. δυοῖν τε καὶ ἀνίσων ἑκάτερον αὐτὸ αὑτῷ ἴσον, ὥστε ἴσα καὶ ἄνισα αὐτὰ
αὑτοῖς.

Ἐμπίπτουσι μὲν οὖν οὗτοι καὶ εἰς ἄλλας λύσεις·
20 καὶ γὰρ τὸ ἄμφω καὶ τὸ ἅπαντα πλείω σημαίνει·
οὔκουν ταὐτόν, πλὴν ὄνομα, συμβαίνει φῆσαι καὶ

---

[1] Reading ἐπειδὴ for ἐπεὶ δ᾽ with Poste.

must not affirm or deny several things of one thing
nor one thing of several things, but one thing of one
thing. But just as in the case of equivocal terms, a
predicate is sometimes true of both meanings and
sometimes of neither, and so, though the question
is not simple, no detriment results if people give a
simple answer, so too with these double questions.
When, therefore, the several predicates are true of one
subject, or one predicate of several subjects, no contradiction is involved in giving a simple answer, though
he has made this mistake. But when the predicate
is true of one subject but not of the other, or several
predicates are true of several subjects, then there is
a sense in which both are true of both but another
sense, on the other hand, in which they are not ; so
one must be on one's guard against this. The following arguments illustrate this : (1) Supposing A is
good and B evil, it is true to say that they are good
and evil and, on the other hand, that they are neither
good nor evil (for A is not evil and B is not good), so
that the same thing is good and evil and neither good
nor evil ; (2) If everything is the same as itself and
different from anything else, since things are not the
same as other things but the same as themselves,
and also different from themselves, the same things
are both different from themselves and the same as
themselves ; (3) Moreover, if that which is good
becomes evil and that which is evil is good, they
would become two ; and of two unequal things each
is equal to itself, so that they are both equal and
unequal to themselves.

These refutations also fall under other solutions ;
for the terms ' both ' and ' all ' have several meanings,
so that to affirm or deny the same thing is verbal only,

181 b

ἀποφῆσαι· τοῦτο δ' οὐκ ἦν ἔλεγχος. ἀλλὰ φανερὸν
ὅτι μὴ μιᾶς ἐρωτήσεως τῶν πλειόνων γινομένης,[1]
ἀλλ' ἓν καθ' ἑνὸς φάντος ἢ ἀποφάντος, οὐκ ἔσται
τὸ ἀδύνατον.

25 XXXI. Περὶ δὲ τῶν ἀπαγόντων εἰς τὸ[2] ταὐτὸ
πολλάκις εἰπεῖν, φανερὸν ὡς οὐ δοτέον τῶν πρός
τι λεγομένων σημαίνειν τι χωριζομένας καθ' αὑτὰς
τὰς κατηγορίας, οἷον διπλάσιον ἄνευ τοῦ διπλάσιον
ἡμίσεος, ὅτι ἐμφαίνεται. καὶ γὰρ τὰ δέκα ἐν τοῖς
30 ἑνὸς δέουσι δέκα καὶ τὸ ποιῆσαι ἐν τῷ μὴ ποιῆσαι,
καὶ ὅλως ἐν τῇ ἀποφάσει ἡ φάσις· ἀλλ' ὅμως οὐκ
εἴ τις λέγοι τοδὶ μὴ εἶναι λευκόν, λέγει αὐτὸ λευκὸν
εἶναι. τὸ δὲ διπλάσιον οὐδὲ σημαίνει οὐδὲν ἴσως,
ὥσπερ οὐδὲ τὸ ἐν τῷ ἡμίσει· εἰ δ' ἄρα καὶ σημαίνει,
ἀλλ' οὐ ταὐτὸ καὶ συνῃρημένον. οὐδ' ἡ ἐπιστήμη
35 ἐν τῷ εἴδει, οἷον εἰ ἔστιν ἡ ἰατρικὴ ἐπιστήμη, ὅπερ
τὸ κοινόν· ἐκεῖνο δ' ἦν ἐπιστήμη ἐπιστητοῦ. ἐν
δὲ τοῖς δι' ὧν δηλοῦται κατηγορουμένοις τοῦτο
λεκτέον, ὡς οὐ τὸ αὐτὸ χωρὶς καὶ ἐν τῷ λόγῳ τὸ
δηλούμενον. τὸ γὰρ κοῖλον κοινῇ μὲν τὸ αὐτὸ
δηλοῖ ἐπὶ τοῦ σιμοῦ καὶ τοῦ ῥοικοῦ, προστιθέμενον
182 a δὲ οὐδὲν κωλύει ἄλλα, τὸ μὲν τῇ ῥινὶ τὸ δὲ τῷ
σκέλει, σημαίνειν[3]· ἔνθα μὲν γὰρ τὸ σιμόν, ἔνθα δὲ

---

[1] Reading γινομένης for γινομένων.
[2] Inserting τὸ before ταὐτό.
[3] Reading σημαίνειν (σημαίνει ABD).

138

and this, as we saw, is not a refutation. But clearly, if one of the several questions is not asked but the answerer affirms or denies a single predicate of a single subject, the reduction to an impossibility will not occur.

XXXI. As regards those who lead one on to repeat the same thing several times over, it is clear that one must not allow that predications of relative terms have any signification in themselves when separated from their correlatives ; for example, that ' double ' apart from the expression ' double of half ' is significant, just because it appears in that expression. For ' ten ' appears in the expression ' ten minus one ' and ' do ' in the expression ' not do,' and affirmations in general in negations ; but, all the same, if one were to say ' this is not white,' one is not saying that it is white. ' Double ' has possibly no signification at all, just as ' the ' in ' the half ' too signifies nothing. If it *has* any signification, it is not the same as in the combined expression. Nor is ' knowledge ' of a specific kind, such as ' medical knowledge,' the same as ' knowledge ' as a general term ; for the latter has always meant ' knowledge of the knowable.' When dealing with terms which are predicated of the terms by means of which they are defined, you must say that the term defined is not the same when taken separately as it is in the combined expression. For ' concave ' has the same general meaning when used of the snub-nosed and of the bandy-legged, but when it is combined in the one case with the nose and in the other with the leg, there is no reason why it should not signify different things, for in the first case it signifies ' snub,' in the other ' bandy,' and it makes

(B) Solution of arguments tending to BABBLING.

139

τὸ ῥαιβὸν σημαίνει· καὶ οὐδὲν διαφέρει εἰπεῖν ῥὶς
σιμὴ ἢ ῥὶς κοίλη. ἔτι οὐ δοτέον τὴν λέξιν κατ'
εὐθύ· ψεῦδος γάρ ἐστιν. οὐ γάρ ἐστι τὸ σιμὸν ῥὶς
5 κοίλη ἀλλὰ ῥινὸς τοδί, οἷον πάθος, ὥστ' οὐδὲν
ἄτοπον, εἰ ἡ ῥὶς ἡ σιμὴ ῥίς ἐστιν ἔχουσα κοιλότητα
ῥινός.

XXXII. Περὶ δὲ τῶν σολοικισμῶν, παρ' ὅ τι
μὲν φαίνονται συμβαίνειν, εἴπομεν πρότερον, ὡς
δὲ λυτέον, ἐπ' αὐτῶν τῶν λόγων ἔσται φανερόν.
10 ἅπαντες γὰρ οἱ τοιοίδε τοῦτο βούλονται κατα-
σκευάζειν. ἆρ' ὃ λέγεις ἀληθῶς, καὶ ἔστι τοῦτο
ἀληθῶς; φῇς δ' εἶναί τι λίθον· ἔστιν ἄρα τι λίθον.
ἢ τὸ λέγειν λίθον οὐκ ἔστι λέγειν ὃ ἀλλ' ὄν, οὐδὲ
τοῦτο ἀλλὰ τοῦτον· εἰ οὖν ἔροιτό τις, ἆρ' ὃν ἀληθῶς
λέγεις, ἔστι τοῦτον, οὐκ ἂν δοκοίη ἑλληνίζειν,
15 ὥσπερ οὐδ' εἰ ἔροιτο, ἆρ' ἣν λέγεις εἶναι, ἔστιν
οὗτος; ξύλον δ' εἰπεῖν οὕτως,[1] ἢ ὅσα μήτε θῆλυ
μήτ' ἄρρεν σημαίνει, οὐδὲν διαφέρει. διὸ καὶ οὐ
γίνεται σολοικισμός, εἰ ὃ λέγεις εἶναι, ἔστι τοῦτο;
ξύλον δὲ λέγεις εἶναι· ἔστιν ἄρα ξύλον. ὁ δὲ λίθος
καὶ τὸ οὗτος ἄρρενος ἔχει κλῆσιν. εἰ δέ[2] τις ἔροιτο,
ἆρ' οὗτός ἐστιν αὕτη; εἶτα πάλιν, τί δ'; οὐχ
20 οὗτός ἐστι Κορίσκος; εἶτ' εἴπειεν, ἔστιν ἄρα οὗτος
αὕτη, οὐ συλλελόγισται τὸν σολοικισμόν, οὐδ' εἰ

---

[1] Reading εἰπεῖν οὕτως for εἶπεν οὗτος.
[2] Reading δέ for δή.

---

[a] 165 b 20 f.

[b] The argument is clear in the original, because Greek is
an inflected language, whereas English does not distinguish

no difference whether you say ' a snub nose ' or ' a concave nose.' Further, the expression must not be allowed to pass without qualification ; for it is a falsehood. For snubness is not a concave nose but something, namely a condition, appertaining to a nose ; so there is nothing absurd in supposing that a snub nose is one which possesses nasal concavity.

XXXII. As regards solecisms, we have already stated[a] the apparent cause of their occurrence ; how they should be solved will be clear in the actual arguments. All the following arguments aim at producing this result : ' Is a thing truly that which you truly affirm it to be ? ' You affirm something to be a stone (accusative masculine)[b] ; therefore something (nominative neuter) is a stone (accusative masculine). Or does speaking of a stone (a masculine word) involve the use of the relative ' whom ' rather than ' which ' and the pronoun ' him ' rather than ' it ' ? If, then, one were to ask, ' Is a stone *him whom* you truly state him to be ?,' he would not be considered to be talking good Greek any more than if he were to ask, ' Is *he* whom you state *her* to be ? ' But the use of the word ' stick,' or any other neuter word, in this way, involves no difference between the nominative and accusative ; therefore no solecism is committed if you say, ' Is this what you affirm it to be ? ' You affirm it to be a stick ; therefore it is a stick. ' Stone,' however, and ' he ' have the masculine gender. Now if one were to ask, ' Can " he " be a " she " ?,' and then again, ' Why ? Is he not Coriscus ? ' and then were to say, ' Then he is a she,' he has not proved the solecism even if Coriscus

(C) Solution of arguments tending to SOLECISM.

between the nominative and accusative except in the personal pronouns and the relative.

τὸ Κορίσκος σημαίνει ὅπερ αὕτη, μὴ δίδωσι δὲ
ὁ ἀποκρινόμενος, ἀλλὰ δεῖ τοῦτο προσερωτηθῆναι.
εἰ δὲ μήτ' ἔστιν μήτε δίδωσιν, οὐ συλλελόγισται
οὔτε τῷ ὄντι οὔτε πρὸς τὸν ἠρωτημένον. ὁμοίως

25 οὖν δεῖ κἀκεῖ τὸν λίθον σημαίνειν οὗτος. εἰ δὲ
μήτε ἔστι μήτε δίδοται, οὐ λεκτέον τὸ συμπέρασμα·
φαίνεται δὲ παρὰ τὸ τὴν ἀνόμοιον πτῶσιν τοῦ
ὀνόματος ὁμοίαν φαίνεσθαι. ἆρ' ἀληθές ἐστιν εἰπεῖν ὅτι ἔστιν αὕτη, ὅπερ εἶναι φῂς αὐτήν; εἶναι
δὲ φῂς ἀσπίδα· ἔστιν ἄρα αὕτη ἀσπίδα. ἢ οὐκ

30 ἀνάγκη, εἰ μὴ τὸ αὕτη ἀσπίδα σημαίνει ἀλλ' ἀσπίς,
τὸ δ' ἀσπίδα ταύτην; οὐδ' εἰ ὃ φῂς εἶναι τοῦτον,
ἐστὶν οὗτος, φῂς δ' εἶναι Κλέωνα, ἔστιν ἄρα οὗτος
Κλέωνα· οὐ γὰρ ἔστιν οὗτος Κλέωνα· εἴρηται γὰρ
ὅτι ὅ φημι εἶναι τοῦτον, ἔστιν οὗτος, οὐ τοῦτον·
οὐδὲ γὰρ ἂν ἑλληνίζοι οὕτως τὸ ἐρώτημα λεχθέν.

35 ἆρ' ἐπίστασαι τοῦτο; τοῦτο δ' ἐστὶ λίθος· ἐπίστασαι ἄρα λίθος. ἢ οὐ ταὐτὸ σημαίνει τὸ τοῦτο
ἐν τῷ ἆρ' ἐπίστασαι τοῦτο καὶ ἐν τῷ τοῦτο δὲ
λίθος, ἀλλ' ἐν μὲν τῷ πρώτῳ τοῦτον, ἐν δὲ τῷ
ὑστέρῳ οὗτος; ἆρ' οὗ ἐπιστήμην ἔχεις, ἐπίστασαι
τοῦτο; ἐπιστήμην δ' ἔχεις λίθου· ἐπίστασαι ἄρα

182 b λίθου. ἢ τὸ μὲν τούτου λίθου λέγεις, τὸ δὲ τοῦτον

---

[a] But Cleon.

signifies a 'she,' though the answerer refuses to concede this ; but this must be the subject of a further question. But if neither this is so nor does he concede it, then the solecism has not been proved either in fact or relatively to the person to whom the question was put. Similarly, therefore, in the first example also, 'he' must signify the stone. If, however, this is neither true nor is conceded, the conclusion must not be stated, though it is apparently true, because the case which is used of the word, which is unlike, appears to be like.—' Is it true to say that this object is what you affirm it to be ? ' You affirm it to be a shield (accusative), therefore it is a shield (accusative). Or is this not necessarily so, if ' this object ' (nominative) signifies not shield (accusative) but shield (nominative), while ' this object ' (accusative) signifies shield (accusative).— Nor again if he is what you affirm him to be, and you affirm him to be Cleona (accusative of Cleon), is he therefore Cleona ? for he is not Cleona [a] ; for the statement was that *he* not *him* is what I affirm him to be. For the question if asked in this form [b] would not be Greek either.—' Do you know this ? ' But this is a stone (nominative) ; therefore you know a stone (nominative). Has not ' this ' a different force in the question ' Do you know this ? ' and in ' This is a stone,' in the first case standing for an accusative and in the second for a nominative ?—When you exercise recognition of an object, do you not recognize it ? You exercise recognition of a stone ; therefore you recognize ' of a stone.' Do you not in the one case put the object in the genitive and say ' of the stone,' and in the other case in the accusative and

[b] *i.e.* with the subject in the accusative.

λίθον· ἐδόθη δ᾽, οὗ ἐπιστήμην ἔχεις, ἐπίστασθαι, οὐ
τούτου, ἀλλὰ τοῦτο, ὥστ᾽ οὐ λίθου ἀλλὰ τὸν λίθον.

Ὅτι μὲν οὖν οἱ τοιοῦτοι τῶν λόγων οὐ συλλογί-
ζονται σολοικισμὸν ἀλλὰ φαίνονται, καὶ διὰ τί τε
5 φαίνονται καὶ πῶς ἀπαντητέον πρὸς αὐτούς,
φανερὸν ἐκ τῶν εἰρημένων.

XXXIII. Δεῖ δὲ καὶ κατανοεῖν ὅτι πάντων τῶν
λόγων οἱ μέν εἰσι ῥᾴους κατιδεῖν οἱ δὲ χαλεπώτεροι, παρὰ τί καὶ ἐν τίνι παραλογίζονται τὸν
ἀκούοντα, πολλάκις οἱ αὐτοὶ ἐκείνοις ὄντες. τὸν αὐ-
10 τὸν γὰρ λόγον δεῖ καλεῖν τὸν παρὰ ταὐτὸ γινό-
μενον· ὁ αὐτὸς δὲ λόγος τοῖς μὲν παρὰ τὴν λέξιν
τοῖς δὲ παρὰ τὸ συμβεβηκὸς τοῖς δὲ παρ᾽ ἕτερον
δόξειεν ἂν εἶναι διὰ τὸ μεταφερόμενον ἕκαστον μὴ
ὁμοίως εἶναι δῆλον. ὥσπερ οὖν ἐν τοῖς παρὰ τὴν
ὁμωνυμίαν, ὅσπερ δοκεῖ τρόπος εὐηθέστατος εἶναι
15 τῶν παραλογισμῶν, τὰ μὲν καὶ τοῖς τυχοῦσίν ἐστι
δῆλα (καὶ γὰρ οἱ λόγοι σχεδὸν οἱ γελοῖοι πάντες εἰσὶ
παρὰ τὴν λέξιν), οἷον ἀνὴρ ἐφέρετο κατὰ κλίμακος
δίφρον, καὶ ὅπου στέλλεσθε; πρὸς τὴν κεραίαν.
καὶ ποτέρα τῶν βοῶν ἔμπροσθεν τέξεται; οὐδετέρα,
ἀλλ᾽ ὄπισθεν ἄμφω. καὶ καθαρὸς ὁ βορέας; οὐ
20 δῆτα· ἀπεκτόνηκε γὰρ τὸν πτωχὸν καὶ τὸν ὠνούμενον. ἆρ᾽ Εὔαρχος; οὐ δῆτα, ἀλλ᾽ Ἀπολλωνίδης.

---

[a] The two meanings of the phrase are uncertain ; the
Oxford translation suggests (1) 'a man got the body of
the car taken off its chassis,' and (2) ' he came a " sitter " (δίφρος)
down from the ladder.'

[b] The reply takes the word in the sense of ' To what do you
fasten the sail when you furl it ? '

[c] The answer understands the question to mean ' which
cow will calve forwards ? '

say ' a stone ' ? But it was granted that, when you exercise recognition of a thing, you recognize ' it ' not ' of it,' so that you recognize not ' of a stone ' but ' a stone.'

That arguments of this kind, then, do not prove solecism but only appear to do so, and why they appear to do so and how you must face them, is clear from what has been said.

XXXIII. It must be noted about arguments in general that in some it is easier and in some more difficult to see why and where they mislead the listener, though often the latter are identical with the former. For an argument must be called identical when it depends on the same principle, but the same argument might be held by some people to depend on diction, by others on accident and by others on something else, because each, when applied in different contexts, is not equally clear. So, just as fallacies due to equivocation, which are generally regarded as the stupidest form of fallacy, some are obvious even to ordinary minds (for almost all the most laughable remarks depend upon diction). For example, ' A man was carried over the standing board of the framework of the chariot '[a]; and ' Whither are you bound ? ' ' To the yard-arm '[b]; ' Which of the two cows will calve in front ? ' ' Neither, but both behind.'[c] ' Is the north wind[d] clear ? ' ' No, certainly not ; for he has killed the beggar and the purchaser.'[e] ' Is he Evarchus ? ' ' Certainly not ; he is Apollonides.'[f]

---

[d] The answerer takes Boreas as a proper name.

[e] καὶ τὸν ὠνούμενον is almost certainly corrupt ; Poste suggests καὶ τίς ὁ ὠνούμενος;

[f] The literal meaning of these names might be rendered ' good-manager ' and ' squanderson.'

182 b

τὸν αὐτὸν δὲ τρόπον καὶ τῶν ἄλλων σχεδὸν οἱ πλεῖστοι, τὰ δὲ καὶ τοὺς ἐμπειροτάτους φαίνεται λαν-
θάνειν· σημεῖον δὲ τούτων ὅτι μάχονται πολλάκις
περὶ τῶν ὀνομάτων, οἷον πότερον ταὐτὸν σημαί-
25 νει κατὰ πάντων τὸ ὂν καὶ τὸ ἓν ἢ ἕτερον. τοῖς
μὲν γὰρ δοκεῖ ταὐτὸν σημαίνειν τὸ ὂν καὶ τὸ ἕν·
οἱ δὲ τὸν Ζήνωνος λόγον καὶ Παρμενίδου λύουσι
διὰ τὸ πολλαχῶς φάναι τὸ ἓν λέγεσθαι καὶ τὸ ὄν.
ὁμοίως δὲ καὶ τῶν παρὰ τὸ συμβεβηκὸς καὶ παρὰ[1]
τῶν ἄλλων ἕκαστον οἱ μὲν ἔσονται ῥᾴους ἰδεῖν οἱ
30 δὲ χαλεπώτεροι τῶν λόγων· καὶ λαβεῖν ἐν τίνι γένει,
καὶ πότερον ἔλεγχος ἢ οὐκ ἔλεγχος, οὐ ῥᾴδιον
ὁμοίως περὶ πάντων.

Ἔστι δὲ δριμὺς λόγος ὅστις ἀπορεῖν ποιεῖ μά-
λιστα· δάκνει γὰρ οὗτος μάλιστα. ἀπορία δ᾽ ἐστὶ
διττή, ἡ μὲν ἐν τοῖς συλλελογισμένοις, ὅ τι ἀνέλῃ
35 τις τῶν ἐρωτημάτων, ἡ δ᾽ ἐν τοῖς ἐριστικοῖς, πῶς
εἴπῃ τις τὸ προταθέν. διόπερ ἐν τοῖς συλλογιστι-
κοῖς οἱ δριμύτεροι λόγοι ζητεῖν μᾶλλον ποιοῦσιν.
ἔστι δὲ συλλογιστικὸς μὲν λόγος δριμύτατος, ἂν ἐξ
ὅτι μάλιστα δοκούντων ὅτι μάλιστα ἔνδοξον ἀναιρῇ.
εἷς γὰρ ὢν ὁ λόγος μετατιθεμένης τῆς ἀντιφάσεως
183 a ἅπαντας ὁμοίους ἕξει τοὺς συλλογισμούς· ἀεὶ γὰρ
ἐξ ἐνδόξων ὁμοίως ἔνδοξον ἀναιρήσει ἢ κατασκευά-
σει, διόπερ ἀπορεῖν ἀναγκαῖον. μάλιστα μὲν οὖν
ὁ τοιοῦτος δριμύς, ὁ ἐξ ἴσου τὸ συμπέρασμα ποιῶν
5 τοῖς ἐρωτήμασι, δεύτερος δ᾽ ὁ ἐξ ἁπάντων ὁμοίων·

---

[1] Reading with Poste τῶν παρὰ τὸ συμβεβηκὸς καὶ παρὰ for
τῶν περὶ τοῦ συμβεβηκότος καὶ περί.

And so on with almost all the rest of the ambiguities, but some even the most expert seem to fail to discern. A proof of this is that people often dispute about the terms used, for example, whether ' Being ' and ' Unity ' always mean the same thing or something different ; for some people hold that ' Being ' and ' Unity ' are identical in meaning, while others solve the argument of Zeno and Parmenides by saying that ' Unity ' and ' Being ' are used in several senses. Similarly, too, of the arguments which are dependent on accident and each of the other classes, some will be easier to detect and others more difficult, and it is not always equally easy to grasp into which class they fall and whether refutation takes place or not.

A shrewd argument is one which causes most embarrassment ; for it bites deepest. Embarrassment is of two kinds. In a reasoned discussion one is in doubt which of the questions one should subvert, whereas in contentious arguments it is about the way in which one is to express the proposition. Hence it is in reasoned discussions that shrewder arguments are more stimulative of inquiry. Now a reasoned argument is shrewdest when from the most generally accepted premises possible it subverts the most generally accepted thesis possible. For the single argument, if the contradictory is changed about, will result in all the syllogisms being alike ; for from generally accepted premises it will subvert or establish an equally generally accepted conclusion ; therefore embarrassment must necessarily arise. Such, then, is the shrewdest argument which puts the conclusion on an equality with the premises. The next shrewdest is that which argues from premises which are all on an equality ; for this will cause an equal

Shrewdness in argument.

οὗτος γὰρ ὁμοίως ποιήσει ἀπορεῖν ὁποῖον τῶν
ἐρωτημάτων ἀναιρετέον. τοῦτο δὲ χαλεπόν· ἀναιρετέον μὲν γάρ, ὅ τι δ' ἀναιρετέον, ἄδηλον. τῶν δ'
ἐριστικῶν δριμύτατος μὲν ὁ πρῶτον εὐθὺς ἄδηλος
πότερον συλλελόγισται ἢ οὔ, καὶ πότερον παρὰ
ψεῦδός ἢ διαίρεσίν ἐστιν ἡ λύσις, δεύτερος δὲ τῶν
10 ἄλλων ὁ δῆλος μὲν ὅτι παρὰ διαίρεσιν ἢ ἀναίρεσίν
ἐστι, μὴ φανερὸς δ' ὢν διὰ τίνος τῶν ἠρωτημένων
ἀναίρεσιν ἢ διαίρεσιν λυτέος ἐστίν, ἀλλ' ἢ[1] πότερον
αὕτη παρὰ τὸ συμπέρασμα ἢ παρά τι τῶν ἐρωτημάτων ἐστίν.

Ἐνίοτε μὲν οὖν ὁ μὴ συλλογισθεὶς λόγος εὐήθης
15 ἐστίν, ἐὰν ᾖ λίαν ἄδοξα ἢ ψευδῆ τὰ λήμματα·
ἐνίοτε δ' οὐκ ἄξιος καταφρονεῖσθαι. ὅταν μὲν γὰρ
ἐλλείπῃ τι τῶν τοιούτων ἐρωτημάτων, περὶ οὗ ὁ
λόγος καὶ δι' ὅ, καὶ μὴ προσλαβὼν τοῦτο καὶ
μὴ συλλογισάμενος εὐήθης ὁ συλλογισμός, ὅταν
20 δὲ τῶν ἔξωθεν, οὐκ εὐκαταφρόνητος οὐδαμῶς, ἀλλ'
ὁ μὲν λόγος ἐπιεικής, ὁ δ' ἐρωτῶν ἠρώτηκεν οὐ
καλῶς.

Ἔστι τε, ὥσπερ λύειν ὁτὲ μὲν πρὸς τὸν λόγον ὁτὲ
δὲ πρὸς τὸν ἐρωτῶντα καὶ τὴν ἐρώτησιν ὁτὲ δὲ
πρὸς οὐδέτερον τούτων, ὁμοίως καὶ ἐρωτᾶν ἔστι
καὶ συλλογίζεσθαι καὶ πρὸς τὴν θέσιν καὶ πρὸς τὸν
25 ἀποκρινόμενον καὶ πρὸς τὸν χρόνον, ὅταν ᾖ πλείονος χρόνου δεομένη ἡ λύσις ἢ τοῦ παρόντος
καιροῦ.[2]

XXXIV. Ἐκ πόσων μὲν οὖν καὶ ποίων γίνονται
τοῖς διαλεγομένοις οἱ παραλογισμοί, καὶ πῶς δεί-
ξομέν τε ψευδόμενον καὶ παράδοξα λέγειν ποιή-

___
[1] Reading ἀλλ' ἢ with Wallies.
[2] Omitting with Waitz τὸ διαλεχθῆναι πρὸς τὴν λύσιν as a gloss.

embarrassment as to which kind of question ought to be subverted. The difficulty lies in this, that something must be subverted but it is not clear what. The shrewdest of contentious arguments is that which, in the first place, immediately makes it uncertain whether the reasoning is conclusive or not, and also whether the solution is due to a false premiss or a distinction. Of the rest, that comes next which clearly depends on a distinction or a subversion, but it is not clear which of the premisses it is on the subversion or distinction of which the solution depends, but only whether this process depends upon the conclusion or one of the premisses.

Now sometimes an inadequately reasoned argu- Stupid
ment is stupid if the premisses assumed are too para- arguments.
doxical or false ; but sometimes it is not deserving
of contempt. For when some question is wanting
such as concerns the argument or the means of
carrying it on, the reasoning which has failed to
supply this and is not properly argued is stupid ; but
when something which is merely extraneous has been
omitted, the reasoning is by no means to be lightly
condemned but is respectable, though the questioner
has not asked his questions well.

As it is possible to address the solution sometimes
to the argument, sometimes to the questioner and
his mode of questioning and sometimes to neither
of these, so likewise also it is possible to address one's
questions and reasonings both to the thesis and to
the answerer and to the time, when the solution needs
more time than the present occasion supplies.

XXXIV. The number, then, and the nature of the EPI-
sources from which fallacies arise in discussion, and LOGUE.
how we are to show up a pretender and make him (1) Summary of
results.

183 a

30 σομεν, ἔτι δ᾿ ἐκ τίνων συμβαίνει ὁ σολοικισμός,[1]
καὶ πῶς ἐρωτητέον καὶ τίς ἡ τάξις τῶν ἐρωτημάτων, ἔτι πρὸς τί χρήσιμοι πάντες εἰσὶν οἱ τοιοῦτοι
λόγοι, καὶ περὶ ἀποκρίσεως ἁπλῶς τε πάσης καὶ
πῶς λυτέον τοὺς λόγους καὶ τοὺς σολοικισμούς,[2]
εἰρήσθω περὶ ἁπάντων ἡμῖν ταῦτα. λοιπὸν δὲ περὶ
35 τῆς ἐξ ἀρχῆς προθέσεως ἀναμνήσασιν εἰπεῖν τι
βραχὺ περὶ αὐτῆς καὶ τέλος ἐπιθεῖναι τοῖς εἰρημένοις.

Προειλόμεθα μὲν οὖν εὑρεῖν δύναμίν τινα συλ-
λογιστικὴν περὶ τοῦ προβληθέντος ἐκ τῶν ὑπαρχόντων ὡς ἐνδοξοτάτων· τοῦτο γὰρ ἔργον ἐστὶ τῆς
183 b διαλεκτικῆς καθ᾿ αὑτὴν καὶ τῆς πειραστικῆς. ἐπεὶ
δὲ προσκατασκευάζεται πρὸς αὐτὴν διὰ τὴν τῆς
σοφιστικῆς γειτνίασιν, ὡς οὐ μόνον πεῖραν δύναται
λαβεῖν διαλεκτικῶς ἀλλὰ καὶ ὡς εἰδώς, διὰ τοῦτο
οὐ μόνον τὸ λεχθὲν ἔργον ὑπεθέμεθα τῆς πραγμα-
5 τείας, τὸ λόγον δύνασθαι λαβεῖν, ἀλλὰ καὶ ὅπως
λόγον ὑπέχοντες φυλάξομεν τὴν θέσιν ὡς δι᾿ ἐνδοξο-
τάτων ὁμοτρόπως. τὴν δ᾿ αἰτίαν εἰρήκαμεν τούτου,
ἐπεὶ καὶ διὰ τοῦτο Σωκράτης ἠρώτα, ἀλλ᾿ οὐκ
ἀπεκρίνετο· ὡμολόγει γὰρ οὐκ εἰδέναι. δεδήλωται
δ᾿ ἐν τοῖς πρότερον καὶ πρὸς πόσα καὶ ἐκ πόσων
10 τοῦτο ἔσται, καὶ ὅθεν εὐπορήσομεν τούτων, ἔτι δὲ
πῶς ἐρωτητέον ἢ τακτέον τὴν ἐρώτησιν πᾶσαν, καὶ

---

[1] Reading with Pacius σολοικισμός for συλλογισμός.

utter paradoxes, and, further, in what circumstances a solecism occurs, and how to ask questions, and what is the right arrangement of questions, and, moreover, what is the use of all such arguments, and also about all answering of questions in general and in particular how to solve arguments and solecisms, on all these subjects let the treatment we have given suffice. There remains to call to mind our original purpose and say a few words about it and then bring our treatise to an end.

Our purpose, then, was to discover a faculty which could reason on the problem set before us from the most generally accepted premisses that exist ; for this is the function of dialectic in itself and of the art of examination. But, since there is further added to it, on account of its close affinity with the art of sophistry, that it can undertake an examination not only dialectically but also with a pretence of knowledge, we therefore proposed as the purpose of our treatise not only the above-mentioned task of being able to conduct an argument but also the discovery how, when supporting an argument, we are to defend our thesis by means of the most generally accepted premisses in a consistent manner. Of this we have given the reason ; for this was why Socrates used to ask questions but never answered them, because he confessed ignorance. An indication has been given, in what has been said above, of the number of cases in which this will apply and of the various kinds of material which can be used for this and the various sources from which we may obtain an abundance of them ; moreover also how questions must be asked and about the arrangement of questions in

(2) Concluding remarks on dialectic.

---

² Reading with Pacius σολοικισμούς for συλλογισμούς.

περί τε ἀποκρίσεων καὶ λύσεων τῶν πρὸς τοὺς
συλλογισμούς. δεδήλωται δὲ καὶ περὶ τῶν ἄλλων,
ὅσα τῆς αὐτῆς μεθόδου τῶν λόγων ἐστίν. πρὸς
δὲ τούτοις περὶ τῶν παραλογισμῶν διεληλύθαμεν,
15 ὥσπερ εἰρήκαμεν ἤδη πρότερον. ὅτι μὲν οὖν ἔχει
τέλος ἱκανῶς ἃ προειλόμεθα, φανερόν· δεῖ δ᾽ ἡμᾶς
μὴ λεληθέναι τὸ συμβεβηκὸς περὶ ταύτην τὴν
πραγματείαν. τῶν γὰρ εὑρισκομένων ἁπάντων τὰ
μὲν παρ᾽ ἑτέρων ληφθέντα πρότερον πεπονημένα
κατὰ μέρος ἐπιδέδωκεν ὑπὸ τῶν παραλαβόντων
20 ὕστερον· τὰ δ᾽ ἐξ ὑπαρχῆς εὑρισκόμενα μικρὰν τὸ
πρῶτον ἐπίδοσιν λαμβάνειν εἴωθε, χρησιμωτέραν
μέντοι πολλῷ τῆς ὕστερον ἐκ τούτων αὐξήσεως.
μέγιστον γὰρ ἴσως ἀρχὴ παντός, ὥσπερ λέγεται· διὸ
καὶ χαλεπώτατον· ὅσῳ γὰρ κράτιστον τῇ δυνάμει,
25 τοσούτῳ μικρότατον ὂν τῷ μεγέθει χαλεπώτατόν
ἐστιν ὀφθῆναι. ταύτης δ᾽ εὑρημένης ῥᾷον τὸ προστιθέναι καὶ συναύξειν τὸ λοιπόν ἐστιν· ὅπερ καὶ
περὶ τοὺς ῥητορικοὺς λόγους συμβέβηκε, σχεδὸν δὲ
καὶ περὶ τὰς ἄλλας πάσας τέχνας. οἱ μὲν γὰρ τὰς
ἀρχὰς εὑρόντες παντελῶς ἐπὶ μικρόν τι προήγαγον·
30 οἱ δὲ νῦν εὐδοκιμοῦντες παραλαβόντες παρὰ πολλῶν
οἷον ἐκ διαδοχῆς κατὰ μέρος προαγαγόντων οὕτως
ηὐξήκασι, Τισίας μὲν μετὰ τοὺς πρώτους, Θρασύ-
μαχος δὲ μετὰ Τισίαν, Θεόδωρος δὲ μετὰ τοῦτον,
καὶ πολλοὶ πολλὰ συνενηνόχασι μέρη· διόπερ οὐδὲν
θαυμαστὸν ἔχειν τι πλῆθος τὴν τέχνην. ταύτης δὲ

general, and about answers and solutions applicable to the reasonings employed. All the other points have also been set forth which belong to the same system of argument. In addition to these we have also explained about fallacies, as we have already remarked above. That what we purposed has been satisfactorily carried through to the end is plain ; but we must not fail to observe what has happened regarding this inquiry. In all discoveries, either the results of other people's work have been taken over and after having been first elaborated have been subsequently advanced step by step by those who took them over, or else they are original inventions which usually make progress which at first is small but of much greater utility than the later development which results from them. It is perhaps a true proverb which says that the beginning of anything is the most important ; hence it is also the most difficult. For, as it is very powerful in its effects, so it is very small in size and therefore very difficult to see. When, however, the first beginning has been discovered, it is easier to add to it and develop the rest. This has happened, too, with rhetorical composition, and also with practically all the other arts. Those who discovered the beginnings of rhetoric carried them forward quite a little way, whereas the famous modern professors of the art, entering into the heritage, so to speak, of a long series of predecessors who had gradually advanced it, have brought it to its present perfection—Tisias following the first inventors, Thrasymachus following Tisias, Theodorus following Thrasymachus, while numerous others have made numerous contributions ; hence it is no wonder that the art possesses a certain amplitude. Of our (3) Originality of the

183 b
35 τῆς πραγματείας οὐ τὸ μὲν ἦν τὸ δ' οὐκ ἦν προεξειρ-
γασμένον, ἀλλ' οὐδὲν παντελῶς ὑπῆρχεν. καὶ γὰρ
τῶν περὶ τοὺς ἐριστικοὺς λόγους μισθαρνούντων
ὁμοία τις ἦν ἡ παίδευσις τῇ Γοργίου πραγματείᾳ.
λόγους γὰρ οἱ μὲν ῥητορικοὺς οἱ δὲ ἐρωτητικοὺς
ἐδίδοσαν ἐκμανθάνειν, εἰς οὓς πλειστάκις ἐμπίπτειν
184 a ᾠήθησαν ἑκάτεροι τοὺς ἀλλήλων λόγους. διόπερ
ταχεῖα μὲν ἄτεχνος δ' ἦν ἡ διδασκαλία τοῖς μαν-
θάνουσι παρ' αὐτῶν· οὐ γὰρ τέχνην ἀλλὰ τὰ ἀπὸ
τῆς τέχνης διδόντες παιδεύειν ὑπελάμβανον, ὥσπερ
5 ἂν εἴ τις ἐπιστήμην φάσκων παραδώσειν ἐπὶ τὸ
μηδὲν πονεῖν τοὺς πόδας, εἶτα σκυτοτομικὴν μὲν
μὴ διδάσκοι, μηδ' ὅθεν δυνήσεται πορίζεσθαι τὰ
τοιαῦτα, δοίη δὲ πολλὰ γένη παντοδαπῶν ὑποδη-
μάτων· οὗτος γὰρ βεβοήθηκε μὲν πρὸς τὴν χρείαν,
τέχνην δ' οὐ παρέδωκεν. καὶ περὶ μὲν τῶν ῥη-
184 b τορικῶν ὑπῆρχε πολλὰ καὶ παλαιὰ τὰ λεγόμενα,
περὶ δὲ τοῦ συλλογίζεσθαι παντελῶς οὐδὲν εἴχομεν
πρότερον ἄλλο λέγειν, ἀλλ' ἢ τριβῇ ζητοῦντες πολὺν
χρόνον ἐπονοῦμεν. εἰ δὲ φαίνεται θεασαμένοις
ὑμῖν ὡς ἐκ τοιούτων ἐξ ἀρχῆς ὑπαρχόντων ἔχειν ἡ
5 μέθοδος ἱκανῶς παρὰ τὰς ἄλλας πραγματείας τὰς
ἐκ παραδόσεως ηὐξημένας, λοιπὸν ἂν εἴη πάντων
ὑμῶν ἢ τῶν ἠκροαμένων ἔργον τοῖς μὲν παραλε-
λειμμένοις τῆς μεθόδου συγγνώμην τοῖς δ' εὑρη-
μένοις πολλὴν ἔχειν χάριν.

present inquiry, however, it is not true to say that present
it had already been partly elaborated and partly treatise.
not ; nay, it did not exist at all. For the training
given by the paid teachers of contentious argument
resembled the system of Gorgias. For some of them
gave their pupils to learn by heart speeches which
were either rhetorical or consisted of questions and
answers, in which both sides thought that the rival
arguments were for the most part included. Hence
the teaching which they gave to their pupils was
rapid but unsystematic ; for they conceived that they
could train their pupils by imparting to them not an
art but the results of an art, just as if one should
claim to be about to communicate knowledge for the
prevention of pain in the feet and then were not to
teach the cobbler's art and the means of providing
suitable foot-gear, but were to offer a selection of
various kinds of shoes ; for he has helped to supply
his need but has not imparted an art to him. Also,
on the subject of rhetoric there already existed much
material enunciated in the past, whereas regarding
reasoning we had absolutely no earlier work to
quote but were for a long time labouring at tentative
researches. If, therefore, on consideration, it appears (4) Appeal
to you that, in view of such original conditions, our to the
reader.
system is adequate when compared with the other
methods which have been built up in the course of
tradition, then the only thing which would remain
for all of you, or those who follow our instruction,
is that you should pardon the lack of complete-
ness of our system and be heartily grateful for our
discoveries.

DE GENERATIONE ET CORRUPTIONE

INTRODUCTION

THAT the *De Generatione et Corruptione* is a genuine work of Aristotle has never been disputed. It belongs to the group of physical treatises which also includes the *Physics*, the *De Caelo* and the *Meteorologica*. Its composition has been generally ascribed to the period covered by Aristotle's residence in the Troad, in Mitylene and in Macedonia, that is, *circa* 347 to 335 B.C.

Professor H. H. Joachim, to whose work I am deeply indebted, tells us that during the preparation of his version for the Oxford Translation of Aristotle he realized that something more was called for. " It soon became evident," he writes, " that a mere translation would be of little or no value, since the intrinsic philosophical interest of the original depends, to a large extent, upon what it implies and presupposes. In short, Aristotle's fascinating and masterly little treatise calls for a commentary in almost every sentence. It is full of allusions to the speculations of his predecessors and contemporaries, and inextricably interwoven with the theories elaborated in his other works, particularly in the *Physics*, *De Caelo* and *Meteorologica*, of which no modern English editions exist." Anyone who attempts to translate the *De Generatione et Corruptione* must feel that a translation by itself is unsatisfactory, but the present translator

159

ARISTOTLE

has found it impossible, within the scope of a Loeb version, to do more than provide brief explanatory notes on some of the major obscurities and to give the references where Aristotle is obviously referring to passages in his other treatises, and to recommend those who require something more to consult Professor Joachim's masterly commentary (*Aristotle on Coming-to-be and Passing-away*, Oxford, 1922).

Amongst the other works which have been consulted most use has been made of the Latin Version of Franciscus Vatablus in vol. iii of the Berlin *Aristotle* and of *Aristotle on Coming-to-be and Passing-away : Some Comments* by Dr. W. T. Verdenius and Dr. T. H. Waszink (Leiden, 1946), which was kindly sent to me by a friend, Dr. H. J. Drossaart Lulof. The summary of the treatise given by Sir W. D. Ross in his *Aristotle* (pp. 99-108) has also been very useful.

The text which has been used is that of I. Bekker in the Berlin *Aristotle*, any divergences from which, except for obvious misprints, have been noted.

The *De Generatione et Corruptione* discusses the πάθη to which the natural bodies in the sublunary sphere are liable, namely, " coming-to-be " (γένεσις) and " passing-away " (φθορά). In Book I these processes are explained and distinguished from alteration (ἀλλοίωσις) and from " growth and diminution " (αὔξησις καὶ φθίσις) ; incidentally the views of Anaxagoras and Empedocles are examined and shown to be inconsistent. In the second half of the book it is shown that what comes-to-be is formed by combination (μίξις) of certain natural constituents, a process which implies " action and passion " (ποιεῖν καὶ πάσχειν), which in their turn imply contact (ἀφή). Book II proves that the material constituents of

160

all that comes-to-be are the elements or " simple bodies," Earth, Air, Fire, and Water, and shows the manner in which they are transformed into one another and how they combine. Aristotle then briefly discusses the material, formal and final causes of " coming-to-be " and " passing-away," in particular criticizing the theory of Socrates in the *Phaedo*. He further states that the efficient cause of the double process is the sun's annual movement, and, in conclusion, shows that what " comes-to-be " is necessary, since absolute necessity is characteristic of a sequence of events which is cyclical, that is to say, continuous and returning upon itself.

MANUSCRIPTS

J = Vindobonensis, phil. Graec. 100 (10th century)
E = Parisiensis Regius 1853 (10th century)
F = Laurentianus 87. 7 (12th century)
H = Vaticanus 1027 (12th century)
L = Vaticanus 253 (14th or 15th century)

Diels = *Die Fragmente der Vorsokratiker*, by Hermann Diels (rec. W. Kranz, 5th edition, Berlin, 1934)

ΑΡΙΣΤΟΤΕΛΟΥΣ ΠΕΡΙ ΓΕΝΕΣΕΩΣ ΚΑΙ ΦΘΟΡΑΣ

Α

1. Περὶ δὲ γενέσεως καὶ φθορᾶς τῶν φύσει γινομένων καὶ φθειρομένων, ὁμοίως κατὰ πάντων, τάς
τε αἰτίας διαιρετέον καὶ τοὺς λόγους αὐτῶν, ἔτι
δὲ περὶ αὐξήσεως καὶ ἀλλοιώσεως, τί ἑκάτερον,
5 καὶ πότερον τὴν αὐτὴν ὑποληπτέον φύσιν εἶναι
ἀλλοιώσεως καὶ γενέσεως, ἢ χωρίς, ὥσπερ διώρισται καὶ τοῖς ὀνόμασιν.

Τῶν μὲν οὖν ἀρχαίων οἱ μὲν τὴν καλουμένην
ἁπλῆν γένεσιν ἀλλοίωσιν εἶναί φασιν, οἱ δ᾽ ἕτερον
ἀλλοίωσιν καὶ γένεσιν. ὅσοι μὲν γὰρ ἕν τι τὸ πᾶν
λέγουσιν εἶναι καὶ πάντα ἐξ ἑνὸς γεννῶσιν, τούτοις
10 μὲν ἀνάγκη τὴν γένεσιν ἀλλοίωσιν φάναι καὶ τὸ
κυρίως γινόμενον ἀλλοιοῦσθαι· ὅσοι δὲ πλείω τὴν
ὕλην ἑνὸς τιθέασιν, οἷον Ἐμπεδοκλῆς καὶ Ἀναξαγόρας καὶ Λεύκιππος, τούτοις δὲ ἕτερον. καίτοι
Ἀναξαγόρας γε τὴν οἰκείαν φωνὴν ἠγνόησεν· λέγει

ARISTOTLE ON
COMING-TO-BE AND PASSING-AWAY

BOOK I

1. In discussing coming-to-be and passing-away of things which by nature come-to-be and pass-away, as exhibited uniformly wherever they occur, we must distinguish their causes and definitions ; further, we must deal with " growth " and " alteration," and inquire what each of these terms means, and whether we are to suppose that the nature of " alteration " and coming-to-be is the same, or whether each is of a separate nature corresponding to the names by which they are distinguished.

Chs. 1-5. *Coming-to-be and Passing-away are not "alteration" nor are they growth and diminution.*

Of the ancient philosophers some assert that what is called " simple " coming-to-be is " alteration," while others hold that " alteration " and coming-to-be are different processes. Those who hold that the universe is a simple entity and who generate all things from a single thing, must necessarily maintain that coming-to-be is " alteration," and that what comes-to-be in the proper sense of the term undergoes " alteration." Those, on the other hand, who hold that the matter of things is more than one, must regard the two processes as different—Empedocles, for example, and Anaxagoras and Leucippus. Anaxagoras, however, misunderstood his own statement ;

Views of the Monists and Pluralists examined.

163

314 a

γοῦν ὡς τὸ γίνεσθαι καὶ ἀπόλλυσθαι ταὐτὸν
15 καθέστηκε τῷ ἀλλοιοῦσθαι. πολλὰ δὲ λέγει τὰ
στοιχεῖα, καθάπερ καὶ ἕτεροι. Ἐμπεδοκλῆς μὲν
γὰρ τὰ μὲν σωματικὰ τέτταρα, τὰ δὲ πάντα μετὰ
τῶν κινούντων ἓξ τὸν ἀριθμόν, Ἀναξαγόρας δὲ
ἄπειρα καὶ Λεύκιππος καὶ Δημόκριτος. ὁ μὲν γὰρ
20 τὰ ὁμοιομερῆ στοιχεῖα τίθησιν, οἷον ὀστοῦν καὶ
σάρκα καὶ μυελόν, καὶ τῶν ἄλλων ὧν ἑκάστου
συνώνυμον τὸ μέρος ἐστίν· Δημόκριτος δὲ καὶ
Λεύκιππος ἐκ σωμάτων ἀδιαιρέτων τἆλλα συγ-
κεῖσθαί φασι, ταῦτα δ' ἄπειρα καὶ τὸ πλῆθος εἶναι
καὶ τὰς μορφάς, αὐτὰ δὲ πρὸς αὑτὰ διαφέρειν τούτοις ἐξ ὧν εἰσὶ καὶ θέσει καὶ τάξει τούτων. ἐναν-
25 τίως δὲ φαίνονται λέγοντες οἱ περὶ Ἀναξαγόραν
τοῖς περὶ Ἐμπεδοκλέα· ὁ μὲν γάρ φησι πῦρ καὶ
ὕδωρ καὶ ἀέρα καὶ γῆν στοιχεῖα τέσσαρα καὶ ἁπλᾶ
εἶναι μᾶλλον ἢ σάρκα καὶ ὀστοῦν καὶ τὰ τοιαῦτα
τῶν ὁμοιομερῶν, οἱ δὲ ταῦτα μὲν ἁπλᾶ καὶ στοιχεῖα, γῆν δὲ καὶ πῦρ καὶ ὕδωρ καὶ ἀέρα σύνθετα·
314 b πανσπερμίαν γὰρ εἶναι τούτων.

Τοῖς μὲν οὖν ἐξ ἑνὸς πάντα κατασκευάζουσιν
ἀναγκαῖον λέγειν τὴν γένεσιν καὶ τὴν φθορὰν ἀλ-
λοίωσιν· ἀεὶ γὰρ μένειν τὸ ὑποκείμενον ταὐτὸ καὶ
ἕν (τὸ δὲ τοιοῦτον ἀλλοιοῦσθαί φαμεν)· τοῖς δὲ τὰ
5 γένη πλείω ποιοῦσι διαφέρειν τὴν ἀλλοίωσιν τῆς

ᵃ Diels, fr. 17.

ᵇ *i.e.* compounds (though, it may be, in different propor-
tions) of the same four simple bodies—Earth, Air, Fire and
Water—such as wood, the metals, and blood, flesh and
marrow in animals. Such compounds, when divided, still
retain the same constituents.

for example, he says that coming-to-be and destruction constitute the same process as " being altered," [a] though, like others, he says that the elements are many. Thus Empedocles holds that the corporeal elements are four, but that all the elements, including those which create motion, are six in number, while Anaxagoras, Leucippus and Democritus hold that their number is infinite. For Anaxagoras puts down as elements things which have like parts,[b] for example bone, flesh and marrow, and anything else of which the part bears the same name as the whole ; whereas Democritus and Leucippus say that all other things are composed of indivisible bodies, and that these are infinite both in number and in the forms which they take, while the compounds differ from one another in their constituents and the position and arrangement of these. Anaxagoras and his school obviously take a view directly opposite to that of Empedocles and his school ; for Empedocles says that Fire, Water, Air and Earth are four elements and are " simple " rather than flesh and bone and similar things which have like parts, whereas Anaxagoras and his school assert that the things which have like parts are " simple " and are elements, but that Earth, Fire, Water and Air are composite, for each of them is, they say, a " general seed-ground " for things which have like parts.

Those, therefore, who construct everything out of a single element must necessarily say that coming-to-be and passing-away are " alteration," for their substratum remains the same and one (and it is such a substratum which we say undergoes " alteration ") ; but those who make the kinds of things more than one must hold that " alteration " differs from coming-

314 b

γενέσεως· συνιόντων γὰρ καὶ διαλυομένων ἡ γένεσις
συμβαίνει καὶ ἡ φθορά. διὸ λέγει τοῦτον τὸν
τρόπον καὶ Ἐμπεδοκλῆς, ὅτι " φύσις οὐδενός
ἐστιν, ἀλλὰ μόνον μίξις τε διάλλαξίς τε μιγέντων."
ὅτι μὲν οὖν οἰκεῖος ὁ λόγος αὐτῶν τῇ ὑποθέσει
10 οὕτω φάναι, δῆλον, καὶ ὅτι λέγουσι τὸν τρόπον
τοῦτον· ἀναγκαῖον δὲ καὶ τούτοις τὴν ἀλλοίωσιν
εἶναι μέν τι φάναι παρὰ τὴν γένεσιν, ἀδύνατον
μέντοι κατὰ τὰ ὑπ' ἐκείνων λεγόμενα. τοῦτο δ'
ὅτι λέγομεν ὀρθῶς, ῥᾴδιον συνιδεῖν. ὥσπερ γὰρ
ὁρῶμεν ἠρεμούσης τῆς οὐσίας ἐν αὐτῇ μεταβολὴν
15 κατὰ μέγεθος, τὴν καλουμένην αὔξησιν καὶ φθίσιν,
οὕτω καὶ ἀλλοίωσιν. οὐ μὴν ἀλλ' ἐξ ὧν λέγουσιν
οἱ πλείους ἀρχὰς ποιοῦντες μιᾶς ἀδύνατον ἀλλοιοῦσθαι. τὰ γὰρ πάθη, καθ' ἃ φαμεν τοῦτο συμβαίνειν, διαφοραὶ τῶν στοιχείων εἰσίν, λέγω δ'
οἷον θερμὸν ψυχρόν, λευκὸν μέλαν, ξηρὸν ὑγρόν,
20 μαλακὸν σκληρὸν καὶ τῶν ἄλλων ἕκαστον, ὥσπερ
καὶ φησὶν Ἐμπεδοκλῆς " ἠέλιον μὲν λευκὸν ὁρᾶν
καὶ θερμὸν ἀπάντῃ, ὄμβρον δ' ἐν πᾶσιν δνοφόεντά
τε ῥιγαλέον τε," ὁμοίως δὲ διορίζει καὶ ἐπὶ τῶν
λοιπῶν. ὥστ' εἰ μὴ δυνατὸν ἐκ πυρὸς γενέσθαι
ὕδωρ μηδ' ἐξ ὕδατος γῆν, οὐδ' ἐκ λευκοῦ μέλαν
25 ἔσται οὐδὲν οὐδ' ἐκ μαλακοῦ σκληρόν· ὁ δ' αὐτὸς
λόγος καὶ περὶ τῶν ἄλλων. τοῦτο δ' ἦν ἀλλοίωσις.
ᾗ καὶ φανερὸν ὅτι μίαν ἀεὶ τοῖς ἐναντίοις ὑπο-

ᵃ Diels, fr. 8.   ᵇ Diels, fr. 21 lines 3 and 5.

to-be, for coming-to-be and passing-away occur when things come together and are dissolved. This is the reason why Empedocles also is speaking to this effect, when he says that " there is no origin of anything, but only a mingling and separation of things which have been mingled." [a] It is clear then, that their description of coming-to-be and passing-away in this way accords with their assumption and that they actually describe them in this way ; they also must, however, admit that " alteration " is something different from coming-to-be, though they cannot possibly do so consistently with the views which they express. It is easy to see that we are correct in saying this ; for just as we see changes in magnitude taking place in a thing while its substance remains unchanged (what we call " increase " and " diminution "), so also we see " alteration " occurring. Nevertheless, the statements of those who suppose the existence of more than one first principle make it impossible for " alteration " to take place. For the qualities, in respect of which we say that " alteration " occurs (for example, hot and cold, white and black, dry and moist, soft and hard, etc.) are differences affecting the elements. As Empedocles says,

> The sun is white to look upon and hot
> In every part, the rain is dark and chill [b] ;

and he likewise characterizes also the other elements. Hence, as it is impossible for Water to come-into-being from Fire, or Earth from Water, neither will black come into existence out of white, nor hard out of soft ; and the same argument applies also to the other qualities. Now this is what " alteration " has always meant. From this it is also clear that it must be assumed that a single matter belongs to the " con-

314 b

θετέον ὕλην, ἄν τε μεταβάλλῃ κατὰ τόπον, ἄν τε
κατ᾽ αὔξησιν καὶ φθίσιν, ἄν τε κατ᾽ ἀλλοίωσιν.
ἔτι δ᾽ ὁμοίως ἀναγκαῖον εἶναι τοῦτο καὶ ἀλλοίωσιν·
315 a εἴτε γὰρ ἀλλοίωσίς ἐστι, καὶ τὸ ὑποκείμενον ἓν
στοιχεῖον καὶ μία ἡ πάντων ὕλη τῶν ἐχόντων εἰς
ἄλληλα μεταβολήν, κἂν εἰ τὸ ὑποκείμενον ἕν, ἔστιν
ἀλλοίωσις.

Ἐμπεδοκλῆς μὲν οὖν ἔοικεν ἐναντία λέγειν καὶ
πρὸς τὰ φαινόμενα καὶ πρὸς αὐτὸν αὑτός. ἅμα
5 μὲν γὰρ οὔ φησιν ἕτερον ἐξ ἑτέρου γίνεσθαι τῶν
στοιχείων οὐδέν, ἀλλὰ τἆλλα πάντα ἐκ τούτων,
ἅμα δ᾽ ὅταν εἰς ἓν συναγάγῃ τὴν ἅπασαν φύσιν
πλὴν τοῦ νείκους, ἐκ τοῦ ἑνὸς γίνεσθαι πάλιν
ἕκαστον. ὥστ᾽ ἐξ ἑνός τινος δῆλον ὅτι διαφοραῖς
τισὶ χωριζομένων καὶ πάθεσιν ἐγένετο τὸ μὲν ὕδωρ
10 τὸ δὲ πῦρ, καθάπερ λέγει τὸν μὲν ἥλιον λευκὸν καὶ
θερμόν, τὴν δὲ γῆν βαρὺ καὶ σκληρόν. ἀφαιρου-
μένων οὖν τούτων τῶν διαφορῶν (εἰσὶ γὰρ ἀφαι-
ρεταὶ γενόμεναί γε) δῆλον ὡς ἀνάγκη γίνεσθαι καὶ
γῆν ἐξ ὕδατος καὶ ὕδωρ ἐκ γῆς, ὁμοίως δὲ καὶ
τῶν ἄλλων ἕκαστον, οὐ τότε μόνον ἀλλὰ καὶ νῦν,
15 μεταβάλλοντά γε τοῖς πάθεσιν. ἔστι δ᾽ ἐξ ὧν
εἴρηκε δυνάμενα προσγίνεσθαι καὶ χωρίζεσθαι πάλιν, ἄλλως τε καὶ μαχομένων ἀλλήλοις ἔτι τοῦ
νείκους καὶ τῆς φιλίας. διόπερ καὶ τότε ἐξ ἑνὸς
ἐγεννήθησαν· οὐ γὰρ δὴ πῦρ γε καὶ γῆ καὶ ὕδωρ

---

^a *i.e.* when the elements originally came-to be.

trary poles," whether they change in respect of place, or of " growth " and " diminution," or of " alteration " ; furthermore, that the existence of a single matter and that of " alteration " are each as necessary as the other, for, if " alteration " takes place, then the substratum is a single element, and so all things which change into one another have a single matter, and, conversely, if the substratum is one, " alteration " takes place.

Empedocles, then, seems to contradict the observed facts and himself as well. For he denies that any one of his elements comes-to-be from any other element, but declares that all other things come-to-be from these elements, and at the same time, after collecting all nature, except Strife, together into one, he declares that each thing again comes-to-be out of the One. Hence it is clear that out of a One, when separation took place owing to certain differences and qualities, one thing came-to-be Water and another Fire, as is shown by his calling the sun " white and hot " and the earth " heavy and hard." If, therefore, these differences are taken away (and it is possible to take them away, since they came-to-be), it is clear that Earth must necessarily come-to-be out of Water, and Water out of Earth, and similarly with each of the other elements, not only then [a] but also now,[b] when they undergo a change in their qualities. According to his statements, the qualities can be attached and can be separated again, especially as Strife and Love are still fighting against one another. This is also the reason why the elements were originally generated from the One ; for, I suppose, Fire, Earth and Water

[b] *i.e.* when according to Empedocles " Strife " is gaining the upper hand.

315 a

ἔτι ὄντα ἓν ἦν τὸ πᾶν. ἄδηλον δὲ καὶ πότερον
20 ἀρχὴν αὐτῶν θετέον τὸ ἓν ἢ τὰ πολλά, λέγω δὲ πῦρ
καὶ γῆν καὶ τὰ σύστοιχα τούτων. ᾗ μὲν γὰρ ὡς
ὕλη ὑπόκειται, ἐξ οὗ μεταβάλλοντα διὰ τὴν κίνησιν
γίνονται γῆ καὶ πῦρ, τὸ ἓν στοιχεῖον· ᾗ δὲ τοῦτο
μὲν ἐκ συνθέσεως γίνεται συνιόντων ἐκείνων,
ἐκεῖνα δ' ἐκ διαλύσεως, στοιχειωδέστερα ἐκεῖνα
25 καὶ πρότερα τὴν φύσιν.

2. Ὅλως τε δὴ περὶ γενέσεως καὶ φθορᾶς τῆς
ἁπλῆς λεκτέον, πότερον ἔστιν ἢ οὐκ ἔστι καὶ πῶς
ἐστίν, καὶ περὶ τῶν ἄλλων ἁπλῶν κινήσεων, οἷον
περὶ αὐξήσεως καὶ ἀλλοιώσεως. Πλάτων μὲν οὖν
30 μόνον περὶ γενέσεως ἐσκέψατο καὶ φθορᾶς, ὅπως
ὑπάρχει τοῖς πράγμασι, καὶ περὶ γενέσεως οὐ
πάσης ἀλλὰ τῆς τῶν στοιχείων· πῶς δὲ σάρκες ἢ
ὀστᾶ ἢ τῶν ἄλλων τι τῶν τοιούτων, οὐδέν· ἔτι
οὔτε περὶ ἀλλοιώσεως οὔτε περὶ αὐξήσεως, τίνα
τρόπον ὑπάρχουσι τοῖς πράγμασιν. ὅλως δὲ παρὰ
τὰ ἐπιπολῆς περὶ οὐδενὸς οὐδεὶς ἐπέστησεν ἔξω
35 Δημοκρίτου. οὗτος δ' ἔοικε μὲν περὶ ἁπάντων
315 b φροντίσαι, ἤδη δὲ ἐν τῷ πῶς διαφέρει. οὔτε γὰρ
περὶ αὐξήσεως οὐδεὶς οὐδὲν διώρισεν, ὥσπερ λέγομεν, ὅ τι μὴ κἂν ὁ τυχὼν εἴπειεν, ὅτι προσιόντος
αὐξάνονται τοῦ ὁμοίου[1] τῷ ὁμοίῳ (πῶς δὲ τοῦτο,

---

[1] τοῦ ὁμοίου addidi.

---

[a] *i.e.* Water and Air.
[b] Namely, that set up by Strife.
[c] *Timaeus* 52 D ff.

170

did not exist separately at all while they were still one. Now it is also not clear whether we must ascribe to him the One as his starting-point, or the Many—by which I mean Fire and Earth and their co-ordinates.[a] For the One, in as much as it forms, as its matter, the substratum from which Earth and Fire come-to-be through the change due to motion,[b] is an element ; on the other hand, in as much as the One comes-to-be through a process of composition, due to the coming together of the Many, whereas the Many are the result of dissolution, the Many are more " elementary " than the One and by nature prior to it.

2. We must, therefore, deal in general with the subject of unqualified coming-to-be and passing-away, and discuss whether they exist or not, and how they exist, and with the other simple motions, such as " growth " and " alteration." Plato,[c] it is true, investigated coming-to-be and passing-away, but only as to the manner in which passing-away is inherent in things, and as regards coming-to-be he did not deal with it in general but only that of the elements ; he never inquired how flesh or bones or any other similar things came-to-be, and, further, he did not discuss how " alteration " and " growth " are present in things. In fact no one at all has applied himself to any of these subjects, except in a superficial manner, with the single exception of Democritus. He seems to have thought about them all, and from first to last he excels in his manner of treatment. For, as we assert, no one else made any definite pronouncement about " growth," except such as any man-in-the-street might make, namely, that things grow by the coming together of like with like (without a word as

Plato's view is too narrow.

Views of Democritus and Leucippus.

οὐκέτι), οὐδὲ περὶ μίξεως, οὐδὲ περὶ τῶν ἄλλων
5 ὡς εἰπεῖν οὐδενός, οἷον τοῦ ποιεῖν καὶ τοῦ πάσχειν,
τίνα τρόπον τὸ μὲν ποιεῖ τὸ δὲ πάσχει τὰς φυσικὰς
ποιήσεις. Δημόκριτος δὲ καὶ Λεύκιππος ποιή-
σαντες τὰ σχήματα τὴν ἀλλοίωσιν καὶ τὴν γένεσιν
ἐκ τούτων ποιοῦσι, διακρίσει μὲν καὶ συγκρίσει
γένεσιν καὶ φθοράν, τάξει δὲ καὶ θέσει ἀλλοίωσιν.
10 ἐπεὶ δ' ᾤοντο τἀληθὲς ἐν τῷ φαίνεσθαι, ἐναντία δὲ
καὶ ἄπειρα τὰ φαινόμενα, τὰ σχήματα ἄπειρα
ἐποίησαν, ὥστε ταῖς μεταβολαῖς τοῦ συγκειμένου
τὸ αὐτὸ ἐναντίον δοκεῖν ἄλλῳ καὶ ἄλλῳ, καὶ μετα-
κινεῖσθαι μικροῦ ἐμμιγνυμένου, καὶ ὅλως ἕτερον
φαίνεσθαι ἑνὸς μετακινηθέντος· ἐκ τῶν αὐτῶν γὰρ
15 τραγῳδία καὶ κωμῳδία γίνεται γραμμάτων.

Ἐπεὶ δὲ δοκεῖ σχεδὸν πᾶσιν ἕτερον εἶναι γένεσις
καὶ ἀλλοίωσις, καὶ γίνεσθαι μὲν καὶ φθείρεσθαι
συγκρινόμενα καὶ διακρινόμενα, ἀλλοιοῦσθαι δὲ
μεταβαλλόντων τῶν παθημάτων, περὶ τούτων ἐπι-
στήσασι θεωρητέον. ἀπορίας γὰρ ἔχει ταῦτα καὶ
20 πολλὰς καὶ εὐλόγους. εἰ μὲν γάρ ἐστι σύγκρισις
ἡ γένεσις, πολλὰ ἀδύνατα συμβαίνει· εἰσὶ δ' αὖ
λόγοι ἕτεροι ἀναγκαστικοὶ καὶ οὐκ εὔποροι διαλύειν
ὡς οὐκ ἐνδέχεται ἄλλως ἔχειν. εἰ δὲ¹ μή ἐστι σύγκρισις ἡ γένεσις, ἢ ὅλως οὐκ ἔστι γένεσις ἢ ἀλ-

to how this happens), and they tell us nothing about
" mixing " and practically nothing about the other
terms, such as " action " and " passion," that is, how
one thing acts upon and another is affected by physical
action. Democritus, however, and Leucippus postulate the " figures " and make " alteration " and
coming-to-be result from these, attributing coming-
to-be and passing-away to their dissociation and
association, and " alteration " to their arrangement
and position ; and, since they held that the truth
consisted in appearance, and appearances are contrary to one another and infinite in number, they
made the " figures " infinite in number, so that, owing
to changes in the compound, the same thing seems
to be contrary to different people and to be " trans-
posed " by the mixing in of a small ingredient and
to appear quite different owing to " transposition "
of one constituent. For a tragedy and a comedy are
composed of the same letters.

Since almost all philosophers think (a) that coming-
to-be and " alteration " are different processes and
(b) that things come-to-be and pass-away by " association " and " dissociation," whereas they undergo
" alteration " by a change of their qualities, we must
fix our attention on these views and examine them ;
for they present many arguable questions for discussion. For if coming-to-be is " association," many
impossible situations arise ; and, on the other hand,
there are other compelling arguments, not easy to
disentangle, to prove that coming-to-be cannot be
anything else. If, on the other hand, coming-to-be
is not " association," either coming-to-be does not

---

[1] εἰ δὲ scripsi : εἴτε codd.

315 b

λοίωσις, ἢ¹ καὶ τοῦτο διαλῦσαι χαλεπὸν ὂν πειρατέον.

25 Ἀρχὴ δὲ τούτων πάντων, πότερον οὕτω γίνεται
καὶ ἀλλοιοῦται καὶ αὐξάνεται τὰ ὄντα καὶ τἀναντία
τούτοις πάσχει, τῶν πρώτων ὑπαρχόντων μεγεθῶν
ἀδιαιρέτων, ἢ οὐδέν ἐστι μέγεθος ἀδιαίρετον· διαφέρει γὰρ τοῦτο πλεῖστον. καὶ πάλιν εἰ μεγέθη,
πότερον, ὡς Δημόκριτος καὶ Λεύκιππος, σώματα
30 ταῦτ' ἐστίν, ἢ ὥσπερ ἐν τῷ Τιμαίῳ, ἐπίπεδα.
τοῦτο μὲν οὖν αὐτό, καθάπερ καὶ ἐν ἄλλοις εἰρήκαμεν, ἄλογον μέχρι ἐπιπέδων διαλῦσαι. διὸ
μᾶλλον εὔλογον σώματα εἶναι ἀδιαίρετα. ἀλλὰ
καὶ ταῦτα πολλὴν ἔχει ἀλογίαν. ὅμως δὲ τούτοις
ἀλλοίωσιν καὶ γένεσιν ἐνδέχεται ποιεῖν, καθάπερ
35 εἴρηται, τροπῇ καὶ διαθιγῇ μετακινοῦντα τὸ αὐτὸ
316 a καὶ ταῖς τῶν σχημάτων διαφοραῖς, ὅπερ ποιεῖ
Δημόκριτος (διὸ καὶ χροιὰν οὔ φησιν εἶναι· τροπῇ
γὰρ χρωματίζεσθαι), τοῖς δ' εἰς ἐπίπεδα διαιροῦσιν
οὐκέτι· οὐδὲν γὰρ γίνεται πλὴν στερεὰ συντιθε-
μένων· πάθος γὰρ οὐδ' ἐγχειροῦσι γεννᾶν οὐδὲν ἐξ
αὐτῶν.

5 Αἴτιον δὲ τοῦ ἐπ' ἔλαττον δύνασθαι τὰ ὁμολογούμενα συνορᾶν ἡ ἀπειρία. διὸ ὅσοι ἐνῳκήκασι μᾶλλον ἐν τοῖς φυσικοῖς, μᾶλλον δύνανται ὑποτίθεσθαι
τοιαύτας ἀρχὰς αἳ ἐπὶ πολὺ δύνανται συνείρειν·

----

¹ εἰ post ἢ omisi cum EH.

ᵃ Plato, *Timaeus* 53 c ff.
ᵇ *De Caelo* 299 a 6 ff.
ᶜ These terms are explained in *Met.* 985 b 15 ff.

exist at all or it is " alteration " ; or else we must try
to unravel this problem too, difficult as it is.

The starting-point for dealing with all these pro- There are
blems is the question, " Do things which exist come- no in-
to-be and ' alter ' and ' grow,' and undergo the divisible
magnitudes.
contrary changes, because the primary existences
are indivisible magnitudes ? Or is no magnitude indivisible ? " For it makes a great difference which
view we take. Again, if primary existences are indivisible magnitudes, are they bodies, as Democritus
and Leucippus assert ? Or are they planes, as is the
view expressed in the *Timaeus* ? [a] To resolve them
into planes and to stop at that point is, as we have
said elsewhere,[b] in itself contrary to reason. Hence
it is more reasonable to hold that they are indivisible
bodies, though this view also involves considerable
irrationality. Nevertheless, as has been said, it is
possible with these bodies to bring about " alteration " and coming-to-be if one " transposes " the
same thing by " turning " and " intercontact " [c] and
by variations of the " figures," as Democritus does
(hence he denies that colour exists, for coloration,
he says is due to the " turning " of the " figures ") ;
but it is impossible for those who divide bodies into
planes to bring about " alteration " and coming-to
be ; for, when planes are put together, nothing can
result except solids ; for they never even try to
generate any quality from them.

The reason why we have not the power to comprehend the admitted facts is our lack of experience.
Hence those who have lived in a more intimate com-
munion with the phenomena of nature are better able
to lay down such principles as can be connected together and cover a wide field ; those, on the other

ARISTOTLE

οἱ δ' ἐκ τῶν πολλῶν λόγων ἀθεώρητοι τῶν ὑπαρ-
10 χόντων ὄντες, πρὸς ὀλίγα βλέψαντες ἀποφαίνονται
ῥᾷον. ἴδοι δ' ἄν τις καὶ ἐκ τούτων ὅσον διαφέρουσιν
οἱ φυσικῶς καὶ λογικῶς σκοποῦντες· περὶ γὰρ
τοῦ ἄτομα εἶναι μεγέθη οἱ μέν φασιν ὅτι τὸ αὐτο-
τρίγωνον πολλὰ ἔσται, Δημόκριτος δ' ἂν φανείη
οἰκείοις καὶ φυσικοῖς λόγοις πεπεῖσθαι. δῆλον δ'
ἔσται ὃ λέγομεν προϊοῦσιν.

15 Ἔχει γὰρ ἀπορίαν, εἴ τις θείη σῶμά τι εἶναι καὶ
μέγεθος πάντη διαιρετόν, καὶ τοῦτο δυνατόν. τί
γὰρ ἔσται ὅπερ τὴν διαίρεσιν διαφεύγει; εἰ γὰρ
πάντη διαιρετόν, καὶ τυτο δυνατόν, κἂν ἅμα εἴη
τοῦτο πάντη διῃρημένον, καὶ εἰ μὴ ἅμα διῄρηται·
κἂν εἰ τοῦτο γένοιτο, οὐδὲν ἂν εἴη ἀδύνατον.
20 οὐκοῦν καὶ κατὰ τὸ μέσον ὡσαύτως, καὶ ὅλως δέ,
εἰ πάντη πέφυκε διαιρετόν, κἂν διαιρεθῇ, οὐδὲν
ἔσται ἀδύνατον γεγονός, ἐπεὶ οὐδ' ἂν εἰς μυρία
μυριάκις διῃρημένα ᾖ, οὐδὲν ἀδύνατον· καίτοι ἴσως
οὐδεὶς ἂν διέλοι. ἐπεὶ τοίνυν πάντη τοιοῦτόν ἐστι
τὸ σῶμα, διῃρήσθω. τί οὖν ἔσται λοιπόν; μέ-
25 γεθος; οὐ γὰρ οἷόν τε· ἔσται γάρ τι οὐ διῃρημένον,
ἦν δὲ πάντη διαιρετόν. ἀλλὰ μὴν εἰ μηδὲν ἔσται

ᵃ i.e. the Platonists.
ᵇ See De Lin. Insec. 968 a 9 ff.

176

hand, who indulge in long discussions without taking the facts into account are more easily detected as men of narrow views. One can see, too, from this the great difference which exists between those whose researches are based on the phenomenon of nature and those who inquire by a dialectical method. For on the subject of atomic magnitudes one school[a] maintains their existence on the ground that otherwise the " ideal triangle " will be many,[b] while Democritus would appear to have been convinced by arguments germane to the subject and founded on the study of nature. What we mean will be clear as we proceed.

If one postulates that a body, that is, a magnitude, is divisible throughout and that such a division is possible, a difficulty arises, namely, what will the body be which escapes division ? If it is divisible throughout and this procedure is possible, it might be simultaneously divided throughout, even though the divisions have not been made simultaneously, and, if this were to result, no impossibility would be involved. Therefore, supposing it is of a nature to be divisible throughout, by a series of similar bisections or on any other principle, nothing impossible will have been achieved if it has actually been divided, since, even if it has been divided into innumerable parts innumerable times, there is no impossibility, though perhaps no one would carry out this division. Since, therefore, the body is divisible throughout, let us suppose that it has been divided. What then will be left ? A magnitude ? No : that is impossible, since then there will be something which has not been divided, and it was divisible *throughout*. But if no body or magnitude is to be left

Difficulty caused by the assumption that bodies are divisible throughout.

177

316 a

σῶμα μηδὲ μέγεθος, διαίρεσις δ' ἔσται, ἢ ἐκ
στιγμῶν ἔσται, καὶ ἀμεγέθη ἐξ ὧν σύγκειται, ἢ
οὐδὲν παντάπασιν, ὥστε κἂν γίνοιτο ἐκ μηδενὸς
κἂν εἴη συγκείμενον, καὶ τὸ πᾶν δὴ οὐδὲν ἀλλ' ἢ
30 φαινόμενον. ὁμοίως δὲ κἂν ᾖ ἐκ στιγμῶν, οὐκ
ἔσται ποσόν. ὁπότε γὰρ ἥπτοντο καὶ ἓν ἦν μέγεθος
καὶ ἅμα ἦσαν, οὐδὲν ἐποίουν μεῖζον τὸ πᾶν. διαι-
ρεθέντος γὰρ εἰς δύο καὶ πλείω, οὐδὲν ἔλαττον οὐδὲ
μεῖζον τὸ πᾶν τοῦ πρότερον, ὥστε κἂν πᾶσαι συν-
τεθῶσιν, οὐδὲν ποιήσουσι μέγεθος. ἀλλὰ μὴν καὶ
316 b εἴ τι διαιρουμένου οἷον ἔκπρισμα γίνεται τοῦ σώματος, καὶ οὕτως ἐκ τοῦ μεγέθους σῶμά τι ἀπέρχεται, ὁ αὐτὸς λόγος, ἐκεῖνο πῶς διαιρετόν; εἰ
δὲ μὴ σῶμα ἀλλ' εἶδός τι χωριστὸν ἢ πάθος ὃ
ἀπῆλθεν, καὶ ἔστι τὸ μέγεθος στιγμαὶ ἢ ἀφαὶ τοδὶ
5 παθοῦσαι, ἄτοπον ἐκ μὴ μεγεθῶν μέγεθος εἶναι.
ἔτι δὲ ποῦ ἔσονται καὶ ἀκίνητοι ἢ κινούμεναι αἱ
στιγμαί; ἀφή τε ἀεὶ μία δυοῖν τινῶν, ὡς ὄντος
τινὸς παρὰ τὴν ἀφὴν καὶ τὴν διαίρεσιν καὶ τὴν
στιγμήν. εἰ δή τις θήσεται ὁτιοῦν ἢ ὁπηλικονοῦν
σῶμα εἶναι πάντῃ διαιρετόν, πάντα ταῦτα συμ-
10 βαίνει. ἔτι ἐὰν διελὼν συνθῶ τὸ ξύλον ἤ τι ἄλλο,
πάλιν ἴσον τε καὶ ἕν. οὐκοῦν οὕτως ἔχει δηλονότι
κἂν τέμω τὸ ξύλον καθ' ὁτιοῦν σημεῖον. πάντῃ
ἄρα διῄρηται δυνάμει. τί οὖν ἔστι παρὰ τὴν διαί-

ᵃ *i.e.* the sum of the separated parts.

and yet division is to take place, the body either will consist of points, and its constituents will be things of no magnitude, or else it will be absolutely nothing ; and so it would come-to-be and be compounded of nothing, and the whole would be nothing but an illusory appearance. Similarly, if it consists of points, it will not be a magnitude ; for when the points were in contact and formed a single magnitude and were together, they did not make the whole any larger. For when it was divided into two or more parts, the whole [a] was no smaller or larger than before ; so that, if all the points were to be put together, they will not make any magnitude. Further, if, when the body is being divided, a minute portion of it, like a piece of saw-dust, is formed and in this way a body is detached from the magnitude, the same argument holds good, and the question arises : " In what sense is this portion divisible ? " If it was not a body which was detached but a separable form or quality, and if the magnitude is points or contacts thus qualified, it is absurd that a magnitude should be composed of things which are not magnitudes. Furthermore, where will the points be ? And, are they motionless or do they move ? Also a contact is always a contact of two things, since there is always something as well as the contact or the division or the point. All this results, if one is going to posit that any body of any size whatever is divisible throughout. Furthermore, if, after having divided a piece of wood or some other object, I put it together again, it is again both equal to what it was and a unity. Obviously this is so at whatever point I cut the wood. The wood has, there-fore, been divided potentially throughout. What then, is there in the wood besides the division ? For

179

ρεσιν; εἰ γὰρ καὶ ἔστι τι πάθος, ἀλλὰ πῶς εἰς
ταῦτα διαλύεται καὶ γίνεται ἐκ τούτων; ἢ πῶς
15 χωρίζεται ταῦτα; ὥστ' εἴπερ ἀδύνατον ἐξ ἀφῶν
ἢ στιγμῶν εἶναι τὰ μεγέθη, ἀνάγκη εἶναι σώματα
ἀδιαίρετα καὶ μεγέθη. οὐ μὴν ἀλλὰ καὶ ταῦτα
θεμένοις οὐχ ἧττον συμβαίνει ἀδύνατον. ἔσκεπται
δὲ περὶ αὐτῶν ἐν ἑτέροις. ἀλλὰ ταῦτα πειρατέον
λύειν· διὸ πάλιν ἐξ ἀρχῆς τὴν ἀπορίαν λεκτέον.

20 Τὸ μὲν οὖν ἅπαν σῶμα αἰσθητὸν εἶναι διαιρετὸν
καθ' ὁτιοῦν σημεῖον καὶ ἀδιαίρετον οὐδὲν ἄτοπον·
τὸ μὲν γὰρ δυνάμει διαιρετόν, τὸ δ' ἐντελεχείᾳ
ὑπάρξει. τὸ δ' εἶναι ἅμα πάντῃ διαιρετὸν δυνάμει
ἀδύνατον δόξειεν ἂν εἶναι. εἰ γὰρ δυνατόν, κἂν
γένοιτο, οὐχ ὥστε εἶναι ἅμα ἄμφω ἐντελεχείᾳ
25 ἀδιαίρετον καὶ διῃρημένον, ἀλλὰ διῃρημένον καθ'
ὁτιοῦν σημεῖον. οὐδὲν ἄρα ἔσται λοιπόν, καὶ εἰς
ἀσώματον ἐφθαρμένον τὸ σῶμα, καὶ γένοιτο δ' ἂν
πάλιν ἤτοι ἐκ στιγμῶν ἢ ὅλως ἐξ οὐδενός. καὶ
τοῦτο πῶς δυνατόν;

Ἀλλὰ μὴν ὅτι γε διαιρεῖται εἰς χωριστὰ καὶ ἀεὶ
εἰς ἐλάττω μεγέθη καὶ εἰς ἀπέχοντα καὶ κεχωρι-
30 σμένα, φανερόν. οὔτε δὴ κατὰ μέρος διαιροῦντι εἴη
ἂν ἄπειρος ἡ θρύψις, οὔτε ἅμα οἷόν τε διαιρεθῆναι
κατὰ πᾶν σημεῖον (οὐ γὰρ δυνατόν) ἀλλὰ μέχρι του.
ἀνάγκη ἄρα ἄτομα ἐνυπάρχειν μεγέθη ἀόρατα,
ἄλλως τε καὶ εἴπερ ἔσται γένεσις καὶ φθορὰ ἡ

---

[a] *i.e.* points of division and quality.
[b] *Phys.* 231 a 21 ff.   [c] *i.e.* uncuttable.

even if there is some quality, how is it dissolved into these constituents [a] and how does it come-to-be out of them ? And how are these constituents separated ? Therefore, since it is impossible for magnitudes to consist of contacts or points, there must be indivisible bodies and magnitudes. However, if we posit these, an equally impossible consequence arises, which has been the subject of discussion elsewhere.[b] But we must try to solve these difficulties, and so the problem must be stated again from the beginning.

It is, then, in no wise absurd that every perceptible body should be divisible at any point whatsoever and also indivisible ; for it will be potentially divisible and actually indivisible. But it would seem impossible that it should be, even potentially, divisible throughout at the same time ; for, if that were possible, it would actually happen, with the result, not that it would actually be simultaneously both things—indivisible and divided—but that it would be divided simultaneously at any and every point. Nothing will, therefore, be left, and the body will have passed-away into a state of incorporeity, and so it also might come-to-be again either from points or absolutely from nothing. And how is this possible ?

It is clear, however, that a body is divided into magnitudes which are separable and grow smaller and smaller and come apart from one another and are separated. If you divide a body piece by piece, the process of breaking it up would not be infinite, nor can it be divided simultaneously at every point (for this is not possible), but the process can only be carried on within a certain limit. There must, then, exist in a body atomic [c] magnitudes which are invisible, especially if coming-to-be and passing-away

μὲν διακρίσει ἡ δὲ συγκρίσει. ὁ μὲν οὖν ἀναγκάζειν
δοκῶν λόγος εἶναι μεγέθη ἄτομα οὗτός ἐστιν· ὅτι
δὲ λανθάνει παραλογιζόμενος, καὶ ᾗ λανθάνει, λέγωμεν.

Ἐπεὶ γὰρ οὐκ ἔστι στιγμὴ στιγμῆς ἐχομένη, τὸ
πάντῃ εἶναι διαιρετὸν ἔστι μὲν ὡς ὑπάρχει τοῖς
μεγέθεσιν, ἔστι δ᾽ ὡς οὔ. δοκεῖ δ᾽ ὅταν τοῦτο
5 τεθῇ, καὶ ὁπῃοῦν καὶ πάντῃ στιγμὴν εἶναι, ὥστ᾽
ἀναγκαῖον εἶναι διαιρεθῆναι τὸ μέγεθος εἰς μηδέν·
πάντῃ γὰρ εἶναι στιγμήν· ὥστε ἢ ἐξ ἀφῶν ἢ ἐκ
στιγμῶν εἶναι. τὸ δ᾽ ἔστιν ὡς ὑπάρχει πάντῃ,
ὅτι μία ὁπῃοῦν ἐστί, καὶ πᾶσαι ὡς ἑκάστη, πλείους
δὲ μιᾶς οὐκ εἰσίν (ἐφεξῆς γὰρ οὐκ εἰσίν), ὥστ᾽ οὐ
10 πάντῃ. εἰ γὰρ κατὰ μέσον διαιρετόν, καὶ κατ᾽
ἐχομένην στιγμὴν ἔσται διαιρετόν· οὐχὶ δέ[1]· οὐ
γάρ ἐστιν ἐχόμενον σημεῖον σημείου ἢ στιγμὴ
στιγμῆς. τοῦτο δ᾽ ἐστὶ διαίρεσις καὶ[2] σύνθεσις.

Ὥστ᾽ ἔστι καὶ διάκρισις καὶ σύγκρισις, ἀλλ᾽ οὔτ᾽
εἰς ἄτομα καὶ ἐξ ἀτόμων (πολλὰ γὰρ τὰ ἀδύνατα)
15 οὔτε οὕτως ὥστε πάντῃ διαίρεσιν γενέσθαι (εἰ
γὰρ ἦν ἐχομένη στιγμὴ στιγμῆς, τοῦτ᾽ ἂν ἦν), ἀλλ᾽
εἰς μικρὰ καὶ ἐλάττω ἐστί, καὶ σύγκρισις ἐξ
ἐλαττόνων. ἀλλ᾽ οὐχ ἡ ἁπλῆ καὶ τελεία γένεσις
συγκρίσει καὶ διακρίσει ὥρισται, ὡς τινές φασιν,
τὴν δ᾽ ἐν τῷ συνεχεῖ μεταβολὴν ἀλλοίωσιν. ἀλλὰ

[1] οὐχὶ δέ J : om. cet. codd.
[2] καὶ H : ἤ.

are going to take place by association and dissociation respectively. This, then, is the argument which
is thought to necessitate the existence of atomic
magnitudes, but let us now show that it conceals a
false inference, and where this false inference lies.

Since no point is contiguous to another point, the
divisibility throughout of a body is possible in one
sense, but not in another sense. When such divisibility is postulated, it is generally held that there is
a point both anywhere and everywhere in it, so that
it follows that the magnitudes must be divided until
nothing is left. For, it is urged, there is a point everywhere in it, so that it consists either of contacts or
of points. But divisibility-throughout is possible only
in the sense that there is one point *anywhere* within
it and that all its points taken separately are within
it ; but there are not more points than one *anywhere*
in it (for the points are not " consecutive "), so that
it is not divisible throughout ; for then, if it was
divisible at its centre, it will also be divisible at a
contiguous point. But it is not ; for one moment
in time is not contiguous to another, nor is one point
to another. So much for division and composition.

Hence both association and dissociation occur but
neither into atomic magnitudes and out of them (for
the impossibilities involved are numerous), nor in
such a way that division-throughout occurs (for this
would be possible only if point were contiguous to
point) ; but dissociation occurs into small, or relatively
small, parts, while association occurs out of relatively
small parts. But unqualified and complete coming-
to-be is not defined as due to association and dissociation, as some people assert, while they say that
change in what is continuous is " alteration." In fact,

Coming-to-
be is not
due to
association
of small
particles
nor passing-
away to
their dis-
sociation.

183

20 τοῦτ' ἐστὶν ἐν ᾧ σφάλλεται πάντα. ἔστι γὰρ
γένεσις ἁπλῆ καὶ φθορὰ οὐ συγκρίσει καὶ διακρίσει,
ἀλλ' ὅταν μεταβάλλῃ ἐκ τοῦδε εἰς τόδε ὅλον. οἱ
δὲ οἴονται ἀλλοίωσιν πᾶσαν εἶναι τὴν τοιαύτην
μεταβολήν· τὸ δὲ διαφέρει. ἐν γὰρ τῷ ὑποκειμένῳ
τὸ μέν ἐστι κατὰ τὸν λόγον, τὸ δὲ κατὰ τὴν ὕλην.
25 ὅταν μὲν οὖν ἐν τούτοις ᾖ ἡ μεταβολή, γένεσις
ἔσται ἢ φθορά, ὅταν δ' ἐν τοῖς πάθεσι καὶ κατὰ
συμβεβηκός, ἀλλοίωσις. διακρινόμενα δὲ καὶ συγκρινόμενα εὔφθαρτα γίνεται. ἐὰν μὲν γὰρ εἰς
ἐλάττω ὑδάτια διαιρεθῇ, θᾶττον ἀὴρ γίνεται, ἐὰν
30 δὲ συγκριθῇ, βραδύτερον. μᾶλλον δ' ἔσται δῆλον
ἐν τοῖς ὕστερον. νῦν δὲ τοσοῦτον διωρίσθω, ὅτι
ἀδύνατον εἶναι τὴν γένεσιν σύγκρισιν, οἵαν δή τινές
φασιν.

3. Διωρισμένων δὲ τούτων, πρῶτον θεωρητέον
πότερον ἔστι τι γινόμενον ἁπλῶς καὶ φθειρόμενον,
ἢ κυρίως μὲν οὐδέν, ἀεὶ δ' ἔκ τινος καὶ τί, λέγω δ'
35 οἷον ἐκ κάμνοντος ὑγιαῖνον καὶ κάμνον ἐξ ὑγιαί-
317 b νοντος, ἢ μικρὸν ἐκ μεγάλου καὶ μέγα ἐκ μικροῦ,
καὶ τἆλλα πάντα τοῦτον τὸν τρόπον. εἰ γὰρ ἁπλῶς
ἔσται γένεσις, ἁπλῶς ἂν γίνοιτο ἐκ μὴ ὄντος, ὥστ'
ἀληθὲς ἂν εἴη λέγειν ὅτι ὑπάρχει τισὶ τὸ μὴ ὄν.

ᵃ 328 a 23–b 22.

this is where the whole mistake occurs ; for unqualified coming-to-be and passing-away are not due to association and dissociation, but take place when something as a whole changes from " this " to " that." But some philosophers hold that all such change is " alteration," whereas there is a difference. For in that which underlies the change there is a factor corresponding to the definition and a material factor ; when, therefore, the change takes place in these, coming-to-be or passing-away will occur, but, when the change is in the qualities (that is to say, there is an accidental change), " alteration " will result. Things which are associated and dissociated become liable to pass-away ; for if drops of water are divided into still smaller drops, air comes-to-be from them more quickly, whereas, if they are associated together, air comes-to-be more slowly. This, however, will be clearer in what follows [a] ; for the moment let us assume this much as established, namely, that coming-into-being cannot be association of the kind which some people assert it to be.

3. Having made the above distinctions, we must first inquire whether there is anything which comes-to-be and passes-away in an unqualified sense, or whether nothing comes-to-be in the strict sense, but everything comes-to-be *something*, and out of *something*—for example, comes-to-be healthy out of being ill, and ill out of being healthy, or small out of being large, and large out of being small, and so on in the other instances which one might give. For, if there is to be coming-to-be without qualification, something must come-to-be out of not-being without qualification, so that it would be true to say that there are things of which " not-being " can be predicated ; for

Do unqualified coming-to-be and passing-away actually occur?

185

τὶς μὲν γὰρ γένεσις ἐκ μὴ ὄντος τινός, οἷον ἐκ
5 μὴ λευκοῦ ἢ μὴ καλοῦ, ἡ δὲ ἁπλῆ ἐξ ἁπλῶς μὴ
ὄντος.

Τὸ δ' ἁπλῶς ἤτοι τὸ πρῶτον σημαίνει καθ'
ἑκάστην κατηγορίαν τοῦ ὄντος, ἢ τὸ καθόλου καὶ
τὸ πάντα περιέχον. εἰ μὲν οὖν τὸ πρῶτον, οὐσίας
ἔσται γένεσις ἐκ μὴ οὐσίας. ᾧ δὲ μὴ ὑπάρχει οὐσία
μηδὲ τόδε, δῆλον ὡς οὐδὲ τῶν ἄλλων οὐδεμία κατη-
10 γοριῶν, οἷον οὔτε ποιὸν οὔτε ποσὸν οὔτε τὸ ποῦ·
χωριστὰ γὰρ ἂν εἴη τὰ πάθη τῶν οὐσιῶν. εἰ δὲ
τὸ μὴ ὂν ὅλως, ἀπόφασις ἔσται καθόλου πάντων,
ὥστε ἐκ μηδενὸς ἀνάγκη γίνεσθαι τὸ γινόμενον.

Περὶ μὲν οὖν τούτων ἐν ἄλλοις τε διηπόρηται καὶ
15 διώρισται τοῖς λόγοις ἐπὶ πλεῖον· συντόμως δὲ καὶ
νῦν λεκτέον, ὅτι τρόπον μέν τινα ἐκ μὴ ὄντος ἁπλῶς
γίνεται, τρόπον δὲ ἄλλον ἐξ ὄντος ἀεί· τὸ γὰρ
δυνάμει ὂν ἐντελεχείᾳ δὲ μὴ ὂν ἀνάγκη προϋπάρχειν
λεγόμενον ἀμφοτέρως. ὃ δὲ καὶ τούτων διωρισμένων ἔχει θαυμαστὴν ἀπορίαν, πάλιν ἐπαναπο-
20 διστέον, πῶς ἔστιν ἁπλῆ γένεσις, εἴτ' ἐκ δυνάμει
ὄντος οὖσα εἴτε καί πως ἄλλως. ἀπορήσειε γὰρ ἄν
τις ἆρ' ἔστιν οὐσίας γένεσις καὶ τοῦ τοῦδε, ἀλλὰ
μὴ τοῦ τοιοῦδε καὶ τοσοῦδε καὶ ποῦ (τὸν αὐτὸν δὲ

---

a *Phys.* i. 6-9.
b *i.e.* as " being " and as " not-being."

186

some kind of coming-to-be proceeds from some kind of not-being, for example, from " not-white " and " not-beautiful," but unqualified coming-to-be proceeds from unqualified not-being.

Now " unqualified " signifies either (a) that which is primary in each category, or (b) that which is universal and universally comprehensive. If, then, it signifies that which is primary, there will be a coming-to-be of substance out of not-substance ; but that which has not a substance or a " this " obviously cannot have any predicate from the other categories, either, for example, quality, quantity or position, for then the properties would exist apart from the substances. If, on the other hand, " unqualified not-being " signifies that which does not exist at all, this will be a general negation of all being, and, therefore, what comes-to-be must come-to-be out of nothing.

The meaning of *unqualified*.

This problem has been discussed and settled at greater length elsewhere [a] ; but a short restatement of it is called for here : In one way things come-to-be out of that which has no unqualified being, in another way they always come-to-be out of what is ; for there must be a pre-existence of that which potentially is, but actually is not, in being, and this is described in both ways.[b] This having been established, a question involving extraordinary difficulty must be re-examined, namely, how can there be " unqualified coming-to-be," whether it comes from what exists potentially or in some other way ? For one might raise the question whether there is a coming-to-be of substance (that is, of the " this ") at all, and not rather of a " such " or a " so-great " or a " somewhere " ; and the same question might be asked

Are coming-to-be and passing-away concerned with substance or with quality ?

317 b

τρόπον καὶ περὶ φθορᾶς). εἰ γάρ τι γίνεται, δῆλον
ὡς ἔσται δυνάμει τις οὐσία, ἐντελεχείᾳ δ' οὔ, ἐξ
25 ἧς ἡ γένεσις ἔσται καὶ εἰς ἣν ἀνάγκη μεταβάλλειν
τὸ φθειρόμενον. πότερον οὖν ὑπάρξει τι τούτῳ
τῶν ἄλλων ἐντελεχείᾳ; λέγω δ' οἷον ἆρ' ἔσται
ποσὸν ἢ ποιὸν ἢ ποῦ τὸ δυνάμει μόνον τόδε καὶ ὄν,
ἁπλῶς δὲ μὴ τόδε μηδ' ὄν; εἰ γὰρ μηδὲν ἀλλὰ
πάντα δυνάμει, χωριστόν τε συμβαίνει τὸ μὴ οὕτως
30 ὄν, καὶ ἔτι, ὃ μάλιστα φοβούμενοι διετέλεσαν οἱ
πρῶτοι φιλοσοφήσαντες, τὸ ἐκ μηδενὸς γίνεσθαι
προϋπάρχοντος· εἰ δὲ τὸ μὲν εἶναι τόδε τι ἢ οὐσίαν
οὐχ ὑπάρξει, τῶν δ' ἄλλων τι τῶν εἰρημένων, ἔσται,
καθάπερ εἴπομεν, χωριστὰ τὰ πάθη τῶν οὐσιῶν.
περί τε τούτων οὖν ὅσον ἐνδέχεται πραγματευτέον,
35 καὶ τίς αἰτία τοῦ γένεσιν ἀεὶ εἶναι, καὶ τὴν ἁπλῆν
καὶ τὴν κατὰ μέρος.

318 a   Οὔσης δ' αἰτίας μιᾶς μὲν ὅθεν τὴν ἀρχὴν εἶναί
φαμεν τῆς κινήσεως, μιᾶς δὲ τῆς ὕλης, τὴν τοιαύτην
αἰτίαν λεκτέον. περὶ μὲν γὰρ ἐκείνης εἴρηται πρότερον ἐν τοῖς περὶ κινήσεως λόγοις, ὅτι ἐστὶ τὸ
5 μὲν ἀκίνητον τὸν ἅπαντα χρόνον, τὸ δὲ κινούμενον
ἀεί. τούτων δὲ περὶ μὲν τῆς ἀκινήτου ἀρχῆς τῆς
ἑτέρας καὶ προτέρας διελεῖν ἐστι φιλοσοφίας ἔργον·

---

[a] In lines 10, 11 above.
[b] i.e. qualified, that is, changing in respect of quality,
quantity or position.
[c] Phys. 258 b 10 ff.

about passing-away also. For, if something comes-to-be, it is clear that there will be substance, not actually but potentially, from which the coming-to-be will proceed and into which that which is passing-away must change. Will any other attribute then belong actually to this supposed substance ? For example, I mean, will that which is only potentially a " this " (and only potentially exists), and which is not a " this " and does not exist *without qualification*, possess size or quality or position ? For, (1) if it actually possessed none of these determinations but possesses them all potentially, the result is (a) that a being which is not a determined being can possess a separate existence, and (b) that coming-to-be arises out of nothing pre-existent—a view which inspired great and continuous alarm in the minds of the early philosophers. On the other hand, (2) if, although it is not to be a " this " or a substance, it is to possess some of the other attributes which we have mentioned, then, as we said,[a] the qualities will be separable from the substance. We must, therefore, deal with these matters to the best of our ability, and also with the causes of continuous coming-to-be, both the unqualified and the partial.[b]

Now there are two meanings of " cause," one being that which, as we say, results in the beginning of motion, and the other the material cause. It is the latter kind with which we have to deal here ; for with cause in the former sense we have dealt in our discussion of Motion,[c] when we said that there is something which remains immovable through all time and something which is always in motion. To come to a decision about the first of these, the immovable original source, is the task of the other and prior

189

περὶ δὲ τοῦ διὰ τὸ συνεχῶς κινεῖσθαι τἄλλα κινοῦν-
τος ὕστερον ἀποδοτέον, τί τοιοῦτον τῶν καθ᾽
ἕκαστα λεγομένων αἴτιόν ἐστιν. νῦν δὲ τὴν ὡς ἐν
10 ὕλης εἴδει τιθεμένην αἰτίαν εἴπωμεν, δι᾽ ἣν ἀεὶ
φθορὰ καὶ γένεσις οὐχ ὑπολείπει τὴν φύσιν· ἅμα
γὰρ ἂν ἴσως τοῦτο γένοιτο δῆλον, καὶ περὶ τοῦ
νῦν ἀπορηθέντος, πῶς ποτὲ δεῖ λέγειν καὶ περὶ τῆς
ἁπλῆς φθορᾶς καὶ γενέσεως.

Ἔχει δ᾽ ἀπορίαν ἱκανὴν καὶ τί τὸ αἴτιον τοῦ
συνείρειν τὴν γένεσιν, εἴπερ τὸ φθειρόμενον εἰς τὸ
15 μὴ ὂν ἀπέρχεται, τὸ δὲ μὴ ὂν μηδέν ἐστιν· οὔτε
γὰρ τὶ οὔτε ποιὸν οὔτε ποσὸν οὔτε ποῦ τὸ μὴ ὄν.
εἴπερ οὖν ἀεί τι τῶν ὄντων ἀπέρχεται, διὰ τί ποτ᾽
οὐκ ἀνήλωται πάλαι καὶ φροῦδον τὸ πᾶν, εἴ γε
πεπερασμένον ἦν ἐξ οὗ γίνεται τῶν γινομένων
ἕκαστον; οὐ γὰρ δὴ διὰ τὸ ἄπειρον εἶναι ἐξ οὗ
20 γίνεται, οὐχ ὑπολείπει· τοῦτο γὰρ ἀδύνατον. κατ᾽
ἐνέργειαν μὲν γὰρ οὐδέν ἐστιν ἄπειρον, δυνάμει
δ᾽ ἐπὶ τὴν διαίρεσιν, ὥστ᾽ ἔδει ταύτην εἶναι μόνην
τὴν μὴ ὑπολείπουσαν τῷ γίνεσθαί τι ἀεὶ ἔλαττον·
νῦν δὲ τοῦτο οὐχ ὁρῶμεν.

Ἆρ᾽ οὖν διὰ τὸ τὴν τοῦδε φθορὰν ἄλλου εἶναι
25 γένεσιν καὶ τὴν τοῦδε γένεσιν ἄλλου εἶναι φθορὰν

---

[a] Usually called πρώτη φιλοσοφία.
[b] See 336 a 13 ff.
[c] Or " specific " causes, as opposed to causes in the
universal sense : cf. *Phys.* 195 a 27 ff.

branch of philosophy,[a] while, regarding that which moves all other things by its own continuous motion, we shall have to explain later [b] which of the individual [c] causes is of this kind. For the moment let us deal with the cause which is placed in the class of matter, owing to which passing-away and coming-to-be never fail to occur in nature ; for perhaps this may be cleared up and it may become evident at the same time what we ought to say about the problem which arose just now, namely, about unqualified passing-away and coming-to-be.

What is the cause of the continuous process of coming-to-be is a perplexing enough problem, if it is really true that what passes-away vanishes into " what is not " and " what is not " is nothing ; for " what is not " is not anything and possesses neither quality nor quantity nor position. If, therefore, some one of the "things-which-are" is constantly vanishing, how is it that the whole of being has not long ago been used up and has not disappeared, provided, of course, that the source of each of the things which come-to-be was limited ? For, I suppose, the fact that coming-to-be never fails is not because the source from which it comes is infinite ; for this is impossible, since nothing is actually infinite but only potentially so for the purpose of division, so that there would have to be only one kind of coming-to-be, namely, one which never fails, because something which comes-to-be is successively smaller and smaller. But, as a matter of fact, we do not see this happening.

What is the cause of coming-to-be and passing-away ?

Is it, then, because the passing-away of one thing is the coming-to-be of another thing, and the coming-to-be of one thing the passing-away of another thing,

Why is the process of change unceasing ?

191

ἄπαυστον ἀναγκαῖον εἶναι τὴν μεταβολήν; περὶ
μὲν οὖν τοῦ γένεσιν εἶναι καὶ φθορὰν ὁμοίως περὶ
ἕκαστον τῶν ὄντων, ταύτην οἰητέον εἶναι πᾶσιν
ἱκανὴν αἰτίαν. διὰ τί δέ ποτε τὰ μὲν ἁπλῶς γίνεσθαι λέγεται καὶ φθείρεσθαι τὰ δ' οὐχ ἁπλῶς,
30 πάλιν σκεπτέον, εἴπερ τὸ αὐτό ἐστι γένεσις μὲν
τουδὶ φθορὰ δὲ τουδί, καὶ φθορὰ μὲν τουδὶ γένεσις
δὲ τουδί· ζητεῖ γάρ τινα τοῦτο λόγον. λέγομεν
γὰρ ὅτι φθείρεται νῦν ἁπλῶς, καὶ οὐ μόνον τοδί·
καὶ αὕτη μὲν γένεσις ἁπλῶς, αὕτη δὲ φθορά. τοδὶ
δὲ γίνεται μέν τι, γίνεται δ' ἁπλῶς οὔ· φαμὲν γὰρ
35 τὸν μανθάνοντα γίνεσθαι μὲν ἐπιστήμονα, γίνεσθαι
δ' ἁπλῶς οὔ.

Καθάπερ οὖν πολλάκις διορίζομεν λέγοντες ὅτι τὰ
μὲν τόδε τι σημαίνει τὰ δ' οὔ, διὰ τοῦτο συμβαίνει
τὸ ζητούμενον· διαφέρει γὰρ εἰς ἃ μεταβάλλει τὸ
μεταβάλλον· οἷον ἴσως ἡ μὲν εἰς πῦρ ὁδὸς γένεσις
5 μὲν ἁπλῆ, φθορὰ δὲ τινός ἐστιν, οἷον γῆς, ἡ δὲ γῆς
γένεσις τὶς γένεσις, γένεσις δ' οὐχ ἁπλῶς, φθορὰ
δ' ἁπλῶς, οἷον πυρός, ὥσπερ Παρμενίδης λέγει δύο
τὸ ὂν καὶ τὸ μὴ ὂν εἶναι φάσκων, πῦρ καὶ γῆν. τὸ
δὴ ταῦτα ἢ τοιαῦθ' ἕτερα ὑποτίθεσθαι διαφέρει
οὐδέν· τὸν γὰρ τρόπον ζητοῦμεν, ἀλλ' οὐ τὸ ὑπο-

---

[a] Fr. 8 lines 53 ff. (Diels), but Parmenides mentions this
theory as being wrong.

that the process of change is necessarily unceasing ? As regards the occurrence of coming-to-be and passing-away in everything which exists alike, the above must be regarded by all as an adequate cause ; but why some things are said to come-to-be and to pass-away *without qualification* and others *with quali-fication*, must be examined once more, if it is true that the same process is a coming-to-be of " this," but a passing-away of " that," and a passing-away of " this " but a coming-to-be of " that " ; for the question calls for discussion. For we say " It is now passing-away " without qualification, and not merely " *This* is passing-away " ; and we call *this* a " coming-to-be," and *that* a " passing-away," without qualifica-tion. But *this* " comes-to-be-something," but does not do so without qualification ; for we say that the student " comes-to-be learned," not " comes-to-be " without qualification.

The dis-tinction between " qualified " and " un-qualified."

Now we often make a distinction, saying that some things signify a " this," and others do not ; and it is because of this that the point which we are examining arises, for it makes a difference *into what* that which is changing changes. For example, perhaps the passage into Fire is " coming-to-be " without quali-fication but " passing-away-of-something " (for in-stance, of Earth), while the coming-to-be of Earth is qualified (not unqualified) coming-to-be, but un-qualified passing-away (for example, of Fire). This agrees with Parmenides' theory,[a] for he says that the things into which change takes place are two and asserts that these two things, what is and what is not, are Fire and Earth. Whether we postulate these or other things of a like kind makes no difference ; for we are seeking not what underlies these changes, but

10 κείμενον. ἡ μὲν οὖν εἰς τὸ μὴ ὂν ἁπλῶς ὁδὸς
φθορὰ ἁπλῆ, ἡ δ' εἰς τὸ ἁπλῶς ὂν γένεσις ἁπλῆ.
οἷς οὖν διώρισται εἴτε πυρὶ καὶ γῇ εἴτε ἄλλοις τισί,
τούτων ἔσται τὸ μὲν ὂν τὸ δὲ μὴ ὄν. ἕνα μὲν οὖν
τρόπον τούτῳ διοίσει τὸ ἁπλῶς τι γίνεσθαι καὶ
φθείρεσθαι τοῦ μὴ ἁπλῶς, ἄλλον δὲ τῇ ὕλῃ ὁποία
15 τις ἂν ᾖ· ἧς μὲν γὰρ μᾶλλον αἱ διαφοραὶ τόδε τι
σημαίνουσι, μᾶλλον οὐσία, ἧς δὲ στέρησιν, μὴ ὄν,
οἷον τὸ μὲν θερμὸν κατηγορία τις καὶ εἶδος, ἡ δὲ
ψυχρότης στέρησις· διαφέρουσι δὲ γῆ καὶ πῦρ καὶ
ταύταις ταῖς διαφοραῖς.

Δοκεῖ δὲ μᾶλλον τοῖς πολλοῖς τῷ αἰσθητῷ καὶ
20 μὴ αἰσθητῷ διαφέρειν· ὅταν μὲν γὰρ εἰς αἰσθητὴν
μεταβάλλῃ ὕλην, γίνεσθαί φασιν, ὅταν δ' εἰς ἀφανῆ,
φθείρεσθαι· τὸ γὰρ ὂν καὶ τὸ μὴ ὂν τῷ αἰσθάνεσθαι
καὶ τῷ μὴ αἰσθάνεσθαι διορίζουσιν, ὥσπερ τὸ μὲν
ἐπιστητὸν ὄν, τὸ δ' ἄγνωστον μὴ ὄν· ἡ γὰρ αἴσθησις
ἐπιστήμης ἔχει δύναμιν. καθάπερ οὖν αὐτοὶ τῷ
25 αἰσθάνεσθαι ἢ τῷ δύνασθαι καὶ ζῆν καὶ εἶναι
νομίζουσιν, οὕτω καὶ τὰ πράγματα, τρόπον τινὰ

the manner in which they take place. The passage, then, into that which " is not " without qualification is unqualified passing-away, while the passage into that which " is " without qualification is unqualified coming-to-be. Hence, whatever it is by which the things which change are distinguished from one another—whether it be Fire and Earth or some other pair—one will be " a being," the other " a not-being." One way, then, in which unqualified will differ from qualified coming-to-be and passing-away is obtained by this method. Another way of distinguishing them is by the special nature of the material of that which changes ; for the more the differences of material signify " a this," the more is it a real being, whereas the more they signify a privation, the more unreal it is. For example, " hot " is a positive predication and a " form," while " cold " is a privation, and Earth and Fire are distinguished from one another by these differences.

In the opinion of most people the difference between qualified and unqualified depends rather on perceptibility and imperceptibility ; for when there is a change to perceptible material, they say that coming-to-be takes place, but, when they change to invisible material, they say that passing-away occurs : for they distinguish between " that which is " and " that which is not " by their perception and non-perception, just as what is knowable *is* and what is unknowable *is not* (for to them perception has the force of knowledge). As, therefore, they themselves think that they live and have their being in virtue of perceiving or having the power to perceive, so, too, they consider that things exist because they perceive them—and, in a way, they are on the right road to

A note on why most people identify the real with the perceptible and the unreal with the imperceptible.

318 b

διώκοντες τἀληθές, αὐτὸ δὲ λέγοντες οὐκ ἀληθές. συμβαίνει δὴ κατὰ δόξαν καὶ κατ' ἀλήθειαν ἄλλως τὸ γίνεσθαί τε ἁπλῶς καὶ τὸ φθείρεσθαι· πνεῦμα γὰρ καὶ ἀὴρ κατὰ μὲν τὴν αἴσθησιν ἧττόν ἐστιν (διὸ 30 καὶ τὰ φθειρόμενα ἁπλῶς τῇ εἰς ταῦτα μεταβολῇ φθείρεσθαι λέγουσιν, γίνεσθαι δ' ὅταν εἰς ἁπτὸν καὶ εἰς γῆν μεταβάλλῃ), κατὰ δ' ἀλήθειαν μᾶλλον τόδε τι καὶ εἶδος ταῦτα τῆς γῆς.

Τοῦ μὲν οὖν εἶναι τὴν μὲν ἁπλῆν γένεσιν φθορὰν οὖσάν τινος, τὴν δὲ φθορὰν τὴν ἁπλῆν γένεσιν οὖσάν 35 τινος, εἴρηται τὸ αἴτιον (διὰ γὰρ τὸ τὴν ὕλην δια-
319 a φέρειν ἢ τῷ οὐσίαν εἶναι ἢ τῷ μή, ἢ τῷ τὴν μὲν μᾶλλον τὴν δὲ μή, ἢ τῷ τὴν μὲν μᾶλλον αἰσθητὴν εἶναι τὴν ὕλην ἐξ ἧς καὶ εἰς ἤν, τὴν δὲ ἧττον εἶναι)· τοῦ δὲ τὰ μὲν ἁπλῶς γίνεσθαι λέγεσθαι, τὰ δέ τι μόνον, μὴ τῇ ἐξ ἀλλήλων γενέσει, καθ' ὃν εἴπομεν 5 νῦν τρόπον (νῦν μὲν γὰρ τοσοῦτον διώρισται, τί δή ποτε πάσης γενέσεως οὔσης φθορᾶς ἄλλου, καὶ πάσης φθορᾶς οὔσης ἑτέρου τινὸς γενέσεως, οὐχ ὁμοίως ἀποδίδομεν τὸ γίνεσθαι καὶ τὸ φθείρεσθαι τοῖς εἰς ἄλληλα μεταβάλλουσιν. τὸ δ' ὕστερον εἰρη-μένον οὐ τοῦτο διαπορεῖ ἀλλὰ τί ποτε τὸ μανθάνον 10 μὲν οὐ λέγεται ἁπλῶς γίνεσθαι ἀλλὰ γίνεσθαι ἐπι-στῆμον, τὸ δὲ φυόμενον γίνεσθαι), ταῦτα δὲ δι-ώρισται ταῖς κατηγορίαις· τὰ μὲν γὰρ τόδε τι

---

[a] τοῦ μὲν (318 b 33) is answered by τοῦ δὲ (319 a 3), and the construction is broken by the parenthesis.

[b] *i.e.* in 318 a 33 ff.

[c] *i.e.* to the question raised in lines 3-5 above.

196

the truth, though what they actually say is not true. Indeed, the popular opinion about the way in which unqualified coming-to-be and passing-away occur, differs from the truth ; for Wind and Air have less reality according to our perception of them (hence, too, things which pass-away are said to do so in an unqualified sense by changing into Wind and Air, and to come-to-be when they change into what is tangible, namely, into Earth), whereas in truth they are more a definite something and a " form " than Earth.

We have now stated the reason why [a] there is unqualified coming-to-be, which is the passing-away of something, and unqualified passing-away, which is the coming-to-be of something (for it depends on the difference of the material, from which and into which the change takes place, and on its being substance or not, or on its having more or less of the nature of substance, or on its being more or less perceptible) ; but why are some things said to come-to-be without qualification, while others come-to-be some particular thing only and not by coming-to-be reciprocally out of one another in the manner which we described just now ? (For up to the present we have only determined this much, namely, why, although all coming-to-be is a passing-away of something else and all passing-away is a coming-to-be of some other thing, we do not attribute coming-to-be and passing-away uniformly to things which change into one another ; but the problem afterwards raised [b] does not discuss this difficulty, but why that which learns is said to come-to-be learned and not to come-to-be without qualification, yet that which grows is said to come-to-be). The answer [c] is that this is determined by the differences of the categories ; for

Summary of the argument. Coming-to-be and passing-away are two sides of a single transformation of substance into substance.

197

319 a

σημαίνει, τὰ δὲ τοιόνδε, τὰ δὲ ποσόν· ὅσα οὖν μὴ
οὐσίαν σημαίνει, οὐ λέγεται ἁπλῶς, ἀλλὰ τὶ γίνεσθαι. οὐ μὴν ἀλλ' ὁμοίως ἐν πᾶσι γένεσις μὲν
15 κατὰ τὰ ἐν τῇ ἑτέρᾳ συστοιχίᾳ λέγεται, οἷον ἐν μὲν
οὐσίᾳ ἐὰν πῦρ ἀλλ' οὐκ ἐὰν γῆ, ἐν δὲ τῷ ποιῷ ἐὰν
ἐπιστῆμον ἀλλ' οὐχ ὅταν ἀνεπιστῆμον.

Περὶ μὲν οὖν τοῦ τὰ μὲν ἁπλῶς γίνεσθαι τὰ δὲ
μή, καὶ ὅλως καὶ ἐν ταῖς οὐσίαις αὐταῖς, εἴρηται,
καὶ διότι τοῦ γένεσιν εἶναι συνεχῶς αἰτία ὡς ὕλη
20 τὸ ὑποκείμενον, ὅτι μεταβλητικὸν εἰς τἀναντία,
καὶ ἔστιν ἡ θατέρου γένεσις ἀεὶ ἐπὶ τῶν οὐσιῶν
ἄλλου φθορὰ καὶ ἡ ἄλλου φθορὰ ἄλλου γένεσις.
ἀλλὰ μὴν οὐδ' ἀπορῆσαι δεῖ διὰ τί γίνεται ἀεὶ
ἀπολλυμένων· ὥσπερ γὰρ καὶ τὸ φθείρεσθαι ἁπλῶς
φασίν, ὅταν εἰς ἀναίσθητον ἔλθῃ καὶ τὸ μὴ ὄν,
25 ὁμοίως καὶ γίνεσθαι ἐκ μὴ ὄντος φασίν, ὅταν ἐξ
ἀναισθήτου. εἴτ' οὖν ὄντος τινὸς τοῦ ὑποκειμένου
εἴτε μή, γίνεται ἐκ μὴ ὄντος. ὥστε ὁμοίως καὶ
γίνεται ἐκ μὴ ὄντος καὶ φθείρεται εἰς τὸ μὴ ὄν.
εἰκότως οὖν οὐχ ὑπολείπει· ἡ γὰρ γένεσις φθορὰ
τοῦ μὴ ὄντος, ἡ δὲ φθορὰ γένεσις τοῦ μὴ ὄντος.

30 Ἀλλὰ τοῦτο τὸ μὴ ὂν ἁπλῶς ἀπορήσειεν ἄν τις

ᵃ *i.e.* the two parallel columns containing co-ordinate
pairs ; see W. D. Ross on *Met.* 1054 b 35.

some things signify a " this," others a " such-and-such," others a " so-much." Those things, therefore, which do not signify substance are not said to come-to-be without qualification, but to come-to-be *some-thing*. However, coming-to-be is said to take place in all things alike when a thing comes-to-be some-thing in *one* of the two columns [a] : in substance if it comes-to-be Fire, but not if it comes-to-be Earth ; in quality, if it comes-to-be learned, but not if it comes-to-be ignorant.

It has already been stated how some things come-to-be without qualification and others do not, both generally and in the substances themselves, and that the substratum is the material cause why coming-to-be is a continuous process because it is subject to change into the contraries, and, in the case of sub-stances, the coming-to-be of one thing is always a passing-away of another, and the passing-away of one thing another's coming-to-be. It is, however, not necessary even to raise the question why coming-to-be goes on when things are being destroyed ; for, just as people use the term passing-away without qualification when a thing has passed into the im-perceptible and into apparent non-existence, so like-wise also they talk of coming-to-be from non-exist-ence, when a thing appears out of imperceptibility. Whether, therefore, the substratum is something or is not, what comes-to-be does so from not-being ; and so it comes-to-be from not-being and passes-away into not-being in the same manner. Therefore it is probable that coming-to-be never fails ; for it is a passing-away of that which is not, and passing-away is a coming-to-be of that which is not.

But about that which " is not," unless you qualify

319 a

πότερον τὸ ἕτερον τῶν ἐναντίων ἐστίν, οἷον γῆ
καὶ τὸ βαρὺ μὴ ὄν, πῦρ δὲ καὶ τὸ κοῦφον[1] ὄν, ἢ
οὔ, ἀλλ᾽ ἔστι καὶ γῆ τὸ ὄν, τὸ δὲ μὴ ὂν ὕλη ἢ τῆς
γῆς, καὶ πυρὸς ὡσαύτως. καὶ ἆρά γε ἑτέρα ἑκα-

319 b τέρου ἡ ὕλη, ἢ οὐκ ἂν γίνοιτο ἐξ ἀλλήλων οὐδ᾽ ἐξ
ἐναντίων; τούτοις γὰρ ὑπάρχει τἀναντία, πυρί, γῇ,
ὕδατι, ἀέρι. ἢ ἔστι μὲν ὡς ἡ αὐτή, ἔστι δ᾽ ὡς ἡ
ἑτέρα· ὃ μὲν γάρ ποτε ὂν ὑπόκειται τὸ αὐτό, τὸ
δ᾽ εἶναι οὐ τὸ αὐτό. περὶ μὲν οὖν τούτων ἐπὶ
5 τοσοῦτον εἰρήσθω.

4. Περὶ δὲ γενέσεως καὶ ἀλλοιώσεως λέγωμεν τί
διαφέρουσιν· φαμὲν γὰρ ἑτέρας εἶναι ταύτας τὰς
μεταβολὰς ἀλλήλων. ἐπειδὴ οὖν ἐστί τι τὸ ὑποκείμενον καὶ ἕτερον τὸ πάθος ὃ κατὰ τοῦ ὑποκειμένου
10 λέγεσθαι πέφυκεν, καὶ ἔστι μεταβολὴ ἑκατέρου
τούτων, ἀλλοίωσις μέν ἐστιν, ὅταν ὑπομένοντος τοῦ
ὑποκειμένου, αἰσθητοῦ ὄντος, μεταβάλλῃ ἐν τοῖς
αὐτοῦ πάθεσιν, ἢ ἐναντίοις οὖσιν ἢ μεταξύ, οἷον
τὸ σῶμα ὑγιαίνει καὶ πάλιν κάμνει ὑπομένον γε
ταὐτό, καὶ ὁ χαλκὸς στρογγύλος, ὁτὲ δὲ γωνιοειδὴς
15 ὁ αὐτός γε ὤν. ὅταν δ᾽ ὅλον μεταβάλλῃ μὴ ὑπομένοντος αἰσθητοῦ τινὸς ὡς ὑποκειμένου τοῦ αὐτοῦ,
ἀλλ᾽ οἷον ἐκ τῆς γονῆς αἷμα πάσης ἢ ἐξ ὕδατος
ἀὴρ ἢ ἐξ ἀέρος παντὸς ὕδωρ, γένεσις ἤδη τὸ τοιοῦτον, τοῦ δὲ φθορά, μάλιστα δέ, ἂν ἡ μεταβολὴ

[1] post κοῦφον add. τὸ EL.

it, one might well be puzzled. Is it one of the two contraries? For example, is Earth, and that which is heavy, " not-being," but Fire, and that which is light, " being " ? Or is this not so, but is Earth also " what is," while " what is not " is matter—the matter of Earth and of Fire alike? And is the matter of each different, or else they would not come-to-be out of one another, that is, contraries out of contraries? For the contraries exist in these things, namely, in Fire, Earth, Water and Air. Or is the matter the same in one sense, but different in another? For their substratum at any particular moment is the same, but their being is not the same. So much, then, on these subjects.

4. Let us now deal with coming-to-be and " alteration " and discuss the difference between them ; for we say these forms of change differ from one another. Since, then, the substratum is one thing and the property which is of such a nature as to be predicated of the substratum is another thing, and since change takes place in each of these, " alteration " occurs when the substratum, which is perceptible, persists, but there is change in its properties, which are either directly or intermediately contrary to one another : for example, the body is healthy and then again sick, though it persists in being the same body, and the bronze is spherical and then again angular, remaining the same bronze. But when the thing as a whole changes, nothing perceptible persisting as identical substratum (for example, when the seed as a whole is converted into blood, or water into air, or air as a whole into water), such a process is a coming-to-be— and a passing-away of the other substance—particularly if the change proceeds from something imper-

γίνηται ἐξ ἀναισθήτου εἰς αἰσθητὸν ἢ ἁφῇ ἢ πάσαις
20 ταῖς αἰσθήσεσιν, οἷον ὅταν ὕδωρ γένηται ἢ φθαρῇ
εἰς ἀέρα· ὁ γὰρ ἀὴρ ἐπιεικῶς ἀναίσθητον. ἐν δὲ
τούτοις ἄν τι ὑπομένῃ πάθος τὸ αὐτὸ ἐναντιώσεως
ἐν τῷ γενομένῳ καὶ τῷ φθαρέντι (οἷον ὅταν ἐξ
ἀέρος ὕδωρ, εἰ ἄμφω διαφανῆ ἢ ψυχρά), οὐ δεῖ
τούτου θάτερον πάθος εἶναι εἰς ὃ μεταβάλλει. εἰ
25 δὲ μή, ἔσται ἀλλοίωσις. οἷον ὁ μουσικὸς ἄνθρωπος
ἐφθάρη, ἄνθρωπος δ' ἄμουσος ἐγένετο, ὁ δ' ἄνθρωπος ὑπομένει τὸ αὐτό. εἰ μὲν οὖν τούτου μὴ πάθος
ἦν καθ' αὑτὸ ἡ μουσικὴ καὶ ἡ ἀμουσία, τοῦ μὲν
γένεσις ἦν ἄν, τοῦ δὲ φθορά· διὸ ἀνθρώπου μὲν
ταῦτα πάθη, ἀνθρώπου δὲ μουσικοῦ καὶ ἀνθρώπου
30 ἀμούσου γένεσις καὶ φθορά· νῦν δὲ πάθος τοῦτο
τοῦ ὑπομένοντος. διὸ ἀλλοίωσις τὰ τοιαῦτα.

Ὅταν μὲν οὖν κατὰ τὸ ποσὸν ᾖ ἡ μεταβολὴ τῆς
ἐναντιώσεως, αὔξη καὶ φθίσις, ὅταν δὲ κατὰ τόπον,
φορά, ὅταν δὲ κατὰ πάθος καὶ τὸ ποιόν, ἀλλοίωσις,
ὅταν δὲ μηδὲν ὑπομένῃ οὗ θάτερον πάθος ἢ συμβεβηκὸς ὅλως, γένεσις, τὸ δὲ φθορά. ἔστι δὲ ὕλη
μάλιστα μὲν καὶ κυρίως τὸ ὑποκείμενον γενέσεως καὶ
φθορᾶς δεκτικόν, τρόπον δέ τινα καὶ τὸ ταῖς ἄλλαις
5 μεταβολαῖς, ὅτι πάντα δεκτικὰ τὰ ὑποκείμενα ἐναν-

ceptible to something perceptible (either to touch or to all the senses), as when water comes-to-be out of, or passes-away into, air ; for air is pretty well imperceptible. But if, in these circumstances, any property belonging to a pair of contraries persists in being the same in the thing which has come-to-be as it was in the thing which has passed-away—if, for instance, when water comes-to-be out of air, both are transparent or cold—that into which it changes is not necessarily another property of this thing ; otherwise the change will be " alteration." For example, the musical man passed-away and an un-musical man came-to-be, but the man persists as identically the same. Now if musicality (and un-musicality) were not in itself a property of man, there would be a coming-to-be of the one and passing-away of the other ; therefore, these are qualities of a man, but the coming-to-be and the passing-away of a musical man and of an unmusical man ; but, in fact, musicality (and unmusicality) are a quality of the persistent identity. Consequently such changes are " alteration."

When, therefore, the change from one contrary to another is quantitative, it is " growth and diminu-tion " ; when it is a change of place, it is " motion "; when it is a change of property (or quality), it is " alteration " ; but when nothing persists of which the resulting state is a property or an accident of any kind, it is a case of coming-to-be, and the contrary change is passing-away. Matter, in the chief and strictest sense of the word, is the substratum which admits of coming-to-be and passing-away ; but the substratum of the other kind of change is also in a sense matter, because all the substrata admit of

320 a

τιώσεών τινων. περὶ μὲν οὖν γενέσεως,[1] εἴτε ἔστιν
εἴτε μή, καὶ πῶς ἔστι, καὶ περὶ ἀλλοιώσεως διωρίσθω τοῦτον τὸν τρόπον.

5. Περὶ δὲ αὐξήσεως λοιπὸν εἰπεῖν, τί τε διαφέρει γενέσεως καὶ ἀλλοιώσεως, καὶ πῶς αὐξάνεται
10 τῶν αὐξανομένων ἕκαστον καὶ φθίνει ὁτιοῦν τῶν
φθινόντων. σκεπτέον δὴ πρῶτον πότερον μόνως
ἐν τῷ περὶ ὅ ἐστιν αὐτῶν ἡ πρὸς ἄλληλα διαφορά,
οἷον ὅτι ἡ μὲν ἐκ τοῦδε εἰς τόδε μεταβολή, οἷον ἐκ
δυνάμει οὐσίας εἰς ἐντελεχείᾳ οὐσίαν, γένεσίς ἐστιν,
ἡ δὲ περὶ μέγεθος αὔξησις, ἡ δὲ περὶ πάθος ἀλ-
15 λοίωσις· ἀμφότερα δὲ ἐκ δυνάμει ὄντων εἰς ἐντελέχειαν μεταβολὴ τῶν εἰρημένων ἐστίν, ἢ καὶ ὁ
τρόπος διαφέρει τῆς μεταβολῆς· φαίνεται γὰρ τὸ
μὲν ἀλλοιούμενον οὐκ ἐξ ἀνάγκης μεταβάλλον κατὰ
τόπον, οὐδὲ τὸ γινόμενον, τὸ δ' αὐξανόμενον καὶ
20 τὸ φθῖνον, ἄλλον δὲ τρόπον τοῦ φερομένου. τὸ μὲν
γὰρ φερόμενον ὅλον ἀλλάττει τόπον, τὸ δ' αὐξανόμενον ὥσπερ τὸ ἐλαυνόμενον· τούτου γὰρ μένοντος τὰ μόρια μεταβάλλει κατὰ τόπον, οὐχ ὥσπερ
τὰ τῆς σφαίρας· τὰ μὲν γὰρ ἐν τῷ ἴσῳ τόπῳ μεταβάλλει τοῦ ὅλου μένοντος, τὰ δὲ τοῦ αὐξανομέ-
25 νου ἀεὶ ἐπὶ πλείω τόπον, ἐπ' ἐλάττω δὲ τὰ τοῦ
φθίνοντος.

---

[1] καὶ φθορᾶς post γενέσεως add. Bekker.

certain kinds of contrariety. Let this, then, be our decision on the question about coming-to-be, whether it exists or not, and how it exists, and about " alteration."

5. It remains, therefore, for us to deal with " growth " and to discuss (*a*) how it differs from coming-to-be and from " alteration," and (*b*) how " growth " takes place in each thing that grows and how " diminution " occurs in each thing that diminishes. First we must consider whether the difference between them lies only in the sphere of each. For example, is it because the change from one thing to another (for instance, from potential to actual substance) is coming-to be, while the change in respect of magnitude is " growth " ; and the change in respect of property is " alteration," and both the last two involve a change from what is-actually to what is-potentially ? Or does the difference also lie in the manner of the change ? For it is manifest that, whereas neither that which is altering nor that which is coming-to-be necessarily changes in respect of position, that which is growing and that which is diminishing *do* change in this respect but in a manner different from that in which that which is moving changes. For that which is moving changes its place as a whole, but that which is growing changes its position like a metal which is being beaten out ; for, while it retains its place, its parts undergo local change, but not in the same manner as the parts of a revolving globe. For the latter change their places while the whole remains in an equal space, whereas the parts of that which is growing change so as to occupy an ever larger space, and the parts of that which is diminishing contract into an ever smaller space.

The nature of growth.

Growth is change in respect of size.

205

320 a

Ὅτι μὲν οὖν ἡ μεταβολὴ διαφέρει οὐ μόνον περὶ
ὃ ἀλλὰ καὶ ὡς τοῦ τε γινομένου καὶ ἀλλοιουμένου
καὶ αὐξανομένου, δῆλον. περὶ δὲ ὅ ἐστιν ἡ μεταβολὴ ἡ τῆς αὐξήσεως καὶ ἡ τῆς φθίσεως (περὶ
μέγεθος δὲ δοκεῖ εἶναι τὸ αὐξάνεσθαι καὶ φθίνειν),
30 ποτέρως ὑποληπτέον, πότερον ἐκ δυνάμει μὲν
μεγέθους καὶ σώματος, ἐντελεχείᾳ δ' ἀσωμάτου
καὶ ἀμεγέθους γίνεσθαι σῶμα καὶ μέγεθος, καὶ
τούτου διχῶς ἐνδεχομένου λέγειν, ποτέρως ἡ
αὔξησις γίνεται; πότερον ἐκ κεχωρισμένης αὐτῆς
καθ' αὑτὴν τῆς ὕλης, ἢ ἐνυπαρχούσης ἐν ἄλλῳ
320 b σώματι; ἢ ἀδύνατον ἀμφοτέρως; χωριστὴ μὲν
γὰρ οὖσα ἢ οὐδένα καθέξει τόπον, [ἢ] οἷον στιγμή
τις, ἢ κενὸν ἔσται ἢ σῶμα οὐκ αἰσθητόν. τούτων
δὲ τὸ μὲν οὐκ ἐνδέχεται, τὸ δὲ ἀναγκαῖον ἔν τινι
εἶναι· ἀεὶ γάρ που ἔσται τὸ γινόμενον ἐξ αὐτοῦ,
5 ὥστε κἀκεῖνο, ἢ καθ' αὑτὸ ἢ κατὰ συμβεβηκός.
ἀλλὰ μὴν εἴ γ' ἔν τινι ὑπάρξει, εἰ μὲν κεχωρισμένον
οὕτως ὥστε μὴ ἐκείνου καθ' αὑτὸ ἢ κατὰ συμβεβηκός τι εἶναι, συμβήσεται πολλὰ καὶ ἀδύνατα.
λέγω δ' οἷον εἰ γίνεται ἀὴρ ἐξ ὕδατος, οὐ τοῦ
ὕδατος ἔσται μεταβάλλοντος, ἀλλὰ διὰ τὸ ὥσπερ
10 ἐν ἀγγείῳ τῷ ὕδατι ἐνεῖναι τὴν ὕλην αὐτοῦ.
ἀπείρους γὰρ οὐδὲν κωλύει ὕλας εἶναι, ὥστε καὶ
γίνεσθαι ἐντελεχείᾳ. ἔτι δ' οὐδ' οὕτω φαίνεται

---

[a] i.e. either as itself occupying a place, or contained in
something else.

It is clear, then, that the changes both of that which comes-to-be and of that which " alters " and of that which " grows," differ not only in sphere but also in manner. But how are we to conceive the sphere of the change which is growth and diminution? Growth and diminution are generally regarded as taking place in the sphere of magnitude. Are we, then, to suppose that body and magnitude come-to-be out of what is potentially body and magnitude but is actually incorporeal and without magnitude? And since this can be meant in two different senses, in which of these senses does growth take place? Does it come from matter which exists separately by itself or matter previously existing in another body? Or is it impossible for growth to take place under either of these conditions? For, since the matter is separate, either it will take up no space, like a point, or else it will be void or, in other words, an imperceptible body. Of these alterations the first is impossible, and in the second the matter must be *in* something. For, in the first case, what comes-to-be from it will always be somewhere, so that the matter too must exist somewhere, either directly or indirectly [a]; in the second case, supposing it is to be in something else, if it is so separated as not to belong to that something, either directly or indirectly, many impossibilities will arise. For example, if Air comes-to-be from Water, it will not be due to any change in the Water but owing to the presence of the matter of the Air in the Water, as in a vessel. For there is nothing to prevent there being an infinite number of matters contained in the Water, so that they might actually come-to-be; and, furthermore, the Air cannot be seen coming-to-be

207

γινόμενος ἀὴρ ἐξ ὕδατος, οἷον ἐξιὼν ὑπομένοντος.

Βέλτιον τοίνυν ποιεῖν πᾶσιν ἀχώριστον τὴν ὕλην ὡς οὖσαν τὴν αὐτὴν καὶ μίαν τῷ ἀριθμῷ, τῷ λόγῳ
15 δὲ μὴ μίαν. ἀλλὰ μὴν οὐδὲ στιγμὰς θετέον οὐδὲ γραμμὰς τὴν τοῦ σώματος ὕλην διὰ τὰς αὐτὰς αἰτίας. ἐκεῖνο δὲ οὗ ταῦτα ἔσχατα, ἡ ὕλη, ἣν οὐδέποτ' ἄνευ πάθους οἷόν τε εἶναι οὐδ' ἄνευ μορφῆς. γίνεται μὲν οὖν ἁπλῶς ἕτερον ἐξ ἑτέρου, ὥσπερ καὶ ἐν ἄλλοις διώρισται, καὶ ὑπό τινος δὲ ἐντελεχείᾳ
20 ὄντος ἢ ὁμοιοειδοῦς ἢ ὁμογενοῦς, οἷον πῦρ ὑπὸ πυρὸς ἢ ἄνθρωπος ὑπ' ἀνθρώπου, ἢ ὑπ' ἐντελεχείας· σκληρὸν γὰρ οὐχ ὑπὸ σκληροῦ γίνεται. ἐπεὶ δ' ἐστὶ καὶ οὐσίας ὕλη σωματικῆς, σώματος δ' ἤδη τοιουδί (σῶμα γὰρ κοινὸν οὐδέν), ἡ αὐτὴ καὶ μεγέθους καὶ πάθους ἐστί, τῷ μὲν λόγῳ χωριστή,
25 τόπῳ δ' οὐ χωριστή, εἰ μὴ καὶ τὰ πάθη χωριστά.

Φανερὸν δὴ ἐκ τῶν διηπορημένων ὅτι οὐκ ἔστιν ἡ αὔξησις μεταβολὴ ἐκ δυνάμει μεγέθυς, ἐντελεχείᾳ δὲ μηδὲν ἔχοντος μέγεθος· χωριστὸν γὰρ ἂν εἴη τὸ κενόν, τοῦτο δ' ὅτι ἀδύνατον, εἴρηται ἐν ἑτέροις πρότερον. ἔτι δ' ἤ γε τοιαύτη μεταβολὴ
30 οὐκ αὐξήσεως ἴδιος ἀλλὰ γενέσεως· ἡ γὰρ αὔξησίς ἐστι τοῦ ἐνυπάρχοντος μεγέθους ἐπίδοσις, ἡ δὲ φθίσις μείωσις (διὸ δὴ ἔχειν τι δεῖ μέγεθος τὸ

ª See *Met.* 1032 a 12 ff.
ᵇ Or " form " ; see *Met. l.c.* 25 ff.
ᶜ In 320 a 27–b 12.
ᵈ *Phys.* iv. 6-9.

in this manner out of Water, namely, issuing forth while the Water is left as it was.

It is better, therefore, to suppose that the matter in anything is inseparable, being the same and numerically one, though not one by definition. Further, for the same reasons also, we ought not to regard the matter of the body as points or lines; matter is that which has points and lines as its *limits* and cannot possibly ever exist without qualities and without form. Now one thing comes-to-be, in the unqualified sense, out of another, as has been determined elsewhere [a] and by the agency of something which is actually either of the same species or of the same genus—for example, Fire comes-to-be through the agency of Fire and Man through that of Man—or through an actuality [b] (for that which is hard does not come-to-be through that which is hard). But since there is also a matter out of which corporeal substance comes-to-be, but already belonging to a body of such-and-such a kind (for there is no such being as body in general), this same matter is also the matter of magnitude and quality, being separable by definition but not in place, unless the properties are also separable.

Now it is clear from the difficulties which we have discussed,[c] that growth is not a change from a potential magnitude which actually has no magnitude; for then, " the void " would be separable, and that is impossible, as has already been stated elsewhere.[d] Moreover, such a change is not peculiar to growth but characteristic of coming-to-be; for growth is an increase, just as diminution is a reduction, of the already existing magnitude (hence that which grows must already possess a certain magni-

320 b

αὐξανόμενον), ὥστ᾿ οὐκ ἐξ ἀμεγέθους ὕλης δεῖ εἶναι
τὴν αὔξησιν εἰς ἐντελέχειαν μεγέθους· γένεσις γὰρ
ἂν εἴη σώματος μᾶλλον, οὐκ αὔξησις. ληπτέον δὴ

321 a μᾶλλον οἷον ἁπτομένους τῆς ζητήσεως ἐξ ἀρχῆς,
ποίου τινὸς ὄντος τοῦ αὐξάνεσθαι ἢ τοῦ φθίνειν τὰ
αἴτια ζητοῦμεν.

Φαίνεται δὴ τοῦ αὐξανομένου ὁτιοῦν μέρος ηὐ-
ξῆσθαι, ὁμοίως δὲ καὶ ἐν τῷ φθίνειν ἔλαττον γεγονέναι, ἔτι δὲ προσιόντος τινὸς αὐξάνεσθαι καὶ
5 ἀπιόντος φθίνειν. ἀναγκαῖον δὴ ἢ ἀσωμάτῳ αὐξάνεσθαι ἢ σώματι. εἰ μὲν οὖν ἀσωμάτῳ, ἔσται
χωριστὸν τὸ κενόν· ἀδύνατον δὲ μεγέθους ὕλην
εἶναι χωριστήν, ὥσπερ εἴρηται πρότερον· εἰ δὲ
σώματι, δύο ἐν τῷ αὐτῷ σώματα τόπῳ ἔσται, τό
τε αὐξόμενον καὶ τὸ αὖξον· ἔστι δὲ καὶ τοῦτο
10 ἀδύνατον. ἀλλὰ μὴν οὐδ᾿ οὕτως ἐνδέχεται λέγειν
γίνεσθαι τὴν αὔξησιν καὶ τὴν φθίσιν, ὥσπερ ὅταν
ἐξ ὕδατος ἀήρ· τότε γὰρ μείζων ὁ ὄγκος γέγονεν·
οὐ γὰρ αὔξησις τοῦτο ἀλλὰ γένεσις μὲν τοῦ εἰς ὃ
μετέβαλεν ἔσται, φθορὰ δὲ τοῦ ἐναντίου· αὔξησις
δὲ οὐδετέρου, ἀλλ᾿ ἢ οὐδενὸς ἢ εἴ τι κοινὸν ἀμφοῖν
15 ὑπάρχει, τῷ γινομένῳ καὶ τῷ φθαρέντι, οἷον εἰ
σῶμα. τὸ δ᾿ ὕδωρ οὐκ ηὔξηται οὐδ᾿ ὁ ἀήρ, ἀλλὰ
τὸ μὲν ἀπόλωλε τὸ δὲ γέγονεν· τὸ σῶμα δέ, εἴπερ,
ηὔξηται. ἀλλὰ καὶ τοῦτ᾿ ἀδύνατον. δεῖ γὰρ σώ-

---

[a] In 320 a 27 ff.   [b] i.e. steam.

tude), so that growth must not be from matter without magnitude to an actuality of magnitude ; for that would be rather a coming-to-be of a body and not a growth. We must, therefore, lay hold more closely and, as it were, get to grips with our inquiry from the beginning as to the nature of growth and diminution, the causes of which we are seeking.

It appears that every part of that which grows has increased, and likewise in diminution every part has become smaller, and, further, that growth occurs when something is added and diminution when something departs. Growth, then, must be due to the addition of something incorporeal or of a body. If it is due to something incorporeal, there will be a void existing separately ; but, as has been stated before,[a] it is impossible for matter of magnitude to exist separately ; whereas, if it grows by the addition of a body, there will be two bodies in the same place, one which grows and the other which causes the growth, and this also is impossible. But neither is it admissible for us to say that growth or diminution occurs in the manner in which it occurs when air [b] is produced from water. For then, the volume has become greater ; for it will not be a case of growth but of a coming-to-be of that into which the change has taken place, and a passing-away of its contrary. It is a growth of neither, but either of nothing or of something (for example, " body ") which belongs in common both to that which is coming-to-be and to that which has passed-away. The water has not grown nor has the air, but the former has perished and the latter has come-to-be ; and the " body," if anything, has grown. But this is also impossible ; for in our account we must preserve the character-

What is added when growth takes place ?

321 a

ζειν τῷ λόγῳ τὰ ὑπάρχοντα τῷ αὐξανομένῳ καὶ
φθίνοντι. ταῦτα δὲ τρία ἐστίν, ὧν ἓν μέν ἐστι τὸ
20 ὁτιοῦν μέρος μεῖζον γίγνεσθαι τοῦ αὐξανομένου
μεγέθους, οἷον εἰ σὰρξ τῆς σαρκός, καὶ προσιόντος
τινός, καὶ τρίτον σωζομένου τοῦ αὐξανομένου καὶ
ὑπομένοντος· ἐν μὲν γὰρ τῷ γίνεσθαί τι ἁπλῶς
ἢ φθείρεσθαι οὐχ ὑπομένει, ἐν δὲ τῷ ἀλλοιοῦσθαι
ἢ αὐξάνεσθαι ἢ φθίνειν ὑπομένει τὸ αὐτὸ τὸ αὐ-
25 ξανόμενον ἢ ἀλλοιούμενον· ἀλλ' ἔνθα μὲν τὸ πάθος
ἔνθα δὲ τὸ μέγεθος τὸ αὐτὸ οὐ μένει. εἰ δὴ ἔσται
ἡ εἰρημένη αὔξησις, ἐνδέχοιτ' ἂν μηδενός γε προσιόντος μηδὲ ὑπομένοντος αὐξάνεσθαι καὶ μηδενὸς
ἀπιόντος φθίνειν καὶ μὴ ὑπομένειν τὸ αὐξανόμενον.
ἀλλὰ δεῖ τοῦτο σώζειν· ὑπόκειται γὰρ ἡ αὔξησις
τοιοῦτον.

30 Ἀπορήσειε δ' ἄν τις καὶ τί ἐστι τὸ αὐξανόμενον, πότερον ᾧ προστίθεταί τι, οἷον εἰ τὴν κνήμην
αὐξάνει, αὕτη μείζων, ᾧ δὲ αὐξάνει, ἡ τροφή, οὔ.
διὰ τί δὴ οὖν οὐκ ἄμφω ηὔξηται; μεῖζον γὰρ καὶ
ὃ καὶ ᾧ, ὥσπερ ὅταν μίξῃς οἶνον ὕδατι· ὁμοίως
γὰρ πλεῖον ἑκάτερον. ἢ ὅτι τοῦ μὲν μένει ἡ οὐσία,
35 τοῦ δ' οὔ, οἷον τῆς τροφῆς, ἐπεὶ καὶ ἐνταῦθα τὸ
321 b ἐπικρατοῦν λέγεται ἐν τῇ μίξει, οἷον ὅτι οἶνος·
ποιεῖ γὰρ τὸ τοῦ οἴνου ἔργον ἀλλ' οὐ τὸ τοῦ ὕδατος
τὸ σύνολον μῖγμα. ὁμοίως δὲ καὶ ἐπ' ἀλλοιώσεως,
εἰ μένει σὰρξ οὖσα καὶ τὸ τί ἐστι, πάθος δέ τι

---

[a] *i.e.* the generation of air from water.
[b] *i.e.* the persistence of that which grows.
[c] In line 22 above.
[d] With λέγεται understand πλεῖον.

istics which belong to what is growing and diminishing. These characteristics are three : (*a*) that every part of the growing magnitude is greater (for example, if flesh grows, every part of it grows) ; (*b*) that it grows by the accession of something ; and (*c*) that it grows because that which grows is preserved and persists. For while a thing does not persist in unqualified coming-to-be or passing-away, in alteration and growth or diminution that which grows or alters persists in its identity, but, in the case of alteration the quality, and, in the case of growth, the magnitude does not remain the same. Now if the change mentioned above [a] is to be growth, it would be possible for something to grow without anything being added to it or persisting and to diminish without anything going away, and for that which grows not to persist. But this quality [b] must be preserved ; for it has been assumed [c] that growth has this characteristic.

One might also raise this difficulty : What is it which grows ? Is it that to which something is added ? For example, if a man grows in his leg, is it his leg which is greater, while that which makes him grow, namely, his food, is not greater ? Why have not both grown ? For both that which is added and that to which the addition was made are greater, just as when you mix wine with water ; for each ingredient is similarly increased. Or is it because the substance of the leg remains unchanged, but that of the other (*i.e.* the food) does not ? For in the mixture of the wine and water it is the prevailing ingredient which is said to increase,[d] namely the wine ; for the mixture as a whole performs the function of wine and not of water. Similarly, too, in the process of " alteration," flesh is " altered," if

What is it that grows ?

213

ὑπάρχει τῶν καθ᾽ αὑτό, ὃ πρότερον οὐχ ὑπῆρχεν,
5 ἠλλοίωται τοῦτο· ᾧ δ᾽ ἠλλοίωται, ὁτὲ μὲν οὐδὲν
πέπονθεν, ὁτὲ δὲ κἀκεῖνο. ἀλλὰ τὸ ἀλλοιοῦν καὶ
ἡ ἀρχὴ τῆς κινήσεως ἐν τῷ αὐξανομένῳ καὶ τῷ
ἀλλοιουμένῳ· ἐν τούτοις γὰρ τὸ κινοῦν, ἐπεὶ καὶ
τὸ εἰσελθὸν γένοιτ᾽ ἄν ποτε μεῖζον, καὶ τὸ ἀπο-
λαῦσαν αὐτοῦ σῶμα, οἷον εἰ εἰσελθὸν γένοιτο
10 πνεῦμα. ἀλλ᾽ ἔφθαρταί γε τοῦτο παθόν, καὶ τὸ
κινοῦν οὐκ ἐν τούτῳ.

Ἐπεὶ δὲ διηπόρηται περὶ αὐτῶν ἱκανῶς, δεῖ καὶ
τῆς ἀπορίας πειρᾶσθαι λύσιν εὑρεῖν, σῴζοντας τὸ
ὑπομένοντός τε τοῦ αὐξανομένου καὶ προσιόντος
τινὸς αὐξάνεσθαι, ἀπιόντος δὲ φθίνειν, ἔτι δὲ τὸ
ὁτιοῦν σημεῖον αἰσθητὸν ἢ μεῖζον ἢ ἔλαττον γεγο-
15 νέναι, καὶ μήτε κενὸν εἶναι τὸ σῶμα μήτε δύο ἐν
τῷ αὐτῷ τόπῳ μεγέθη μήτε ἀσωμάτῳ αὐξάνεσθαι.
ληπτέον δὲ τὸ αἴτιον διορισαμένοις πρῶτον ἓν μὲν
ὅτι τὰ ἀνομοιομερῆ αὐξάνεται τῷ τὰ ὁμοιομερῆ
αὐξάνεσθαι (σύγκειται γὰρ ἐκ τούτων ἕκαστον),
20 ἔπειθ᾽ ὅτι σὰρξ καὶ ὀστοῦν καὶ ἕκαστον τῶν τοιούτων μορίων ἐστὶ διττόν, ὥσπερ καὶ τῶν ἄλλων τῶν
ἐν ὕλῃ εἶδος ἐχόντων· καὶ γὰρ ἡ ὕλη λέγεται καὶ
τὸ εἶδος σὰρξ ἢ ὀστοῦν. τὸ οὖν ὁτιοῦν μέρος
αὐξάνεσθαι καὶ προσιόντος τινὸς κατὰ μὲν τὸ εἶδός
ἐστιν ἐνδεχόμενον, κατὰ δὲ τὴν ὕλην οὐκ ἔστιν.

---

^a *i.e.* the organic parts. ^b *i.e.* the tissue.

it remains flesh and its substance remains the same, but some inherent quality now belongs to it which did not belong before ; but that by which it has been altered sometimes has not been affected but sometimes has also been affected. But that which causes alteration and the source of movement reside in that which grows and in that which is altered (for the motive agent is within them) ; for that which has entered might sometimes become greater as well as the body which benefits by it (for example, if, after entering in, it were to become wind), but after having undergone this process, it has passed-away and the motive agent is not in it.

Now that the difficulties have been adequately discussed, we must try to find a solution of the problem. In doing so we must maintain the doctrine that growth occurs, when that which grows persists and grows by the accession of something (and diminishes by the departure of something), and that every perceptible particle has become greater (or less), and that the body is not void, and that there are not two magnitudes in the same place, and that growth does not take place by the addition of anything incorporeal. We must grasp the cause of growth by making the distinctions (i) that the parts which are not uniform *a* grow by the growth of the parts which are uniform *b*—for each part is composed of these—and (ii) that flesh and bone and every such part, like all other things which have their form in matter, are of a double nature ; for the form as well as the matter is called flesh or bone. It is quite possible, then, that any part can grow in respect of *form* by the addition of something, but not in respect of *matter* ; for we must regard the process as like that

Conclusions about growth.

215

321 b

δεῖ γὰρ νοῆσαι ὥσπερ εἴ τις μετροίη τῷ αὐτῷ
25 μέτρῳ ὕδωρ· ἀεὶ γὰρ ἄλλο καὶ ἄλλο τὸ γινόμενον.
οὕτω δ' αὐξάνεται ἡ ὕλη τῆς σαρκός, καὶ οὐχ
ὁτῳοῦν παντὶ προσγίνεται, ἀλλὰ τὸ μὲν ὑπεκρεῖ
τὸ δὲ προσέρχεται, τοῦ δὲ σχήματος καὶ τοῦ εἴδους
ὁτῳοῦν μορίῳ. ἐπὶ δὲ τῶν ἀνομοιομερῶν τοῦτο
μᾶλλον δῆλον, οἷον χειρός, ὅτι ἀνάλογον ηὔξηται·
30 ἡ γὰρ ὕλη ἑτέρα οὖσα δήλη μᾶλλον τοῦ εἴδους
ἐνταῦθα ἢ ἐπὶ σαρκὸς καὶ τῶν ὁμοιομερῶν· διὸ
καὶ τεθνεῶτος μᾶλλον ἂν δόξειεν εἶναι ἔτι σὰρξ
καὶ ὀστοῦν ἢ χεὶρ καὶ βραχίων. ὥστε ἔστι μὲν
ὡς ὁτιοῦν τῆς σαρκὸς ηὔξηται, ἔστι δ' ὡς οὔ.
κατὰ μὲν γὰρ τὸ εἶδος ὁτῳοῦν προσελήλυθεν, κατὰ
35 δὲ τὴν ὕλην οὔ. μεῖζον μέντοι τὸ ὅλον γέγονε
322 a προσελθόντος μέν τινος, ὃ καλεῖται τροφὴ καὶ
ἐναντίον, μεταβάλλοντος δὲ εἰς τὸ αὐτὸ εἶδος, οἷον
εἰ ξηρῷ προσίοι ὑγρόν, προσελθὸν δὲ μεταβάλοι
καὶ γένοιτο ξηρόν· ἔστι μὲν γὰρ ὡς τὸ ὅμοιον
ὁμοίῳ αὐξάνεται, ἔστι δ' ὡς τὸ ἀνόμοιον[1] ἀνο-
μοίῳ.
5 Ἀπορήσειε δ' ἄν τις ποῖόν τι δεῖ εἶναι τὸ ᾧ
αὐξάνεται. φανερὸν δὴ ὅτι δυνάμει ἐκεῖνο, οἷον
εἰ σάρξ, δυνάμει σάρκα. ἐντελεχείᾳ ἄρα ἄλλο·
φθαρὲν δὴ τοῦτο σὰρξ γέγονεν. οὐκοῦν οὐκ αὐτὸ
καθ' αὑτό (γένεσις γὰρ ἂν ἦν, οὐκ αὔξησις)· ἀλλὰ

[1] τὸ ἀνόμοιον addidi.

216

which happens when a man measures water with the same measure, for there is first one portion and then another in constant succession. It is in this way that the matter of the flesh grows ; something flows out and something flows in, but there is not an addition made to every particle of it, but to every part of its figure and " form." That the growth has taken place proportionally is more obvious in the parts which are not uniform, for instance, in the hand ; for there the matter, being distinct from the form, is more noticeable than in the flesh and the parts which are uniform ; for this reason one is more likely to think of a corpse as still possessing flesh and bone than that it has a hand and an arm. Therefore, in one sense it is true that every part of the flesh has grown, but in another sense it is untrue ; for in respect to its form there has been an accession to every part, but not in respect to its matter ; the whole, however, has become greater (a) by the accession of something which is called food, the " contrary " of flesh, and (b) by the change of this food into the same form as that of the flesh, just as if moist were to be added to dry, and, after having been added, were to change and become dry ; for, it is possible that " like grows by like " and also that " unlike grows by unlike."

One might raise the question what must be the nature of that by which a thing grows. It is clear that it must be potentially that which is growing, for example, potentially flesh, if it is flesh which is growing ; actually, then, it is something different. This, therefore, has passed-away and come-to-be flesh—not alone by itself (for that would have been a coming-to-be and not growth) ; but it is that which

322 a

τὸ αὐξανόμενον τούτῳ. τί οὖν παθὸν ὑπὸ τούτου
[ηὐξήθη]¹; ἢ μιχθέν, ὥσπερ οἴνῳ εἴ τις ἐπιχέοι
10 ὕδωρ, ὁ δὲ δύναιτο οἶνον ποιεῖν τὸ μιχθέν; καὶ
ὥσπερ τὸ πῦρ ἁψάμενον τοῦ καυστοῦ, οὕτως ἐν
τῷ αὐξανομένῳ καὶ ὄντι ἐντελεχείᾳ σαρκὶ τὸ ἐνὸν
αὐξητικὸν προσελθόντος δυνάμει σαρκὸς ἐποίησεν
ἐντελεχείᾳ σάρκα. οὐκοῦν ἅμα ὄντος· εἰ γὰρ χωρίς,
γένεσις. ἔστι μὲν γὰρ οὕτω πῦρ ποιῆσαι ἐπὶ τὸ
15 ὑπάρχον ἐπιθέντα ξύλα. ἀλλ' οὕτω μὲν αὔξησις,
ὅταν δὲ αὐτὰ τὰ ξύλα ἀφθῇ, γένεσις.

Ποσὸν δὲ τὸ μὲν καθόλου οὐ γίνεται, ὥσπερ
οὐδὲ ζῷον ὃ μήτ' ἄνθρωπος μήτε τῶν καθ' ἕκαστα·
ἀλλ' ὡς ἐνταῦθα τὸ καθόλου, κἀκεῖ τὸ ποσόν.
σὰρξ δὲ ἢ ὀστοῦν ἢ χεὶρ καὶ τούτων τὰ ὁμοιομερῆ,
20 προσελθόντος μὲν δή τινος ποσοῦ, ἀλλ' οὐ σαρκὸς
ποσῆς. ᾗ μὲν οὖν δυνάμει τὸ συναμφότερον, οἷον
ποσὴ σάρξ, ταύτῃ μὲν αὔξει· καὶ γὰρ ποσὴν δεῖ
γενέσθαι καὶ σάρκα· ᾗ δὲ μόνον σάρξ, τρέφει·
ταύτῃ γὰρ διαφέρει τροφὴ καὶ αὔξησις τῷ λόγῳ.
διὸ τρέφεται μὲν ἕως ἂν σώζηται καὶ φθῖνον,²
25 αὐξάνεται δὲ οὐκ ἀεί. καὶ ἡ τροφὴ τῇ αὐξήσει τὸ
αὐτὸ μέν, τὸ δ' εἶναι ἄλλο· ᾗ μὲν γάρ ἐστι τὸ

¹ ηὐξήθη seclusit Joachim.
² φθῖνον L : φθίνει F : φθίνῃ H.

ᵃ And not a growth of already existent tissue.

218

grows which now comes-to-be flesh owing to the food. How has the food been affected by the growing thing ? Is it by admixture, as if one were to pour water into wine, and the latter were able to convert the mixture into wine ? And like fire when it takes hold of inflammable material, so the principle of growth present in that which grows (*i.e.* in what is actually flesh) lays hold of the added food which is potentially flesh, and turns it into actual flesh. The added food must, therefore, be together with that which grows ; for, if it is separate, it would be a case of coming-to-be.[a] For it is possible to produce fire by placing logs on the fire which is already in existence ; in this case there is growth, but, when the logs themselves are set on fire, there is a coming-to-be of fire.

" Quantum-in-general " does not come-to-be, just as " animal," which is neither man nor any other particular animal, does not come-to-be ; but what " animal-in-general " is in coming-to-be, that " quantum-in-general " is in growth. But what comes-to-be in growth is flesh or bone or hand and the uniform parts of these, by the accession of such-and-such a quantity of something, but not of such-and-such a quantity of flesh. In so far, then, as the combination of the two, *e.g.*, so much flesh, is a potentiality, it produces growth ; for both quantity and flesh must come-to-be, but in so far as it is potentially flesh only, it nourishes ; for it is here that nutrition and growth differ in their definition. Therefore the body is nourished as long as it is kept alive, even when it is diminishing, but it is not always growing ; and nutrition, though it is the same as growth, is different in its being ; for, in so far as that which is added is

322 a

προσιὸν δυνάμει ποσὴ σάρξ, ταύτῃ μὲν αὐξητικὸν σαρκός, ᾗ δὲ μόνον δυνάμει σάρξ, τροφή.

Τοῦτο δὲ τὸ εἶδος [ἄνευ ὕλης],[1] οἷον αὐλός,[2] δύναμίς τις ἐν ὕλῃ ἐστίν. ἐὰν δέ τις προσίῃ ὕλη, οὖσα
30 δυνάμει αὐλός,[2] ἔχουσα καὶ τὸ ποσὸν δυνάμει, οὗτοι ἔσονται μείζους αὐλοί.[2] ἐὰν δὲ μηκέτι ποιεῖν δύνηται, ἀλλ' οἷον ὕδωρ οἴνῳ ἀεὶ πλεῖον μιγνύμενον τέλος ὑδαρῆ ποιεῖ καὶ ὕδωρ, τότε φθίσιν ποιεῖται τοῦ ποσοῦ, τὸ δ' εἶδος μένει.

322 b   6. Ἐπεὶ δὲ πρῶτον δεῖ περὶ τῆς ὕλης καὶ τῶν καλουμένων στοιχείων εἰπεῖν, εἴτ' ἔστιν εἴτε μή, καὶ πότερον ἀΐδιον ἕκαστον ἢ γίνεταί πως, καὶ εἰ γίνεται, πότερον ἐξ ἀλλήλων γίνεται πάντα τὸν
5 αὐτὸν τρόπον ἤ τι πρῶτον ἕν αὐτῶν ἐστίν, ἀνάγκη δὴ πρότερον εἰπεῖν περὶ ὧν ἀδιορίστως λέγεται νῦν. πάντες γὰρ οἵ τε τὰ στοιχεῖα γεννῶντες καὶ οἱ τὰ ἐκ τῶν στοιχείων διακρίσει χρῶνται καὶ συγκρίσει καὶ τῷ ποιεῖν καὶ πάσχειν. ἔστι δ' ἡ σύγκρισις μίξις· πῶς δὲ μίγνυσθαι λέγομεν, οὐ διώρισται σαφῶς. ἀλλὰ μὴν οὐδ' ἀλλοιοῦσθαι
10 δυνατόν, οὐδὲ διακρίνεσθαι καὶ συγκρίνεσθαι, μηδενὸς ποιοῦντος μηδὲ πάσχοντος· καὶ γὰρ οἱ πλείω τὰ στοιχεῖα ποιοῦντες γεννῶσι τῷ ποιεῖν καὶ πάσχειν ὑπ' ἀλλήλων, καὶ τοῖς ἐξ ἑνὸς ἀνάγκη

---

[1] ἄνευ ὕλης seclusit Joachim.
[2] αὐλός ... αὐλός ... αὐλοί Joachim : ἄυλος ... ἄυλος ... ἄυλοι codd : tibia ... tibia ... tibiae vertit Vatablus.

---

[a] In 321 b 22 ff.
[b] i.e. the Pluralists, like Anaxagoras, Democritus and Plato, who regard Earth, Air, Fire and Water as composed of some prior constituents.
[c] i.e. other Pluralists, like Empedocles, who regard them as actual elements.

potentially so much flesh, it is productive of the growth of flesh, but, in so far as it is only potentially flesh, it is nutriment.

This " form " of which we spoke [a] is a kind of power present in matter, as it were a channel. If, therefore, matter is added which is potentially a channel and also potentially possesses such-and-such a quantity, these channels will become bigger. But if the " form " is no longer able to function, but, as water mixed with wine in ever-increasing quantities eventually makes the wine waterish and converts it into water, it will cause a diminution of the quantity, though the " form " still persists.

6. We must first deal with the *matter* and the so-called " elements " and determine whether they exist or not, and whether each is eternal, or whether there is a sense in which they come-to-be, and, if so, whether they all come-to-be in the same manner out of one another, or whether one among them is something primary. We must, therefore, first deal with matters about which people at present speak only vaguely. For all those who generate the elements [b] and those who generate the bodies composed of the elements,[c] apply the terms " dissociation " and " association " and " action " and " passion." Now " association " is a process of mixing ; but what we mean by mixing has not yet been clearly defined. But there cannot be " alteration " any more than there can be " dissociation " and " association " without an " agent " and a " patient." For those who suppose the elements to be several in number ascribe the generation of composite bodies to the reciprocal " action " and " passion " of these elements, whereas those who derive them from a

*Chs. 6-10.
That which comes-to-be is formed of material constituents by their combination. Combination involves " action " and " passion " which involve " contact."*

221

λέγειν τὴν ποίησιν, καὶ τοῦτ' ὀρθῶς λέγει Διο-
γένης, ὅτι εἰ μὴ ἐξ ἑνὸς ἦν ἅπαντα, οὐκ ἂν ἦν τὸ
15 ποιεῖν καὶ τὸ πάσχειν ὑπ' ἀλλήλων, οἷον τὸ θερμὸν
ψύχεσθαι καὶ τοῦτο θερμαίνεσθαι πάλιν· οὐ γὰρ
ἡ θερμότης μεταβάλλει καὶ ἡ ψυχρότης εἰς ἄλληλα,
ἀλλὰ δῆλον ὅτι τὸ ὑποκείμενον. ὥστε ἐν οἷς τὸ
ποιεῖν ἐστὶ καὶ τὸ πάσχειν, ἀνάγκη τούτων μίαν
εἶναι τὴν ὑποκειμένην φύσιν. τὸ μὲν οὖν πάντ'
20 εἶναι τοιαῦτα φάσκειν οὐκ ἀληθές, ἀλλ' ἐν ὅσοις
τὸ ὑπ' ἀλλήλων ἐστίν.

Ἀλλὰ μὴν εἰ περὶ τοῦ ποιεῖν καὶ πάσχειν καὶ
περὶ μίξεως θεωρητέον, ἀνάγκη καὶ περὶ ἁφῆς·
οὔτε γὰρ ποιεῖν ταῦτα καὶ πάσχειν δύναται κυρίως
ἃ μὴ οἷόν τε ἅψασθαι ἀλλήλων, οὔτε μὴ ἁψάμενά
25 πως ἐνδέχεται μιχθῆναι πρῶτον. ὥστε περὶ τριῶν
τούτων διοριστέον, τί ἁφὴ καὶ τί μίξις καὶ τί
ποίησις.

Ἀρχὴν δὲ λάβωμεν τήνδε. ἀνάγκη γὰρ τῶν
ὄντων ὅσοις ἐστὶ μίξις, εἶναι ταῦτ' ἀλλήλων ἁπτικά·
κἂν εἴ τι ποιεῖ, τὸ δὲ πάσχει κυρίως, καὶ τούτοις
ὡσαύτως. διὸ πρῶτον λεκτέον περὶ ἁφῆς. σχεδὸν
30 μὲν οὖν, ὥσπερ καὶ τῶν ἄλλων ὀνομάτων ἕκαστον
λέγεται πολλαχῶς, καὶ τὰ μὲν ὁμωνύμως τὰ δὲ
θάτερα ἀπὸ τῶν ἑτέρων καὶ τῶν προτέρων, οὕτως
ἔχει καὶ περὶ ἁφῆς. ὅμως δὲ τὸ κυρίως λεγόμενον
323 a ὑπάρχει τοῖς ἔχουσι θέσιν. θέσις δ' οἷσπερ καὶ

---

^a Fr. 2 (Diels).

single element must necessarily hold that there is
" action " ; and Diogenes [a] is right in saying that
there could not be reciprocal action and passion,
unless all things were derived from one. For example,
what is hot would not become cold, and the cold
become hot again ; for it is not heat and cold which
change into one another, but it is obviously the
substratum which changes ; so that, where action
and passion exist, their underlying nature must be
one. It is not, however, true to say that *all* things
are of this kind ; but it is true of all things between
which there is reciprocal action and passion.

But if we must go into the question of " action " and " passion " and of " commingling," we must also investigate " contact." For action and passion ought properly to be possible only for such things as can touch one another ; nor can things be mixed with one another in the first instance without coming in some kind of contact. Hence we must decide about these three things, namely, what is " contact," what is " mixture," and what is " action." What is contact ?

Let us take this as our starting-point. All existing
things which can undergo mixture must be able to
come into contact with one another, and this must
also be true of any pair of things, one of which acts
and the other is acted upon in the proper sense of
the word. Therefore we must first speak about
" contact." Practically speaking, just as every other
term which is used in several senses is so used owing
to verbal coincidence or because the different senses
are derived from different prior meanings, so it is
also with " contact." Nevertheless, " contact " in
its proper sense belongs only to things which have
" position," and " position " belongs to those things

τόπος· καὶ γὰρ τοῖς μαθηματικοῖς ὁμοίως ἀποδοτέον ἀφὴν καὶ τόπον, εἴτ᾽ ἐστὶ κεχωρισμένον ἕκαστον αὐτῶν εἴτ᾽ ἄλλον τρόπον. εἰ οὖν ἐστίν, ὥσπερ
διωρίσθη πρότερον, τὸ ἅπτεσθαι τὸ τὰ ἔσχατα
5 ἔχειν ἅμα, ταῦτα ἂν ἅπτοιτο ἀλλήλων ὅσα διωρι-
σμένα μεγέθη καὶ θέσιν ἔχοντα ἅμα ἔχει τὰ ἔσχατα.
ἐπεὶ δὲ θέσις μὲν ὅσοις καὶ τόπος ὑπάρχει, τόπου
δὲ διαφορὰ πρώτη τὸ ἄνω καὶ κάτω καὶ τὰ τοιαῦτα
τῶν ἀντικειμένων, ἅπαντα τὰ ἀλλήλων ἁπτόμενα
βάρος ἂν ἔχοι ἢ κουφότητα, ἢ ἄμφω ἢ θάτερον.
10 τὰ δὲ τοιαῦτα παθητικὰ καὶ ποιητικά· ὥστε φανερὸν
ὅτι ταῦτα ἅπτεσθαι πέφυκεν ἀλλήλων, ὧν διῃρη-
μένων μεγεθῶν ἅμα τὰ ἔσχατά ἐστιν, ὄντων κινη-
τικῶν καὶ κινητῶν ὑπ᾽ ἀλλήλων. ἐπεὶ δὲ τὸ κινοῦν
οὐχ ὁμοίως κινεῖ τὸ κινούμενον, ἀλλὰ τὸ μὲν ἀνάγκη
κινούμενον καὶ αὐτὸ κινεῖν, τὸ δ᾽ ἀκίνητον ὄν, δῆ-
15 λον ὅτι καὶ ἐπὶ τοῦ ποιοῦντος ἐροῦμεν ὡσαύτως·
καὶ γὰρ τὸ κινοῦν ποιεῖν τί φασι καὶ τὸ ποιοῦν
κινεῖν. οὐ μὴν ἀλλὰ διαφέρει γε καὶ δεῖ διορίζειν·
οὐ γὰρ οἷόν τε πᾶν τὸ κινοῦν ποιεῖν, εἴπερ τὸ
ποιοῦν ἀντιθήσομεν τῷ πάσχοντι, τοῦτο δ᾽ οἷς ἡ
κίνησις πάθος, πάθος δὲ καθ᾽ ὅσον ἀλλοιοῦται

---

which have also a " place " ; for " place," just as much
as " contact," must be attributed to mathematical
objects, whether each exists in separation or in some
other manner. If, therefore, as has been defined in
a previous work,[a] for things to be in " contact " they
must have their extremities together, only those
things would be in contact with one another, which,
possessing definite magnitudes and a definite position, have their extremities together. Now, since
position belongs to such things as also have a " place,"
and the primary differentiation of " place " is " above "
and " below " and other such pairs of opposites, all
things which are in contact with one another would
have " weight " and " lightness," either both of these
qualities or one or other of them. Now such things
are capable of " acting " and " being acted upon " ;
so that it is clear that those things are of a nature
to be in contact with one another, the extremities
of whose separate magnitudes are " together " and
which are capable of moving one another and being
moved by one another. But, since that which moves
does not always move that which is moved in the
same way, but one mover must move by being itself moved, and another while itself remaining unmoved, it is clear that we must speak in the same
terms about that which " acts " ; for the " moving
thing " is said to " act " (in a sense) and the " acting
thing " to " move." There is, however, a difference,
and a distinction must be made ; for not every
" mover " can " act," if we are going to employ the
term " agent " in contrast to the term " patient,"
and the term " patient " is applied only to those
things for which the movement is an " affection " [b]

[b] See *Met*. x. 1022 b 15 ff.

323 a

20 μόνον, οἷον τὸ λευκὸν καὶ τὸ θερμόν· ἀλλὰ τὸ κινεῖν
ἐπὶ πλέον τοῦ ποιεῖν ἐστίν. ἐκεῖνο δ' οὖν φανερόν,
ὅτι ἔστι μὲν ὡς τὰ κινοῦντα τῶν κινητῶν ἅπτοιτ'
ἄν, ἔστι δ' ὡς οὔ. ἀλλ' ὁ διορισμὸς τοῦ ἅπτεσθαι
καθόλου μὲν ὁ τῶν θέσιν ἐχόντων καὶ τοῦ μὲν
κινητικοῦ τοῦ δὲ κινητοῦ, πρὸς ἄλληλα δέ, κινη-
25 τικοῦ καὶ κινητοῦ ἐν οἷς ὑπάρχει τὸ ποιεῖν καὶ τὸ
πάσχειν. ἔστι μὲν οὖν ὡς ἐπὶ τὸ πολὺ τὸ ἁπτόμενον ἁπτομένου ἁπτόμενον· καὶ γὰρ κινεῖ κινούμενα πάντα σχεδὸν τὰ ἐμποδών, ὅσοις ἀνάγκη καὶ
φαίνεται τὸ ἁπτόμενον ἅπτεσθαι ἁπτομένου· ἔστι
δ', ὡς ἐνίοτέ φαμεν, τὸ κινοῦν ἅπτεσθαι μόνον τοῦ
κινουμένου, τὸ δ' ἁπτόμενον μὴ ἅπτεσθαι ἁπτο-
30 μένου· ἀλλὰ διὰ τὸ κινεῖν κινούμενα τὰ ὁμογενῆ,
ἀνάγκη δοκεῖ εἶναι ἁπτομένου ἅπτεσθαι. ὥστε εἴ
τι κινεῖ ἀκίνητον ὄν, ἐκεῖνο μὲν ἂν ἅπτοιτο τοῦ
κινητοῦ, ἐκείνου δὲ οὐδέν· φαμὲν γὰρ ἐνίοτε τὸν
λυποῦντα ἅπτεσθαι ἡμῶν, ἀλλ' οὐκ αὐτοὶ ἐκείνου.
περὶ μὲν οὖν ἁφῆς τῆς ἐν τοῖς φυσικοῖς διωρίσθω
τοῦτον τὸν τρόπον.

323 b   7. Περὶ δὲ τοῦ ποιεῖν καὶ πάσχειν λεκτέον ἐφεξῆς, παρειλήφαμεν δὲ παρὰ τῶν πρότερον ὑπεναν-

(an " affection," that is, such as whiteness and heat, in virtue of which they only undergo " alteration "), whereas to " move " is a wider term than to " act." But this, at any rate, is clear, that there is a sense in which the things which move can come into contact with the things which are capable of being moved, and a sense in which they cannot do so. But the distinction between contact in the most general sense and " reciprocal contact " is that, in the first sense, two objects should have position and that one should be capable of moving and the other of being moved ; in the second sense, that there should be one thing capable of moving and another of being moved, possessing, respectively, the qualities of " agent " and " patient." Generally, no doubt, if one thing touches another, the latter also touches the former ; for almost all things, when they move, cause motion in the things which stand in their way, and in these cases that which touches must, and obviously *does*, touch that which touches it. But it is possible, as we say sometimes, for that which causes motion merely to touch that which is moved, and that which touches need not touch something which touches it ; but because things of the same kind impart motion by being moved, it seems to follow necessarily that they touch that which touches them. Hence, if anything causes motion without being itself moved, it might touch that which is moved, though not itself touched by anything ; for we say sometimes that a man who grieves us " touches " us, though we ourselves do not " touch " him. So much for our definition of contact in the realm of Nature.

7. Next we must deal with " action " and " passion." We have inherited conflicting accounts from " Action " and " Passion ";

τίους ἀλλήλοις λόγους. οἱ μὲν γὰρ πλεῖστοι τοῦτό
γε ὁμονοητικῶς λέγουσιν, ὡς τὸ μὲν ὅμοιον ὑπὸ
5 τοῦ ὁμοίου πᾶν ἀπαθές ἐστι διὰ τὸ μηδὲν μᾶλλον ποιητικὸν ἢ παθητικὸν εἶναι θάτερον θατέρου
(πάντα γὰρ ὁμοίως ὑπάρχειν ταὐτὰ τοῖς ὁμοίοις),
τὰ δ᾽ ἀνόμοια καὶ τὰ διάφορα ποιεῖν καὶ πάσχειν
εἰς ἄλληλα πέφυκεν. καὶ γὰρ ὅταν τὸ ἔλαττον
πῦρ ὑπὸ τοῦ πλείονος φθείρηται, διὰ τὴν ἐναντίωσιν
10 τοῦτό φασι πάσχειν· ἐναντίον γὰρ εἶναι τὸ πολὺ
τῷ ὀλίγῳ. Δημόκριτος δὲ παρὰ τοὺς ἄλλους ἰδίως
ἔλεξε μόνος· φησὶ γὰρ τὸ αὐτὸ καὶ ὅμοιον εἶναι
τό τε ποιοῦν καὶ τὸ πάσχον· οὐ γὰρ ἐγχωρεῖν τὰ
ἕτερα καὶ διαφέροντα πάσχειν ὑπ᾽ ἀλλήλων, ἀλλὰ
κἂν ἕτερα ὄντα ποιῇ τι εἰς ἄλληλα, οὐχ ᾗ ἕτερα
15 ἀλλ᾽ ᾗ ταὐτόν τι ὑπάρχει, ταύτῃ τοῦτο συμβαίνειν
αὐτοῖς.

Τὰ μὲν οὖν λεγόμενα ταῦτ᾽ ἐστίν, ἐοίκασι δὲ
οἱ τοῦτον τὸν τρόπον λέγοντες ὑπεναντία φαίνεσθαι λέγειν. αἴτιον δὲ τῆς ἐναντιολογίας ὅτι
δέον ὅλον τι θεωρῆσαι μέρος τι τυγχάνουσι λέγοντες ἑκάτεροι· τό τε γὰρ ὅμοιον καὶ τὸ πάντῃ
20 πάντως ἀδιάφορον εὔλογον μὴ πάσχειν ὑπὸ τοῦ
ὁμοίου μηδέν (τί γὰρ μᾶλλον θάτερον ἔσται ποιητικὸν ἢ θάτερον; εἴ τε[1] ὑπὸ τοῦ ὁμοίου τι πάσχειν
δυνατόν, καὶ αὐτὸ ὑφ᾽ αὑτοῦ· καίτοι τούτων οὕτως
ἐχόντων οὐδὲν ἂν εἴη οὔτε ἄφθαρτον οὔτε ἀκίνητον, εἴπερ τὸ ὅμοιον ᾗ ὅμοιον ποιητικόν, αὐτὸ γὰρ

---

[1] εἴ τε Bonitz : εἴτε Bekker.

our predecessors. For most of them agree in de- claring that (i) like is always unaffected by like because, of two things which are like, neither is, they argue, at all more liable than the other to act or to be acted upon (for all the same properties belong in a like degree to things which are like), and (ii) things which are unlike and different are naturally disposed to reciprocal action and passion ; for, when the lesser fire is destroyed by the greater, it is said to be thus affected owing to its contrariety, the great being the contrary of the small. Democritus, however, in disagreement with all other philosophers, held a view peculiar to himself ; for he says that the agent and the patient are the same and alike, for (he declares) it is not possible for things which are " other " and different to be affected by one another, but even if two things which are " other " do act in any way upon one another, this occurs to them not in as much as they are " other," but because some identical property belongs to them both.

These, then, are the views expressed, and it appears that those who so expressed them were obviously in opposition to one another. But the reason of this opposition is that each school, when they ought to have viewed the problem as a whole, in fact only stated part of the truth. For, firstly, it is reasonable to hold that that which is like another thing, that is, in every respect absolutely without difference from it, cannot be in any way affected by the other thing which is like it. (For why should one be more likely to act than the other ? And if like can be affected by like, it can also be affected by itself ; yet, if that were so—if like were liable to act *qua* like—nothing would be indestructible or immovable, for everything

323 b

25 αὐτὸ κινήσει πᾶν)· τό τε παντελῶς ἕτερον καὶ
τὸ μηδαμῇ ταὐτὸν ὡσαύτως. οὐδὲν γὰρ ἂν πάθοι
λευκότης ὑπὸ γραμμῆς ἢ γραμμὴ ὑπὸ λευκότητος,
πλὴν εἰ μή που κατὰ συμβεβηκός, οἷον εἰ συμβέβηκε λευκὴν ἢ μέλαιναν εἶναι τὴν γραμμήν· οὐκ
ἐξίστησι γὰρ ἄλληλα τῆς φύσεως ὅσα μήτ' ἐναντία
30 μήτ' ἐξ ἐναντίων ἐστίν. ἀλλ' ἐπεὶ οὐ τὸ τυχὸν
πέφυκε πάσχειν καὶ ποιεῖν, ἀλλ' ὅσα ἢ ἐναντία
ἐστὶν ἢ ἐναντίωσιν ἔχει, ἀνάγκη καὶ τὸ ποιοῦν καὶ
τὸ πάσχον τῷ γένει μὲν ὅμοιον εἶναι καὶ ταὐτό,
τῷ δ' εἴδει ἀνόμοιον καὶ ἐναντίον (πέφυκε γὰρ
σῶμα μὲν ὑπὸ σώματος, χυμὸς δ' ὑπὸ χυμοῦ,
324 a χρῶμα δ' ὑπὸ χρώματος πάσχειν, ὅλως δὲ τὸ
ὁμογενὲς ὑπὸ τοῦ ὁμογενοῦς. τούτου δ' αἴτιον ὅτι
τἀναντία ἐν ταὐτῷ γένει πάντα, ποιεῖ δὲ καὶ πάσχει τἀναντία ὑπ' ἀλλήλων), ὥστ' ἀνάγκη πῶς μὲν
εἶναι ταὐτὰ τό τε ποιοῦν καὶ τὸ πάσχον, πῶς δ'
5 ἕτερα καὶ ἀνόμοια ἀλλήλοις. ἐπεὶ δὲ καὶ τὸ πάσχον καὶ τὸ ποιοῦν τῷ μὲν γένει ταὐτὰ καὶ ὅμοια
τῷ δ' εἴδει ἀνόμοια, τοιαῦτα δὲ τἀναντία, φανερὸν
ὅτι παθητικὰ καὶ ποιητικὰ ἀλλήλων ἐστὶ τά τ'
ἐναντία καὶ τὰ μεταξύ· καὶ γὰρ ὅλως φθορὰ καὶ
γένεσις ἐν τούτοις.

10 Διὸ καὶ εὔλογον ἤδη τό τε πῦρ θερμαίνειν καὶ
τὸ ψυχρὸν ψύχειν, καὶ ὅλως τὸ ποιητικὸν ὁμοιοῦν
ἑαυτῷ τὸ πάσχον· τό τε γὰρ ποιοῦν καὶ τὸ πάσχον
ἐναντία ἐστί, καὶ ἡ γένεσις εἰς τοὐναντίον. ὥστ'

230

will move itself.) And, secondly, the same thing happens if there is complete difference and no kind of identity. For whiteness could not be affected in any degree by line, or line by whiteness, except perhaps incidentally, if, for example, it happened that the line was white or black ; for unless the two things are contraries or made up of contraries, one cannot displace the other from its natural condition. But, since only such things as possess contrariety or are themselves actual contraries—and not any chance things—are naturally adapted to be acted upon and to act, both " agent " and " patient " must be alike and identical in kind, but unlike and contrary in species. For body is by nature adapted so as to be affected by body, flavour by flavour, colour by colour, and in general that which is of the same kind by something else of the same kind ; and the reason of this is that contraries are always within the same kind, and it is contraries which act and are acted upon reciprocally. Hence " agent " and " patient " are necessarily in one sense the same, and in another sense " other " and unlike one another ; and since " agent " and " patient " are identical in kind and like, but unlike in species, and it is contraries which have these characteristics, it is clear that contraries and their " intermediates " are capable of being affected and of acting reciprocally—indeed it is entirely these processes which constitute passing-away and coming-to-be.

It is, then, now reasonable to hold both that fire heats and that what is cold cools and, in general, that what is active assimilates that which is passive to itself ; for the agent and patient are contrary to one another, and coming-to-be is a process into the

Aristotle's definition of " agent " and " patient."

ἀνάγκη τὸ πάσχον εἰς τὸ ποιοῦν μεταβάλλειν·
οὕτω γὰρ ἔσται εἰς τοὐναντίον ἡ γένεσις. καὶ
15 κατὰ λόγον δὴ τὸ μὴ ταὐτὰ λέγοντας ἀμφοτέρους
ὅμως ἅπτεσθαι τῆς φύσεως. λέγομεν γὰρ πάσχειν
ὁτὲ μὲν τὸ ὑποκείμενον (οἷον ὑγιάζεσθαι τὸν ἄνθρωπον καὶ θερμαίνεσθαι καὶ ψύχεσθαι καὶ τἆλλα τὸν
αὐτὸν τρόπον), ὁτὲ δὲ θερμαίνεσθαι μὲν τὸ ψυχρόν,
ὑγιάζεσθαι δὲ τὸ κάμνον· ἀμφότερα δ' ἐστὶν ἀληθῆ
20 (τὸν αὐτὸν δὲ τρόπον καὶ ἐπὶ τοῦ ποιοῦντος· ὁτὲ
μὲν γὰρ τὸν ἄνθρωπόν φαμεν θερμαίνειν, ὁτὲ δὲ
τὸ θερμόν· ἔστι μὲν γὰρ ὡς ἡ ὕλη πάσχει, ἔστι δ'
ὡς τοὐναντίον). οἱ μὲν οὖν εἰς ἐκεῖνο βλέψαντες
ταὐτόν τι δεῖν ᾠήθησαν τὸ ποιοῦν ἔχειν καὶ τὸ
πάσχον, οἱ δ' εἰς θάτερα τοὐναντίον.

25 Τὸν αὐτὸν δὲ λόγον ὑποληπτέον εἶναι περὶ τοῦ
ποιεῖν καὶ πάσχειν ὅνπερ καὶ περὶ τοῦ κινεῖν καὶ
κινεῖσθαι. διχῶς γὰρ λέγεται καὶ τὸ κινοῦν· ἐν
ᾧ τε γὰρ ἡ ἀρχὴ τῆς κινήσεως, δοκεῖ τοῦτο κινεῖν
(ἡ γὰρ ἀρχὴ πρώτη τῶν αἰτίων), καὶ πάλιν τὸ
ἔσχατον πρὸς τὸ κινούμενον καὶ τὴν γένεσιν.
ὁμοίως δὲ καὶ περὶ τοῦ ποιοῦντος· καὶ γὰρ τὸν
30 ἰατρόν φαμεν ὑγιάζειν καὶ τὸν οἶνον. τὸ μὲν οὖν
πρῶτον κινοῦν οὐδὲν κωλύει ἐν μὲν κινήσει ἀκίνητον εἶναι (ἐπ' ἐνίων δὲ καὶ ἀναγκαῖον), τὸ δ'
ἔσχατον ἀεὶ κινεῖν κινούμενον, ἐπὶ δὲ ποιήσεως

---

a *i.e.* immediately next to that which is moved.

contrary, so that the patient must change into the agent, since only thus will coming-to-be be a process into the contrary. And it is reasonable to suppose that both schools, though they do not express the same views, are yet in touch with the nature of things. For we sometimes say that it is the substratum which is acted upon (for example, we talk of a man as being restored to health and warmed and chilled and so on), and sometimes we say that what is cold is being warmed and what is ill is being restored to health. Both these ways of putting the case are true (and similarly with the agent : for at one time we say that it is the man that causes heat, and at another time that it is that which is hot ; for in one sense it is the matter which is acted upon and in another sense it is the " contrary "). One school, therefore, directed its attention to the substratum and thought that the agent and patient must possess something identical, the other school, with its attention on the contraries, held the opposite view.

We must suppose that the same account holds good of " action " and " passion " as about moving and being moved. For " move " is also used in two senses ; for that in which the original source of motion resides is generally held to cause motion (for the original source is the first of causes), and so also is that which is last in relation to that which is moved [a] and to the process of coming-to-be. Similarly, too, in the case of the agent ; for we speak of the doctor, and also of wine, as healing. Now, in motion, there is nothing to prevent the first mover being unmoved (in fact in some cases it is actually necessary), but the last mover always causes motion by itself being moved ; and in action, there is nothing to prevent

324 a

τὸ μὲν πρῶτον ἀπαθές, τὸ δ' ἔσχατον καὶ αὐτὸ
πάσχον· ὅσα γὰρ μὴ ἔχει τὴν αὐτὴν ὕλην, ποιεῖ
35 ἀπαθῆ ὄντα (οἷον ἡ ἰατρική, αὐτὴ γὰρ ποιοῦσα
324 b ὑγίειαν οὐδὲν πάσχει ὑπὸ τοῦ ὑγιαζομένου)· τὸ
δὲ σιτίον ποιοῦν καὶ αὐτὸ πάσχει τι· ἢ γὰρ θερμαί-
νεται ἢ ψύχεται ἢ ἄλλο τι πάσχει ἅμα ποιοῦν.
ἔστι δὲ ἡ μὲν ἰατρικὴ ὡς ἀρχή, τὸ δὲ σιτίον τὸ
ἔσχατον καὶ ἁπτόμενον.

5 Ὅσα μὲν οὖν μὴ ἐν ὕλῃ ἔχει τὴν μορφήν, ταῦτα
μὲν ἀπαθῆ τῶν ποιητικῶν, ὅσα δ' ἐν ὕλῃ, παθητικά. τὴν μὲν γὰρ ὕλην λέγομεν ὁμοίως ὡς εἰπεῖν
τὴν αὐτὴν εἶναι τῶν ἀντικειμένων ὁποτερουοῦν,
ὥσπερ γένος ὄν, τὸ δὲ δυνάμενον θερμὸν εἶναι
παρόντος τοῦ θερμαντικοῦ καὶ πλησιάζοντος ἀνάγκη
10 θερμαίνεσθαι· διό, καθάπερ εἴρηται, τὰ μὲν τῶν
ποιητικῶν ἀπαθῆ τὰ δὲ παθητικά. καὶ ὥσπερ
ἐπὶ κινήσεως, τὸν αὐτὸν ἔχει τρόπον καὶ ἐπὶ τῶν
ποιητικῶν· ἐκεῖ τε γὰρ τὸ πρώτως κινοῦν ἀκίνητον,
καὶ ἐπὶ τῶν ποιητικῶν τὸ πρῶτον ποιοῦν ἀπαθές.
ἔστι δὲ τὸ ποιητικὸν αἴτιον ὡς ὅθεν ἡ ἀρχὴ τῆς
15 κινήσεως. τὸ δ' οὗ ἕνεκα οὐ ποιητικόν (διὸ ἡ
ὑγίεια οὐ ποιητικόν, εἰ μὴ κατὰ μεταφοράν)· καὶ
γὰρ τοῦ μὲν ποιοῦντος ὅταν ὑπάρχῃ, γίνεταί τι
τὸ πάσχον, τῶν δ' ἕξεων παρουσῶν οὐκέτι γίνεται,
ἀλλ' ἔστιν ἤδη· τὰ δ' εἴδη καὶ τὰ τέλη ἕξεις τινές.

---

[a] Of which the two opposites are species.
[b] Such as " health " or " disease."

the first agent being unaffected, but the last agent is itself also affected. For those things which have not the same matter act without being themselves affected (for example, the art of the physician which, while it causes health, is not itself acted upon by that which is being healed), but food, while it acts, is itself all somehow acted upon, for, while it acts, it is at the same time being heated or cooled or affected in some other way. Now the art of the physician is, as it were, an original source, while the food is, as it were, the final mover and in contact with that which is moved.

Of the things, then, which are capable of acting, those of which the form does not consist in matter are not affected, but those of which the form consists in matter are liable to be affected ; for we say that the matter of either of the two opposed things alike is the same, so to speak, being, as it were, a kind ^{a} ; and that which is capable of being hot must become hot, if that which is capable of heating is present and near to it. Therefore, as has been said, some of the active agencies are unaffected, while others are liable to be acted upon ; and what holds good of motion is also true of the active agencies ; for as in motion the first mover is unmoved, so among active agencies the first agent is unaffected. The active agency is a cause, as being the source from which the origin of the movement comes, but the end in view is not " active " (hence health is not active, except meta-phorically) ; for, when the agent is present, the patient becomes something, but when " states " ^{b} are present, the patient no longer " becomes " but already " is," and the " forms," that is the " ends," are a kind of " state," but the matter, *qua* matter,

ἡ δ' ὕλη ᾗ ὕλη παθητικόν. τὸ μὲν οὖν πῦρ ἔχει ἐν
20 ὕλῃ τὸ θερμόν· εἰ δέ τι εἴη θερμὸν χωριστόν, τοῦτο
οὐδὲν ἂν πάσχοι. τοῦτο μὲν οὖν ἴσως ἀδύνατον
εἶναι χωριστόν· εἰ δ' ἐστὶν ἔνια τοιαῦτα, ἐπ' ἐκείνων ἂν εἴη τὸ λεγόμενον ἀληθές. τί μὲν οὖν τὸ
ποιεῖν καὶ πάσχειν ἐστὶ καὶ τίσιν ὑπάρχει καὶ διὰ
τί καὶ πῶς, διωρίσθω τοῦτον τὸν τρόπον.

25 8. Πῶς δὲ ἐνδέχεται τοῦτο συμβαίνειν, πάλιν
λέγωμεν. τοῖς μὲν οὖν δοκεῖ πάσχειν ἕκαστον διά
τινων πόρων εἰσιόντος τοῦ ποιοῦντος ἐσχάτου καὶ
κυριωτάτου, καὶ τοῦτον τὸν τρόπον καὶ ὁρᾶν καὶ
ἀκούειν ἡμᾶς φασὶ καὶ τὰς ἄλλας αἰσθήσεις αἰσθάνεσθαι πάσας, ἔτι δὲ ὁρᾶσθαι διά τε ἀέρος καὶ ὕδα-
30 τος καὶ τῶν διαφανῶν, διὰ τὸ πόρους ἔχειν ἀοράτους
μὲν διὰ μικρότητα, πυκνοὺς δὲ καὶ κατὰ στοῖχον,
καὶ μᾶλλον ἔχειν τὰ διαφανῆ μᾶλλον.

Οἱ μὲν οὖν ἐπί τινων οὕτω διώρισαν, ὥσπερ
καὶ Ἐμπεδοκλῆς, οὐ μόνον ἐπὶ τῶν ποιούντων
καὶ πασχόντων, ἀλλὰ καὶ μίγνυσθαί φασιν ὅσων
35 οἱ πόροι σύμμετροι πρὸς ἀλλήλους εἰσίν· ὁδῷ
325 a δὲ μάλιστα καὶ περὶ πάντων ἑνὶ λόγῳ διωρί-
κασι Λεύκιππος καὶ Δημόκριτος, ἀρχὴν ποιησά-
μενοι κατὰ φύσιν ἥπερ ἐστίν. ἐνίοις γὰρ τῶν
ἀρχαίων ἔδοξε τὸ ὂν ἐξ ἀνάγκης ἓν εἶναι καὶ
ἀκίνητον· τὸ μὲν γὰρ κενὸν οὐκ ὄν, κινηθῆναι δ'
5 οὐκ ἂν δύνασθαι μὴ ὄντος κενοῦ κεχωρισμένου,
οὐδ' αὖ πολλὰ εἶναι μὴ ὄντος τοῦ διείργοντος.

---

[a] Namely, Parmenides and Melissus.

is passive. Now fire holds the heat embodied in matter : but, if there were such a thing as " the hot " apart from matter, it could not be acted upon at all. Heat, therefore, perhaps cannot exist separately ; but, if there are any such separate existences, what we are saying would be true of them also. Let this, then, be our explanation of " action " and " passion," and when they exist, and why and how.

8. Let us now go back and discuss how it is possible for action and passion to occur. Some people hold that each patient is acted upon when the last agent —the agent in the strictest sense—enters in through certain pores, and they say that it is in this way that we also see and hear and employ our other senses. Furthermore, they say that things are seen through air and water and the other transparent bodies, because they have pores, which, owing to their minuteness, are invisible, but are set close together and in rows, and are more transparent the closer together and in more serried array they are. *How do " action " and " passion " occur ?*

Some philosophers (including Empedocles) held this theory as regards certain bodies, not confining it to those which act and are acted upon ; but mixture also, they assert, takes place only between bodies whose pores are symmetrical with one another. The most methodical theory, however, and the one of most general application has been that enunciated by Leucippus and Democritus, taking what is the natural starting-point. For some of the ancient thinkers [a] held that " what is " must necessarily be one and immovable ; for they argued that the void does not exist, but that, if there is not a void existing separately, " what is " could not be moved ; nor, again, could there be a multiplicity of things, since *The " pores " theory of Empedocles.*

325 a

τοῦτο δ' οὐδὲν διαφέρειν, εἴ τις οἴεται μὴ συνεχὲς
εἶναι τὸ πᾶν ἀλλ' ἅπτεσθαι διῃρημένον, τοῦ φάναι
πολλὰ καὶ μὴ ἓν εἶναι καὶ κενόν. εἰ μὲν γὰρ πάντῃ
διαιρετόν, οὐδὲν εἶναι ἕν, ὥστε οὐδὲ πολλά, ἀλλὰ
10 κενὸν τὸ ὅλον· εἰ δὲ τῇ μὲν τῇ δὲ μή, πεπλασμένῳ
τινὶ τοῦτ' ἐοικέναι· μέχρι πόσου γὰρ καὶ διὰ τί
τὸ μὲν οὕτως ἔχει τοῦ ὅλου καὶ πλῆρές ἐστι, τὸ
δὲ διῃρημένον; ἔτι ὁμοίως φάναι ἀναγκαῖον μὴ
εἶναι κίνησιν. ἐκ μὲν οὖν τούτων τῶν λόγων,
ὑπερβάντες τὴν αἴσθησιν καὶ παριδόντες αὐτὴν ὡς
15 τῷ λόγῳ δέον ἀκολουθεῖν, ἓν καὶ ἀκίνητον τὸ πᾶν
εἶναί φασι, καὶ ἄπειρον ἔνιοι· τὸ γὰρ πέρας περ-
αίνειν ἂν πρὸς τὸ κενόν. οἱ μὲν οὖν οὕτως καὶ
διὰ ταύτας τὰς αἰτίας ἀπεφήναντο περὶ τῆς ἀλη-
θείας· ἔτι δὲ ἐπὶ μὲν τῶν λόγων δοκεῖ ταῦτα συμβαίνειν, ἐπὶ δὲ τῶν πραγμάτων μανία παραπλήσιον
20 εἶναι τὸ δοξάζειν οὕτως· οὐδένα γὰρ τῶν μαινο-
μένων ἐξεστάναι τοσοῦτον ὥστε τὸ πῦρ ἓν εἶναι
δοκεῖν καὶ τὸν κρύσταλλον, ἀλλὰ μόνον τὰ καλὰ
καὶ τὰ φαινόμενα διὰ συνήθειαν, ταῦτ' ἐνίοις διὰ
τὴν μανίαν οὐδὲν δοκεῖ διαφέρειν.

Λεύκιππος δ' ἔχειν ᾠήθη λόγους οἵτινες πρὸς τὴν
αἴσθησιν ὁμολογούμενα λέγοντες οὐκ ἀναιρήσουσιν
25 οὔτε γένεσιν οὔτε φθορὰν οὔτε κίνησιν καὶ τὸ πλῆθος
τῶν ὄντων. ὁμολογήσας δὲ ταῦτα μὲν τοῖς φαινομένοις, τοῖς δὲ τὸ ἓν κατασκευάζουσιν ὡς οὐκ[1] ἂν

---

[1] οὐκ Ε : οὔτε FHJL.

---

[a] *i.e.* the Monists.

there is nothing which keeps them apart; and they declare that, if one holds that the universe is not continuous but maintains contact in separation, this does not differ from saying that things are " many " (and not " one ") and that there is a void. For if the universe is divisible throughout, there is no " one," and therefore no " many," but the whole is void; but to suppose that it is divisible at one point but not at another seems like a baseless invention. For how far is it divisible? And why is part of the whole indivisible and a *plenum*, and part divided? Moreover, they say that it is equally necessary to deny the existence of motion. As a result, then, of these arguments, going beyond and disregarding sense-perception, on the plea that they ought to follow reason, they assert that the universe is one and immovable; some add that it is infinite as well, for the limit would be a limit against the void. Some philosophers, then, set forth their views about the truth in this manner and based them on these grounds. Furthermore, though these opinions seem to follow logically from the arguments, yet, in view of the facts, to hold them seems almost madness; for no madman is so out of his senses as to hold that fire and ice are " one "; it is only between things which *are* good and things which, through habit, *seem* to be good, that some people, in their madness, see no difference.

Leucippus, however, thought that he had arguments, which, while agreeing with sense-perception, would not do away with coming-to-be and passing-away, or motion, or the multiplicity of things which are. While making these concessions to things as they appear, and conceding to those who postulate the oneness of things [a] that there could not be motion

The " atoms and void " theory of Leucippus and Democritus.

325 a

κίνησιν οὖσαν ἄνευ κενοῦ τό τε κενὸν μὴ ὄν, καὶ τοῦ
ὄντος οὐδὲν μὴ ὂν φησιν εἶναι. τὸ γὰρ κυρίως ὂν
παμπληθὲς ὄν· ἀλλ' εἶναι τὸ τοιοῦτον οὐχ ἕν, ἀλλ'
30 ἄπειρα τὸ πλῆθος καὶ ἀόρατα διὰ σμικρότητα τῶν
ὄγκων. ταῦτα δ' ἐν τῷ κενῷ φέρεσθαι (κενὸν γὰρ
εἶναι), καὶ συνιστάμενα μὲν γένεσιν ποιεῖν, δια-
λυόμενα δὲ φθοράν. ποιεῖν δὲ καὶ πάσχειν ᾗ τυγ-
χάνουσιν ἁπτόμενα (ταύτῃ γὰρ οὐχ ἓν εἶναι), καὶ
35 συντιθέμενα δὲ καὶ περιπλεκόμενα γεννᾶν· ἐκ δὲ
τοῦ κατ' ἀλήθειαν ἑνὸς οὐκ ἂν γενέσθαι πλῆθος, οὐδ'
ἐκ τῶν ἀληθῶς πολλῶν ἕν, ἀλλ' εἶναι τοῦτ' ἀδύνα-
325 b τον, ἀλλ' ὥσπερ Ἐμπεδοκλῆς καὶ τῶν ἄλλων τινές
φασι πάσχειν διὰ πόρων, οὕτω πᾶσαν ἀλλοίωσιν
καὶ πᾶν τὸ πάσχειν τοῦτον γίνεσθαι τὸν τρόπον, διὰ
τοῦ κενοῦ γινομένης τῆς διαλύσεως καὶ τῆς φθο-
5 ρᾶς, ὁμοίως δὲ καὶ τῆς αὐξήσεως, ὑπεισδυομένων
στερεῶν.

Σχεδὸν δὲ καὶ Ἐμπεδοκλεῖ ἀναγκαῖον λέγειν,
ὥσπερ καὶ Λεύκιππός φησιν· εἶναι γὰρ ἄττα στερεά,
ἀδιαίρετα δέ, εἰ μὴ πάντῃ πόροι συνεχεῖς εἰσίν.
τοῦτο δ' ἀδύνατον· οὐδὲν γὰρ ἔσται ἕτερον στερεὸν
παρὰ τοὺς πόρους, ἀλλὰ πᾶν κενόν. ἀνάγκη ἄρα
10 τὰ μὲν ἁπτόμενα εἶναι ἀδιαίρετα, τὰ δὲ μεταξὺ
αὐτῶν κενά, οὓς ἐκεῖνος λέγει πόρους. οὕτως δὲ
καὶ Λεύκιππος λέγει περὶ τοῦ ποιεῖν καὶ πάσχειν.

Οἱ μὲν οὖν τρόποι καθ' οὓς τὰ μὲν ποιεῖ τὰ δὲ
πάσχει, σχεδὸν οὗτοι λέγονται· καὶ περὶ μὲν τού-

without a void, he declares that the void is " not being," and nothing of " what is " is " not being " ; for " what is " in the strictest sense is a complete *plenum*. " But this ' *plenum*,' " he says, " is not one but many things of infinite number, and invisible owing to the minuteness of their bulk. These are carried along in the void (for there *is* a void) and, when they come together, they cause coming-to-be and, when they dissolve, they cause passing-away. They act and are acted upon where they happen to come into contact (for there they are not one), and they generate when they are placed together and intertwined. But from that which is truly one, a multiplicity could never come-into-being, nor a one from the truly many ; but this is impossible. But " (just as Empedocles and some of the other philosophers say that things are acted upon through their pores) " all ' alteration ' and all ' passion ' occur in this way, dissolution and passing-away taking place by means of the void, and likewise also growth, when solids creep into the voids."

Empedocles, too, is almost compelled to take the same view as Leucippus ; for he says that there are certain solids, but they are indivisible, unless there are continuous pores throughout. But this is impossible ; for then there will be nothing solid except the pores, but the whole will be void. It necessarily follows, therefore, that those things which are in contact are indivisible, but the spaces between them, which he calls pores, must be void. This is also Leucippus' view about " action " and " passion."

These, then, are, roughly speaking, the accounts given of the way in which some things " act " and other things are " acted upon." As regards this

των, καὶ πῶς λέγουσι, δῆλον, καὶ πρὸς τὰς αὐτῶν
15 θέσεις αἷς χρῶνται σχεδὸν ὁμολογουμένως φαίνεται συμβαῖνον. τοῖς δ' ἄλλοις ἧττον, οἷον Ἐμπεδοκλεῖ τίνα τρόπον ἔσται γένεσις καὶ φθορὰ καὶ
ἀλλοίωσις, οὐ δῆλον. τοῖς μὲν γάρ ἐστιν ἀδιαίρετα
τὰ πρῶτα τῶν σωμάτων, σχήματι διαφέροντα
μόνον, ἐξ ὧν πρώτων σύγκειται καὶ εἰς ἃ ἔσχατα
20 διαλύεται· Ἐμπεδοκλεῖ δὲ τὰ μὲν ἄλλα φανερὸν
ὅτι μέχρι τῶν στοιχείων ἔχει τὴν γένεσιν καὶ τὴν
φθοράν, αὐτῶν δὲ τούτων πῶς γίνεται καὶ φθείρεται τὸ σωρευόμενον μέγεθος, οὔτε δῆλον οὔτε
ἐνδέχεται λέγειν αὐτῷ μὴ λέγοντι καὶ τοῦ πυρὸς
εἶναι στοιχεῖον, ὁμοίως δὲ καὶ τῶν ἄλλων ἁπάντων,
25 ὥσπερ ἐν τῷ Τιμαίῳ γέγραφε Πλάτων· τοσοῦτον
γὰρ διαφέρει τοῦ μὴ τὸν αὐτὸν τρόπον Λευκίππῳ
λέγειν, ὅτι ὁ μὲν στερεὰ ὁ δ' ἐπίπεδα λέγει τὰ
ἀδιαίρετα, καὶ ὁ μὲν ἀπείροις ὡρίσθαι σχήμασι
[τῶν ἀδιαιρέτων στερεῶν ἕκαστον], ὁ δὲ ὡρισμένοις,
ἐπεὶ ἀδιαίρετά γε ἀμφότεροι λέγουσι καὶ ὡρισμένα
30 σχήμασιν. ἐκ δὴ τούτων αἱ γενέσεις καὶ αἱ δια-
κρίσεις Λευκίππῳ μὲν [δύο τρόποι ἂν εἶεν,] διά τε
τοῦ κενοῦ καὶ διὰ τῆς ἁφῆς (ταύτῃ γὰρ διαιρετὸν
ἕκαστον), Πλάτωνι δὲ κατὰ τὴν ἁφὴν μόνον· κενὸν
γὰρ οὐκ εἶναί φησιν.

Καὶ περὶ μὲν τῶν ἀδιαιρέτων ἐπιπέδων εἰρήκαμεν ἐν τοῖς πρότερον λόγοις· περὶ δὲ τῶν ἀδι-
35 αιρέτων στερεῶν τὸ μὲν ἐπὶ πλέον θεωρῆσαι τὸ

---

[a] *i.e.* Leucippus and the other Atomists.
[b] *i.e.* the Atomists.

school,[a] it is obvious what their views are and how they state them, and they are clearly more or less consistent with the suppositions which they adopt. This is less clearly the case with the other school; for example, it is not clear how, in the view of Empedocles, there are to be coming-to-be and passing-away and "alteration." For to the other school [b] the primary bodies, from which originally bodies are composed and into which ultimately they are dissolved, are indivisible, differing only in structure; but to Empedocles, it is clear that all the other bodies, down to the elements, have their coming-to-be and passing-away, but it is not evident how the accumulated mass of the elements themselves comes-to-be and passes-away; nor is it possible for him to give an explanation without asserting that there is also an element of fire and likewise of all the other kinds, as Plato has stated in the *Timaeus*.[c] For Plato is so far from giving the same account as Leucippus that, while both of them declare that the elementary constituents are indivisible and determined of figures, (*a*) Leucippus holds that the indivisibles are solid, Plato that they are planes, and (*b*) Leucippus declares that they are determined by an infinite number of figures, Plato by a definite number. It is from these indivisibles that the comings-to-be and dissolutions result: according to Leucippus, through the void and through the contact (for it is at the point of contact that each body is divisible); according to Plato, as a result of contact only, for he denies that a void exists.

Now we have dealt with indivisible planes in earlier discussions [d]; but with regard to indivisible solids, let us leave for the moment further discussion

Plato's view compared with that of Leucippus.

Neither the theory of Empedocles nor that

[c] 53 A ff.   [d] *De Caelo* 298 b 33 ff.

325 b

326 a

συμβαῖνον ἀφείσθω τὸ νῦν, ὡς δὲ μικρὸν παρεκ-
βᾶσιν εἰπεῖν, ἀναγκαῖον ἀπαθές τε ἕκαστον λέγειν
τῶν ἀδιαιρέτων (οὐ γὰρ οἷόν τε πάσχειν ἀλλ' ἢ
διὰ τοῦ κενοῦ) καὶ μηδενὸς ποιητικὸν πάθους· οὔτε
γὰρ ψυχρὸν οὔτε σκληρὸν οἷόν τ' εἶναι. καίτοι
τοῦτό γε ἄτοπον, τὸ μόνον ἀποδοῦναι τῷ περι-
5 φερεῖ σχήματι τὸ θερμόν· ἀνάγκη γὰρ καὶ τοὐναντίον τὸ ψυχρὸν ἄλλῳ τινὶ προσήκειν τῶν σχημάτων.
ἄτοπον δὲ κἂν εἰ ταῦτα μὲν ὑπάρχει, λέγω δὲ
θερμότης καὶ ψυχρότης, βαρύτης δὲ καὶ κουφότης
καὶ σκληρότης καὶ μαλακότης μὴ ὑπάρξει· καίτοι
βαρύτερόν γε κατὰ τὴν ὑπεροχὴν φησιν εἶναι
10 Δημόκριτος ἕκαστον τῶν ἀδιαιρέτων, ὥστε δῆλον
ὅτι καὶ θερμότερον. τοιαῦτα δ' ὄντα μὴ πάσχειν
ὑπ' ἀλλήλων ἀδύνατον, οἷον ὑπὸ τοῦ πολὺ ὑπερ-
βάλλοντος θερμοῦ τὸ ἠρέμα θερμόν. ἀλλὰ μὴν
εἰ σκληρόν, καὶ μαλακόν. τὸ δὲ μαλακὸν ἤδη τῷ
πάσχειν τι λέγεται· τὸ γὰρ ὑπεικτικὸν μαλακόν.
15 ἀλλὰ μὴν ἄτοπον καὶ εἰ μηδὲν ὑπάρχει ἀλλ' ἢ
μόνον σχῆμα· καὶ εἰ ὑπάρχει, ἓν δὲ μόνον, οἷον τὸ
μὲν ψυχρὸν τὸ δὲ θερμόν· οὐδὲ γὰρ ἂν μία τις εἴη
ἡ φύσις αὐτῶν. ὁμοίως δὲ ἀδύνατον καὶ εἰ πλείω
τῷ ἑνί· ἀδιαίρετον γὰρ ὂν ἐν τῷ αὐτῷ ἕξει τὰ πάθη,
20 ὥστε καὶ ἐὰν πάσχῃ εἴπερ ψύχεται, ταύτῃ τι[1]
καὶ ἄλλο ποιήσει ἢ πείσεται. τὸν αὐτὸν δὲ τρόπον
καὶ ἐπὶ τῶν ἄλλων παθημάτων· τοῦτο γὰρ καὶ

---

[1] ταύτῃ τι J : ταύτη τι EL : ταύτη τοι F : ταύτο τι H.

---

[a] i.e. of the Atomists.

of what they involve and deal with them in a short of the
digression. It is a necessary part of the theory [a] that
each " indivisible " is incapable of being acted upon
(for it cannot be acted upon except through the void)
and incapable of producing an effect on anything
else ; for it cannot be either cold or hard. Yet it
is certainly strange that heat can only be attributed
to the spherical figure ; for then it necessarily
follows that its contrary, cold, must belong to another
of the figures. It is also strange if these properties,
I mean heat and cold, belong to the indivisibles,
while heaviness and lightness and hardness and soft-
ness are not going to belong. Yet Democritus says
that the more each of the indivisibles exceeds, the
heavier it is, so that clearly it is also hotter. Being
of this kind, it is impossible that the indivisibles should
not be acted upon by one another, for example, the
slightly hot should be acted upon by what far sur-
passes it in heat. Again, if an indivisible can be
hard, it can also be soft ; and the soft is always
so-called because it can be acted upon ; for that
which yields to pressure is soft. But, further, it is
strange that no property except figure should attach
to the indivisible ; and that, if properties do attach
to them, only one should attach to each, *e.g.* that one
" indivisible " should be cold and another hot ; for,
then, neither would their substance be uniform. It
is equally impossible, too, that more than one property should belong to one indivisible, for, being
indivisible, it will possess these properties in the
same place ; so that if it is acted upon by being
chilled, it will also, in this way, act or be acted upon
in some other way. And similarly with the other
properties also ; for this problem also confronts in

245

326 a

τοῖς στερεὰ καὶ τοῖς ἐπίπεδα λέγουσιν ἀδιαίρετα
συμβαίνει τὸν αὐτὸν τρόπον· οὔτε γὰρ μανότερα
οὔτε πυκνότερα οἷόν τε γίνεσθαι κενοῦ μὴ ὄντος
25 ἐν τοῖς ἀδιαιρέτοις. ἔτι δ' ἄτοπον καὶ τὸ μικρὰ
μὲν ἀδιαίρετα εἶναι, μεγάλα δὲ μή· νῦν μὲν γὰρ
εὐλόγως τὰ μείζω θραύεται μᾶλλον τῶν μικρῶν· τὰ
μὲν γὰρ διαλύεται ῥᾳδίως, οἷον τὰ μεγάλα· προσ-
κόπτει γὰρ πολλοῖς· τὸ δὲ ἀδιαίρετον ὅλως διὰ
τί μᾶλλον ὑπάρχει τῶν μεγάλων τοῖς μικροῖς; ἔτι
30 δὲ πότερον μία πάντων ἡ φύσις ἐκείνων τῶν
στερεῶν, ἢ διαφέρει θάτερα τῶν ἑτέρων, ὥσπερ
ἂν εἰ τὰ μὲν εἴη πύρινα, τὰ δὲ γήϊνα τὸν ὄγκον;
εἰ μὲν γὰρ μία φύσις ἐστὶν ἁπάντων, τί τὸ χωρί-
σαν; ἢ διὰ τί οὐ γίνεται ἁψάμενα ἕν, ὥσπερ
ὕδωρ ὕδατος ὅταν θίγῃ; οὐδὲν γὰρ διαφέρει τὸ ὕσ-
35 τερον τοῦ προτέρου. εἰ δ' ἕτερα, ποῖα ταῦτα; καὶ
326 b δῆλον ὡς ταῦτα θετέον ἀρχὰς καὶ αἰτίας τῶν συμ-
βαινόντων μᾶλλον ἢ τὰ σχήματα. ἔτι δὲ διαφέροντα τὴν φύσιν, κἂν ποιῇ κἂν πάσχῃ θιγγάνοντα
ἀλλήλων. ἔτι δὲ τί τὸ κινοῦν; εἰ μὲν γὰρ ἕτερον,
παθητικά[1]· εἰ δ' αὐτὸ αὑτὸ ἕκαστον, ἢ διαιρετὸν
5 ἔσται, κατ' ἄλλο μὲν κινοῦν κατ' ἄλλο δὲ κινούμενον, ἢ κατὰ ταὐτὸ τἀναντία ὑπάρξει, καὶ ἡ ὕλη
οὐ μόνον ἀριθμῷ ἔσται μία ἀλλὰ καὶ δυνάμει.

Ὅσοι μὲν οὖν διὰ τῆς τῶν πόρων κινήσεώς φασι

---

[1] παθητικά EHL : -όν F.

---

the same way both those who assert that " indivisibles " are solid and those who say they are planes, for they cannot become either rarer or denser, because there can be no void in the " indivisibles." Further, it is strange that there should be small " indivisibles " but not large ones ; for it is natural to suppose at this stage that the larger bodies are more liable to be shattered than the small, for the former, like large things in general, are easily dissolved, since they come into collision with many other bodies. But why should indivisibility in general attach to small things rather than large ? Furthermore, is the substance of all these solids uniform or does it differ in different groups, as if, for example, some were fiery and some earthy in their bulk ? For if they are all of one substance, what has separated them from one another ? Or why do they not become one when they come into contact, just as water does when it touches water ? For there is no difference between the two cases. But if they belong to different classes, what are their different qualities ? Indeed it is clear that we ought to postulate that these classes rather than the " figures " are the origins and causes of the resulting phenomena. Moreover, if they were different in substance they would act and be acted upon reciprocally if they touched one another. Again, what sets these in motion ? For if it is something other than themselves, they must be liable to be acted upon ; but, if each is its own mover either it will be divisible, in part causing motion and in part being moved, or contraries will belong to it in the same respect, and the matter of it will be not only arithmetically but also potentially one.[a]

As for those who say that the processes of being

247

τὰ πάθη συμβαίνειν, εἰ μὲν καὶ πεπληρωμένων
τῶν πόρων, περίεργον οἱ πόροι· εἰ γὰρ ταύτῃ τι
10 πάσχει τὸ πᾶν, κἂν μὴ πόρους ἔχον ἀλλ' αὐτὸ
συνεχὲς ὂν πάσχοι τὸν αὐτὸν τρόπον. ἔτι δὲ πῶς
ἐνδέχεται περὶ τοῦ διορᾶν συμβαίνειν ὡς λέγουσιν;
οὔτε γὰρ κατὰ τὰς ἀφὰς ἐνδέχεται διιέναι διὰ τῶν
διαφανῶν, οὔτε διὰ τῶν πόρων, εἰ πλήρης ἕκαστος·
τί γὰρ διοίσει τοῦ μὴ ἔχειν πόρους; πᾶν γὰρ
15 ὁμοίως ἔσται πλῆρες. ἀλλὰ μὴν εἰ καὶ κενὰ μὲν
ταῦτα (ἀνάγκη δὲ σώματα ἐν αὐτοῖς ἔχειν), ταὐτὸ
συμβήσεται πάλιν. εἰ δὲ τηλικαῦτα τὸ μέγεθος
ὥστε μὴ δέχεσθαι σῶμα μηδέν, γελοῖον τὸ μικρὸν
μὲν οἴεσθαι κενὸν εἶναι, μέγα δὲ μὴ μηδ' ὁπηλικονοῦν, ἢ τὸ κενὸν ἄλλο τι οἴεσθαι λέγειν πλὴν
20 χώραν σώματος, ὥστε δῆλον ὅτι παντὶ σώματι τὸν
ὄγκον ἴσον ἔσται κενόν.

Ὅλως δὲ τὸ πόρους ποιεῖν περίεργον· εἰ μὲν γὰρ
μηδὲν ποιεῖ κατὰ τὴν ἀφήν, οὐδὲ διὰ τῶν πόρων
ποιήσει διιόν· εἰ δὲ τῷ ἅπτεσθαι, καὶ μὴ πόρων
ὄντων τὰ μὲν πείσεται τὰ δὲ ποιήσει τῶν πρὸς
25 ἄλληλα τοῦτον τὸν τρόπον πεφυκότων. ὅτι μὲν
οὖν οὕτως λέγειν τοὺς πόρους ὥς τινες ὑπολαμ-
βάνουσιν, ἢ ψεῦδος ἢ μάταιον, φανερὸν ἐκ τούτων
ἐστίν· διαιρετῶν δ' ὄντων πάντῃ τῶν σωμάτων
πόρους ποιεῖν γελοῖον· ᾗ γὰρ διαιρετά, δύναται
χωρίζεσθαι.

---

^a *i.e.* the body is none the less impenetrable, even if it is
held that the pores, though they contain bodies, are themselves, *qua* pores, empty channels.

^b *i.e.* the very fact that a body is everywhere divisible
makes it possible to open up a channel in it.

acted upon occur through movement in the pores, if this happens although the pores are filled, the pores are an unnecessary supposition; for if the whole body is acted upon at all in this way, it would be acted upon in the same way even if it had no pores, in its own continuous self. Again, how is it possible to carry out the process of seeing through a medium as they describe it? For it is not possible to penetrate through the transparent bodies either at the points of contact or through the pores, if each pore is full. For how will this condition differ from the possession of no pores at all? For the whole will be equally full throughout. Furthermore, if these channels, though they must contain bodies, are void, the same result will occur again [a]; but if they are of such a size that they cannot admit any body, it is absurd to suppose that there is a small void but not a big one, of whatever size it be, or to think that "a void" means anything except a space for a body; so that it is clear that there will be a void equal in cubic capacity to every body.

In general, then, it is superfluous to postulate the existence of pores; for if the agent effects nothing by contact, neither will it effect anything by passing through pores. If, however, it effects anything by contact, then, even without there being any pores, some of those things which are by nature adapted for reciprocal effect of this kind will be acted upon, while others will act. It is clear, therefore, from what we have said that it is either false or useless to talk of pores of the kind which some people suppose to exist, and, since bodies are everywhere divisible, it is ridiculous to postulate pores at all; for since bodies are divisible, they can be separated into parts.[b]

9. Τίνα δὲ τρόπον ὑπάρχει τοῖς οὖσι γεννᾶν καὶ
30 ποιεῖν καὶ πάσχειν, λέγωμεν λαβόντες ἀρχὴν τὴν
πολλάκις εἰρημένην. εἰ γάρ ἐστι τὸ μὲν δυνάμει
τὸ δ' ἐντελεχείᾳ τοιοῦτον, πέφυκεν οὐ τῇ μὲν τῇ
δ' οὔ πάσχειν, ἀλλὰ πάντῃ καθ' ὅσον ἐστὶ τοιοῦτον,
ἧττον δὲ καὶ μᾶλλον ᾗ τοιοῦτον μᾶλλόν ἐστι καὶ
ἧττον· καὶ ταύτῃ πόρους ἄν τις λέγοι μᾶλλον,
35 καθάπερ ἐν τοῖς μεταλλευομένοις διατείνουσι τοῦ
327 a παθητικοῦ φλέβες συνεχεῖς. συμφυὲς μὲν οὖν ἕκαστον καὶ ἓν ὂν ἀπαθές. ὁμοίως δὲ καὶ μὴ θιγγάνοντα μήτε αὑτῶν μήτ' ἄλλων, ἃ ποιεῖν πέφυκε
καὶ πάσχειν. λέγω δ' οἷον οὐ μόνον ἁπτόμενον
θερμαίνει τὸ πῦρ, ἀλλὰ κἂν ἄποθεν ᾖ· τὸν μὲν γὰρ
5 ἀέρα τὸ πῦρ, ὁ δ' ἀὴρ τὸ σῶμα θερμαίνει, πεφυκὼς
ποιεῖν καὶ πάσχειν. τὸ δὲ τῇ μὲν οἴεσθαι πάσχειν
τῇ δὲ μή, διορίσαντας ἐν ἀρχῇ τοῦτο λεκτέον. εἰ
μὲν γὰρ μὴ πάντῃ διαιρετὸν τὸ μέγεθος, ἀλλ' ἔστι
σῶμα ἀδιαίρετον ἢ πλάτος, οὐκ ἂν εἴη πάντῃ
10 παθητικόν, ἀλλ' οὐδὲ συνεχὲς οὐδέν· εἰ δὲ τοῦτο
ψεῦδος καὶ πᾶν σῶμα διαιρετόν, οὐδὲν διαφέρει
διῃρῆσθαι μὲν ἅπτεσθαι δέ, ἢ διαιρετὸν εἶναι· εἰ
γὰρ διακρίνεσθαι δύναται κατὰ τὰς ἁφάς, ὥσπερ
φασί τινες, κἂν μήπω ᾖ διῃρημένον, ἔσται διῃρη-

---

[a] It is difficult to extract any meaning from this sentence as it stands. Joachim supposes a lacuna after τῇ δὲ μή.

9. Let us now deal with the question about the way in which existences have the power of generating and of acting and being acted upon, starting from the principle which we have often enunciated. For if there exists that which is potentially of a certain kind as well as that which is actually so, it is of a nature, in so far as it is what it is, to be acted upon in every part, and not in some part but not in another, and to a more or a less extent according as it is more or less of that particular nature ; and one might speak of pores as having a particular nature in a greater degree, just as there are veins of substance which can be acted upon which stretch continuously in metals which are being mined. Every body, then, which is coherent and one is not acted upon ; and this is equally true of bodies which do not touch either each other or other bodies which are of a nature to act or be acted upon. Fire is an example of what I mean : it heats not only when it is in contact with something, but also if it is at a distance ; for it heats the air, and the air heats the body, being of a nature both to act and to be acted upon. But having enunciated the theory that a body is acted upon in one part but not in another, we must first make the following declaration [a] : if the magnitude is not everywhere divisible, but there is a divisible body or plane, no body would be liable to be acted upon throughout, but neither would any body be continuous ; but, if this is not true and every body is divisible, there is no difference between " having been divided but being in contact " and " being divisible " ; for if it is possible for a body to be " separated at the points of contact "—a phrase which some people use—then, even if it has not yet been divided,

Aristotle's explanation of " action-and-passion."

251

327 a

μένον· δυνατὸν γὰρ διαιρεθῆναι· γίνεται γὰρ οὐδὲν
15 ἀδύνατον. ὅλως δὲ τὸ τοῦτον γίνεσθαι τὸν τρόπον
σχιζομένων τῶν σωμάτων ἄτοπον· ἀναιρεῖ γὰρ οὗτος ὁ λόγος ἀλλοίωσιν, ὁρῶμεν δὲ τὸ αὐτὸ σῶμα
συνεχὲς ὂν ὁτὲ μὲν ὑγρὸν ὁτὲ δὲ πεπηγός, οὐ διαιρέσει καὶ συνθέσει τοῦτο παθόν, οὐδὲ τροπῇ καὶ
διαθιγῇ, καθάπερ λέγει Δημόκριτος· οὔτε γὰρ
20 μετατεθὲν οὔτε μεταβαλὸν τὴν φύσιν πεπηγὸς ἐξ
ὑγροῦ γέγονεν· οὐδ' ἐνυπάρχει τὰ σκληρὰ καὶ πε-
πηγότα ἀδιαίρετα τοὺς ὄγκους· ἀλλ' ὁμοίως ἅπαν
ὑγρόν, ὁτὲ δὲ σκληρὸν καὶ πεπηγός ἐστιν. ἔτι
δ' οὐδ' αὔξησιν οἷόν τ' εἶναι καὶ φθίσιν· οὐ γὰρ
ὁτιοῦν ἔσται γεγονὸς μεῖζον, εἴπερ ἔσται πρόσθεσις,
25 καὶ μὴ πᾶν μεταβεβληκός, ἢ μιχθέντος τινὸς ἢ
καθ' αὑτὸ μεταβαλόντος.

Ὅτι μὲν οὖν ἔστι τὸ γεννᾶν καὶ τὸ ποιεῖν καὶ τὸ
γίνεσθαί τε καὶ πάσχειν ὑπ' ἀλλήλων, καὶ τίνα
τρόπον ἐνδέχεται, καὶ τίνα φασὶ μέν τινες οὐκ
ἐνδέχεται δέ, διωρίσθω τοῦτον τὸν τρόπον.

30 10. Λοιπὸν δὲ θεωρῆσαι περὶ μίξεως κατὰ τὸν
αὐτὸν τρόπον τῆς μεθόδου· τοῦτο γὰρ ἦν τρίτον
τῶν προτεθέντων ἐξ ἀρχῆς. σκεπτέον δὲ τί τ'
ἐστὶν ἡ μίξις καὶ τί τὸ μικτόν, καὶ τίσιν ὑπάρχει
τῶν ὄντων καὶ πῶς, ἔτι δὲ πότερον ἔστι μίξις ἢ
τοῦτο ψεῦδος· ἀδύνατον γάρ ἐστι μιχθῆναί τι ἕτε-
35 ρον ἑτέρῳ, καθάπερ λέγουσί τινες· ὄντων μὲν γὰρ
327 b ἔτι τῶν μιχθέντων καὶ μὴ ἠλλοιωμένων οὐδὲν μᾶλ-

ᵃ The other two being ἁφή (ch. 6) and ποιεῖν καὶ πάσχειν
(chs. 7-9).

it will be in a condition of having been divided ; for since it *can* be divided, nothing impossible results. And, in general, it is strange that it should happen in this way only, namely, if the bodies are being split ; for this theory does away with " alteration," whereas we see the same body remaining in a state of continuity, though it is at one time liquid and at another solid, and it has not undergone this change by " division " or " composition," nor yet by " turning "and " mutual contact," as Democritus declares ; for it has not become solid instead of liquid through any change of arrangement or alteration of its substance, nor do there exist in it those hard and congealed particles which are indivisible in their bulk, but it is liquid and at another time hard and congealed uniformly throughout. Furthermore, it is also impossible for there to be growth and diminution ; for if there shall be any addition—as opposed to a change in the whole, either by the admixture of something or by a change in the body itself—no part of it will have become greater.

Let this, then, be our explanation of the way in which things generate and act and come into being and are acted upon by one another, and the manner in which these processes *can* occur and the impossible theories which some philosophers enunciate.

10. It now remains to consider " mixture " by the same kind of method ; for this is the third of the subjects originally proposed.[a] We must consider what " mixture " is and what it is that can be mixed and of what things mixture is a property and how ; and, further, whether there is such a thing as mixture, or is it a fiction. For, according to some people, it is impossible for one thing to be mixed with another ; for (a) if the ingredients still exist and are not altered

The nature of " mixture " or " combination " and how it takes place.

253

λον νῦν μεμῖχθαί φασιν ἢ πρότερον, ἀλλ' ὁμοίως
ἔχειν, θατέρου δὲ φθαρέντος οὐ μεμῖχθαι, ἀλλὰ τὸ
μὲν εἶναι τὸ δ' οὐκ εἶναι, τὴν δὲ μίξιν ὁμοίως
5 ἐχόντων εἶναι· τὸν αὐτὸν δὲ τρόπον καὶ εἰ ἀμφοτέρων συνελθόντων ἔφθαρται τῶν μιγνυμένων
ἑκάτερον· οὐ γὰρ εἶναι μεμιγμένα τά γε ὅλως οὐκ
ὄντα.

Οὗτος μὲν οὖν ὁ λόγος ἔοικε ζητεῖν διορίσαι τί
διαφέρει μίξις γενέσεως καὶ φθορᾶς, καὶ τί τὸ μικτὸν τοῦ γεννητοῦ καὶ φθαρτοῦ· δῆλον γὰρ ὡς δεῖ
10 διαφέρειν, εἴπερ ἔστιν. ὥστε τούτων ὄντων φανερῶν τὰ διαπορηθέντα λύοιντ' ἄν.

Ἀλλὰ μὴν οὐδὲ τὴν ὕλην τῷ πυρὶ μεμῖχθαί
φαμεν οὐδὲ μίγνυσθαι καιομένην, οὔτ' αὐτὴν αὐτῆς
τοῖς μορίοις οὔτε τῷ πυρί, ἀλλὰ τὸ μὲν πῦρ γίνεσθαι,
τὴν δὲ φθείρεσθαι. τὸν αὐτὸν δὲ τρόπον οὔτε τῷ
15 σώματι τὴν τροφὴν οὔτε τὸ σχῆμα τῷ κηρῷ μιγνύμενον σχηματίζειν τὸν ὄγκον· οὐδὲ τὸ σῶμα καὶ τὸ
λευκὸν οὐδ' ὅλως τὰ πάθη καὶ τὰς ἕξεις οἷόν τε
μίγνυσθαι τοῖς πράγμασιν· σωζόμενα γὰρ ὁρᾶται.
ἀλλὰ μὴν οὐδὲ τὸ λευκόν γε καὶ τὴν ἐπιστήμην
ἐνδέχεται μιχθῆναι, οὐδ' ἄλλο τῶν μὴ χωριστῶν
20 οὐδέν. ἀλλὰ τοῦτο λέγουσιν οὐ καλῶς οἱ πάντα
ποτὲ ὁμοῦ φάσκοντες εἶναι καὶ μεμῖχθαι· οὐ γὰρ

---

[a] *i.e.* "white" and "knowledge" cannot exist by them-

at all, they are no more mixed than they were before, but are in a similar state ; and (b) if one ingredient is destroyed, they have not been mixed, but one ingredient exists while the other does not, whereas mixture is composed of ingredients which remain what they were before ; and in the same way (c) even if, both the ingredients having come together, each of them has been destroyed, there is no mixture ; for things which have no existence at all cannot have been mixed.

This argument, then, seems to seek to define in what respect " mixing " differs from coming-to-be and passing-away, and how that which is " mixed " differs from that which comes-to-be and passes-away ; for obviously " mixture," if there is such a thing, must be something different. When, therefore, these questions have been cleared up, our difficulties would be solved.

Now we do not say that wood has mixed with fire nor that it mixes, when it is burning, either with its own particles or with the fire, but we say that the fire comes-to-be and the wood passes-away. Similarly we do not say that the food mixes with the body or that the shape mixes with the wax and so forms the lump. Nor can " body " and " white " be " mixed " together, nor, in general, can " properties " and " states " be mixed with " things " ; for we see them persisting unchanged. Again, " white " and " knowledge " cannot be mixed together, nor any of the terms which cannot be used separately.[a] This is what is wrong in the theory of those who hold that formerly all things were together and mixed ; for

selves ; a man can be " white " and " learned," but these attributes can only exist as properties of someone.

327 b

ἅπαν ἅπαντι μικτόν, ἀλλ' ὑπάρχειν δεῖ χωριστὸν
ἑκάτερον τῶν μιχθέντων· τῶν δὲ παθῶν οὐδὲν
χωριστόν. ἐπεὶ δ' ἐστὶ τὰ μὲν δυνάμει τὰ δ'
ἐνεργείᾳ τῶν ὄντων, ἐνδέχεται τὰ μιχθέντα εἶναί
25 πως καὶ μὴ εἶναι, ἐνεργείᾳ μὲν ἑτέρου ὄντος τοῦ
γεγονότος ἐξ αὐτῶν, δυνάμει δ' ἔτι ἑκατέρου ἅπερ
ἦσαν πρὶν μιχθῆναι, καὶ οὐκ ἀπολωλότα· τοῦτο
γὰρ ὁ λόγος διηπόρει πρότερον· φαίνεται δὲ τὰ
μιγνύμενα πρότερόν τε ἐκ κεχωρισμένων συνιόντα
καὶ δυνάμενα χωρίζεσθαι πάλιν. οὔτε διαμένουσιν
30 οὖν ἐνεργείᾳ ὥσπερ τὸ σῶμα καὶ τὸ λευκόν, οὔτε
φθείρονται, οὔτε θάτερον οὔτ' ἄμφω· σῴζεται γὰρ
ἡ δύναμις αὐτῶν. διὸ ταῦτα μὲν ἀφείσθω· τὸ
δὲ συνεχὲς τούτοις ἀπόρημα διαιρετέον, πότερον ἡ
μίξις πρὸς τὴν αἴσθησιν τί ἐστιν.

Ὅταν γὰρ οὕτως εἰς μικρὰ διαιρεθῇ τὰ μιγνύ-
35 μενα, καὶ τεθῇ παρ' ἄλληλα τοῦτον τὸν τρόπον
ὥστε μὴ δῆλον ἕκαστον εἶναι τῇ αἰσθήσει, τότε
328 a μέμικται ἢ οὔ, ἀλλ' ἔστιν ὥστε ὁτιοῦν παρ' ὁτιοῦν εἶναι μόριον τῶν μιχθέντων; λέγεται μὲν οὖν
ἐκείνως, οἷον κριθὰς μεμῖχθαι πυροῖς, ὅταν ἡτισοῦν
παρ' ὁντινοῦν τεθῇ. εἰ δ' ἐστὶ πᾶν σῶμα διαιρετόν,
εἴπερ καὶ ἔστι σῶμα σώματι μικτὸν ὁμοιομερές,
5 ὁτιοῦν ἂν δέοι μέρος γίνεσθαι παρ' ὁτιοῦν. ἐπεὶ

256

everything cannot be mixed with everything, but each of the ingredients which are mixed must originally exist separately, and no property can have a separate existence. Since, however, some things have a potential, and other things an actual, existence, it is possible for things which combine in a mixture to " be " in one sense and " not-be " in another, the resulting compound formed from them being actually something different but each ingredient being still potentially what it was before they were mixed and not destroyed. (This is the difficulty which arose in our earlier argument, and it is clear that the ingredients of a mixture first come together after having been separate and can be separated again.) They do not actually persist as " body " and " white," nor are they destroyed (either one or both of them), for their potentiality is preserved. Let us, therefore, dismiss these questions, but the problem closely connected with them must be discussed, namely, whether mixture is something relative to perception.

When the ingredients of the mixture have been divided into such small particles and so set side by side with one another that each is not apparent to the sense-perception, have they then been mixed ? Or is this not so, and is mixture of such a nature that every particle of one ingredient is side by side with a particle of the other ingredient ? The term certainly is used in the former sense ; for instance, we say that barley is mixed with wheat when each grain of barley is placed side by side with a grain of wheat. But if every body is divisible, then since body mixed with body is made up of like parts, every part of each ingredient ought to be side by side with a part of the other. But since it is not possible for a body to be

328 a

δ' οὐκ ἔστιν εἰς τἀλάχιστα διαιρεθῆναι, οὔτε σύνθεσις ταὐτὸ καὶ μίξις ἀλλ' ἕτερον, δῆλον ὡς οὔτε
κατὰ μικρὰ σωζόμενα δεῖ τὰ μιγνύμενα φάναι
μεμῖχθαι (σύνθεσις γὰρ ἔσται καὶ οὐ κρᾶσις οὐδὲ
10 μίξις, οὐδ' ἕξει τὸν αὐτὸν λόγον τῷ ὅλῳ τὸ μόριον.
φαμὲν δὲ δεῖν,[1] εἴπερ μέμικται,[2] τὸ μιχθὲν ὁμοιο-
μερὲς εἶναι, καὶ ὥσπερ τοῦ ὕδατος τὸ μέρος ὕδωρ,
οὕτω καὶ τοῦ κραθέντος. ἂν δ' ᾖ κατὰ μικρὰ
σύνθεσις ἡ μίξις, οὐθὲν συμβήσεται τούτων, ἀλλὰ
μόνον μεμιγμένα πρὸς τὴν αἴσθησιν· καὶ τὸ αὐτὸ
15 τῷ μὲν μεμιγμένον, ἐὰν μὴ βλέπῃ ὀξύ, τῷ Λυγ-
κεῖ δ' οὐδὲν μεμιγμένον) οὔτε τῇ διαιρέσει ὥστε
ὁτιοῦν παρ' ὁτιοῦν μέρος· ἀδύνατον γὰρ οὕτω διαιρεθῆναι. ἢ οὖν οὐκ ἔστι μίξις, ἢ λεκτέον τοῦτο
πῶς ἐνδέχεται γίνεσθαι πάλιν.

Ἔστι δή, ὡς ἔφαμεν, τῶν ὄντων τὰ μὲν ποιητικά,
τὰ δ' ὑπὸ τούτων παθητικά. τὰ μὲν οὖν ἀντι-
20 στρέφει, ὅσων ἡ αὐτὴ ὕλη ἐστί, καὶ ποιητικὰ ἀλλήλων καὶ παθητικὰ ὑπ' ἀλλήλων· τὰ δὲ ποιεῖ
ἀπαθῆ ὄντα, ὅσων μὴ ἡ αὐτὴ ὕλη. τούτων μὲν
οὖν οὐκ ἔστι μίξις· διὸ οὐδ' ἡ ἰατρικὴ ποιεῖ ὑγίειαν
οὐδ' ἡ ὑγίεια μιγνυμένη τοῖς σώμασιν. τῶν δὲ

---

[1] δ' EL.
[2] μέμικται F : μεμῖχθαι E : δεῖ μεμῖχθαί τι L.

---

[a] One of the Argonauts, famous for his keen sight
(Apollonius Rhodius i. 153 ff.).

divided into its smallest parts and " composition "
and mixture are not the same thing but different, it
is clear (a) that we must not say that the ingredients,
if they are preserved in small particles, are mixed
(for this will be " composition " and not " blending "
or " mixing," nor will the part show the same ratio
between its constituents as the whole ; but we say
that, if mixing has taken place, the mixture ought
to be uniform throughout, and, just as any part of
water is water, so any part of what is blended should
be the same as the whole. But if mixing is a composition of small particles, none of these things will
happen, but the ingredients will only be mixed
according to the standard of sense-perception, and
the same thing will be a mixture to one man, if he
has not sharp sight, but to the eyes of Lynceus [a]
will not be mixed) ; it is also clear (b) that we must
not say that things are mixed by means of a division
whereby every part of one ingredient is set by the
side of a part of the other ; for it is impossible for
them to be thus divided. Either, then, there is no
mixing, or another explanation must be given of the
way in which it occurs.

Now, as we maintained, some of those things which
exist are capable of action and others capable of
being acted upon by them. Some things, then,
namely, those whose matter is the same, " recipro-
cate," that is, are capable of acting and being acted
upon by one another, while other things, namely,
those which have not the same matter, act but are
not liable to be acted upon. Of the latter, then, no
mixing is possible ; hence, neither the art of healing
nor health mixing with the patients' bodies can produce health. But of things which are capable of

ποιητικῶν καὶ παθητικῶν ὅσα εὐδιαίρετα, πολλὰ
25 μὲν ὀλίγοις καὶ μεγάλα μικροῖς συντιθέμενα οὐ
ποιεῖ μίξιν, ἀλλ' αὔξησιν τοῦ κρατοῦντος· μεταβάλλει γὰρ θάτερον εἰς τὸ κρατοῦν, οἷον σταλαγμὸς
οἴνου μυρίοις χοεῦσιν ὕδατος οὐ μίγνυται· λύεται
γὰρ τὸ εἶδος καὶ μεταβάλλει εἰς τὸ πᾶν ὕδωρ.
ὅταν δὲ ταῖς δυνάμεσιν ἰσάζῃ πως, τότε μετα-
30 βάλλει μὲν ἑκάτερον εἰς τὸ κρατοῦν ἐκ τῆς αὑτοῦ
φύσεως, οὐ γίνεται δὲ θάτερον, ἀλλὰ μεταξὺ καὶ
κοινόν.

Φανερὸν οὖν ὅτι ταῦτ' ἐστὶ μικτὰ ὅσα ἐναντίωσιν
ἔχει τῶν ποιούντων· ταῦτα γὰρ δὴ ὑπ' ἀλλήλων
ἐστὶ παθητικά. καὶ μικρὰ δὲ μικροῖς παρατιθέμενα
μίγνυται μᾶλλον· ῥᾷον γὰρ καὶ θᾶττον ἄλληλα
35 μεθίστησιν. τὸ δὲ πολὺ καὶ ὑπὸ πολλοῦ χρονίως
328 b τοῦτο δρᾷ. διὸ τὰ εὐόριστα τῶν διαιρετῶν καὶ
παθητικῶν μικτά (διαιρεῖται γὰρ εἰς μικρὰ ταῦτα
ῥᾳδίως· τοῦτο γὰρ ἦν τὸ εὐορίστῳ εἶναι), οἷον τὰ
ὑγρὰ μικτὰ μάλιστα τῶν σωμάτων· εὐόριστον γὰρ
μάλιστα τὸ ὑγρὸν τῶν διαιρετῶν, ἐὰν μὴ γλίσχρον
5 ᾖ· ταῦτα γὰρ δὴ πλείω καὶ μείζω μόνον ποιεῖ
τὸν ὄγκον. ὅταν δ' ᾖ θάτερον μόνον παθητικὸν ἢ
σφόδρα, τὸ δὲ πάμπαν ἠρέμα, ἢ οὐδὲν πλεῖον τὸ

action and capable of being acted upon, those which are easily divisible, when many of one of them are compounded with few of another or a large bulk with a small, do not produce a mixture but an increase of the predominant ingredient, for there is a change of the other ingredient into the predominant. (For example, a drop of wine does not mix with ten thousand measures of water, for its form is dissolved and it changes so as to become part of the total volume of water.) But when there is some sort of balance between the " active powers," then each changes from its own nature into the predominant ingredient, without, however, becoming the other but something between the two with common properties.

It is clear, therefore, that those agents are capable of admixture which show contrariety, for these can be acted upon by one another ; and they mix all the better if small particles of the one ingredient are set side by side with small particles of the other, for then they more easily and more quickly cause a change in one another, whereas a large quantity of one takes a long time to be affected in this way by a large quantity of the other. Hence, those of the divisible and susceptible materials whose form is easily modified are capable of mixture ; for they are easily divided into small particles (for that is what " to be easily modified in form " means) ; for example, the liquids are the most " mixable " of bodies, since of " divisibles " liquid is the most easily modified in form, provided it is not viscous (for viscous liquids merely increase the volume and bulk). But when one only of the ingredients is susceptible to action— or is excessively susceptible, while the other ingredient is only slightly so—the result of the mixture

Aristotle's view of "mixture."

328 b

μιχθὲν ἐξ ἀμφοῖν ἢ μικρόν, ὅπερ συμβαίνει περὶ
τὸν καττίτερον καὶ τὸν χαλκόν. ἔνια γὰρ ψελλί-
10 ζεται πρὸς ἄλληλα τῶν ὄντων καὶ ἐπαμφοτερίζει·
φαίνεται γάρ πως καὶ μικτὰ ἠρέμα, καὶ ὡς
θάτερον μὲν δεκτικὸν θάτερον δ' εἶδος. ὅπερ ἐπὶ
τούτων συμβαίνει· ὁ γὰρ καττίτερος ὡς πάθος τι
ὢν ἄνευ ὕλης τοῦ χαλκοῦ σχεδὸν ἀφανίζεται, καὶ
μιχθεὶς ἄπεισι χρωματίσας μόνον. ταὐτὸ δὲ τοῦτο
συμβαίνει καὶ ἐφ' ἑτέρων.

15 Φανερὸν τοίνυν ἐκ τῶν εἰρημένων καὶ ὅτι ἔστι
μίξις καὶ τί ἐστι καὶ διὰ τί, καὶ ποῖα μικτὰ τῶν
ὄντων, ἐπείπερ ἐστὶν ἔνια τοιαῦτα οἷα παθητικά
τε ὑπ' ἀλλήλων καὶ εὐόριστα καὶ εὐδιαίρετα· ταῦτα
γὰρ οὔτ' ἐφθάρθαι ἀνάγκη μεμιγμένα οὔτ' ἔτι
ταὐτὰ ἁπλῶς εἶναι, οὔτε σύνθεσιν εἶναι τὴν μίξιν
20 αὐτῶν, οὔτε πρὸς τὴν αἴσθησιν· ἀλλ' ἔστι μικτὸν
μὲν ὃ ἂν εὐόριστον ὂν παθητικὸν ᾖ καὶ ποιητικὸν
καὶ τοιούτῳ μικτόν (πρὸς ὁμώνυμον γὰρ τὸ μικτόν),
ἡ δὲ μίξις τῶν μικτῶν ἀλλοιωθέντων ἕνωσις.

of the two is no greater in volume or very little greater, as happens when tin and copper are mixed. For some things adopt a hesitant and wavering attitude towards one another, for they appear somehow to be only slightly " mixable," one, as it were, acting in a "receptive" manner, the other as a "form." This is what happens with these metals ; the tin almost disappears as though it were a property of the copper without any material of its own and, after being mixed, almost vanishes, having only given its colour to the copper. And the same thing happens in other instances too.

It is clear, then, from what has been said, that there is such a process as mixing, and what it is, and how it occurs, and what kind of existing things are " mixable," seeing that some things are of such a nature as to be acted upon by one another and easily modified in shape and easily divisible. For it does not necessarily follow either that they are destroyed by having been mixed, or that they simply remain still the same, or that their " mixture " is composition, or only dependent on perception ; but anything is " mixable " which, being easily modified in shape, is capable of acting or being acted upon, and is " mixable " with something of the same kind as itself (for the term " mixable " is used in relation to something else which is also called " mixable "), and mixture is the union of " mixables," when they have undergone alteration.

B

328 b 26   1. Περὶ μὲν οὖν μίξεως καὶ ἀφῆς καὶ τοῦ ποιεῖν
καὶ πάσχειν εἴρηται πῶς ὑπάρχει τοῖς μεταβάλλουσι κατὰ φύσιν, ἔτι δὲ περὶ γενέσεως καὶ φθορᾶς τῆς ἁπλῆς, πῶς καὶ τίνος¹ ἐστὶ καὶ διὰ τίν'
30 αἰτίαν. ὁμοίως δὲ καὶ περὶ ἀλλοιώσεως εἴρηται, τί
τὸ ἀλλοιοῦσθαι καὶ τίν' ἔχει διαφορὰν αὐτῶν. λοιπὸν
δὲ θεωρῆσαι περὶ τὰ καλούμενα στοιχεῖα τῶν σωμάτων.

Γένεσις μὲν γὰρ καὶ φθορὰ πάσαις ταῖς φύσει
συνεστώσαις οὐσίαις οὐκ ἄνευ τῶν αἰσθητῶν σω-
μάτων· τούτων δὲ τὴν ὑποκειμένην ὕλην οἱ μέν
35 φασιν εἶναι μίαν, οἷον ἀέρα τιθέντες ἢ πῦρ ἤ τι
329 a μεταξὺ τούτων, σῶμά τε ὂν καὶ χωριστόν, οἱ δὲ
πλείω τὸν ἀριθμὸν ἑνός, οἱ μὲν πῦρ καὶ γῆν, οἱ
δὲ ταῦτά τε καὶ ἀέρα τρίτον, οἱ δὲ καὶ ὕδωρ τούτων
τέταρτον, ὥσπερ Ἐμπεδοκλῆς· ἐξ ὧν συγκρινο-
μένων καὶ διακρινομένων ἢ ἀλλοιουμένων συμ-
5 βαίνειν τὴν γένεσιν καὶ τὴν φθορὰν τοῖς πράγμασιν.

Ὅτι μὲν οὖν τὰ πρῶτα ἀρχὰς καὶ στοιχεῖα καλῶς ἔχει λέγειν, ἔστω συνομολογούμενον, ἐξ ὧν
μεταβαλλόντων ἢ κατὰ σύγκρισιν καὶ διάκρισιν ἢ

---

¹ πῶς καὶ τίνος J¹Dᵇ : τίνος καὶ πῶς EJ² : καὶ τίνος καὶ
πῶς HL.

264

BOOK II

1. WE have now dealt with the way in which mixture, contact and action-and-passion are attributable to things which undergo natural change ; we have, moreover, explained how unqualified coming-to-be and passing-away exist, and with what they are concerned and owing to what cause they occur. Similarly, we have dealt with "alteration" and explained how it differs from coming-to-be and passing-away. It remains to consider the so-called elements of bodies.

Chapters 1-8. *What comes-to-be and passes-away consists of elements, that is, simple bodies. What are they and how do they combine ?*

Coming-to-be and passing-away occur in all naturally constituted substances, if we presuppose the existence of perceptible bodies. Some people assert that the matter underlying these bodies is one ; for example, they suppose it to be Air or Fire, or an intermediate between these two, but still a single separate body. Others hold that there are more than one material, some thinking that they are Fire and Earth, others adding Air as a third, others (like Empedocles) adding Water as a fourth ; and it is, they say, from the association and separation or alteration of these that coming-to-be and passing-away of things comes about.

Views held by various schools.

Let us, then, be agreed that the primary materials from the changes of which, either by association or by separation or by some other kind of change,

265

329 a

κατ' ἄλλην μεταβολὴν συμβαίνει γένεσιν εἶναι καὶ
φθοράν. . ἀλλ' οἱ μὲν ποιοῦντες μίαν ὕλην παρὰ
10 τὰ εἰρημένα, ταύτην δὲ σωματικὴν καὶ χωριστήν,
ἁμαρτάνουσιν· ἀδύνατον γὰρ ἄνευ ἐναντιώσεως εἶναι τὸ σῶμα τοῦτο αἰσθητῆς¹· ἢ γὰρ κοῦφον ἢ
βαρὺ ἢ ψυχρὸν ἢ θερμὸν ἀνάγκη εἶναι τὸ ἄπειρον
τοῦτο, ὃ λέγουσί τινες εἶναι τὴν ἀρχήν. ὡς δ' ἐν
τῷ Τιμαίῳ γέγραπται, οὐδένα ἔχει διορισμόν· οὐ
15 γὰρ εἴρηκε σαφῶς τὸ πανδεχές, εἰ χωρίζεται τῶν
στοιχείων. οὐδὲ χρῆται οὐδέν, φήσας εἶναι ὑπο-
κείμενόν τι τοῖς καλουμένοις στοιχείοις πρότερον,
οἷον χρυσὸν τοῖς ἔργοις τοῖς χρυσοῖς. (καίτοι καὶ
τοῦτο οὐ καλῶς λέγεται τοῦτον τὸν τρόπον λεγόμενον, ἀλλ' ὧν μὲν ἀλλοίωσις, ἔστιν οὕτως, ὧν
20 δὲ γένεσις καὶ φθορά, ἀδύνατον ἐκεῖνο προσαγο-
ρεύεσθαι ἐξ οὗ γέγονεν. καίτοι γέ φησι μακρῷ
ἀληθέστατον εἶναι χρυσὸν λέγειν ἕκαστον εἶναι.)
ἀλλὰ τῶν στοιχείων ὄντων στερεῶν μέχρι ἐπιπέδων
ποιεῖται τὴν ἀνάλυσιν· ἀδύνατον δὲ τὴν τιθήνην
καὶ τὴν ὕλην τὴν πρώτην τὰ ἐπίπεδα εἶναι. ἡμεῖς
25 δὲ φαμὲν μὲν εἶναί τινα ὕλην τῶν σωμάτων τῶν
αἰσθητῶν, ἀλλὰ ταύτην οὐ χωριστὴν ἀλλ' ἀεὶ μετ'
ἐναντιώσεως, ἐξ ἧς γίνεται τὰ καλούμενα στοιχεῖα.
διώρισται δὲ περὶ αὐτῶν ἐν ἑτέροις ἀκριβέστερον.
οὐ μὴν ἀλλ' ἐπειδὴ καὶ τὸν τρόπον τοῦτόν ἐστιν
ἐκ τῆς ὕλης τὰ σώματα τὰ πρῶτα, διοριστέον καὶ
30 περὶ τούτων, ἀρχὴν μὲν καὶ πρώτην οἰομένοις εἶναι

¹ αἰσθητῆς HJ : αἰσθητόν E : τὸ αἰσθητόν F : αἰσθητὸν ὄν L.

ᵃ Plato, *Timaeus* 51 A.　　ᵇ *Ibid.* 49 D—50 C.
ᶜ *Ibid.* 53 C ff.　　ᵈ *Ibid.* 49 A.
ᵉ *Phys.* i. 6 and 7.

coming-to-be and passing-away occur, are rightly described as " sources " and " elements." But (a) those who postulate that there is a single matter, besides the bodies which we have mentioned, and that this is corporeal and separable, are mistaken ; for it is impossible that this body can exist without " perceptible contrariety," for this " infinite," which some say must be the source of reality, must be either light or heavy, or hot or cold. And (b) what is written in the *Timaeus* [a] is not accurately defined ; for Plato has not clearly stated whether his " omnirecipient " has any existence apart from the elements, nor does he make any use of it, after saying that it is a *substratum* prior to the so-called elements, just as gold is the *substratum* of objects made of gold. (Yet put in this way the statement is not a happy one. Things of which there is coming-to-be and passing-away cannot be called after that out of which they have come-to-be, though it is possible for things which are altered to keep the name of that of which they are alterations. However, what he actually says [b] is that by far the truest account is to say that each of the objects is " gold.") However, he carries the analysis of the elements,[c] though they are solids, back to " planes," and it is impossible for the " Nurse," [d] that is the primary matter, to consist of planes. Our theory is that there is matter of which the perceptible bodies consist, but that it is not separable but always accompanied by contrariety, and it is from this that the so-called elements come into being ; but a more accurate account of these things has been given elsewhere.[e] However, since the primary bodies are also derived in this way from matter, we must explain about these also, reckoning as a source and as primary

Aristotle's view that the elements are primary matter and certain " contrarieties."

267

329 a

τὴν ὕλην τὴν ἀχώριστον μέν, ὑποκειμένην δὲ τοῖς
ἐναντίοις· οὔτε γὰρ τὸ θερμὸν ὕλη τῷ ψυχρῷ οὔτε
τοῦτο τῷ θερμῷ, ἀλλὰ τὸ ὑποκείμενον ἀμφοῖν.
ὥστε πρῶτον μὲν τὸ δυνάμει σῶμα αἰσθητὸν ἀρχή,
δεύτερον δ᾽ αἱ ἐναντιώσεις, λέγω δ᾽ οἷον θερμότης
35 καὶ ψυχρότης, τρίτον δ᾽ ἤδη πῦρ καὶ ὕδωρ καὶ τὰ
329 b τοιαῦτα· ταῦτα μὲν γὰρ μεταβάλλει εἰς ἄλληλα,
καὶ οὐχ ὡς Ἐμπεδοκλῆς καὶ ἕτεροι λέγουσιν (οὐδὲ
γὰρ ἂν ἦν ἀλλοίωσις), αἱ δ᾽ ἐναντιώσεις οὐ μεταβάλλουσιν. ἀλλ᾽ οὐδὲν ἧττον καὶ ὡς σώματος
ποίας καὶ πόσας λεκτέον ἀρχάς· οἱ μὲν γὰρ ἄλ-
5 λοι ὑποθέμενοι χρῶνται, καὶ οὐδὲν λέγουσι διὰ τί
αὗται ἢ τοσαῦται.

2. Ἐπεὶ οὖν ζητοῦμεν αἰσθητοῦ σώματος ἀρχάς,
τοῦτο δ᾽ ἐστὶν ἁπτοῦ, ἁπτὸν δ᾽ οὗ ἡ αἴσθησις ἁφή,
φανερὸν ὅτι οὐ πᾶσαι αἱ ἐναντιώσεις σώματος
10 εἴδη καὶ ἀρχὰς ποιοῦσιν, ἀλλὰ μόνον αἱ κατὰ τὴν
ἁφήν· κατ᾽ ἐναντίωσίν τε γὰρ διαφέρουσι, καὶ κατὰ
ἁπτὴν ἐναντίωσιν. διὸ οὔτε λευκότης καὶ μελανία
οὔτε γλυκύτης καὶ πικρότης, ὁμοίως δ᾽ οὐδὲ τῶν
ἄλλων τῶν αἰσθητῶν ἐναντιώσεων οὐδὲν ποιεῖ
στοιχεῖον. καίτοι πρότερον ὄψις ἁφῆς, ὥστε καὶ
15 τὸ ὑποκείμενον πρότερον. ἀλλ᾽ οὐκ ἔστι σώματος
ἁπτοῦ πάθος ᾗ ἁπτόν, ἀλλὰ καθ᾽ ἕτερον, καὶ εἰ
ἔτυχε τῇ φύσει πρότερον.

Αὐτῶν δὲ πρῶτον τῶν ἁπτῶν διαιρετέον ποῖαι
πρῶται διαφοραὶ καὶ ἐναντιώσεις. εἰσὶ δ᾽ ἐναντιώσεις κατὰ τὴν ἁφὴν αἵδε, θερμὸν ψυχρόν, ξηρὸν

the matter which is inseparable from, but underlies, the contrarieties ; for " the hot " is not matter for " the cold," nor " the cold " for " the hot," but the *substratum* is matter for them both. Therefore, firstly, the potentially perceptible body, secondly, the contrarieties (for example, heat and cold), and thirdly, Fire and Water and the like are " sources." For the bodies in this third class change into one another and are not as Empedocles and others describe them [a] (otherwise alteration could not have taken place), whereas the contrarieties do not change. Nevertheless, even so the question must be decided what kinds of contrariety and how many of them there are which are sources of body ; for all other philosophers assume and make use of them without stating why they are these and why they are of a particular number.

2. Since, therefore, we are seeking the sources of perceptible bodies, and this means tangible, and tangible is that of which the perception is touch, it is clear that not all the contrarieties constitute " forms " and " sources " of body, but only those connected with touch ; for it is in the matter of contrariety that they differ, that is, tangible contrariety. Therefore neither whiteness and blackness, nor sweetness and bitterness, nor any of the other perceptible contrarieties constitute an element. Yet sight is prior to touch, so that its subject is also prior ; but it is a quality of tangible body not in virtue of its tangibility but because of something else, even though it happens to be naturally prior.

Of the tangible differences and contrarieties themselves we must distinguish which are primary. The following are contrarieties according to touch : hot

The " contrarieties " are " hot and cold " and " dry and moist."

---

[a] *i.e.* as immutable.

20 ὑγρόν, βαρὺ κοῦφον, σκληρὸν μαλακόν, γλίσχρον
κραῦρον, τραχὺ λεῖον, παχὺ λεπτόν. τούτων δὲ
βαρὺ μὲν καὶ κοῦφον οὐ ποιητικὰ οὐδὲ παθητικά·
οὐ γὰρ τῷ ποιεῖν τι ἕτερον ἢ πάσχειν ὑφ᾿ ἑτέρου
λέγονται. δεῖ δὲ ποιητικὰ εἶναι ἀλλήλων καὶ
παθητικὰ τὰ στοιχεῖα· μίγνυται γὰρ καὶ μετα-
25 βάλλει εἰς ἄλληλα. θερμὸν δὲ καὶ ψυχρὸν καὶ
ὑγρὸν καὶ ξηρὸν τὰ μὲν τῷ ποιητικὰ εἶναι τὰ δὲ
τῷ παθητικὰ λέγεται· θερμὸν γάρ ἐστι τὸ συγκρῖνον τὰ ὁμογενῆ (τὸ γὰρ διακρίνειν, ὅπερ φασὶ
ποιεῖν τὸ πῦρ, συγκρίνειν ἐστὶ τὰ ὁμόφυλα· συμβαίνει γὰρ ἐξαιρεῖν τὰ ἀλλότρια), ψυχρὸν δὲ τὸ
30 συνάγον καὶ συγκρῖνον ὁμοίως τά τε συγγενῆ καὶ
τὰ μὴ ὁμόφυλα, ὑγρὸν δὲ τὸ ἀόριστον οἰκείῳ ὅρῳ
εὐόριστον ὄν, ξηρὸν δὲ τὸ εὐόριστον μὲν οἰκείῳ
ὅρῳ, δυσόριστον δέ. τὸ δὲ λεπτὸν καὶ παχὺ καὶ
γλίσχρον καὶ κραῦρον καὶ σκληρὸν καὶ μαλακὸν
καὶ αἱ ἄλλαι διαφοραὶ ἐκ τούτων· ἐπεὶ γὰρ τὸ
35 ἀναπληστικόν ἐστι τοῦ ὑγροῦ διὰ τὸ μὴ ὡρίσθαι
330 a μὲν εὐόριστον δ᾿ εἶναι καὶ ἀκολουθεῖν τῷ ἁπτο-
μένῳ, τὸ δὲ λεπτὸν ἀναπληστικόν (λεπτομερὲς
γάρ, καὶ τὸ μικρομερὲς ἀναπληστικόν· ὅλον γὰρ

and cold, dry and moist, heavy and light, hard and soft, viscous and brittle, rough and smooth, coarse and fine. Of these heavy and light are not active nor yet passive ; for they do not get their names because they act on something else or are acted upon by something else ; elements, on the other hand, must be mutually active and passive, for they mix and change into one another. But hot and cold, and dry and moist are terms of which the first pair get their names because they are active, the second pair because they are passive ; for " hot " is that which associates things of the same kind (for to " dissociate," which, they say, is an action of Fire, is to associate things of the same class, since the result is to destroy things which are foreign), but cold is that which brings together and associates alike both things which are of the same kind and things which are not of the same class. Moist[a] is that which, though easily adaptable to form, cannot be confined within limits of its own, while dry is that which is easily confined within its own limits but is not easily adaptable in form. From the moist and the dry are derived the fine and the coarse, the viscous and the brittle, the hard and the soft and the other contrasted pairs. For since " capacity for filling up something " is characteristic of the moist, because it is not confined within bounds but is adaptable in form and follows the shape of that which comes into contact with it,[b] and that which is " fine " is " capable of filling up something " (for it consists of small particles, and that which consists of small particles is capable of filling up something, for the whole is in

---

[a] Aristotle means liquid.

[b] *e.g.*, water conforms with the shape of the vessel into which it is poured.

330 a

ὅλου ἅπτεται· τὸ δὲ λεπτὸν μάλιστα τοιοῦτον),
φανερὸν ὅτι τὸ μὲν λεπτὸν ἔσται τοῦ ὑγροῦ, τὸ δὲ
5 παχὺ τοῦ ξηροῦ. πάλιν δὲ τὸ μὲν γλίσχρον τοῦ
ὑγροῦ (τὸ γὰρ γλίσχρον ὑγρὸν πεπονθός τί ἐστιν,
οἷον τὸ ἔλαιον), τὸ δὲ κραῦρον τοῦ ξηροῦ· κραῦρον
γὰρ τὸ τελέως ξηρόν, ὥστε καὶ πεπηγέναι δι᾽
ἔλλειψιν ὑγρότητος. ἔτι τὸ μὲν μαλακὸν τοῦ ὑγροῦ
(μαλακὸν γὰρ τὸ ὑπεῖκον εἰς ἑαυτὸ καὶ μὴ μεθιστά-
10 μενον, ὅπερ ποιεῖ τὸ ὑγρόν· διὸ καὶ οὐκ ἔστι τὸ
ὑγρὸν μαλακόν, ἀλλὰ τὸ μαλακὸν τοῦ ὑγροῦ), τὸ
δὲ σκληρὸν τοῦ ξηροῦ· σκληρὸν γάρ ἐστι τὸ πεπηγός, τὸ δὲ πεπηγὸς ξηρόν. λέγεται δὲ ξηρὸν
καὶ ὑγρὸν πλεοναχῶς· ἀντίκειται γὰρ τῷ ξηρῷ καὶ
τὸ ὑγρὸν καὶ τὸ διερόν, καὶ πάλιν τῷ ὑγρῷ καὶ τὸ
15 ξηρὸν καὶ τὸ πεπηγός· ἅπαντα δὲ ταῦτ᾽ ἐστὶ τοῦ
ξηροῦ καὶ τοῦ ὑγροῦ τῶν πρώτων λεχθέντων. ἐπεὶ
γὰρ ἀντίκειται τῷ διερῷ τὸ ξηρόν, καὶ διερὸν μέν
ἐστι τὸ ἔχον ἀλλοτρίαν ὑγρότητα ἐπιπολῆς, βεβρεγμένον δὲ τὸ εἰς βάθος, ξηρὸν δὲ τὸ ἐστερημένον
ταύτης, φανερὸν ὅτι τὸ μὲν διερὸν ἔσται τοῦ ὑγροῦ,
20 τὸ δ᾽ ἀντικείμενον ξηρὸν τοῦ πρώτου ξηροῦ. πάλιν
δὲ τὸ ὑγρὸν καὶ τὸ πεπηγὸς ὡσαύτως· ὑγρὸν μὲν
γάρ ἐστι τὸ ἔχον οἰκείαν ὑγρότητα, βεβρεγμένον
δὲ τὸ ἔχον ἀλλοτρίαν ὑγρότητα ἐν τῷ βάθει, πεπηγὸς δὲ τὸ ἐστερημένον ταύτης. ὥστε καὶ τούτων ἔσται τὸ μὲν ξηροῦ τὸ δὲ ὑγροῦ. δῆλον τοίνυν
25 ὅτι πᾶσαι αἱ ἄλλαι διαφοραὶ ἀνάγονται εἰς τὰς

ᵃ See 329 b 30 ff.

contact with the whole, and that which is fine consists of the smallest possible particles), it is clear that the fine is derived from the moist and the coarse derived from the dry. Again, the viscous is derived from the moist (for that which is viscous is moisture which has undergone a certain treatment, as in the case of oil), and the brittle is derived from the dry ; for the completely dry is brittle, so that it has become solid through lack of moisture. Further, the soft is derived from the moist (for the soft is that which gives way and sinks into itself but does not change its position, as does the moist ; hence, too, the moist is not soft, but the soft is derived from the moist). The hard, on the other hand, is derived from the dry ; for that which has solidified is hard, and the solid is dry. Now " dry " and " moist " are used in several senses ; for both moist and damp are opposed to dry, and, again, solid as well as dry is opposed to moist. But all these qualities are derived from the dry and the moist which we mentioned originally.[a] For the dry is opposed to the damp, and the damp is that which has foreign moisture on its surface, soaked being that which is damp to its innermost depth, while dry is that which is deprived of foreign moisture. Therefore, clearly the damp will be derived from the moist, and the dry, which is opposed to it, will be derived from the primary dry. So likewise, on the other hand, with the moist and the solidified ; for moist is that which contains its own moisture in its depth, while soaked is that which contains foreign moisture there, and solidified is that which has lost its foreign moisture ; so that of these the latter derives from the dry, the former from the moist. It is clear, then, that all the other differences are re-

330 a

πρώτας τέτταρας. αὗται δὲ οὐκέτι εἰς ἐλάττους·
οὔτε γὰρ τὸ θερμὸν ὅπερ ὑγρὸν ἢ ὅπερ ξηρόν, οὔτε
τὸ ὑγρὸν ὅπερ θερμὸν ἢ ὅπερ ψυχρόν, οὔτε τὸ
ψυχρὸν καὶ τὸ ξηρὸν οὔθ' ὑπ' ἄλληλ' οὔθ' ὑπὸ τὸ
θερμὸν καὶ τὸ ὑγρόν εἰσιν· ὥστ' ἀνάγκη τέτταρας
εἶναι ταύτας.

30 3. Ἐπεὶ δὲ τέτταρα τὰ στοιχεῖα, τῶν δὲ τεττάρων ἓξ αἱ συζεύξεις, τὰ δ' ἐναντία οὐ πέφυκε
συνδυάζεσθαι (θερμὸν γὰρ καὶ ψυχρὸν εἶναι τὸ αὐτὸ
καὶ πάλιν ξηρὸν καὶ ὑγρὸν ἀδύνατον), φανερὸν
ὅτι τέτταρες ἔσονται αἱ τῶν στοιχείων συζεύξεις,
330 b θερμοῦ καὶ ξηροῦ, καὶ θερμοῦ καὶ ὑγροῦ, καὶ πάλιν
ψυχροῦ καὶ ὑγροῦ, καὶ ψυχροῦ καὶ ξηροῦ. καὶ
ἠκολούθηκε κατὰ λόγον τοῖς ἁπλοῖς φαινομένοις
σώμασι, πυρὶ καὶ ἀέρι καὶ ὕδατι καὶ γῇ· τὸ μὲν
γὰρ πῦρ θερμὸν καὶ ξηρόν, ὁ δ' ἀὴρ θερμὸν καὶ
5 ὑγρόν (οἷον ἀτμὶς γὰρ ὁ ἀήρ), τὸ δ' ὕδωρ ψυχρὸν
καὶ ὑγρόν, ἡ δὲ γῆ ψυχρὸν καὶ ξηρόν, ὥστ' εὐλόγως
διανέμεσθαι τὰς διαφορὰς τοῖς πρώτοις σώμασι,
καὶ τὸ πλῆθος αὐτῶν εἶναι κατὰ λόγον. ἅπαντες
γὰρ οἱ τὰ ἁπλᾶ σώματα στοιχεῖα ποιοῦντες οἱ μὲν
ἕν, οἱ δὲ δύο, οἱ δὲ τρία, οἱ δὲ τέτταρα ποιοῦσιν.
10 ὅσοι μὲν οὖν ἓν μόνον λέγουσιν, εἶτα πυκνώσει
καὶ μανώσει τἆλλα γεννῶσι, τούτοις συμβαίνει δύο
ποιεῖν τὰς ἀρχάς, τό τε μανὸν καὶ τὸ πυκνὸν ἢ
τὸ θερμὸν καὶ τὸ ψυχρόν· ταῦτα γὰρ τὰ δημιουρ-
γοῦντα, τὸ δ' ἓν ὑπόκειται καθάπερ ὕλη. οἱ δ'
εὐθὺς δύο ποιοῦντες, ὥσπερ Παρμενίδης πῦρ καὶ
15 γῆν, τὰ μεταξὺ μίγματα ποιοῦσι τούτων, οἷον
ἀέρα καὶ ὕδωρ. ὡσαύτως δὲ καὶ οἱ τρία λέγοντες,

---

^a *i.e.* are *mathematically* possible.

duced to the first four, and these cannot be further reduced to a lesser number ; for the hot is not that which is essentially moist or essentially dry, nor is the moist essentially hot or essentially cold, nor do the cold and the dry fall in the category of one another nor in that of the hot and moist ; hence these must necessarily be four of these elementary qualities.

3. Now since the elementary qualities are four in number and of these four six couples can be formed,[a] but contraries are not of a nature which permits of their being coupled—for the same thing cannot be hot and cold, or again, moist and dry—it is clear that the pairs of elementary qualities will be four in number, hot and dry, hot and moist, and, again, cold and moist, and cold and dry. And, according to theory, they have attached themselves to the apparently simple bodies, Fire, Air, Water and Earth ; for Fire is hot and dry, Air is hot and moist (Air, for example, is vapour), Water is cold and moist, and Earth is cold and dry. Thus the variations are reasonably distributed among the primary bodies, and the number of these is according to theory. For all those who make out that the simple bodies are elements make them either one or two or three or four. Therefore (a) those who hold that there is only *one* and then generate everything else by condensation and rarefaction, as a result make the sources two in number, the rare and the dense or the hot and the cold ; for these are the creative forces, and " the one " underlies them as matter. But (b) those who hold that there are *two* from the beginning— as Parmenides held that there were Fire and Earth —make the intermediates, Air and Water, mixtures of these ; and (c) the same thing is done also by

The four elementary qualities (hot, cold, dry, moist) by being coupled together in different ways, constitute four simple bodies, Earth, Air, Fire and Water.

ARISTOTLE

καθάπερ Πλάτων ἐν ταῖς διαιρέσεσιν· τὸ γὰρ μέσον
μῖγμα ποιεῖ. καὶ σχεδὸν ταὐτὰ λέγουσιν οἵ τε
δύο καὶ οἱ τρία ποιοῦντες· πλὴν οἱ μὲν τέμνουσιν
εἰς δύο τὸ μέσον, οἱ δ' ἓν μόνον ποιοῦσιν. ἔνιοι
20 δ' εὐθὺς τέτταρα λέγουσιν, οἷον Ἐμπεδοκλῆς. συνάγει δὲ καὶ οὗτος εἰς τὰ δύο· τῷ γὰρ πυρὶ τἆλλα
πάντα ἀντιτίθησιν.

Οὐκ ἔστι δὲ τὸ πῦρ καὶ ὁ ἀὴρ καὶ ἕκαστον
τῶν εἰρημένων ἁπλοῦν, ἀλλὰ μικτόν. τὰ δ' ἁπλᾶ
τοιαῦτα μέν ἐστιν, οὐ μέντοι ταὐτά, οἷον εἴ τι τῷ
πυρὶ ὅμοιον, πυροειδές, οὐ πῦρ, καὶ τὸ τῷ ἀέρι
25 ἀεροειδές· ὁμοίως δὲ κἀπὶ τῶν ἄλλων. τὸ δὲ πῦρ
ἐστὶν ὑπερβολὴ θερμότητος, ὥσπερ καὶ κρύσταλλος
ψυχρότητος· ἡ γὰρ πῆξις καὶ ἡ ζέσις ὑπερβολαί
τινές εἰσιν, ἡ μὲν ψυχρότητος, ἡ δὲ θερμότητος.
εἰ οὖν ὁ κρύσταλλός ἐστι πῆξις ὑγροῦ ψυχροῦ, καὶ
τὸ πῦρ ἔσται ζέσις ξηροῦ θερμοῦ. διὸ καὶ οὐδὲν
30 οὔτ' ἐκ κρυστάλλου γίνεται οὔτ' ἐκ πυρός.

Ὄντων δὲ τεττάρων τῶν ἁπλῶν σωμάτων, ἑκάτερον τοῖν δυοῖν ἑκατέρου τῶν τόπων ἐστίν· πῦρ
μὲν γὰρ καὶ ἀὴρ τοῦ πρὸς τὸν ὅρον φερομένου, γῆ
δὲ καὶ ὕδωρ τοῦ πρὸς τὸ μέσον. καὶ ἄκρα μὲν
καὶ εἰλικρινέστατα πῦρ καὶ γῆ, μέσα δὲ καὶ με-
331 a μιγμένα μᾶλλον ὕδωρ καὶ ἀήρ. καὶ ἑκάτερα ἑκα-
τέροις ἐναντία· πυρὶ μὲν γὰρ ἐναντίον ὕδωρ, ἀέρι
δὲ γῆ· ταῦτα γὰρ ἐκ τῶν ἐναντίων παθημάτων

---

[a] It is doubtful what is meant here. The commentator
Philoponos suggests that it was a collection of otherwise
unpublished doctrines of Plato and thinks that Aristotle is
referring to a theory of Plato that there was "the great" and
"the small" and a third ἀρχή, which was a mixture of these
and served as matter; but there is nothing to support this
theory. H. H. Joachim takes "the Divisions" to mean the

276

those who hold that there are *three*, as Plato does in the " Divisions," [a] for he makes " the middle " a mixture. Those who hold that there are two and those who postulate *three* say practically the same things, except that the former divide the middle into two, while the latter treat it as one. But (d) some declare that there are four from the start, for instance Empedocles, though he also reduces these to two, for he too opposes all the others to Fire.

Fire, however, and Air and each of the other bodies which we have mentioned are not simple but mixed, while the simple forms of them are similar to them but not the same as they are ; for example, that which is like fire is " fiery," not fire, and that which is like air is " air-like," and similarly with the rest. But fire is an excess of heat, just as ice is an excess of cold ; for freezing and boiling are excesses, the former of cold, the latter of heat. If, therefore, ice is a freezing of moist and cold, so fire will be a boiling of dry and hot ; and that is why nothing comes to be from ice or from fire.

The simple bodies, then, being four in number, make up two pairs belonging to two regions ; for Fire and Air form the body which is carried along towards the " limit," while Earth and Water form the body which is carried along towards the centre [b] ; and Fire and Earth are extremes and very pure, while Water and Air are intermediates and more mixed. Further, the members of each pair are contrary to the members of the other pair, Water being the contrary of Fire, and Earth of Air, for they are

sections in the *Timaeus* (35 A ff.), where Plato makes the middle of his three kinds of substance a blend of the other two. [b] *Cf. De Caelo* 308 a 14 ff.

συνέστηκεν. οὐ μὴν ἀλλ' ἁπλῶς γε τέτταρα ὄντα
ἑνὸς ἕκαστόν ἐστι, γῆ μὲν ξηροῦ μᾶλλον ἢ ψυχροῦ,
5 ὕδωρ δὲ ψυχροῦ μᾶλλον ἢ ὑγροῦ, ἀὴρ δ' ὑγροῦ
μᾶλλον ἢ θερμοῦ, πῦρ δὲ θερμοῦ μᾶλλον ἢ ξηροῦ.

4. Ἐπεὶ δὲ διώρισται πρότερον ὅτι τοῖς ἁπλοῖς
σώμασιν ἐξ ἀλλήλων ἡ γένεσις, ἅμα δὲ καὶ κατὰ
τὴν αἴσθησιν φαίνεται γινόμενα (οὐ γὰρ ἂν ἦν ἀλ-
10 λοίωσις· κατὰ γὰρ τὰ τῶν ἁπτῶν πάθη ἡ ἀλλοίωσίς
ἐστιν), λεκτέον τίς ὁ τρόπος τῆς εἰς ἄλληλα μεταβολῆς, καὶ πότερον ἅπαν ἐξ ἅπαντος γίνεσθαι
δυνατὸν ἢ τὰ μὲν δυνατὸν τὰ δ' ἀδύνατον. ὅτι μὲν
οὖν ἅπαντα πέφυκεν εἰς ἄλληλα μεταβάλλειν, φανε-
ρόν· ἡ γὰρ γένεσις εἰς ἐναντία καὶ ἐξ ἐναντίων, τὰ
15 δὲ στοιχεῖα πάντα ἔχει ἐναντίωσιν πρὸς ἄλληλα
διὰ τὸ τὰς διαφορὰς ἐναντίας εἶναι· τοῖς μὲν γὰρ
ἀμφότεραι ἐναντίαι, οἷον πυρὶ καὶ ὕδατι (τὸ μὲν
γὰρ ξηρὸν καὶ θερμόν, τὸ δ' ὑγρὸν καὶ ψυχρόν),
τοῖς δ' ἡ ἑτέρα μόνον, οἷον ἀέρι καὶ ὕδατι (τὸ μὲν
20 γὰρ ὑγρὸν καὶ θερμόν, τὸ δὲ ὑγρὸν καὶ ψυχρόν).
ὥστε καθόλου μὲν φανερὸν ὅτι πᾶν ἐκ παντὸς γίνεσθαι πέφυκεν, ἤδη δὲ καθ' ἕκαστον οὐ χαλεπὸν
ἰδεῖν πῶς· ἅπαντα μὲν γὰρ ἐξ ἁπάντων ἔσται,
διοίσει δὲ τῷ θᾶττον καὶ βραδύτερον καὶ τῷ ῥᾷον
καὶ χαλεπώτερον. ὅσα μὲν γὰρ ἔχει σύμβολα
25 πρὸς ἄλληλα, ταχεῖα τούτων ἡ μετάβασις, ὅσα δὲ

---

^a *De Caelo* 304 b 23 ff.

made up of different qualities. However, since they are four, each is described simply as possessing a single quality, Earth a dry rather than a cold quality, Water a cold rather than a moist, Air a moist rather than a hot, and Fire a hot rather than a dry.

4. Since it has been determined in a former discussion [a] that the coming-to-be of simple bodies is out of one another, and at the same time, too, it is evident from sense-perception that they *do* come-to-be (for otherwise there would have been no alteration—for alteration is concerned with the qualities of tangible things), we must state (*a*) what is the manner of their reciprocal change, and (*b*) whether any one of them can come-to-be out of any other one of them, or some can do so and others cannot. Now it is manifest that all of them are of such a nature as to change into one another ; for coming-to-be is a process into contraries and out of contraries, and all the elements are characterized by contrarieties one to another, because their distinguishing qualities are contrary. In some of them both qualities are contrary, for example, in Fire and Water (for the former is dry and hot, the latter is moist and cold), in others only one, for example, in Air and Water (for the former is moist and hot, the latter is moist and cold). Hence, it is clear, if we take a general view, that every one of them naturally comes-to-be out of every one of them and, if we take them separately, it is not difficult now to see how this happens ; for all will be the product of all, but there will be a difference owing to the greater and less speed and the greater and less difficulty of the process. For the change will be quick in those things which have qualities which correspond with one

The four simple bodies change into one another in various manners.

279

μὴ ἔχει, βραδεῖα, διὰ τὸ ῥᾷον εἶναι τὸ ἐν ἢ τὰ
πολλὰ μεταβάλλειν, οἷον ἐκ πυρὸς μὲν ἔσται ἀὴρ
θατέρου μεταβάλλοντος (τὸ μὲν γὰρ ἦν θερμὸν καὶ
ξηρόν, τὸ δὲ θερμὸν καὶ ὑγρόν, ὥστε ἂν κρατηθῇ
τὸ ξηρὸν ὑπὸ τοῦ ὑγροῦ, ἀὴρ ἔσται). πάλιν δὲ ἐξ
30 ἀέρος ὕδωρ, ἐὰν κρατηθῇ τὸ θερμὸν ὑπὸ τοῦ ψυχροῦ
(τὸ μὲν γὰρ ἦν θερμὸν καὶ ὑγρόν, τὸ δὲ ψυχρὸν καὶ
ὑγρόν, ὥστε μεταβάλλοντος τοῦ θερμοῦ ὕδωρ ἔσται).
τὸν αὐτὸν δὲ τρόπον καὶ ἐξ ὕδατος γῆ καὶ ἐκ γῆς
πῦρ· ἔχει γὰρ ἄμφω πρὸς ἄμφω σύμβολα· τὸ μὲν
35 γὰρ ὕδωρ ὑγρὸν καὶ ψυχρόν, ἡ δὲ γῆ ψυχρὸν καὶ
ξηρόν, ὥστε κρατηθέντος τοῦ ὑγροῦ γῆ ἔσται. καὶ
331 b πάλιν ἐπεὶ τὸ μὲν πῦρ ξηρὸν καὶ θερμόν, ἡ δὲ γῆ
ψυχρὸν καὶ ξηρόν, ἐὰν φθαρῇ τὸ ψυχρόν, πῦρ ἔσται
ἐκ γῆς.

Ὥστε φανερὸν ὅτι κύκλῳ τε ἔσται ἡ γένεσις
τοῖς ἁπλοῖς σώμασι, καὶ ῥᾷστος οὗτος ὁ τρόπος
τῆς μεταβολῆς διὰ τὸ σύμβολα ἐνυπάρχειν τοῖς
5 ἐφεξῆς. ἐκ πυρὸς δὲ ὕδωρ καὶ ἐξ ἀέρος γῆν καὶ
πάλιν ἐξ ὕδατος καὶ γῆς ἀέρα καὶ πῦρ ἐνδέχεται
μὲν γίνεσθαι, χαλεπώτερον δὲ διὰ τὸ πλειόνων
εἶναι τὴν μεταβολήν· ἀνάγκη γάρ, εἰ ἔσται ἐξ
ὕδατος πῦρ, φθαρῆναι καὶ τὸ ψυχρὸν καὶ τὸ ὑγρόν,
καὶ πάλιν εἰ ἐκ γῆς ἀήρ, φθαρῆναι καὶ τὸ ψυχρὸν
10 καὶ τὸ ξηρόν. ὡσαύτως δὲ καὶ εἰ ἐκ πυρὸς καὶ
ἀέρος ὕδωρ καὶ γῆ, ἀνάγκη ἀμφότερα μεταβάλλειν.
αὕτη μὲν οὖν χρονιωτέρα ἡ γένεσις· ἐὰν δ' ἑκα-

ᵃ σύμβολα was originally used of two pieces of wood or
bone broken away from one another and kept by the two
parties to a contract as a means of identification.

another,[a] but slow when these do not exist, because it is easier for one thing to change than for many; for example, Air will result from Fire by the change of one quality; for Fire, as we said, is hot and dry, while Air is hot and moist, so that Air will result if the dry is overpowered by the moist. Again, Water will result from Air, if the hot is overpowered by the cold; for Air, as we said, is hot and moist, while Water is cold and moist, so that Water will result if the hot undergoes a change. In the same way, too, Earth will result from Water, and Fire from Earth; for both members of each pair have qualities which correspond to one another, since Water is moist and cold, and Earth is cold and dry, and so, when the moist is overpowered, Earth will result. Again, since Fire is dry and hot, and Earth is cold and dry, if the cold were to pass away, Fire will result from Earth.

It is clear, therefore, that the coming-to-be of simple bodies will be cyclical; and this manner of change will be very easy, because the corresponding qualities are already present in the elements which are next to one another. The change, however, from Fire to Water and from Air to Earth, and again from Water and Earth to Air and Fire *can* take place, but is more difficult, because the change involves more stages. For if Fire is to be produced from Water, both the cold and the moist must be made to pass-away; and, again, if Air is to be produced from Earth, both the cold and the dry must be made to pass-away. In like manner, too, if Water and Earth are to be produced from Fire and Air, there must be a change of both qualities. This method of coming-to-be is, therefore, a lengthier process; but if one

τέρου φθαρῇ θάτερον, ῥᾴων μέν, οὐκ εἰς ἄλληλα
δὲ ἡ μετάβασις, ἀλλ' ἐκ πυρὸς μὲν καὶ ὕδατος
ἔσται γῆ καὶ ἀήρ, ἐξ ἀέρος δὲ καὶ γῆς πῦρ καὶ
15 ὕδωρ. ὅταν μὲν γὰρ τοῦ ὕδατος φθαρῇ τὸ ψυχρὸν
τοῦ δὲ πυρὸς τὸ ξηρόν, ἀὴρ ἔσται (λείπεται γὰρ
τοῦ μὲν τὸ θερμὸν τοῦ δὲ τὸ ὑγρόν), ὅταν δὲ τοῦ
μὲν πυρὸς τὸ θερμὸν τοῦ δ' ὕδατος τὸ ὑγρόν, γῆ
διὰ τὸ λείπεσθαι τοῦ μὲν τὸ ξηρὸν τοῦ δὲ τὸ
ψυχρόν. ὡσαύτως δὲ καὶ ἐξ ἀέρος καὶ γῆς πῦρ
20 καὶ ὕδωρ· ὅταν μὲν γὰρ τοῦ ἀέρος φθαρῇ τὸ θερμὸν
τῆς δὲ γῆς τὸ ξηρόν, ὕδωρ ἔσται (λείπεται γὰρ
τοῦ μὲν τὸ ὑγρὸν τῆς δὲ τὸ ψυχρόν), ὅταν δὲ τοῦ
μὲν ἀέρος τὸ ὑγρὸν τῆς δὲ γῆς τὸ ψυχρόν, πῦρ
διὰ τὸ λείπεσθαι τοῦ μὲν τὸ θερμὸν τῆς δὲ τὸ ξηρόν,
ἅπερ ἦν πυρός. ὁμολογουμένη δὲ καὶ τῇ αἰσθήσει
25 ἡ τοῦ πυρὸς γένεσις· μάλιστα μὲν γὰρ πῦρ ἡ φλόξ,
αὕτη δ' ἐστὶ καπνὸς καιόμενος, ὁ δὲ καπνὸς ἐξ
ἀέρος καὶ γῆς.

Ἐν δὲ τοῖς ἐφεξῆς οὐκ ἐνδέχεται φθαρέντος ἐν
ἑκατέρῳ θατέρου τῶν στοιχείων γενέσθαι μετά-
βασιν εἰς οὐδὲν τῶν σωμάτων διὰ τὸ λείπεσθαι ἐν
ἀμφοῖν ἢ ταὐτὰ ἢ τἀναντία. ἐξ οὐδετέρων δὲ
30 ἐγχωρεῖ γίνεσθαι σῶμα, οἷον εἰ τοῦ μὲν πυρὸς
φθαρείη τὸ ξηρόν, τοῦ δ' ἀέρος τὸ ὑγρόν· λείπεται
γὰρ ἐν ἀμφοῖν τὸ θερμόν· ἐὰν δ' ἐξ ἑκατέρου τὸ
θερμόν, λείπεται τἀναντία, ξηρὸν καὶ ὑγρόν.

---

[a] *i.e.* those which pass into one another by the " cyclical "
process described in 331 b 2 ff.

quality of each element were to be made to pass away, the change will be easier but not reciprocal ; but from Fire and Water will come Earth and (alternatively) Air, and from Air and Earth Fire and (alternatively) Water ; for when the cold of the Water and the dryness of the Fire have passed-away, there will be Air (for the heat of the Fire and the moisture of the Water are left), but, when the heat of the Fire and the moisture of the Water have passed-away, there will be Earth, because the dryness of the Fire and the cold of the Water are left. In the same manner also Fire and Water will result from Air and Earth ; for when the heat of the Air and the dryness of the Earth pass-away, there will be Water (for the moisture of the Air and the cold of the Earth are left), but when the moisture of the Air and the cold of the Earth have passed-away, there will be Fire, because the heat of the Air and the dryness of the Earth, which are, as we saw, the constituents of Fire, are left. Now the manner in which Fire comes-to-be is confirmed by our sense-perception ; for flame is the most evident form of Fire, and flame is burning smoke, and smoke is composed of Air and Earth.

No change, however, into any of the bodies can take place from the passing-away of one of the elements in each of them taken in their consecutive order,[a] because either the same or the contrary qualities are left in the pair, and a body cannot come-to-be out of identical or contrary qualities ; for example, it would not result if the dryness of Fire and the moisture of the Air were to pass-away (for the heat is left in both), but, if the heat passes-away from both, the contraries, dryness and moisture, are

331 b

ὁμοίως δὲ καὶ ἐν τοῖς ἄλλοις· ἐν ἅπασι γὰρ τοῖς
ἐφεξῆς ἐνυπάρχει τὸ μὲν ταὐτὸ τὸ δ' ἐναντίον.
35 ὥσθ' ἅμα δῆλον ὅτι τὰ μὲν ἐξ ἑνὸς εἰς ἓν μετα-
βαίνοντα ἑνὸς φθαρέντος γίνεται, τὰ δ' ἐκ δυοῖν
332 a εἰς ἓν πλειόνων. ὅτι μὲν οὖν ἅπαντα ἐκ παντὸς
γίνεται, καὶ τίνα τρόπον εἰς ἄλληλα μετάβασις
γίνεται, εἴρηται.

5. Οὐ μὴν ἀλλ' ἔτι καὶ ὧδε θεωρήσωμεν περὶ
αὐτῶν. εἰ γάρ ἐστι τῶν φυσικῶν σωμάτων ὕλη,
5 ὥσπερ καὶ δοκεῖ ἐνίοις, ὕδωρ καὶ ἀὴρ καὶ τὰ
τοιαῦτα, ἀνάγκη ἤτοι ἓν ἢ δύο εἶναι ταῦτα ἢ πλείω.
ἓν μὲν δὴ πάντα οὐχ οἷόν τε, οἷον ἀέρα πάντα ἢ
ὕδωρ ἢ πῦρ ἢ γῆν, εἴπερ ἡ μεταβολὴ εἰς τἀναντία.
εἰ γὰρ εἴη ἀήρ, εἰ μὲν ὑπομένει, ἀλλοίωσις ἔσται
ἀλλ' οὐ γένεσις. ἅμα δ' οὐδ' οὕτω δοκεῖ, ὥστε
10 ὕδωρ εἶναι ἅμα καὶ ἀέρα ἢ ἄλλ' ὁτιοῦν. ἔσται δή
τις ἐναντίωσις καὶ διαφορὰ ἧς ἕξει τι θάτερον
μόριον τὸ πῦρ οἷον θερμότητα. ἀλλὰ μὴν οὐκ
ἔσται τό γε πῦρ ἀὴρ θερμός· ἀλλοίωσίς τε γὰρ τὸ
τοιοῦτον, καὶ οὐ φαίνεται. ἅμα δὲ πάλιν εἰ ἔσται
15 ἐκ πυρὸς ἀήρ, τοῦ θερμοῦ εἰς τοὐναντίον μεταβάλλοντος ἔσται. ὑπάρξει ἄρα τῷ ἀέρι τοῦτο,
καὶ ἔσται ὁ ἀὴρ ψυχρόν τι. ὥστε ἀδύνατον τὸ
πῦρ ἀέρα θερμὸν εἶναι· ἅμα γὰρ τὸ αὐτὸ θερμὸν

ᵃ See *Phys.* 224 a 21 ff.

left. So likewise with the others too ; for in all the consecutive elements there exists one identical and one contrary quality. It is, therefore, at the same time clear that some elements come-to-be by being transformed from one into one by the passing-away of one quality, but others come-to-be by being transformed from two into one by the passing-away of more than one quality. We have now stated that all the elements come-to-be from any one of them, and how their change into one another takes place.

5. Let us, however, proceed to discuss the following points about them. If Water, Air and the like are, as some people hold, matter for the natural bodies, there must be either one or two or more than two of them. Now they cannot all of them be *one* (for example, they cannot all be Air or Water or Fire or Earth), because change is into contraries.[a] For if they were all Air, then, if Air continues to exist, " alteration " will take place and not coming-to-be. Furthermore, no one holds that Water is at the same time also Air or any other element. There will, then, be a contrariety (or difference),[b] and the other member of this contrariety will belong to some other element, for example, heat will belong to Fire. Fire, however, will certainly not be " hot air " ; for such a change is an " alteration " and also is not observed to happen. Another reason, too, is that, if Air is to be produced from Fire, it will be due to the changing of heat into its contrary. This contrary, therefore, will belong to Air, and Air will be something cold ; hence it is impossible for Fire to be " hot air," for, in that case,

Restatement of the doctrine of chapter 4, and additional evidence.

[b] *e.g.*, if Air is to alter into Fire, we must assign one of a pair of contrary qualities to Air and the other to Fire.

καὶ ψυχρὸν ἔσται. ἄλλο τι ἄρ' ἀμφότερα τὸ αὐτὸ
ἔσται, καὶ ἄλλη τις ὕλη κοινή.

ὁ δ' αὐτὸς λόγος περὶ ἁπάντων, ὅτι οὐκ ἔστιν
20 ἐν τούτων ἐξ οὗ τὰ πάντα. οὐ μὴν οὐδ' ἄλλο τί
γε παρὰ ταῦτα, οἷον μέσον τι ἀέρος καὶ ὕδατος ἢ
ἀέρος καὶ πυρός, ἀέρος μὲν παχύτερον καὶ πυρός,
τῶν δὲ λεπτότερον· ἔσται γὰρ ἀὴρ καὶ πῦρ ἐκεῖνο
μετ' ἐναντιότητος· ἀλλὰ στέρησις τὸ ἕτερον τῶν ἐν-
αντίων· ὥστ' οὐκ ἐνδέχεται μονοῦσθαι ἐκεῖνο οὐδέ-
25 ποτε, ὥσπερ φασί τινες τὸ ἄπειρον καὶ τὸ περιέχον.
ὁμοίως ἄρα ὁτιοῦν τούτων ἢ οὐδέν.

Εἰ οὖν μηδὲν αἰσθητόν γε πρότερον τούτων, ταῦτα ἂν εἴη πάντα. ἀνάγκη τοίνυν ἢ ἀεὶ μένοντα καὶ
ἀμετάβλητα εἰς ἄλληλα, ἢ μεταβάλλοντα, καὶ ἢ
ἅπαντα, ἢ τὰ μὲν τὰ δ' οὔ, ὥσπερ ἐν τῷ Τιμαίῳ
30 Πλάτων ἔγραψεν. ὅτι μὲν τοίνυν μεταβάλλειν
ἀνάγκη εἰς ἄλληλα, δέδεικται πρότερον· ὅτι δ' οὐχ
ὁμοίως ταχέως ἄλλο ἐξ ἄλλου, εἴρηται πρότερον,
ὅτι τὰ μὲν ἔχοντα σύμβολον θᾶττον γίνεται ἐξ
ἀλλήλων, τὰ δ' οὐκ ἔχοντα βραδύτερον. εἰ μὲν
τοίνυν ἡ ἐναντιότης μία ἐστὶ καθ' ἣν μεταβάλ-
35 λουσιν, ἀνάγκη δύο εἶναι· ἡ γὰρ ὕλη τὸ μέσον

ͣ Aristotle's πρώτη ὕλη.
ᵇ *i.e.* without having some quality attached to it.
ᶜ This was the doctrine of Anaximander.
ᵈ The " boundless " cannot exist without being qualified
by a contrary ; if it is qualified by a contrary, it is one of the
elements.
ᵉ *i.e.* there can be no simple bodies but Earth, Air, Fire
and Water.　　ᶠ *Timaeus* 54 ʙ-ᴅ.　　ᵍ 331 a 12 ff.
ʰ See 331 a 23 ff. and note.

the same thing will be hot and cold. Both Fire and Air will, therefore, be something else which is the same, that is, there will be some other " matter " [a] which is common to both.

The same argument holds good of all the elements and shows that there is no single one of them from which all are derived. Yet neither is there anything other than these from which they come, for example, an intermediate between air and water (coarser than Air, but finer than Water) or between Air and Fire (coarser than Fire, but finer than Air). For the intermediate will be Air and Fire with the addition of a pair of contraries ; but one of the contraries will be a privation, so that it is impossible for the intermediate to exist by itself,[b] as some people [c] declare that the " boundless " or " all-embracing " exists ; it is, therefore, one of the elements (it does not matter which), or nothing.[d]

If, therefore, there is nothing—nothing perceptible at any rate—prior to the four elements, these must be all that there are [e] ; it follows, therefore, necessarily, that they must either persist and be unable to change into one another, or they must undergo change, either all of them or some of them only, as Plato wrote in the *Timaeus*.[f] Now it has been shown above [g] that they must change into one another ; and it has previously been stated that they do not come-to-be equally quickly from one another, because elements which have a corresponding quality [h] come-to-be more quickly out of one another, while those which have not this do so more slowly. If, therefore, the contrariety, in virtue of which they change, is *one*, the elements must be two ; for the matter, which is imperceptible and inseparable, is the intermediate

332 b ἀναίσθητος οὖσα καὶ ἀχώριστος. ἐπεὶ δὲ πλείω
ὁρᾶται ὄντα, δύο ἂν εἶεν αἱ ἐλάχισται. δύο δ᾽
ὄντων οὐχ οἷόν τε τρία εἶναι, ἀλλὰ τέσσαρα, ὥσπερ φαίνεται· τοσαῦται γὰρ αἱ συζυγίαι· ἐξ γὰρ
5 οὐσῶν τὰς δύο ἀδύνατον γενέσθαι διὰ τὸ ἐναντίας
εἶναι ἀλλήλαις.

Περὶ μὲν οὖν τούτων εἴρηται πρότερον· ὅτι δ᾽
ἐπειδὴ μεταβάλλουσιν εἰς ἄλληλα, ἀδύνατον ἀρχήν
τινα εἶναι αὐτῶν ἢ ἐπὶ τῷ ἄκρῳ ἢ μέσῳ, ἐκ τῶνδε
δῆλον. ἐπὶ μὲν οὖν τοῖς ἄκροις οὐκ ἔσται, ὅτι
πῦρ ἔσται ἢ γῆ πάντα· καὶ ὁ αὐτὸς λόγος τῷ φάναι
10 ἐκ πυρὸς ἢ γῆς εἶναι πάντα· ὅτι δ᾽ οὐδὲ μέσον,
ὥσπερ δοκεῖ τισὶν ἀὴρ μὲν καὶ εἰς πῦρ μεταβάλλειν
καὶ εἰς ὕδωρ, ὕδωρ δὲ καὶ εἰς ἀέρα καὶ εἰς γῆν,
τὰ δ᾽ ἔσχατα οὐκέτι εἰς ἄλληλα ἐκ τῶνδε δῆλον[1]·
δεῖ μὲν γὰρ στῆναι καὶ μὴ εἰς ἄπειρον τοῦτο ἰέναι
ἐπ᾽ εὐθείας ἐφ᾽ ἑκάτερα· ἄπειροι γὰρ αἱ ἐναντιό-
15 τητες ἐπὶ τοῦ ἑνὸς ἔσονται. γῆ ἐφ᾽ ᾧ Γ, ὕδωρ
ἐφ᾽ ᾧ Υ, ἀὴρ ἐφ᾽ ᾧ Α, πῦρ ἐφ᾽ ᾧ Π. εἰ δὴ τὸ Α
μεταβάλλει εἰς τὸ Π καὶ Υ, ἐναντιότης ἔσται τῶν
ΑΠ. ἔστω ταῦτα λευκότης καὶ μελανία. πάλιν
εἰ εἰς τὸ Υ τὸ Α, ἔσται ἄλλη· οὐ γὰρ ταὐτὸ τὸ Υ
καὶ Π. ἔστω δὲ ξηρότης καὶ ὑγρότης, τὸ μὲν
20 Ξ ξηρότης, τὸ δὲ Υ ὑγρότης. οὐκοῦν εἰ μὲν μένει
τὸ λευκόν, ὑπάρξει τὸ ὕδωρ ὑγρὸν καὶ λευκόν, εἰ
δὲ μή, μέλαν ἔσται τὸ ὕδωρ· εἰς τἀναντία γὰρ ἡ
μεταβολή. ἀνάγκη ἄρα ἢ λευκὸν ἢ μέλαν εἶναι

---

[1] ἐκ τῶνδε δῆλον add. Joachim.

[a] Bk. II. chs. 2 and 3.

between them. But since the elements are seen to be more than two, the contrarieties would be at least two ; but if the latter are two, the elements cannot be three but must be four, as is evidently the case ; for the couples are of that number, since, though six are possible, two of these cannot occur because they are contrary to one another.

These matters have been dealt with before,[a] but that, when the elements change into one another, it is impossible for any one of them, whether at the end or in the middle of the series, to be a " source " is clear from the following considerations. There will be no " source " at the ends, since they will all be Fire or Earth ; and this is the same as arguing that all things are derived from Fire or Earth. That the " source " cannot be in the middle either—as some people hold that Air changes both into Fire and into Water, and Water both into Air and into Earth, while the end-elements are not further changed into one another—is clear from these considerations. There must be a halt, and the process cannot continue in either direction in a straight line to infinity ; for, otherwise, the number of contrarieties belonging to a single element will be infinite. Let E stand for Earth, W for Water, A for Air and F for Fire. Then (a), if A changes into F and W, there will be a contrariety attaching to AF. Let this contrariety be whiteness and blackness. Again (b), if A changes into W, there will be another contrariety ; for W is not the same as F. Let this contrariety be dryness (D) and moisture (M). If, then, the whiteness persists, Water will be moist and white ; if not, Water will be black, for change is into contraries. Water, therefore, must be either white or black. Let it, then, be the

τὸ ὕδωρ. ἔστω δὴ τὸ πρῶτον. ὁμοίως τοίνυν
καὶ τῷ Π τὸ Ξ ὑπάρξει ἡ ξηρότης. ἔσται ἄρα
25 καὶ τῷ Π τῷ πυρὶ μεταβολὴ εἰς τὸ ὕδωρ· ἐναντία
γὰρ ὑπάρχει· τὸ μὲν γὰρ πῦρ τὸ πρῶτον μέλαν ἦν,
ἔπειτα δὲ ξηρόν, τὸ δ' ὕδωρ ὑγρόν, ἔπειτα δὲ
λευκόν. φανερὸν δὴ ὅτι πᾶσιν ἐξ ἀλλήλων ἔσται
ἡ μεταβολή, καὶ ἐπί γε τούτων, ὅτι καὶ ἐν τῷ Γ
τῇ γῇ ὑπάρξει τὰ λοιπὰ καὶ δύο σύμβολα, τὸ
30 μέλαν καὶ τὸ ὑγρόν· ταῦτα γὰρ οὐ συνδεδύασταί
πως.

Ὅτι δ' εἰς ἄπειρον οὐχ οἷόν τ' ἰέναι, ὅπερ μελ-
λήσαντες δείξειν ἐπὶ τοῦτο ἔμπροσθεν ἤλθομεν, δῆλον ἐκ τῶνδε. εἰ γὰρ πάλιν τὸ πῦρ, ἐφ' ᾧ Π, εἰς
ἄλλο μεταβαλεῖ καὶ μὴ ἀνακάμψει, οἷον εἰς τὸ Ψ,
ἐναντιότης τις τῷ πυρὶ καὶ τῷ Ψ ἄλλη ὑπάρξει
35 τῶν εἰρημένων· οὐδενὶ γὰρ τὸ αὐτὸ ὑπόκειται τῶν
333 a Γ Υ Α Π τὸ Ψ. ἔστω δὴ τῷ μὲν Π τὸ Κ, τῷ δὲ
Ψ τὸ Φ. τὸ δὴ Κ πᾶσιν ὑπάρξει τοῖς Γ Υ Α Π·
μεταβάλλουσι γὰρ εἰς ἄλληλα. ἀλλὰ γὰρ τοῦτο
μὲν ἔστω μήπω δεδειγμένον· ἀλλ' ἐκεῖνο δῆλον,
5 ὅτι εἰ πάλιν τὸ Ψ εἰς ἄλλο, ἄλλη ἐναντιότης καὶ
τῷ Ψ ὑπάρξει καὶ τῷ πυρὶ τῷ Π. ὁμοίως δ'
ἀεὶ μετὰ τοῦ προστιθεμένου ἐναντιότης τις ὑπάρξει
τοῖς ἔμπροσθεν, ὥστ' εἰ ἄπειρα, καὶ ἐναντιότητες
ἄπειροι τῷ ἑνὶ ὑπάρξουσιν. εἰ δὲ τοῦτο, οὐκ ἔσται
οὔτε ὁρίσασθαι οὐδὲν οὔτε γενέσθαι· δεήσει γάρ,
εἰ ἄλλο ἔσται ἐξ ἄλλου, τοσαύτας διεξελθεῖν ἐν-
10 αντιότητας, καὶ ἔτι πλείους, ὥστ' εἰς ἔνια μὲν

first of these. Similarly, D will also belong to F; there fore a change into Water will be possible also for Fire (F); for it has qualities which are contrary to those of Water, since Fire was first black and then dry, while Water was first moist and then white. It is clear, then, that the change of all the elements from one another will be possible, and that, in the above examples, E (Earth) will possess also the two remaining " corresponding qualities," blackness and moisture (for these have not yet been in any way coupled together).

That the process cannot go on to infinity—which was the thesis that we were about to prove when we digressed to the above discussion—will be clear from the following considerations. If Fire (F) is to change in turn into something else and not to revert again, for example into Z, another contrariety other than those already mentioned will belong to Fire and Z; for it has been laid down that Z is not the same as any of the four, E, W, A and F. Let K belong to F, and Φ to Z; then K will belong to EWAF; for they change into one another. But, let us admit that this has not yet been demonstrated; yet this is evident that, if Z in turn is to be changed into another element, another contrariety will belong both to Z and also to Fire (F). Similarly, with each addition which is made, a fresh contrariety will attach to the preceding elements of the series, so that if the elements are infinite in number, infinitely numerous contrarieties will also attach *to the single element*. But if this is the case, it will be impossible to define any element and for any element to come-to-be. For if one is to result from another, it will have to pass through so many contrarieties and then through still more. Therefore (*a*), change into some elements

291

οὐδέποτ' ἔσται μεταβολή, οἷον εἰ ἄπειρα τὰ μεταξύ·
ἀνάγκη δ', εἴπερ ἄπειρα τὰ στοιχεῖα· ἔτι δ' οὐδ'
ἐξ ἀέρος εἰς πῦρ, εἰ ἄπειροι αἱ ἐναντιότητες. γίνεται δὲ καὶ πάντα ἕν· ἀνάγκη γὰρ πάσας ὑπάρχειν
τοῖς μὲν κάτω τοῦ Π τὰς τῶν ἄνωθεν, τούτοις δὲ
15 τὰς τῶν κάτωθεν, ὥστε πάντα ἓν ἔσται.

6. Θαυμάσειε δ' ἄν τις τῶν λεγόντων πλείω
ἑνὸς τὰ στοιχεῖα τῶν σωμάτων ὥστε μὴ μεταβάλλειν εἰς ἄλληλα, καθάπερ Ἐμπεδοκλῆς φησί,
πῶς ἐνδέχεται λέγειν αὐτοῖς εἶναι συμβλητὰ τὰ
20 στοιχεῖα. καίτοι λέγει οὕτω· " ταῦτα γὰρ ἰσά τε
πάντα." εἰ μὲν οὖν κατὰ τὸ ποσόν, ἀνάγκη ταὐτό
τι εἶναι ὑπάρχον ἅπασι τοῖς συμβλητοῖς ᾧ με-
τροῦνται, οἷον εἰ ἐξ ὕδατος κοτύλης εἶεν ἀέρος
δέκα· τὸ αὐτό τι ἦν ἄρα ἄμφω, εἰ μετρεῖται τῷ
αὐτῷ. εἰ δὲ μὴ οὕτω κατὰ τὸ ποσὸν συμβλητὰ
25 ὡς ποσὸν ἐκ ποσοῦ, ἀλλ' ὅσον δύναται, οἷον εἰ
κοτύλη ὕδατος ἴσον δύναται ψύχειν καὶ δέκα ἀέρος,
καὶ οὕτως κατὰ τὸ ποσὸν οὐχ ᾗ ποσὸν συμβλητά,
ἀλλ' ᾗ δύναταί τι. εἴη δ' ἂν καὶ μὴ τῷ τοῦ ποσοῦ μέτρῳ συμβάλλεσθαι τὰς δυνάμεις, ἀλλὰ κατ'
ἀναλογίαν, οἷον ὡς τόδε λευκὸν τόδε θερμόν. τὸ
30 δ' ὡς τόδε σημαίνει ἐν μὲν ποιῷ τὸ ὅμοιον, ἐν δὲ
ποσῷ τὸ ἴσον. ἄτοπον δὴ φαίνεται, εἰ τὰ σώματα
ἀμετάβλητα ὄντα μὴ ἀναλογίᾳ συμβλητά ἐστιν,

---

[a] Fr. 17 line 27 (Diels).

[b] *i.e.* if one element is as hot as another is white, they have
" by analogy " the same amount, one of heat, the other of
whiteness.

will never take place, for instance, if the intermediates are infinite in number (and they must be so if the elements are infinite) : and further (*b*), there will not even be a change from Air into Fire, if the contrarieties are infinitely many : and (*c*) all the elements become one, for all the contrarieties of the elements above F must belong to those below F, and *vice versa* ; they will all, therefore, be one.

6. One may well express astonishment at those who, like Empedocles, declare that the elements of bodies are more than one (and, therefore, do not change into one another), and ask them how they can assert that the elements are comparable. Yet Empedocles says,[a] " For these are all not only equal. . . ." Now (*a*) if what is meant is that they are equal in amount, all the " comparables " must all possess something identical by means of which they are measured, if, for instance one pint of Water is equivalent to ten pints of Air, in which case both have always had something identical about them, since they were measured by the same standard. But (*b*) if they are not comparable in amount (in the sense that so much of the one is produced from so much of the other), but in power (for instance, if a pint of water and ten pints of air have an equal cooling power), even so they *are* comparable in amount, though not *qua* amount, but *qua* so much power. And (*c*) it would be possible also to compare their power not by the measure of quantity, but by an " analogy ": for example, " as X is hot, so Y is white." [b] But " analogy," while it signifies similarity in quality, signifies equality in quantity. Now it is obviously absurd that the bodies, though unchangeable, are comparable not merely by " analogy," but by the

293

333 a

ἀλλὰ μέτρῳ τῶν δυνάμεων καὶ τῷ εἶναι ἴσως[1]
θερμὸν ἢ ὁμοίως[2] πυρὸς τοσονδὶ καὶ ἀέρος πολλα-
πλάσιον· τὸ γὰρ αὐτὸ πλεῖον τῷ ὁμογενὲς εἶναι
τοιοῦτον ἕξει τὸν λόγον.

35 Ἀλλὰ μὴν οὐδ' αὔξησις ἂν εἴη κατ' Ἐμπε-
333 b δοκλέα, ἀλλ' ἢ κατὰ πρόσθεσιν· πυρὶ γὰρ αὔξει
τὸ πῦρ· " αὔξει δὲ χθὼν μὲν σφέτερον δέμας,[3]
αἰθέρα δ' αἰθήρ." ταῦτα δὲ προστίθεται· δοκεῖ
δ' οὐχ οὕτως αὔξεσθαι τὰ αὐξανόμενα. πολὺ δὲ
χαλεπώτερον ἀποδοῦναι περὶ γενέσεως τῆς κατὰ
5 φύσιν. τὰ γὰρ γινόμενα φύσει πάντα γίνεται ἢ
ἀεὶ ὡδὶ ἢ ὡς ἐπὶ τὸ πολύ, τὰ δὲ παρὰ τὸ ἀεὶ καὶ
ὡς ἐπὶ τὸ πολὺ ἀπὸ ταὐτομάτου καὶ ἀπὸ τύχης.
τί οὖν τὸ αἴτιον τοῦ ἐξ ἀνθρώπου ἄνθρωπον ἢ ἀεὶ
ἢ ὡς ἐπὶ τὸ πολύ, καὶ ἐκ τοῦ πυροῦ πυρὸν ἀλλὰ
μὴ ἐλαίαν; ἢ καί, ἐὰν ὡδὶ συντεθῇ, ὀστοῦν; οὐ
10 γὰρ ὅπως ἔτυχε συνελθόντων οὐδὲν γίνεται, καθ' ἃ[4]
ἐκεῖνός φησιν, ἀλλὰ λόγῳ τινί. τί οὖν τούτων
αἴτιον; οὐ γὰρ δὴ πῦρ γε ἢ γῆ. ἀλλὰ μὴν οὐδ'
ἡ φιλία καὶ τὸ νεῖκος· συγκρίσεως γὰρ μόνον, τὸ
δὲ διακρίσεως αἴτιον. τοῦτο δ' ἐστὶν ἡ οὐσία ἡ
ἑκάστου, ἀλλ' οὐ μόνον " μίξις τε διάλλαξίς τε
15 μιγέντων," ὥσπερ ἐκεῖνός φησιν. τύχη δ' ἐπὶ
τούτων ὀνομάζεται, ἀλλ' οὐ λόγος· ἔστι γὰρ μιχθῆναι ὡς ἔτυχεν. τῶν δὴ φύσει ὄντων αἴτιον

---

[1] ἴσως : ἴσον codd.   [2] ὁμοίως E : ὅμοιον FHL.
[3] δέμας H : γένος EFL.   [4] καθὰ EHL : καθάπερ F.

---

[a] Empedocles, fr. 37 (Diels).

294

measure of their powers ; that is, that so much Fire and many times as much Air are comparable because they are equally or similarly hot. For the same thing, if greater in amount, will, by being of the same kind, have its ratio increased correspondingly.

Further, according to Empedocles, growth, too, would be impossible except by addition : for in his view Fire increases by Fire and " Earth increases its own body, and ether increases ether," [a] and these are additions ; and it is not generally held that things which increase do so in this way. And it is much more difficult for him to give an account of coming-to-be by a natural process. For the things which come-to-be naturally all come-to-be, either always or generally, in a particular way, and exceptions or violations of the invariable or general rule are the results of chance and luck. What, then, is the reason why man always or generally comes-to-be from man, and why wheat (and not an olive) comes-to-be from wheat ? Or does bone come-to be, if the elements are put together in a certain manner ? For, according to Empedocles, nothing comes-to-be by their coming together by chance but by their coming together in a certain proportion. What, then, is the cause of this ? It is certainly not Fire or Earth ; but neither is it Love and Strife, for the former is a cause of " association " only and the latter of dissociation only. No : the cause is the substance of each thing and not merely, as he says, " a mingling and separation of things mingled " [b] ; and chance, not proportion, is the name applied to these happenings : for it is possible for things to be mixed by chance. The cause, then, of things which exist naturally is that they are in

[b] Empedocles, fr. 8 (Diels) ; see also above, 314 b 7 f.

333 b

τὸ οὕτως ἔχειν, καὶ ἡ ἑκάστου φύσις αὕτη, περὶ
ἧς οὐδὲν λέγει. οὐδὲν ἄρα περὶ φύσεως λέγει.
ἀλλὰ μὴν καὶ τὸ εὖ τοῦτο καὶ ἀγαθόν· ὁ δὲ τὴν
20 μίξιν μόνον ἐπαινεῖ. καίτοι τά γε στοιχεῖα δια-
κρίνει οὐ τὸ νεῖκος, ἀλλ' ἡ φιλία τὰ φύσει πρότερα
τοῦ θεοῦ· θεοὶ δὲ καὶ ταῦτα.

Ἔτι δὲ περὶ κινήσεως ἁπλῶς λέγει· οὐ γὰρ
ἱκανὸν εἰπεῖν διότι ἡ φιλία καὶ τὸ νεῖκος κινεῖ, εἰ
μὴ τοῦτ' ἦν φιλίᾳ εἶναι τὸ κινήσει τοιᾳδί, νείκει
25 δὲ τὸ τοιᾳδί. ἔδει οὖν ἢ ὁρίσασθαι ἢ ὑποθέσθαι
ἢ ἀποδεῖξαι, ἢ ἀκριβῶς ἢ μαλακῶς, ἢ ἄλλως γέ
πως. ἔτι δ' ἐπεὶ φαίνεται καὶ βίᾳ καὶ παρὰ φύσιν
κινούμενα τὰ σώματα, καὶ κατὰ φύσιν (οἷον τὸ
πῦρ ἄνω μὲν οὐ βίᾳ, κάτω δὲ βίᾳ), τῷ δὲ βίᾳ τὸ
κατὰ φύσιν ἐναντίον, ἔστι δὲ τὸ βίᾳ, ἔστιν ἄρα
30 καὶ τὸ κατὰ φύσιν κινεῖσθαι. ταύτην οὖν ἡ φιλία
κινεῖ, ἢ οὔ; τοὐναντίον γὰρ τὴν γῆν κάτω[1] καὶ
διακρίσει ἔοικεν· καὶ μᾶλλον τὸ νεῖκος αἴτιον τῆς
κατὰ φύσιν κινήσεως ἢ ἡ φιλία. ὥστε καὶ ὅλως
παρὰ φύσιν ἡ φιλία ἂν εἴη μᾶλλον. ἁπλῶς δὲ εἰ
μὴ ἡ φιλία ἢ τὸ νεῖκος κινεῖ, αὐτῶν τῶν σωμάτων
35 οὐδεμία κίνησίς ἐστιν οὐδὲ μονή. ἀλλ' ἄτοπον.
334 a ἔτι δὲ καὶ φαίνεται κινούμενα· διέκρινε μὲν γὰρ
τὸ νεῖκος, ἠνέχθη δ' ἄνω ὁ αἰθὴρ οὐχ ὑπὸ τοῦ
νείκους, ἀλλ' ὁτὲ μέν φησιν ὥσπερ ἀπὸ τύχης

---

[1] κάτω EH : ἄνω FL.

[a] Although it is entitled περὶ Φύσεως.
[b] i.e. natural motion.

296

such and-such a condition, and this is what constitutes the nature of each thing, about which he says nothing. There is nothing " About the Nature of Things " in his treatise.[a] And yet it is this which is the excellence and the good of each thing, whereas he gives all the credit to the mixing process. (Yet it is not Strife but Love that dissociates the elements which are by nature prior to God, and they are also gods.)

Further, his account of motion is superficial. For it is not enough to say that Love and Strife move things, unless Love has been given a certain faculty of movement and Strife a certain other. He should, then, have either defined or laid down or demonstrated their powers of movement either accurately or loosely, or at any rate in some manner. Furthermore, since the bodies are seen to move by compulsion (that is, unnaturally) and also naturally (for example, Fire moves upwards without compulsion, but downwards by compulsion), and that which is natural is contrary to that which is by compulsion, and movement by compulsion actually occurs, it follows that natural motion also occurs. Is this, then, the motion which Love sets going, or not ? No : for, on the contrary, it [b] moves the Earth downwards and resembles " dissociation," and Strife rather than Love is the cause of natural motion ; and so, generally speaking, Love rather than Strife would be contrary to nature, and unless Love or Strife is actually setting them in motion, the simple bodies themselves have no motion or rest at all. But this is strange ; and, moreover, they are actually seen to move. For although Strife caused dissociation, it was not by Strife that the ether was carried upwards, but at one time Empedocles talks as if it were due to chance,

("οὕτω γὰρ συνέκυρσε θέων τότε, πολλάκι δ'
ἄλλως"), ὁτὲ δέ φησι πεφυκέναι τὸ πῦρ ἄνω
5 φέρεσθαι, ὁ δ' αἰθήρ, φησί, "μακρῇσι κατὰ χθόνα
δύετο ῥίζαις." ἅμα δὲ καὶ τὸν κόσμον ὁμοίως
ἔχειν φησὶν ἐπί τε τοῦ νείκους νῦν καὶ πρότερον
ἐπὶ τῆς φιλίας. τί οὖν ἐστι τὸ κινοῦν πρῶτον καὶ
αἴτιον τῆς κινήσεως; οὐ γὰρ δὴ ἡ φιλία καὶ τὸ
νεῖκος, ἀλλά τινος κινήσεως ταῦτα αἴτια, εἴ ἐστιν[1]
ἐκεῖνο ἀρχή.

10 Ἄτοπον δὲ καὶ εἰ ἡ ψυχὴ ἐκ τῶν στοιχείων ἢ
ἕν τι αὐτῶν· αἱ γὰρ ἀλλοιώσεις αἱ τῆς ψυχῆς πῶς
ἔσονται, οἷον τὸ μουσικὸν εἶναι καὶ πάλιν ἄμουσον,
ἢ μνήμη ἢ λήθη; δῆλον γὰρ ὅτι εἰ μὲν πῦρ ἡ
ψυχή, τὰ πάθη ὑπάρξει αὐτῇ ὅσα πυρὶ ᾗ πῦρ· εἰ
δὲ μικτόν, τὰ σωματικά· τούτων δ' οὐδὲν σωμα-
15 τικόν.

7. Ἀλλὰ περὶ μὲν τούτων ἑτέρας ἔργον ἐστὶ
θεωρίας. περὶ δὲ τῶν στοιχείων ἐξ ὧν τὰ σώματα
συνέστηκεν, ὅσοις μὲν δοκεῖ τι εἶναι κοινὸν ἢ μεταβάλλειν εἰς ἄλληλα, ἀνάγκη εἰ θάτερον τούτων,
καὶ θάτερον συμβαίνειν· ὅσοι δὲ μὴ ποιοῦσιν ἐξ
ἀλλήλων γένεσιν μηδ' ὡς ἐξ ἑκάστου, πλὴν ὡς ἐκ
20 τοίχου πλίνθους, ἄτοπον πῶς ἐξ ἐκείνων ἔσονται
σάρκες καὶ ὀστᾶ καὶ τῶν ἄλλων ὁτιοῦν. ἔχει δὲ
τὸ λεγόμενον ἀπορίαν καὶ τοῖς ἐξ ἀλλήλων γεν-

---

[1] εἴ ἐστι EHJ : ἔστιν F : εἰ δ' ἔστι.

saying, " For thus in its rush it encountered them then, but oft-times in other wise," [a] whereas on another occasion he says that it is the nature of Fire to be borne upwards, and ether, he says, " sank with long roots into the Earth." [b] At the same time he also says that the Earth is in the same condition now under the rule of Strife as it was formerly under that of Love. What, then, is the " prime mover " and cause of motion ? It certainly is not Love and Strife ; but these are the causes of a secondary motion, if the " prime mover " is the original source.

It is also strange that the soul should consist of the elements or be one of them ; for how, then, will the " alterations " in the soul take place ? How, for example, could the change from being musical to being unmusical occur, or could memory or forgetfulness occur ? For evidently, if the soul is Fire, only such effects will be produced upon it as can be produced by Fire *qua* Fire ; whereas, if it is a mixture of elements, only the corporeal effects will be produced ; but no one of these effects is corporeal.

7. The discussion, however, of these questions is the task of another investigation. But, as regards the elements of which bodies are composed, those who think that they all have something in common or that they change into each other, if they hold one of these views, must necessarily hold the other. For those, on the other hand, who do not make them come-to-be out of each other nor one from another taken singly (except in the sense that bricks come-to-be out of a wall), there is the paradox as to how flesh and bones and any of the other compounds will result from the elements. This suggestion involves a difficulty also for those who generate the elements

How single bodies are combined to form compounds.

299

νῶσιν, τίνα τρόπον γίνεται ἐξ αὐτῶν ἕτερόν τι
παρ' αὐτά. λέγω δ' οἷον ἔστιν ἐκ πυρὸς ὕδωρ
καὶ ἐκ τούτου γίνεσθαι πῦρ· ἔστι γάρ τι κοινὸν
25 τὸ ὑποκείμενον. ἀλλὰ δὴ καὶ σὰρξ ἐξ αὐτῶν
γίνεται καὶ μυελός· ταῦτα δὴ γίνεται πῶς; ἐκείνοις τε γὰρ τοῖς λέγουσιν ὡς Ἐμπεδοκλῆς τίς
ἔσται τρόπος; ἀνάγκη γὰρ σύνθεσιν εἶναι καθάπερ
ἐκ πλίνθων καὶ λίθων τοῖχος· καὶ τὸ μῖγμα δὲ
τοῦτο ἐκ σωζομένων μὲν ἔσται τῶν στοιχείων,
30 κατὰ μικρὰ δὲ παρ' ἄλληλα συγκειμένων. οὕτω
δὴ σὰρξ καὶ τῶν ἄλλων ἕκαστον. συμβαίνει δὴ
μὴ ἐξ ὁτουοῦν μέρους σαρκὸς γίνεσθαι πῦρ καὶ
ὕδωρ, ὥσπερ ἐκ κηροῦ γένοιτ' ἂν ἐκ μὲν τουδὶ
τοῦ μέρους σφαῖρα, πυραμὶς δ' ἐξ ἄλλου τινός·
ἀλλ' ἐνεδέχετό γε ἐξ ἑκατέρου ἑκάτερον γενέσθαι.
35 τοῦτο μὲν δὴ τοῦτον γίνεται τὸν τρόπον ἐκ τῆς
σαρκὸς ἐξ ὁτουοῦν ἄμφω· τοῖς δ' ἐκείνως λέγουσιν
οὐκ ἐνδέχεται, ἀλλ' ὡς ἐκ τοίχου λίθος καὶ πλίνθος,
ἑκάτερον ἐξ ἄλλου τόπου καὶ μέρους. ὁμοίως δὲ
καὶ τοῖς ποιοῦσι μίαν αὐτῶν ὕλην ἔχει τινὰ ἀπορίαν, πῶς ἔσται τι ἐξ ἀμφοτέρων, οἷον ψυχροῦ καὶ
5 θερμοῦ ἢ πυρὸς καὶ γῆς. εἰ γάρ ἐστιν ἡ σὰρξ ἐξ
ἀμφοῖν καὶ μηδέτερον ἐκείνων, μηδ' αὖ σύνθεσις
σωζομένων, τί λείπεται πλὴν ὕλην εἶναι τὸ ἐξ

from each other, namely, in what manner does anything else other than the elements themselves come-to-be out of them. The following is an example of what I mean : Water can come-to-be out of Fire and Fire out of Water (for their *substratum* is something common to both), but flesh, too, and marrow come-to-be out of them ; how do they come-to-be ? What manner of coming-to-be is ascribed to them by those who hold such a view as that of Empedocles ? They must maintain that the process is composition, just as a wall comes-to-be from bricks and stones ; moreover, this "mixture" will consist of the elements preserved intact but placed side by side with one another in minute particles. This, supposedly, is what happens in the case of flesh and each of the other compounds. The result is that Fire and Water do not come-to-be out of any and every part of the flesh ; for example, while a sphere might come-to-be from one part of a piece of wax and a pyramid from another, yet it was possible for either shape to have come-to-be out of either part of the material. This, then, is how coming-to-be occurs when both Fire and Water come-to-be out of any part of the flesh. But for those who hold the above view this is impossible, but the process can only take place as stone and brick come-to-be out of a wall, that is, each out of a different place and part. Similarly, a difficulty arises also for those who make out that the elements have a single matter, namely, how anything will result from two of them taken together, for instance, cold and hot or Fire and Earth. For if flesh consists of both and yet is neither of them, and again is not a compound in which they are preserved intact, what possibility remains except that the result of their composition

301

ἐκείνων; ἡ γὰρ θατέρου φθορὰ ἢ θάτερον ποιεῖ ἢ
τὴν ὕλην.

Ἆρ' οὖν ἐπειδή ἐστι καὶ μᾶλλον καὶ ἧττον θερμὸν
καὶ ψυχρόν, ὅταν μὲν ἁπλῶς ᾖ θάτερον ἐντελεχείᾳ,
10 δυνάμει θάτερον ἔσται· ὅταν δὲ μὴ παντελῶς, ἀλλ'
ὡς μὲν θερμὸν ψυχρόν, ὡς δὲ ψυχρὸν θερμὸν διὰ
τὸ μιγνύμενα φθείρειν τὰς ὑπεροχὰς ἀλλήλων, τότε
οὔθ' ἡ ὕλη ἔσται οὔτε ἐκείνων τῶν ἐναντίων ἑκάτερον ἐντελεχείᾳ ἁπλῶς, ἀλλὰ μεταξύ· κατὰ δὲ τὸ
15 δυνάμει μᾶλλον εἶναι θερμὸν ἢ ψυχρὸν ἢ τοὐναντίον,
κατὰ τοῦτον τὸν λόγον διπλασίως θερμὸν δυνάμει
ἢ ψυχρόν, ἢ τριπλασίως, ἢ κατ' ἄλλον τρόπον
τοιοῦτον; ἔσται δὴ μιχθέντων τἆλλ' ἐκ τῶν ἐναντίων ἢ τῶν στοιχείων, καὶ τὰ στοιχεῖα ἐξ ἐκείνων
δυνάμει πως ὄντων, οὐχ οὕτω δὲ ὡς ἡ ὕλη, ἀλλὰ
20 τὸν εἰρημένον τρόπον· καὶ ἔστιν οὕτω μὲν μίξις,
ἐκείνως δὲ ὕλη τὸ γινόμενον. ἐπεὶ δὲ καὶ πάσχει
τἀναντία κατὰ τὸν ἐν τοῖς πρώτοις διορισμόν·
ἔστι γὰρ τὸ ἐνεργείᾳ θερμὸν δυνάμει ψυχρὸν καὶ
τὸ ἐνεργείᾳ ψυχρὸν δυνάμει θερμόν, ὥστε ἐὰν μὴ
ἰσάζῃ, μεταβάλλει εἰς ἄλληλα. ὁμοίως δὲ καὶ ἐπὶ
25 τῶν ἄλλων ἐναντίων· καὶ πρῶτον οὕτω τὰ στοιχεῖα μεταβάλλει, ἐκ δὲ τούτων σάρκες καὶ ὀστᾶ
καὶ τὰ τοιαῦτα, τοῦ μὲν θερμοῦ γινομένου ψυχροῦ, τοῦ δὲ ψυχροῦ θερμοῦ, ὅταν πρὸς τὸ μέσον

---

a It is difficult to see any meaning in the words and they
should perhaps be omitted.

b *i.e.* the case where one contrary destroys the other,
(lines 6, 7).

c See 323 b 1 ff., where the law of the reciprocal action-
and-passion of contraries is stated.

302

is matter ? For the passing-away of either of them produces either the other or the matter.

Is the following a possible solution based on the fact that there are greater and less degrees in hot and cold ? When one of them is actually in being without qualification, the other will be potentially in existence ; but when neither completely exists but (because they mix and destroy one another's excesses) there is a hot which, for a hot, is cold, and a cold which, for a cold, is hot, then the result will be that neither their matter nor either of the two contraries will be actually in existence without qualification but an intermediate, and according as it is potentially more hot than cold or, *vice versa*, it will possess a power of heating greater in proportion — whether double or treble or in some such ratio— than its power of cooling. The other bodies will result from the contraries (that is, from the elements)[a] when mixed together, and the elements will result from the contraries existing somehow potentially— not in the sense in which matter exists potentially but in the manner already explained. Thus " mixture " takes place, whereas what comes-to-be in the other case [b] is matter. But since the contraries also are acted upon according to the definition given in the first part of this treatise [c]—for the actually hot is potentially cold, and the actually cold is potentially hot, so that, unless the hot and cold are equalized, they change into one another (and the like happens in the case of the other contraries)—thus in the first place the elements are transformed ; but out of them flesh and bones and the like come-to-be when the hot is becoming cold and the cold becoming hot and they reach the mean, for at that point there is neither hot

334 b

ἔλθῃ· ἐνταῦθα γὰρ οὐδέτερον, τὸ δὲ μέσον πολὺ
καὶ οὐκ ἀδιαίρετον. ὁμοίως δὲ καὶ τὸ ξηρὸν καὶ
30 ὑγρὸν καὶ τὰ τοιαῦτα κατὰ μεσότητα ποιοῦσι
σάρκα καὶ ὀστοῦν καὶ τἆλλα.

8. Ἅπαντα δὲ τὰ μικτὰ σώματα, ὅσα περὶ τὸν
τοῦ μέσου τόπον ἐστίν, ἐξ ἁπάντων σύγκειται τῶν
ἁπλῶν. γῆ μὲν γὰρ ἐνυπάρχει πᾶσι διὰ τὸ ἕκαστον
εἶναι μάλιστα καὶ πλεῖστον ἐν τῷ οἰκείῳ τόπῳ,
35 ὕδωρ δὲ διὰ τὸ δεῖν μὲν ὁρίζεσθαι τὸ σύνθετον,
335 a μόνον δ᾿ εἶναι τῶν ἁπλῶν εὐόριστον τὸ ὕδωρ, ἔτι
δὲ καὶ τὴν γῆν ἄνευ τοῦ ὑγροῦ μὴ δύνασθαι συμ-
μένειν, ἀλλὰ τοῦτ᾿ εἶναι τὸ συνέχον· εἰ γὰρ ἐξ-
αιρεθείη τελέως ἐξ αὐτῆς τὸ ὑγρόν, διαπίπτοι ἄν.

Γῇ μὲν οὖν καὶ ὕδωρ διὰ ταύτας ἐνυπάρχει τὰς
5 αἰτίας, ἀὴρ δὲ καὶ πῦρ, ὅτι ἐναντία ἐστὶ γῇ καὶ
ὕδατι· γῆ μὲν γὰρ ἀέρι, ὕδωρ δὲ πυρὶ ἐναντίον ἐστίν,
ὡς ἐνδέχεται οὐσίαν οὐσίᾳ ἐναντίαν εἶναι. ἐπεὶ
οὖν αἱ γενέσεις ἐκ τῶν ἐναντίων εἰσίν, ἐνυπάρχει
δὲ θάτερα ἄκρα τῶν ἐναντίων, ἀνάγκη καὶ θάτερα
ἐνυπάρχειν, ὥστ᾿ ἐν ἅπαντι τῷ συνθέτῳ πάντα τὰ
10 ἁπλᾶ ἐνέσται. μαρτυρεῖν δ᾿ ἔοικε καὶ ἡ τροφὴ
ἑκάστων· ἅπαντα μὲν γὰρ τρέφεται τοῖς αὐτοῖς ἐξ
ὧνπερ ἐστίν, ἅπαντα δὲ πλείοσι τρέφεται. καὶ γὰρ
ἅπερ ἂν δόξειεν ἑνὶ μόνῳ τρέφεσθαι, τῷ ὕδατι τὰ
φυτά, πλείοσι τρέφεται· μέμικται γὰρ τῷ ὕδατι

---

[a] *i.e.* the Earth as the centre of the universe.
[b] *i.e.* because the region in which mixed bodies exist consists mainly of earth.
[c] *i.e.* cold-dry (Earth) and cold-moist (Water).
[d] *i.e.* hot-moist (Air) and hot-dry (Fire).

nor cold. (The mean, however, has considerable extension and is not indivisible.) In like manner also it is in virtue of being in a "mean" condition that the dry and the moist and the like produce flesh and bone and the other compounds.

8. All the mixed bodies, which exist about the region of the centre,[a] are compounds of all the simple bodies. For Earth enters into their composition, because every simple body exists specially and in the greatest quantity in its own place[b]; and Water forms part of them, because that which is composite must have limits, and Water is the only one of the simple bodies which is easily confined within limits, and furthermore, the Earth cannot remain coherent without moisture, and this is what holds it together; for if the moisture were entirely removed from it, it would fall apart.

Earth, therefore, and Water enter into the composition of simple bodies for these reasons; so also do Air and Fire because they are contraries of Earth and Water—Earth of Air, and Water of Fire, in the sense in which one substance can be contrary to another substance. Since, then, comings-to-be result from contraries, and one pair of extreme contraries is already present,[c] the other pair[d] must also be present, so that all the simple bodies are found in every compound. The food of each compound serves to supply evidence of this; for they are all nourished by foods which are identical with their constituents, and all are nourished by more than one food. For indeed the plants, which would seem to be nourished by one food only, namely, Water, are fed by more than one food, for there is Earth mixed with the Water—and this, too, is why farmers experiment by

Every compound body must have all four simple bodies as its constituents.

335 a

γῆ· διὸ καὶ οἱ γεωργοὶ πειρῶνται μίξαντες ἄρδειν.
15 ἐπεὶ δ' ἐστὶν ἡ μὲν τροφὴ τῆς ὕλης, τὸ δὲ τρεφό-
μενον συνειλημένον τῇ ὕλῃ ἡ μορφὴ καὶ τὸ εἶδος,
εὔλογον ἤδη τὸ μόνον τῶν ἁπλῶν σωμάτων τρέφεσθαι τὸ πῦρ ἁπάντων ἐξ ἀλλήλων γινομένων,
ὥσπερ καὶ οἱ πρότεροι λέγουσιν· μόνον γάρ ἐστι
καὶ μάλιστα τοῦ εἴδους τὸ πῦρ διὰ τὸ πεφυκέναι
20 φέρεσθαι πρὸς τὸν ὅρον. ἕκαστον δὲ πέφυκεν εἰς
τὴν ἑαυτοῦ χώραν φέρεσθαι· ἡ δὲ μορφὴ καὶ τὸ
εἶδος ἁπάντων ἐν τοῖς ὅροις. ὅτι μὲν οὖν ἅπαντα
τὰ σώματα ἐξ ἁπάντων συνέστηκε τῶν ἁπλῶν,
εἴρηται.

9. Ἐπεὶ δ' ἐστὶν ἔνια γενητὰ καὶ φθαρτά, καὶ
25 ἡ γένεσις τυγχάνει οὖσα ἐν τῷ περὶ τὸ μέσον τόπῳ, λεκτέον περὶ πάσης γενέσεως ὁμοίως πόσαι τε
καὶ τίνες αὐτῆς αἱ ἀρχαί· ῥᾷον γὰρ οὕτω τὰ καθ'
ἕκαστον θεωρήσομεν, ὅταν περὶ τῶν καθόλου λάβωμεν πρῶτον.

Εἰσὶν οὖν καὶ τὸν ἀριθμὸν ἴσαι καὶ τῷ γένει αἱ
30 αὐταὶ αἵπερ ἐν τοῖς ἀϊδίοις τε καὶ πρώτοις· ἡ μὲν
γάρ ἐστιν ὡς ὕλη, ἡ δ' ὡς μορφή. δεῖ δὲ καὶ τὴν
τρίτην ἔτι προσυπάρχειν· οὐ γὰρ ἱκαναὶ πρὸς τὸ
γεννῆσαι αἱ δύο, καθάπερ οὐδ' ἐν τοῖς πρώτοις.
ὡς μὲν οὖν ὕλη τοῖς γενητοῖς ἐστιν αἴτιον τὸ δυνατὸν εἶναι καὶ μὴ εἶναι. τὰ μὲν γὰρ ἐξ ἀνάγκης
35 ἐστίν, οἷον τὰ ἀΐδια, τὰ δ' ἐξ ἀνάγκης οὐκ ἔστιν.

ᵃ See 321 b 16 ff.

making mixtures and use them for watering. Now whereas food is of the nature of matter, and that which is fed is the "shape" and "form" taken together with the matter,[a] it is reasonable to suppose that of the simple bodies, while all come-to-be out of one another, Fire is the only one which is fed, as is the view also of the earlier philosophers. For Fire alone—and to a greater extent than the rest—is of the nature of "form," because it naturally tends to be borne towards the limit. Now each of the simple bodies tends to be borne to its own place, and the "shape" and "form" of all of them depend on their limits. It has now been explained that all the compound bodies are composed of the simple bodies.

9. Since some things are of a nature to come-to-be and to pass-away, and since coming-to-be actually takes place in the region about the centre, we must discuss the number and the nature of the sources of all coming-to-be alike ; for we shall more easily form a theory about the particulars when we have first grasped the universals.

Chapters 9 and 10. *What causes coming-to-be and passing-away ?* Material, formal and final causes.

These sources, then, are equal in number to and identical in kind with those which exist among eternal and primary things. For there is one in the sense of material cause, a second in the sense of formal cause, and the third too must be present also ; for the two sources are not enough to generate things which come-to-be, just as they are not enough in the case of primary things either. Now cause in the sense of matter for things which are of a nature to come-to-be is " the possibility of being and not-being." For some things exist of necessity, for example, the things which are eternal, and some things of necessity do *not* exist ; and of these two classes it is impossible

307

τούτων δὲ τὰ μὲν ἀδύνατον μὴ εἶναι, τὰ δὲ ἀδύ-
335 b νατον εἶναι διὰ τὸ μὴ ἐνδέχεσθαι παρὰ τὸ ἀναγκαῖον
ἄλλως ἔχειν. ἔνια δὲ καὶ εἶναι καὶ μὴ εἶναι δυνατά,
ὅπερ ἐστὶ τὸ γενητὸν καὶ φθαρτόν· ποτὲ μὲν γάρ
ἐστι τοῦτο, ποτὲ δ' οὐκ ἔστιν. ὥστ' ἀνάγκη γέ-
5 νεσιν εἶναι καὶ φθορὰν περὶ τὸ δυνατὸν εἶναι καὶ
μὴ εἶναι. διὸ καὶ ὡς μὲν ὕλη τοῦτ' ἐστὶν αἴτιον
τοῖς γενητοῖς, ὡς δὲ τὸ οὗ ἕνεκεν ἡ μορφὴ καὶ τὸ
εἶδος· τοῦτο δ' ἐστὶν ὁ λόγος ὁ τῆς ἑκάστου οὐσίας.

Δεῖ δὲ προσεῖναι καὶ τὴν τρίτην, ἣν ἅπαντες
μὲν ὀνειρώττουσι, λέγει δ' οὐδείς, ἀλλ' οἱ μὲν
10 ἱκανὴν ᾠήθησαν αἰτίαν εἶναι πρὸς τὸ γίνεσθαι τὴν
τῶν εἰδῶν φύσιν, ὥσπερ ὁ ἐν Φαίδωνι Σωκράτης·
καὶ γὰρ ἐκεῖνος, ἐπιτιμήσας τοῖς ἄλλοις ὡς οὐδὲν
εἰρηκόσιν, ὑποτίθεται ὅτι ἐστὶ τῶν ὄντων τὰ μὲν
εἴδη τὰ δὲ μεθεκτικὰ τῶν εἰδῶν, καὶ ὅτι εἶναι μὲν
ἕκαστον λέγεται κατὰ τὸ εἶδος, γίνεσθαι δὲ κατὰ
15 τὴν μετάληψιν καὶ φθείρεσθαι κατὰ τὴν ἀποβολήν,
ὥστ' εἰ ταῦτα ἀληθῆ, τὰ εἴδη οἴεται ἐξ ἀνάγκης
αἴτια εἶναι καὶ γενέσεως καὶ φθορᾶς. οἱ δ' αὐτὴν
τὴν ὕλην· ἀπὸ ταύτης γὰρ εἶναι τὴν κίνησιν. οὐ-
δέτεροι δὲ λέγουσι καλῶς. εἰ μὲν γάρ ἐστιν αἴτια
τὰ εἴδη, διὰ τί οὐκ ἀεὶ γεννᾷ συνεχῶς, ἀλλὰ ποτὲ
20 μὲν ποτὲ δ' οὔ, ὄντων καὶ τῶν εἰδῶν ἀεὶ καὶ τῶν

ᵃ Plato, *Phaedo* 96 ᴀ—99 c.

for the first *not to be*, while for the second it is impossible *to be*, because they cannot be other than they are in violation of the law of necessity. Some things, however, can both *be* and *not be*. This is the case with that which can come-to-be and pass-away; for at one moment it exists, at another it does not exist. So coming-to-be and passing-away must occur in the sphere of what can-be-and-not-be. This, then, is the cause, in the sense of material cause, of things which are of a nature to come-to-be, whereas cause, in the sense of their " end in view," is their shape and form; and this is the definition of the essential nature of each of them.

But the third source must also be present, of which everyone dreams but never puts into words. But some people have thought the nature of the " forms " was enough to account for coming-to-be. Socrates, for instance, did so in the *Phaedo* [a]; for he, after finding fault with the other philosophers for having made no pronouncement on the subject, lays it down that some of the things which exist are " forms " and others " partakers in the forms," and that each thing is said to exist in virtue of the " form " and to come-to-be in virtue of its participation in the " form " and to pass-away because of its rejection of it. Hence he thinks that, if this is true, the " forms " are necessarily the causes of both coming-to-be and passing-away. On the other hand, some have thought that the matter in itself was the cause; for it is from this, they said, that movement arises. But neither of these schools of thought is right. For, if the " forms " are causes, why do they not always generate continually but only intermittently, since the " forms " and the partakers in them are always there ? Further-

Criticism of the theory proposed in Plato's *Phaedo*, and the materialist theory.

335 b

μεθεκτικῶν; ἔτι δ' ἐπ' ἐνίων θεωροῦμεν ἄλλο
τὸ αἴτιον ὄν· ὑγίειαν γὰρ ὁ ἰατρὸς ἐμποιεῖ καὶ
ἐπιστήμην ὁ ἐπιστήμων, οὔσης καὶ ὑγιείας αὐτῆς
καὶ ἐπιστήμης καὶ τῶν μεθεκτικῶν· ὡσαύτως
δὲ καὶ ἐπὶ τῶν ἄλλων τῶν κατὰ δύναμιν πρατ-
τομένων. εἰ δὲ τὴν ὕλην τις φήσειε γεννᾶν διὰ
25 τὴν κίνησιν, φυσικώτερον μὲν ἂν λέγοι τῶν οὕτω
λεγόντων· τὸ γὰρ ἀλλοιοῦν καὶ τὸ μετασχηματίζον
αἰτιώτερόν τε τοῦ γεννᾶν, καὶ ἐν ἅπασιν εἰώθαμεν
τοῦτο λέγειν τὸ ποιοῦν, ὁμοίως ἔν τε τοῖς φύσει
καὶ ἐν τοῖς ἀπὸ τέχνης, ὃ ἂν ᾖ κινητικόν. οὐ μὴν
ἀλλὰ καὶ οὗτοι οὐκ ὀρθῶς λέγουσιν· τῆς μὲν
30 γὰρ ὕλης τὸ πάσχειν ἐστὶ καὶ τὸ κινεῖσθαι, τὸ δὲ
κινεῖν καὶ τὸ ποιεῖν ἑτέρας δυνάμεως (δῆλον δὲ
καὶ ἐπὶ τῶν τέχνῃ καὶ ἐπὶ τῶν φύσει γινομένων·
οὐ γὰρ αὐτὸ ποιεῖ τὸ ὕδωρ ζῷον ἐξ αὑτοῦ, οὐδὲ
τὸ ξύλον κλίνην, ἀλλ' ἡ τέχνη). ὥστε καὶ οὗτοι
διὰ τοῦτο λέγουσιν οὐκ ὀρθῶς, καὶ ὅτι παραλεί-
35 πουσι τὴν κυριωτέραν αἰτίαν· ἐξαιροῦσι γὰρ τὸ τί
336 a ἦν εἶναι καὶ τὴν μορφήν. ἔτι δὲ καὶ τὰς δυνάμεις
ἀποδιδόασι τοῖς σώμασι, δι' ἃς γεννῶσι, λίαν
ὀργανικῶς, ἀφαιροῦντες τὴν κατὰ τὸ εἶδος αἰτίαν.
ἐπειδὴ γὰρ πέφυκεν, ὥς φασι, τὸ μὲν θερμὸν διακρίνειν τὸ δὲ ψυχρὸν συνιστάναι, καὶ τῶν ἄλλων
5 ἕκαστον τὸ μὲν ποιεῖν τὸ δὲ πάσχειν, ἐκ τούτων
λέγουσι καὶ διὰ τούτων ἅπαντα τἆλλα γίνεσθαι

more, in some cases we see that something else is the cause ; for it is the physician who implants health and the scientific man who implants scientific know-ledge, although health itself and science itself exist and also the participants in them ; and the same thing is true of the other operations carried out in virtue of a special faculty. On the other hand, if one were to say that matter generates by means of its movement, he would speak more in accordance with the facts of nature than those who state the view given above ; for that which " alters " and transforms is a more potent cause of bringing things into being, and we are always accustomed, in the products alike of nature and of art, to make out that whatever can cause motion is the acting cause. However, these thinkers are also wrong ; for to be acted upon, that is, to be moved, is characteristic of matter, but to move, that is to act, is the function of another power. (This is evident both in the things which come-to-be by art and in those which come-to-be by nature ; for water does not itself produce an animal out of itself, nor does wood produce a bed, but art). So, for this reason, these thinkers are not correct in what they say, and also because they omit the most potent cause ; for they exclude the essential nature and the " form." Moreover, also, when they do away with the formal cause, the powers which they attribute to bodies and which enable them to bring things into being are too instrumental in character. For since, as they assert, it is the nature of the hot to separate and of the cold to bring together and of each of the other qualities the one to act and the other to be acted upon, it is out of these and by means of these, so they say, that all the other things come-to-be and

καὶ φθείρεσθαι· φαίνεται δὲ καὶ τὸ πῦρ αὐτὸ κινούμενον καὶ πάσχον. ἔτι δὲ παραπλήσιον ποιοῦσιν
ὥσπερ εἴ τις τῷ πρίονι καὶ ἑκάστῳ τῶν ὀργάνων
10 ἀπονέμοι τὴν αἰτίαν τῶν γινομένων· ἀνάγκη γὰρ
πρίοντος διαιρεῖσθαι καὶ ξέοντος λεαίνεσθαι, καὶ
ἐπὶ τῶν ἄλλων ὁμοίως. ὥστ᾽ εἰ ὅτι μάλιστα
ποιεῖ καὶ κινεῖ τὸ πῦρ, ἀλλὰ πῶς κινεῖ οὐ προσ-
θεωροῦσιν,[1] ὅτι χεῖρον ἢ τὰ ὄργανα. ἡμῖν δὲ καθόλου τε πρότερον εἴρηται περὶ τῶν αἰτίων, καὶ νῦν
διώρισται περί τε τῆς ὕλης καὶ τῆς μορφῆς.

15 10. Ἔτι δὲ ἐπεὶ ἡ κατὰ τὴν φορὰν κίνησις δέδεικται ὅτι ἀΐδιος, ἀνάγκη τούτων ὄντων καὶ γένεσιν εἶναι συνεχῶς· ἡ γὰρ φορὰ ποιήσει τὴν γένεσιν
ἐνδελεχῶς διὰ τὸ προσάγειν καὶ ἀπάγειν τὸ γεν-
νητικόν. ἅμα δὲ δῆλον ὅτι καὶ τὰ πρότερον καλῶς
20 εἴρηται, τὸ πρώτην τῶν μεταβολῶν τὴν φορὰν
ἀλλὰ μὴ τὴν γένεσιν εἰπεῖν· πολὺ γὰρ εὐλογώ-
τερον τὸ ὂν τῷ μὴ ὄντι γενέσεως αἴτιον εἶναι ἢ τὸ
μὴ ὂν τῷ ὄντι τοῦ εἶναι. τὸ μὲν οὖν φερόμενον
ἔστι, τὸ δὲ γινόμενον οὐκ ἔστιν· διὸ καὶ ἡ φορὰ
προτέρα τῆς γενέσεως. ἐπεὶ δ᾽ ὑπόκειται καὶ δέ-
25 δεικται συνεχὴς οὖσα τοῖς πράγμασι καὶ γένεσις
καὶ φθορά, φαμὲν δ᾽ αἰτίαν εἶναι τὴν φορὰν τοῦ
γίνεσθαι, φανερὸν ὅτι μιᾶς μὲν οὔσης τῆς φορᾶς
οὐκ ἐνδέχεται γίνεσθαι ἄμφω διὰ τὸ ἐναντία εἶναι·

[1] οὐ προσθεωροῦσι : οὐ προσθεωροῖσιν E : οὐ προθεωροῦσιν H :
οὐχ ὁρῶσιν FL.

---

[a] *Phys.* ii. 3-9.   [b] See 335 a 32-b 7.
[c] *Phys.* viii. 7-9.   [d] *i.e.* the sun, see below.
          [e] *Phys.* 260 a 26 ff.

pass-away. But it is evident that Fire itself is moved and is acted upon; moreover, they are doing much the same thing as if one were to ascribe to the saw or to any other tool the causation of objects which are brought into being; for division must take place when a man saws and smoothing when he uses a plane, and a similar effect must be produced by the use of the other tools. Hence, however much Fire is active and causes motion, yet they fail to observe *how* it moves things, namely, in a manner inferior to that in which the tools act. We have ourselves dealt with causes in general in a previous work,[a] and we have now [b] distinguished between matter and form.

10. Moreover, since the change caused by motion has been proved to be eternal,[c] it necessarily follows, if that is so, that coming-to-be goes on continuously; for the movement will produce coming-to-be uninterruptedly by bringing near and withdrawing the "generator."[d] At the same time it is evident that our statement in a former work [e] was also right in which we spoke of motion, not coming-to-be, as the "primary kind of change." For it is far more reasonable that that which *is* should be a cause of coming-to-be of that which *is not*, than that that which *is not* should be cause of being to that which *is*. For that which is being moved exists, but that which is coming-to-be does not exist; therefore movement is prior to coming-to-be. Now since it has been suggested and proved [f] that coming-to-be and passing-away happen to things continuously, and we maintain that motion is the cause of coming-to-be, it is clear that, if motion is simple, both processes cannot go on because they are contrary to one another; for nature has ordained

The efficient cause of coming-to-be and passing-away is the sun's annual movement in the ecliptic circle.

---

[f] *Cf.* 317 b 33 ff.

336 a

τὸ γὰρ αὐτὸ καὶ ὡσαύτως ἔχον ἀεὶ τὸ αὐτὸ πέφυκε
ποιεῖν. ὥστε ἤτοι γένεσις ἀεὶ ἔσται ἢ φθορά. δεῖ
30 δὲ πλείους εἶναι τὰς κινήσεις καὶ ἐναντίας, ἢ τῇ
φορᾷ ἢ τῇ ἀνωμαλίᾳ· τῶν γὰρ ἐναντίων τἀναντία
αἴτια.

Διὸ καὶ οὐχ ἡ πρώτη φορὰ αἰτία ἐστὶ γενέσεως
καὶ φθορᾶς, ἀλλ' ἡ κατὰ τὸν λοξὸν κύκλον· ἐν
ταύτῃ γὰρ καὶ τὸ συνεχές ἐστι καὶ τὸ κινεῖσθαι
δύο κινήσεις· ἀνάγκη γάρ, εἴ γε ἀεὶ ἔσται συνεχὴς
336 b γένεσις καὶ φθορά, ἀεὶ μέν τι κινεῖσθαι, ἵνα μὴ
ἐπιλείπωσιν αὗται αἱ μεταβολαί, δύο δ', ὅπως μὴ
θάτερον συμβαίνῃ μόνον. τῆς μὲν οὖν συνεχείας
ἡ τοῦ ὅλου φορὰ αἰτία, τοῦ δὲ προσιέναι καὶ
ἀπιέναι ἡ ἔγκλισις· συμβαίνει γὰρ ὁτὲ μὲν πόρρω
5 γίνεσθαι ὁτὲ δ' ἐγγύς. ἀνίσου δὲ τοῦ διαστή-
ματος ὄντος ἀνώμαλος ἔσται ἡ κίνησις· ὥστ' εἰ
τῷ προσιέναι καὶ ἐγγὺς εἶναι γεννᾷ, τῷ ἀπιέναι
ταὐτὸν τοῦτο καὶ πόρρω γίνεσθαι φθείρει, καὶ εἰ
τῷ πολλάκις προσιέναι γεννᾷ, καὶ τῷ πολλάκις
ἀπελθεῖν φθείρει· τῶν γὰρ ἐναντίων τἀναντία αἴτια.
10 καὶ ἐν ἴσῳ χρόνῳ καὶ ἡ φθορὰ καὶ ἡ γένεσις ἡ
κατὰ φύσιν. διὸ καὶ οἱ χρόνοι καὶ οἱ βίοι ἑκάστων
ἀριθμὸν ἔχουσι καὶ τούτῳ διορίζονται· πάντων γάρ
ἐστι τάξις, καὶ πᾶς βίος καὶ χρόνος μετρεῖται
περιόδῳ, πλὴν οὐ τῇ αὐτῇ πάντες, ἀλλ' οἱ μὲν

---

^a The revolution of the πρῶτος οὐρανός or outermost sphere
which revolves once every twenty-four hours.

^b The annual course of the sun in the ecliptic circle.

^c i.e. of the πρῶτος οὐρανός, which also involves the revolu-
tion of the concentric spheres.

^d The inclination of the ecliptic to the equator of the outer-

that the same thing, as long as it remains in the same state, always produces the same result, so that either coming-to-be or passing-away will always result. The movements, however, must be more than one and contrary to one another either in the direction of their motion or in their irregularity ; for contraries are the causes of contraries.

It is not, therefore, the primary motion [a] which is the cause of coming-to-be and passing-away, but the motion along the inclined circle [b] ; for in this there is both continuity and also double movement, for it is essential, if there is always to be continuous coming-to-be and passing-away, that there should be something always moving, in order that this series of changes may not be broken, and double movement, in order that there may not be only one change occurring. The movement of the whole [c] is the cause of the continuity, and the inclination [d] causes the approach and withdrawal of the moving body ; for since the distance is unequal, the movement will be irregular. Therefore, if it generates by approaching and being near, this same body causes destruction by withdrawing and becoming distant, and if by frequently approaching it generates, by frequently withdrawing it destroys ; for contraries are the cause of contraries, and natural passing-away and coming-to-be take place in an equal period of time. Therefore the periods, that is the lives, of each kind of living thing have a number and are thereby distinguished ; for there is an order for everything, and every life and span is measured by a period, though this is not the same for all, but some are

most sphere ; according to Aristotle, the equator of the Universe is in the same plane as the earth's equator.

336 b

ἐλάττονι οἱ δὲ πλείονι· τοῖς μὲν γὰρ ἐνιαυτός, τοῖς
15 δὲ μείζων, τοῖς δὲ ἐλάττων περίοδός¹ ἐστι τὸ
μέτρον.

Φαίνεται δὲ καὶ τὰ² κατὰ τὴν αἴσθησιν ὁμολογούμενα τοῖς παρ' ἡμῶν λόγοις· ὁρῶμεν γὰρ ὅτι
προσιόντος μὲν τοῦ ἡλίου γένεσίς ἐστιν, ἀπιόντος
δὲ φθίσις, καὶ ἐν ἴσῳ χρόνῳ ἑκάτερον· ἴσος γὰρ ὁ
χρόνος τῆς φθορᾶς καὶ τῆς γενέσεως τῆς κατὰ
20 φύσιν. ἀλλὰ συμβαίνει πολλάκις ἐν ἐλάττονι
φθείρεσθαι διὰ τὴν πρὸς ἄλληλα σύγκρασιν· ἀνω-
μάλου γὰρ οὔσης τῆς ὕλης καὶ οὐ πανταχοῦ τῆς
αὐτῆς ἀνάγκη καὶ τὰς γενέσεις ἀνωμάλους εἶναι
καὶ τὰς μὲν θάττους τὰς δὲ βραδυτέρας, ὥστε
συμβαίνει διὰ τὴν τούτων γένεσιν ἄλλοις γίνεσθαι
φθοράν.

25 Ἀεὶ δ', ὥσπερ εἴρηται, συνεχὴς ἔσται ἡ γένεσις
καὶ ἡ φθορά, καὶ οὐδέποτε ὑπολείψει δι' ἣν εἴπομεν
αἰτίαν. τοῦτο δ' εὐλόγως συμβέβηκεν· ἐπεὶ γὰρ
ἐν ἅπασιν ἀεὶ τοῦ βελτίονος ὀρέγεσθαί φαμεν τὴν
φύσιν, βέλτιον δὲ τὸ εἶναι ἢ τὸ μὴ εἶναι (τὸ δ' εἶναι
30 ποσαχῶς λέγομεν, ἐν ἄλλοις εἴρηται), τοῦτο δ'
ἀδύνατον ἐν ἅπασιν ὑπάρχειν διὰ τὸ πόρρω τῆς
ἀρχῆς ἀφίστασθαι, τῷ λειπομένῳ τρόπῳ συνε-
πλήρωσε τὸ ὅλον ὁ θεός, ἐνδελεχῆ³ ποιήσας τὴν
γένεσιν· οὕτω γὰρ ἂν μάλιστα συνείροιτο τὸ εἶναι
διὰ τὸ ἐγγύτατα εἶναι τῆς οὐσίας τὸ γίνεσθαι ἀεὶ
337 a καὶ τὴν γένεσιν. τούτου δ' αἴτιον, ὥσπερ εἴρηται

---

¹ ἡ ante περίοδός omisi.
² τὰ addidi.
³ ἐνδελεχῆ FH : ἐντελεχῆ E.

ᵃ See 318 a 9 ff.
ᵇ Metaphysics, passim.

measured by a smaller and some by a greater period ; for some the measure is a year, for others a greater or a lesser period.

The evidence of sense-perception clearly agrees with our views ; for we see that coming-to-be occurs when the sun approaches, and passing-away when it withdraws, and the two processes take an equal time ; for the space of time occupied by natural passing-away and coming-to-be is equal. It often happens, however, that things pass away in too short a time owing to the commingling of things with one another ; for, their matter being irregular and not everywhere the same, their comings-to-be must also be irregular, sometimes too quick and sometimes too slow. The result is that the coming-to-be of certain things becomes the cause of the passing-away of other things.

As has already been remarked, coming-to-be and passing-away will take place continuously, and will never fail owing to the cause which we have given.[a] This has come about with good reason. For nature, as we maintain, always and in all things strives after the better ; and " being " (we have stated elsewhere the different meanings of " being "[b]) is better than " not-being," but it is impossible that " being " can be present in all things, because they are too far away from the " original source." God, therefore, following the course which still remained open, perfected the universe by making coming-to-be a perpetual pro-process ; for in this way " being " would acquire the greatest possible coherence, because the continual coming-to-be of coming-to-be is the nearest approach to eternal being. The cause of this continuous process, as has been frequently remarked, is cyclical

Aristotle claims that his theory explains how coming-to-be and passing-away maintain their continuous alteration.

πολλάκις, ἡ κύκλῳ φορά· μόνη γὰρ συνεχής. διὸ
καὶ τἆλλα ὅσα μεταβάλλει εἰς ἄλληλα κατὰ τὰ
πάθη καὶ τὰς δυνάμεις, οἷον τὰ ἁπλᾶ σώματα,
μιμεῖται τὴν κύκλῳ φοράν· ὅταν γὰρ ἐξ ὕδατος
5 ἀὴρ γένηται καὶ ἐξ ἀέρος πῦρ καὶ πάλιν ἐκ πυρὸς
ὕδωρ, κύκλῳ φαμὲν περιεληλυθέναι τὴν γένεσιν διὰ
τὸ πάλιν ἀνακάμπτειν. ὥστε καὶ ἡ εὐθεῖα φορὰ
μιμουμένη τὴν κύκλῳ συνεχής ἐστιν.

Ἅμα δὲ δῆλον ἐκ τούτων ὅ τινες ἀποροῦσιν,
διὰ τί, ἑκάστου τῶν σωμάτων εἰς τὴν οἰκείαν φε-
10 ρομένου χώραν, ἐν τῷ ἀπείρῳ χρόνῳ οὐ διεστᾶσι
τὰ σώματα. αἴτιον γὰρ τούτου ἐστὶν ἡ εἰς ἄλληλα
μετάβασις· εἰ γὰρ ἕκαστον ἔμενεν ἐν τῇ αὑτοῦ
χώρᾳ καὶ μὴ μετέβαλλεν ὑπὸ τοῦ πλησίον, ἤδη
ἂν διεστήκεσαν. μεταβάλλει μὲν οὖν διὰ τὴν
φορὰν διπλῆν οὖσαν· διὰ δὲ τὸ μεταβάλλειν οὐκ
15 ἐνδέχεται μένειν οὐδὲν αὐτῶν ἐν οὐδεμιᾷ χώρᾳ
τεταγμένῃ.

Διότι μὲν οὖν ἔστι γένεσις καὶ φθορὰ καὶ διὰ
τίν' αἰτίαν, καὶ τί τὸ γενητὸν καὶ φθαρτόν, φανερὸν ἐκ τῶν εἰρημένων. ἐπεὶ δ' ἀνάγκη εἶναί
τι τὸ κινοῦν, εἰ κίνησις ἔσται, ὥσπερ εἴρηται πρότερον ἐν ἑτέροις, καὶ εἰ ἀεί, ὅτι ἀεί τι δεῖ εἶναι, καὶ
20 εἰ συνεχής, ἓν τὸ αὐτὸ καὶ ἀκίνητον καὶ ἀγένητον καὶ ἀναλλοίωτον· καὶ εἰ πλείους εἶεν αἱ κύκλῳ
κινήσεις, πλείους μέν, πάσας δέ πως εἶναι ταύτας
ἀνάγκη ὑπὸ μίαν ἀρχήν· συνεχοῦς δ' ὄντος τοῦ

ᵃ Phys. 255 b 31 ff.

motion, the only motion which is continuous. Hence also the other things which change into one another, for instance, the simple bodies, by being acted upon or having power to act, imitate cyclical movement. For when Air comes-to-be from Water, and Fire from Air, and Water again from Fire, we say that coming-to-be has completed the cycle, because it has come back to its starting-point. Hence motion in a straight line is also continuous because it imitates cyclical motion.

This at the same time clears up a point which some people find puzzling, namely, the reason why, since each of the bodies is being borne along towards its own place, the bodies have not become separated in the infinity of time. The reason is their reciprocal change of position ; for if each remained in its own place and was not transformed by its neighbour, they would have long ago been parted. Their transformation, then, is due to the movement of a double kind ; and, owing to their transformation, none of them can remain in any fixed position.

From what has been said, it is evident that coming-to-be and passing-away take place, and why this is so, and what it is that comes-to-be and passes-away. But if there is to be movement, there must, as has been explained elsewhere in an earlier treatise,[a] be something which causes movement, and if movement is to go on always, that which causes it must go on always and, if it is to be continuous, that which causes it must be one and the same and unmoved, ungenerated and unalterable ; and if the cyclical movements are to be more than one, they must, in spite of being more than one, be all subject somehow to one cause ; and since time is continuous, the move-

χρόνου ἀνάγκη τὴν κίνησιν συνεχῆ εἶναι, εἴπερ
ἀδύνατον χρόνον χωρὶς κινήσεως εἶναι. συνεχοῦς
25 ἄρα τινὸς ἀριθμὸς ὁ χρόνος, τῆς κύκλῳ ἄρα, καθάπερ ἐν τοῖς ἐν ἀρχῇ λόγοις διωρίσθη. συνεχὴς
δ' ἡ κίνησις πότερον τῷ τὸ κινούμενον συνεχὲς
εἶναι ἢ τῷ τὸ ἐν ᾧ κινεῖται, οἷον τὸν τόπον λέγω
ἢ τὸ πάθος; δῆλον δὴ ὅτι τῷ τὸ κινούμενον· πῶς
γὰρ τὸ πάθος συνεχὲς ἀλλ' ἢ τῷ τὸ πρᾶγμα ᾧ
συμβέβηκε συνεχὲς εἶναι; εἰ δὲ καὶ τῷ ἐν ᾧ,
30 μόνῳ τοῦτο τῷ τόπῳ ὑπάρχει· μέγεθος γάρ τι ἔχει.
τούτου δὲ τὸ κύκλῳ μόνον συνεχές, ὥστε αὐτὸ
αὑτῷ ἀεὶ συνεχές. τοῦτο ἄρα ἐστὶν ὃ ποιεῖ συνεχῆ
κίνησιν, τὸ κύκλῳ σῶμα φερόμενον· ἡ δὲ κίνησις
τὸν χρόνον.

11. Ἐπεὶ δ' ἐν τοῖς συνεχῶς κινουμένοις κατὰ
35 γένεσιν ἢ ἀλλοίωσιν ἢ ὅλως μεταβολὴν ὁρῶμεν
337 b τὸ ἐφεξῆς ὂν καὶ γινόμενον τόδε μετὰ τόδε ὥστε
μὴ διαλείπειν, σκεπτέον πότερον ἔστι τι ὃ ἐξ
ἀνάγκης ἔσται, ἢ οὐδέν, ἀλλὰ πάντα ἐνδέχεται μὴ
γενέσθαι. ὅτι μὲν γὰρ ἔνια, δῆλον, καὶ εὐθὺς τὸ
ἔσται καὶ τὸ μέλλον ἕτερον διὰ τοῦτο· ὃ μὲν γὰρ
5 ἀληθὲς εἰπεῖν ὅτι ἔσται, δεῖ τοῦτο εἶναί ποτε ἀληθὲς
ὅτι ἔστιν· ὃ δὲ νῦν ἀληθὲς εἰπεῖν ὅτι μέλλει, οὐδὲν

---

[a] *Phys.* 217 b 29 ff.

ment must be continuous, because it is impossible
for there to be time without movement. Time, then,
is a way of reckoning some kind of continuous movement and, therefore, of cyclical movement, as was
laid down in our original discussion.[a] But is movement continuous because that which is moved is
continuous or because that in which it moves is continuous (for example, the place or the quality)?
Clearly because that which is moved is continuous;
for how could the quality be continuous except
because the thing to which it belongs is continuous?
And if it is because the place in which it occurs is
continuous, continuity is to be found only in the place
in which it occurs; for it has a certain magnitude.
But of that which moves, only that which moves in a
circle is continuous in such a way that it is always
continuous with itself. This, then, is what produces
continuous motion, namely, the body which is moved
in a circle, and its movement makes time continuous.

11. When in things which are moved continuously
in the course of coming-to-be or alteration or change
generally, we observe a sequence, that is, one thing
coming-to-be after another in such a way that there
is no cessation, we must inquire whether there is
anything which will necessarily exist in the future
or whether there is no such thing, or whether any
one of them may possibly fail to come-to-be. For
it is evident that some of them fail to come-to-be,
and the readiest example is the difference which for
this reason exists between " something will be " and
" something is about to be "; for if it is true to say
" something will be," it must be true at some future
date to say that it *is*. On the other hand, though it is
true now to say that " something is about to happen,"

Things which come-to-be do so " of necessity " because a cyclical series of changes is absolutely " of necessity."

κωλύει μὴ γενέσθαι· μέλλων γὰρ ἂν βαδίζειν τις
οὐκ ἂν βαδίσειεν. ὅλως δ᾽, ἐπεὶ ἐνδέχεται ἔνια
τῶν ὄντων καὶ μὴ εἶναι, δῆλον ὅτι καὶ τὰ γινόμενα
10 οὕτως ἕξει, καὶ οὐκ ἐξ ἀνάγκης τοῦτ᾽ ἔσται. πότερον οὖν ἅπαντα τοιαῦτα ἢ οὔ, ἀλλ᾽ ἔνια ἀναγκαῖον
ἁπλῶς γίνεσθαι, καὶ ἔστιν ὥσπερ ἐπὶ τοῦ εἶναι
τὰ μὲν ἀδύνατα μὴ εἶναι τὰ δὲ δυνατά, οὕτως καὶ
περὶ τὴν γένεσιν; οἷον τροπὰς ἄρα ἀνάγκη γενέσθαι, καὶ οὐχ οἷόν τε μὴ ἐνδέχεσθαι.

Εἰ δὴ τὸ πρότερον ἀνάγκη γενέσθαι, εἰ τὸ
15 ὕστερον ἔσται (οἷον εἰ οἰκία, θεμέλιον, εἰ δὲ
τοῦτο, πηλόν), ἆρ᾽ οὖν καὶ εἰ θεμέλιος γέγονεν,
ἀνάγκη οἰκίαν γενέσθαι; ἢ οὐκέτι, εἰ μὴ κἀκεῖνο
ἀνάγκη γενέσθαι ἁπλῶς; εἰ δὲ τοῦτο, ἀνάγκη καὶ
θεμελίου γενομένου γενέσθαι οἰκίαν· οὕτω γὰρ ἦν
τὸ πρότερον ἔχον πρὸς τὸ ὕστερον, ὥστ᾽ εἰ ἐκεῖνο
20 ἔσται, ἀνάγκη ἐκεῖνο πρότερον. εἰ τοίνυν ἀνάγκη
γενέσθαι τὸ ὕστερον, καὶ τὸ πρότερον ἀνάγκη· καὶ
εἰ τὸ πρότερον, καὶ τὸ ὕστερον τοίνυν ἀνάγκη, ἀλλ᾽
οὐ δι᾽ ἐκεῖνο, ἀλλ᾽ ὅτι ὑπέκειτο ἐξ ἀνάγκης ἐσό-
μενον. ἐν οἷς ἄρα τὸ ὕστερον ἀνάγκη εἶναι, ἐν
τούτοις ἀντιστρέφει, καὶ ἀεὶ τοῦ προτέρου γενο-
25 μένου ἀνάγκη γενέσθαι τὸ ὕστερον.

there is nothing to prevent its not happening—a man might not go for a walk, though he is now " about to " do so. In general, since it is possible for some of the things which " are " also " not to be," obviously things which are coming-to-be are also in this case and their coming-to-be will not necessarily take place. Are, then, all the things which come-to-be of this kind ? Or is this not so, but it is absolutely necessary for some of them to come-to-be ? And does the same thing happen in the sphere of coming-to-be as in that of being, where there are some things for which it is impossible " not to be " and for others which it is possible ? For example, solstices must come-to-be and it is impossible that they should be unable to occur.

If it is necessary for that which is prior to come-to-be if that which is posterior is to be—for example, foundations must have come-to-be if a house is to exist, and there must be clay if there are to be foundations—does it follow that, if the foundations have come-to-be, the house must necessarily do so ? Or is this no longer so, if there is no such absolute necessity ? In this case, however, if the foundations have come-to-be, the house must come-to-be ; for such was the assumed relation of the prior to the posterior that, if the posterior is to be, the prior must have preceded it. If, therefore, it is necessary that the posterior should come-to-be, it is necessary also that the prior should have come-to-be, and, if the prior, then also the posterior, not, however, because of the prior, but because the future being of the posterior was assumed as necessary. Hence, whenever the posterior is necessary, the reverse is also true, and always when the prior has come-to-be, the posterior must also come-to-be.

337 b

Εἰ μὲν οὖν εἰς ἄπειρον εἰσιν ἐπὶ τὸ κάτω, οὐκ ἔσται ἀνάγκη τὸ ὕστερον τόδε γενέσθαι ἁπλῶς, ἀλλ' ἐξ ὑποθέσεως· ἀεὶ γὰρ ἕτερον ἔμπροσθεν ἀνάγκη ἔσται, δι' ὃ ἐκεῖνο ἀνάγκη γενέσθαι. ὥστ' εἰ μή ἐστιν ἀρχὴ τοῦ ἀπείρου, οὐδὲ πρῶτον ἔσται

30 οὐδέν, δι' ὃ ἀναγκαῖον ἔσται γενέσθαι. ἀλλὰ μὴν οὐδ' ἐν τοῖς πέρας ἔχουσι τοῦτ' ἔσται εἰπεῖν ἀληθῶς, ὅτι ἁπλῶς ἀνάγκη γενέσθαι, οἷον οἰκίαν, ὅταν θεμέλιος γένηται· ὅταν γὰρ γένηται, εἰ μὴ ἀεὶ τοῦτο ἀνάγκη γίνεσθαι, συμβήσεται ἀεὶ εἶναι τὸ ἐνδεχόμενον μὴ ἀεὶ εἶναι. ἀλλὰ δεῖ τῇ γενέσει ἀεὶ

35 εἶναι, εἰ ἐξ ἀνάγκης αὐτοῦ ἐστιν ἡ γένεσις· τὸ γὰρ

338 a ἐξ ἀνάγκης καὶ ἀεὶ ἅμα· ὃ γὰρ εἶναι ἀνάγκη οὐχ οἷόν τε μὴ εἶναι· ὥστ' εἰ ἔστιν ἐξ ἀνάγκης, ἀΐδιόν ἐστι, καὶ εἰ ἀΐδιον, ἐξ ἀνάγκης. καὶ εἰ ἡ γένεσις τοίνυν ἐξ ἀνάγκης, ἀΐδιος ἡ γένεσις τούτου, καὶ εἰ ἀΐδιος, ἐξ ἀνάγκης.

Εἰ ἄρα τινὸς ἐξ ἀνάγκης ἁπλῶς ἡ γένεσις,

5 ἀνάγκη ἀνακυκλεῖν καὶ ἀνακάμπτειν. ἀνάγκη γὰρ ἤτοι πέρας ἔχειν τὴν γένεσιν ἢ μή, καὶ εἰ μή, ἢ

---

[a] The argument is as follows : let *x* be one of the future members of the series of events, *x*'s occurrence is contingent on the future occurrence of a still later member of the series, which is itself contingent on a still later member, *y*. The occurrence of every subsequent member of the infinite series is therefore conditionally, not absolutely, necessary. If *x*'s occurrence were absolutely necessary, *x* would be the begin-

Now if the series is to go on indefinitely downwards, any particular later member of the series must come-to-be not by absolute, but only by conditional, necessity; for it will always be necessary that another later member of the series should exist first in order to make it necessary that the earlier member of the series should come-to-be. Hence, since the infinite has no beginning, neither will there be any primary member of the series which will make it necessary for the other members to come-to-be.[a] And further, it will not be possible to say with truth, even in the case of members of a series which is limited, that there is an absolute necessity that they should come-to-be. For example, a house will not necessarily come-to-be when its foundations have come-to-be; for unless it is always necessary for a house to come-to-be, the result will be that when its foundations have come-to-be, a thing, which need not always be, must always be. No: if its coming-to-be is of necessity, there must be an " always " about its coming-to-be; for what must *necessarily* be, must at the same time *always* be, since what " must necessarily be " cannot " not-be "; hence, if a thing is " of necessity," it is eternal, and, if it is eternal, it is " of necessity "; if, therefore, the coming-to-be of a thing is " of necessity," it is eternal and, if it is eternal, it is " of necessity."

If, then, the coming-to-be of anything is absolutely necessary, it must be cyclical and return upon itself; for coming-to-be must either have a limit or not have a limit, and if it has not a limit, it must proceed either

ning of the series (*i.e.* would necessitate the earlier members); but the series is infinite and therefore has no beginning or end.

338 a

εἰς εὐθὺ ἢ κύκλῳ. τούτων δ' εἴπερ ἔσται ἀΐδιος,
οὐκ εἰς εὐθὺ οἷόν τε διὰ τὸ μηδαμῶς εἶναι ἀρχὴν
μήτ' ἂν κάτω, ὡς ἐπὶ τῶν ἐσομένων, λαμβάνομεν,
μήτ' ἄνω, ὡς ἐπὶ τῶν γινομένων· ἀνάγκη δ' εἶναι
10 ἀρχήν, μὴ πεπερασμένης οὔσης, καὶ ἀΐδιον εἶναι.
διὸ ἀνάγκη κύκλῳ εἶναι. ἀντιστρέφειν ἄρα ἀνάγκη
ἔσται, οἷον εἰ τοδὶ ἐξ ἀνάγκης, καὶ τὸ πρότερον
ἄρα· ἀλλὰ μὴν εἰ τοῦτο, καὶ τὸ ὕστερον ἀνάγκη
γενέσθαι. καὶ τοῦτο ἀεὶ δὴ συνεχῶς· οὐδὲν γὰρ
τοῦτο διαφέρει λέγειν διὰ δύο ἢ πολλῶν. ἐν τῇ
15 κύκλῳ ἄρα κινήσει καὶ γενέσει ἐστὶ τὸ ἐξ ἀνάγκης
ἁπλῶς· καὶ εἴτε κύκλῳ, ἀνάγκη ἕκαστον γίνεσθαι
καὶ γεγονέναι, καὶ εἰ ἀνάγκη, ἡ τούτων γένεσις
κύκλῳ.

Ταῦτα μὲν δὴ εὐλόγως, ἐπεὶ ἀΐδιος καὶ ἄλλως
ἐφάνη ἡ κύκλῳ κίνησις καὶ ἡ τοῦ οὐρανοῦ, ὅτι
338 b ταῦτα ἐξ ἀνάγκης γίνεται καὶ ἔσται, ὅσαι ταύτης
κινήσεις καὶ ὅσαι διὰ ταύτην· εἰ γὰρ τὸ κύκλῳ
κινούμενον ἀεί τι κινεῖ, ἀνάγκη καὶ τούτων κύκλῳ
εἶναι τὴν κίνησιν, οἷον τῆς ἄνω φορᾶς οὔσης κύκλῳ ὁ ἥλιος[1] ὡδί, ἐπεὶ δ' οὕτως, αἱ ὧραι διὰ τοῦτο

---

[1] κύκλῳ ὁ ἥλιος F, Bonitz.

---

[a] Rectilinear movement, proceeding *ad infinitum*, does

in a straight line or in a circle. But of these alternatives, if it is to be eternal, it cannot proceed in a straight line, because it can have no source,[a] whether we take the members of the series downwards as future events or upwards as past events. But there must be a source of coming-to-be, though without coming-to-be itself being limited, and it must be eternal. Therefore, it must be a cyclical process. It will, therefore, have to return upon itself; for example, if a certain member of the series is necessary, then the one before it is also necessary, and further, if the latter is necessary, then the one which follows must necessarily come-to-be. And this goes on always continuously; for it makes no difference whether we speak of a sequence of two or many members of the series. Therefore, it is in cyclical movement and cyclical coming-to-be that absolute necessity is present, and if the process is cyclical, each member must necessarily come-to-be and have come-to-be, and, if this necessity exists, their coming-to-be is cyclical.

This conclusion is only reasonable, since cyclical movement, that is, the movement of the heavens, has been shown [b] on other grounds to be eternal, because its own movements and the movements which it causes come-to-be of necessity and will continue to do so; for if that which moves in a cycle is continually seeking something else in motion, the movement of those things which it moves must also be cyclical. For example, since the upper revolution is cyclical, the sun moves in a particular way, and since this is so the seasons come-to-be in a cycle and

not involve an ἀρχή from which coming-to-be might derive its necessity.　　　　　[b] *Phys.* viii. 7-9.

338 b

5 κύκλῳ γίνονται καὶ ἀνακάμπτουσιν, τούτων δ' οὕτω γινομένων πάλιν τὰ ὑπὸ τούτων.

Τί οὖν δή ποτε τὰ μὲν οὕτω φαίνεται, οἷον ὕδατα
καὶ ἀὴρ κύκλῳ γινόμενα, καὶ εἰ μὲν νέφος ἔσται,
δεῖ ὗσαι, καὶ εἰ ὕσει γε, δεῖ καὶ νέφος εἶναι, ἄνθρωποι δὲ καὶ ζῷα οὐκ ἀνακάμπτουσιν εἰς αὑτοὺς ὥστε
10 πάλιν γίνεσθαι τὸν αὐτόν (οὐ γὰρ ἀνάγκη, εἰ ὁ
πατὴρ ἐγένετο, σὲ γενέσθαι· ἀλλ' εἰ σύ, ἐκεῖνον,
εἰς εὐθὺ δὲ ἔοικεν εἶναι αὕτη ἡ γένεσις); ἀρχὴ δὲ
τῆς σκέψεως πάλιν αὕτη, πότερον ὁμοίως ἅπαντα
ἀνακάμπτει ἢ οὔ, ἀλλὰ τὰ μὲν ἀριθμῷ τὰ δὲ εἴδει
μόνον. ὅσων μὲν οὖν ἄφθαρτος ἡ οὐσία ἡ κινου-
15 μένη, φανερὸν ὅτι καὶ ἀριθμῷ ταὐτὰ ἔσται (ἡ γὰρ
κίνησις ἀκολουθεῖ τῷ κινουμένῳ), ὅσων δὲ μὴ ἀλλὰ
φθαρτή, ἀνάγκη τῷ εἴδει, ἀριθμῷ δὲ μὴ ἀνακάμπτειν. διὸ ὕδωρ ἐξ ἀέρος καὶ ἀὴρ ἐξ ὕδατος
εἴδει ὁ αὐτός, οὐκ ἀριθμῷ. εἰ δὲ καὶ ταῦτα
ἀριθμῷ, ἀλλ' οὐχ ὧν ἡ οὐσία γίνεται οὖσα τοιαύτη
οἷα ἐνδέχεσθαι μὴ εἶναι.

---

[a] The sun moves in a circle in the ecliptic, and solar motion
causes the cyclical changes of season, on which depend the
vital periods of living things upon the earth.

[b] And not to be cyclical.

[c] In some cycles the same individual always recurs, in
others successive individuals of the same species.

[d] As was the doctrine of Empedocles (*cf.* 315 a 4 ff.).

return upon themselves ; and since they come-to-be in this manner, so do those things which they cause to come-to-be.[a]

Why, then, is it that some things evidently come-to-be cyclically, for example rains and air, and if there is to be cloud, it must rain, and if it is to rain, there must also be a cloud, yet men and animals do not return upon themselves, so that the same creature comes-to-be a second time ? For there is no necessity, because your father came-to-be, that you should come-to-be ; but if you are to come-to-be, he must have done so ; and in this case the course of coming-to-be seems to be in a straight line.[b] The starting-point for the discussion of this problem is this, to ask the question again whether all things alike return upon themselves, or whether some things recur *numerically* and others only specifically.[c] Therefore, obviously, those things of which the substance (which is what is moved) is imperishable will be numerically the same ; for the nature of the movement depends on that of the thing moved ; but those things which are not of this kind but perishable must recur specifically and not numerically. Hence, when Water comes-to-be from Air or Air from Water, the Water or the Air is the same specifically but not numerically ; and if these things also do seem numerically the same,[d] yet this is not true of those things whose " substance " comes-to-be, when it is such that it is possible for it not to be.

PSEUDO-ARISTOTLE
DE MUNDO

INTRODUCTION

ANALYSIS

THE treatise opens with a short introductory chapter, commending to Alexander the study of " the cosmos and the greatest things in the cosmos," and continues with a description of the various parts of the cosmos, working from the region of the aether on the outside of the sphere to the earth at the centre. Chapter 2 describes the shape, the arrangement and the material of the heavens, and indicates very briefly the nature of the " fiery element " and the air that lie inside the outer sphere of aether. Chapter 3 describes the geography of the sea and the earth ; the author naturally concentrates on the " inhabited world," though he maintains that there are other inhabited worlds also, beyond the seas. Chapter 4 is a very summary account of the " most notable phenomena in and about the inhabited world " ; a section on meteorology, including an elaborate catalogue of winds, is followed by a description of the things that happen on or in the earth or sea—volcanic eruptions, earthquakes, tidal waves, etc.

The last sentence of Chapter 4 introduces the main theme of the work : there are many changes in the sublunary world, but the system as a whole remains constant, and is subject neither to generation nor to

destruction. In Chapter 5 the language is heightened in what is virtually a hymn to the eternal cosmos. Chapters 6 and 7 tell of the cause that ensures its eternity—the god who rules everything with his all-pervading power. This god is described in Chapter 6 by means of a series of similes, which show how a remote and transcendent god can maintain the order and arrangement of the cosmos without personal intervention ; Chapter 7 lists a number of names by which God is known and shows how they arise from various aspects of his function.

PHILOSOPHY AND RELIGION

Before examining the problem of the authorship and date of the *De Mundo*, we must consider its purpose and its philosophical position. It is an open letter, written with the most careful attention to style and language, summarizing persuasively the results of a study of the cosmos. The open letter was a common form of literary expression, particularly for protreptic discourses ; the outstanding examples are Isocrates' *Ad Nicoclem* and Aristotle's lost *Protrepticus*, addressed to Themison, the prince of Cyprus. The *De Mundo* shows many similarities to these protreptic addresses in style ; but the author's purpose, emphasized several times, is to provide a summary of his subject, and in this he approaches the pattern of Epicurus's letters or the popular " Introductions " (εἰσαγωγαί) of the Hellenistic period.

The author's attitude of mind is given in a word in the first chapter : " let us theologize (θεολογῶμεν) about all these things." A.-J. Festugière has shown [a]

---

[a] *Le Dieu cosmique*, pp. 341 ff.

how typical this is of that " *koine* spirituelle " which grew in the late Hellenistic age and flowered in the Roman Empire ; nature is explored, not as the object of scientific enquiry, but as the expression of the cosmic deity, and the results are presented straightforwardly as dogma.

The theology and cosmology of the *De Mundo* is, in general, Peripatetic, but the author borrows his details from many schools. Parallel passages and possible sources have been analysed in great detail by W. Capelle, W. L. Lorimer and Joseph P. Maguire,[a] and there is no need to repeat their analysis. Capelle traced many of the details to Posidonius, and this view was for many years generally accepted. Maguire, however, found no reason to believe that anything came from Posidonius except some of the meteorology, and showed that the closest parallels are in the Neo-Pythagorean writers ; he established at least that we cannot attribute a doctrine to Posidonius simply because it occurs in the *De Mundo*, but it would be surprising if a work written after the time of Posidonius were not considerably influenced by him. The paramount difficulty is that the author was an eclectic, living in an age when eclecticism was the fashion and there was a great deal of common ground between different schools ; it is therefore sometimes impossible to say which authors, or even which schools, were chosen as sources.

The scientific chapters of the *De Mundo* are typical of many " introductions " and summaries, and very likely are themselves derived from similar elementary handbooks rather than from the detailed expositions of original authors. The doctrine of the cosmic deity,

[a] See Bibliographical Note, below.

which is the climax of the book, developed gradually in the history of Greek religion. Its chief exponents were the Stoics, and no doubt the *De Mundo* is influenced by Stoic religious thought. But the author rejects an important part of the Stoic doctrine : his god is not immanent in the world, interpenetrating all things, but remote, unmoved and impassive. He maintains the order of the cosmos by means of an undefined " power," which relieves him of the dishonourable necessity of personal intervention.

Clearly we have here a development, however remote, of Aristotle's Unmoved Mover. At first sight the god of the *De Mundo* seems far removed from the god of *Physics* viii and *Metaphysics* Λ, who is inferred as the necessary result of a theory of motion, whose only activity is thought which has itself as its object, and who moves " as the object of love." Aristotle himself, however, seems to have spoken with a rather different voice in his published works. In the *De Philosophia* he said that the orderly movement of the heavenly bodies was one of the reasons for man's belief in gods. Cicero reports an elaborate passage from Aristotle to this effect [a] : suppose there were men who had lived all their lives in caves under the earth and were then released ; " when they saw, suddenly, the earth and seas and sky, when they learnt the vastness of the clouds and the force of the winds, when they beheld the sun and learnt its great size and beauty and the efficacy of its work, that it spreads its light over all the sky and makes day, and when night darkened the lands and then they saw the whole sky adorned with a pattern of stars, and the changes in the moon's light

[a] Cic. *De Nat. Deor.* ii. 37 = Arist. fr. 12 Rose.

as it waxes and wanes, and the rising and setting of them all, and their courses planned and immutable for all eternity—when they saw this, they would think at once that there are gods and that these mighty works are the works of gods." This is close to the spirit of the *De Mundo*.

In one other important respect the author sides with the Peripatetics and Neo-Pythagoreans against the Stoics. Most of the Stoics believed that the element of fire was more powerful than the other elements, and that it periodically enveloped the cosmos in a universal conflagration (ἐκπύρωσις). Pseudo-Aristotle is emphatic in his rejection of this doctrine : the elements are equally balanced and there is no universal conflagration, nor any other kind of cosmic destruction. The eternity of the cosmos was maintained by Aristotle in the lost *De Philosophia*,[a] and in the *De Caelo*.[b] In Hellenistic times it was believed by the Stoic Panaetius, but his successor Posidonius apparently reverted again to ἐκπύρωσις. There are two Hellenistic treatises extant which argue that the cosmos is eternal—*De Universi Natura*, falsely attributed to the Pythagorean Ocellus of Lucania, and Philo (or Pseudo-Philo), *De Aeternitate Mundi*.

AUTHOR AND DATE

It is almost universally agreed that this treatise is not a genuine work of Aristotle. The style and various details of doctrine all make it unthinkable that it was written either by Aristotle himself or during his lifetime ; but no such certainty is possible about the identity of the author or the date of composition.

[a] *Cf.* fr. 22 Rose.   [b] Bk. I. 10-12.

The first problem to be decided is whether the treatise was attributed to Aristotle by the author or by someone else. The probability is that it was a deliberate forgery. Attempts have been made to show that the Alexander to whom the work is addressed is someone other than Alexander the Great : but it is difficult to find another Alexander who might be called " the best of princes." [a] Probably the author followed the example of an earlier forger, the author of the *Rhetoric to Alexander*, in the hope that his work might be taken as a respectful tribute from the master to his most famous pupil.

The late Hellenistic author Demetrius [b] says that Aristotle's letters to Alexander were more like treatises (σνγγράμματα) than real letters. A man called Artemon, who is mentioned by Demetrius, arranged the letters then supposed to be by Aristotle into eight books. We can conclude from this that at the time of Demetrius, who was roughly contemporary with Pseudo-Aristotle, there was in circulation a collection of Aristotle's letters, which included letters to Alexander which were in the form of " treatises." It would seem therefore that the author of the *De Mundo* had ample precedent for the form of his work, whether the *De Mundo* was known to Demetrius or not.

The habit of attributing one's writings to an older and greater author in the same tradition was par-

---

[a] Max Pohlenz (*Die Stoa*, 1948, pp. 361-362) returns to a suggestion of Bernays that the addressee is Tiberius Alexander, nephew of Philo and governor of Egypt soon after A.D. 63.

[b] *On Style* iv. 234. Demetrius wrote some time after 100 B.C. (see J. F. Lockwood, in *C.R.* lii (1938), p. 59) and probably before A.D. 100.

ticularly common among the Pythagoreans of the Hellenistic age ; the author of the *De Mundo* owes much to these Neo-Pythagoreans, and he certainly reproduces enough genuinely Aristotelian thought to make it reasonable that he should wish to usurp Aristotle's name.

This is an important point. Those who have proved that the work is a forgery have sometimes overlooked that it is a forgery of *Aristotle*, and that in this fact we might find a little help in dating the treatise. For if the author is imitating Aristotle at all, it is surely the Aristotle of the *Protrepticus* and *De Philosophia*, the Aristotle whose " flumen orationis aureum " was praised by Cicero,[a] rather than the Aristotle of the school-treatises which survive to-day. The school-treatises were either lost or disregarded after the death of Theophrastus, and did not begin to occupy the attention of the learned world again until the appearance of Andronicus's edition in the late first century B.C.[b]

These considerations will be variously interpreted. Those who believe that knowledge of Aristotle's work was *absolutely* confined to the published writings until Andronicus's edition, will say that the author of the *De Mundo* shows knowledge of doctrines (*e.g.* of the Unmoved Mover, if this was not contained in the *De Philosophia*, and various meteorological details) which were known only after Andronicus. But it is likely that much of Aristotle's doctrine was known throughout the period, at least in his own school,

[a] *Acad. Pr.* ii. 38. 119.
[b] The date usually given for this is *c.* 40 B.C. I. Düring (*Notes on the History of the Transmission of Aristotle's Writings*, Göteborg, 1950) thinks this is the earliest possible date, and would prefer 40–20 B.C.

even though it did not appear in the published works.
I am inclined to believe that the author of the *De
Mundo* could have known all the Aristotelian matter
that he reproduces *before* the publication of Andronicus's edition, and that the style and manner of
the work indicate a date before this edition made
Aristotle's school-treatises more widely known.

Other evidence for the date is confused and difficult. It is certain that Apuleius *De Mundo* is a
translation of the Greek, but it is not quite certain
that this is genuinely by Apuleius. If it is, we have
a *terminus ante quem* of *c.* A.D. 140. The work seems
to have been known to Maximus of Tyre and must
therefore be before A.D. 180–190. From other reports,
references and imitations in later authors nothing
firmer than this can be deduced.

To reach a *terminus post quem* by an analysis of the
sources is equally difficult, since it is usually hard to
say who was the first to express a particular doctrine.
Nevertheless some of the meteorology appears to
depend on Posidonius and his pupil Asclepiodotus,
and we might therefore give *c.* 50 B.C. as the *terminus.*
There is no agreement about the date of the Neo-
Pythagorean sources. Attempts have been made
to argue from the silence of Cicero, Seneca and Pliny,
but arguments from silence do not carry much
weight.

The date has been given by various scholars as
follows : Zeller, 1st cent. A.D. ; Diels, in the reign
of Augustus ; Wilamowitz, in the Julio-Claudian
dynasty ; Capelle, the first half of the 2nd cent. A.D. ;
Lorimer, probably A.D. 40–140 ; Maguire and Festugière, the first few decades of the 1st cent. A.D. In
my view there is some slight reason for saying that

it was written before or not long after Andronicus's edition, and virtually no reason for choosing any other time within the limits already mentioned.[a]

BIBLIOGRAPHICAL NOTE

The *editio princeps* (1497) was based on a single MS., and this remained the common text until Bekker added the results of collation of four more MSS. in the Berlin *Aristotle* (1831). Parts of the treatise were edited by Wilamowitz and Wendland and printed in Wilamowitz's *Griechisches Lesebuch*, Text II (1906), pp. 188-199.

W. L. Lorimer took into account the readings of over seventy MSS., the quotations in Stobaeus and others, the Latin version of Apuleius, the Armenian and Syriac versions, and two mediaeval Latin versions. He published his results in three books : *The Text Tradition of Ps.-Aristotle " De Mundo "* (St. Andrews University Publications, xviii, 1924) ; *Some Notes on the Text of Ps.-Aristotle " De Mundo "* (St. Andrews University Publications, xxi, 1925) ; and *Aristotelis De Mundo* (Paris, 1933). The last of these contains the Greek text with a very detailed *apparatus criticus* and a German translation by E. König of the Syriac version (chaps. v-vii only).

On the sources, the most important works are : W. Capelle, " Die Schrift von der Welt," *Neue Jahrb. f. d. klass. Alt.* xv (1905), pp. 529-568 ; and Joseph P. Maguire, " The Sources of Ps.-Aristotle ' De Mundo,' " *Yale Classical Studies*, vi (1939).

The important article by Hans Strohm, " Studien

[a] Prof. E. H. Warmington has pointed out to me that the geography of ch. 3 confirms an early date.

zur Schrift von der Welt," *Mus. Helv.* ix (1952), pp. 137-175, did not reach me until this book was in proof. Strohm agrees with me in minimizing the influence of Posidonius and in marking the connexions with early Aristotle.

The late Prof. E. S. Forster translated the *De Mundo* for the Oxford translation of Aristotle (1914). A.-J. Festugière translates most of it into French, and adds important comments, in *La Révélation d'Hermes Trismégiste*, vol. ii, *Le Dieu cosmique* (Paris, 1949).

I am indebted to all these, and particularly (as all students of the *De Mundo* must be) to W. L. Lorimer.

TEXT

The text is based on Bekker's edition in the Berlin *Aristotle* ; I have indicated deviations from Bekker, except those that seem trivial.

The four mss. used by Bekker are designated as follows :

> O = Vat. 316.
> P = Vat. 1339.
> Q = Marc. 200.
> R = Paris. 1102.

Where necessary I have added references to mss. collated by Lorimer, as follows :

> B = Hieros. Patr. 108.
> C = Laur. 87, 14.
> D = Paris. 1302.
> E = Vat. Urbin. 125.
> F = Laur. 87, 16.
> G = Vat. 1025.
> W = Paris. 1038.
> Z = Paris. 2381.

Stob. = Stobaeus.   Ap. indicates reading confirmed
by the Latin of Apuleius, *De Mundo*.

Nearly all the deviations from Bekker follow
Lorimer ; to avoid complicating the notes unduly,
where I have followed Lorimer against Bekker and
the MSS. are fairly equally divided, I have used the
abbreviations " Bekk. " and " Lor." without listing
the MSS.   " Lor. (*Notes*) " refers to the second and
" Lor. (*De Mundo*) " to the third of Lorimer's works
cited in the Bibliographical Note above.

I wish to record my indebtedness to Professor
T. B. L. Webster for reading my work in typescript ;
I am very grateful for his criticisms and suggestions.

D. J. F.

ΑΡΙΣΤΟΤΕΛΟΥΣ
ΠΕΡΙ ΚΟΣΜΟΥ

1. Πολλάκις μὲν ἔμοιγε θεῖόν τι καὶ δαιμόνιον
ὄντως χρῆμα, ὦ Ἀλέξανδρε, ἡ φιλοσοφία ἔδοξεν
εἶναι, μάλιστα δὲ ἐν οἷς μόνη διαραμένη πρὸς τὴν
τῶν ὅλων θέαν ἐσπούδασε γνῶναι τὴν ἐν αὐτοῖς
5 ἀλήθειαν, καὶ τῶν ἄλλων ταύτης ἀποστάντων διὰ
τὸ ὕψος καὶ τὸ μέγεθος, αὕτη τὸ πρᾶγμα οὐκ
ἔδεισεν οὐδ᾽ αὐτὴν τῶν καλλίστων ἀπηξίωσεν,
ἀλλὰ καὶ συγγενεστάτην ἑαυτῇ καὶ μάλιστα πρέ-
πουσαν ἐνόμισεν εἶναι τὴν ἐκείνων μάθησιν. ἐπειδὴ
γὰρ οὐχ οἷόν τε ἦν τῷ σώματι εἰς τὸν οὐράνιον
ἀφικέσθαι τόπον καὶ τὴν γῆν ἐκλιπόντα τὸν οὐρά-
10 νιον ἐκεῖνον χῶρον κατοπτεῦσαι, καθάπερ οἱ ἀνόη-
τοί ποτε ἐπενόουν Ἀλωάδαι, ἡ γοῦν ψυχὴ διὰ
φιλοσοφίας, λαβοῦσα ἡγεμόνα τὸν νοῦν, ἐπεραιώθη
καὶ ἐξεδήμησεν, ἀκοπίατόν τινα ὁδὸν εὑροῦσα, καὶ
τὰ πλεῖστον ἀλλήλων ἀφεστῶτα τοῖς τόποις τῇ
διανοίᾳ συνεφρόνησε, ῥᾳδίως, οἶμαι, τὰ συγγενῆ
15 γνωρίσασα, καὶ θείῳ ψυχῆς ὄμματι τὰ θεῖα κατα-

ᵃ See Introduction, p. 338.

ARISTOTLE
ON THE COSMOS

1. I have often thought, Alexander,[a] that philosophy is a divine and really god-like activity, particularly in those instances when it alone has exalted itself to the contemplation of the universe and sought to discover the truth that is in it; the other sciences shunned this field of inquiry because of its sublimity and extensiveness; philosophy has not feared the task or thought itself unworthy of the noblest things, but has judged that the study of these is by nature most closely related to it and most fitting. It was not possible by means of the body to reach the heavenly region or to leave the earth and explore that heavenly place, in the manner once attempted by the foolish Aloadae [b] : so the soul, by means of philosophy, taking the mind as its guide, has crossed the frontier, and made the journey out of its own land by a path that does not tire the traveller. It has embraced in thought the things that are most widely separated from each other in place ; for it had no difficulty, I think, in recognizing things that were related to it, and with " the soul's divine eye " [c] it

[b] Otus and Ephialtes, the mythical Giants, who tried to reach heaven by piling Pelion on Ossa.

[c] Probably a quotation : *cf.* the eye of the soul in Plato, *Rep.* 533 D.

391 a

λαβοῦσα, τοῖς τε ἀνθρώποις προφητεύουσα. τοῦτο
δὲ ἔπαθε, καθ' ὅσον οἷόν τε ἦν, πᾶσιν ἀφθόνως
μεταδοῦναι βουληθεῖσα τῶν παρ' αὐτῇ τιμίων. διὸ
καὶ τοὺς μετὰ σπουδῆς διαγράψαντας ἡμῖν ἑνὸς
τόπου φύσιν ἢ μιᾶς σχῆμα πόλεως ἢ ποταμοῦ μέγε-
20 θος ἢ ὄρους κάλλος, οἷά τινες ἤδη πεποιήκασι,
φράζοντες οἱ μὲν τὴν Ὄσσαν, οἱ δὲ τὴν Νύσσαν,[1]
οἱ δὲ τὸ Κωρύκιον ἄντρον, οἱ δὲ ὁτιοῦν ἔτυχε τῶν
ἐπὶ μέρους, οἰκτίσειεν ἄν τις τῆς μικροψυχίας, τὰ
τυχόντα ἐκπεπληγμένους καὶ μέγα φρονοῦντας ἐπὶ
25 θεωρίᾳ μικρᾷ. τοῦτο δὲ πάσχουσι διὰ τὸ ἀθέατοι
τῶν κρειττόνων εἶναι, κόσμου λέγω καὶ τῶν ἐν
κόσμῳ μεγίστων· οὐδέποτε γὰρ ἂν τούτοις γνη-
391 b σίως ἐπιστήσαντες ἐθαύμαζόν τι τῶν ἄλλων, ἀλλὰ
πάντα αὐτοῖς τὰ ἄλλα μικρὰ κατεφαίνετο ἂν καὶ
οὐδενὸς ἄξια πρὸς τὴν τούτων ὑπεροχήν.

Λέγωμεν δὴ ἡμεῖς καί, καθ' ὅσον ἐφικτόν,
θεολογῶμεν περὶ τούτων συμπάντων, ὡς ἕκαστον
5 ἔχει φύσεως καὶ θέσεως καὶ κινήσεως. πρέπειν δέ
γε οἶμαι καὶ σοί, ὄντι ἡγεμόνων ἀρίστῳ, τὴν τῶν
μεγίστων ἱστορίαν μετιέναι, φιλοσοφίᾳ τε μηδὲν
μικρὸν ἐπινοεῖν, ἀλλὰ τοῖς τοιούτοις δώροις δεξι-
οῦσθαι τοὺς ἀρίστους.

2. Κόσμος μὲν οὖν ἐστι σύστημα ἐξ οὐρανοῦ καὶ
10 γῆς καὶ τῶν ἐν τούτοις περιεχομένων φύσεων.
λέγεται δὲ καὶ ἑτέρως κόσμος ἡ τῶν ὅλων τάξις τε
καὶ διακόσμησις, ὑπὸ θεοῦ[2] τε καὶ διὰ θεὸν[3] φυλατ-

---

[1] Νύσσαν Lor. : Νύσαν Bekk.
[2] θεοῦ codd. Stob. Lor. : θεῶν codd. al. Bekk.
[3] θεὸν codd. Lor. : θεῶν codd. al. Stob. Bekk.

---

[a] Cf. Pausanias x. 32. 2.
[b] Cf. Introduction, p. 334.

grasped things divine, and interpreted them for mankind. This came about because it wished to impart to all unsparingly, as far as possible, a share of its own privileges. So those who have earnestly described to us the nature of a single place, or the plan of a single city, or the size of a river, or the beauty of a mountain, as some have done before now—some of them tell us of Ossa, some of Nyssa, others of the Corycian cave,[a] or whatever other detail it happens to be—all these might well be pitied for their meanness of spirit, since they are overawed by commonplaces and pride themselves on insignificant observations. The reason is that they are blind to the nobler things—I mean the cosmos and the greatest features of the cosmos. For if they once genuinely gave their attention to these things, they would never wonder at any other ; everything else would appear small and worthless to them, in comparison with the matchless superiority of these.

Let us, then, take up the subject, and so far as they are attainable let us theologize [b] about all the greatest features of the cosmos, discussing the nature, position and motion of each. It is right, I think, that even you, the best of princes, should undertake the study of the greatest things, and that philosophy should have no humble intentions, but should greet the most excellent men with worthy gifts.

2. *Cosmos*, then, means a system composed of heaven and earth and the elements contained in them.[c] In another sense, *cosmos* is used to signify the orderly arrangement of the universe, which is preserved by God and through God. The centre of

[c] So also Chrysippus *ap.* Arius Didymus fr. 31 (Diels, *Dox. Graec.* pp. 465-466), and Posidonius *ap.* Diog. Laert. vii. 138.

347

τομένη. ταύτης δὲ τὸ μὲν μέσον, ἀκίνητόν τε καὶ
ἑδραῖον ὄν, ἡ φερέσβιος εἴληχε γῆ, παντοδαπῶν
ζῴων ἑστία τε οὖσα καὶ μήτηρ. τὸ δὲ ὕπερθεν
15 αὐτῆς, πᾶν τε καὶ πάντῃ πεπερατωμένον εἰς¹ τὸ
ἀνωτάτω, θεῶν οἰκητήριον, οὐρανὸς ὠνόμασται.
πλήρης δὲ ὢν σωμάτων θείων, ἃ δὴ καλεῖν ἄστρα
εἰώθαμεν, κινούμενος κίνησιν ἀίδιον, μιᾷ περιαγωγῇ
καὶ κύκλῳ συναναχορεύει πᾶσι τούτοις ἀπαύστως
δι' αἰῶνος. τοῦ δὲ σύμπαντος οὐρανοῦ τε καὶ
20 κόσμου σφαιροειδοῦς ὄντος καὶ κινουμένου, καθάπερ εἶπον, ἐνδελεχῶς, δύο ἀκίνητα ἐξ ἀνάγκης
ἐστι σημεῖα, καταντικρὺ ἀλλήλων, καθάπερ τῆς ἐν
τόρνῳ κυκλοφορουμένης σφαίρας, στερεὰ μένοντα
καὶ συνέχοντα τὴν σφαῖραν, περὶ ἃ ὁ πᾶς ὄγκος
25 κύκλῳ στρέφεται²· καλοῦνται δὲ οὗτοι πόλοι· δι'
ὧν εἰ νοήσαιμεν ἐπεζευγμένην εὐθεῖαν, ἥν τινες
392 a ἄξονα καλοῦσι, διάμετρος ἔσται τοῦ κόσμου, μέσον³
μὲν ἔχουσα τὴν γῆν, τοὺς δὲ δύο πόλους πέρατα.
τῶν δὲ ἀκινήτων πόλων τούτων ὁ μὲν ἀεὶ φανερός
ἐστιν ὑπὲρ κορυφὴν ὢν κατὰ τὸ βόρειον κλίμα,
ἀρκτικὸς καλούμενος, ὁ δὲ ὑπὸ γῆν ἀεὶ κατακέ-
5 κρυπται, κατὰ τὸ νότιον, ἀνταρκτικὸς καλούμενος.

Οὐρανοῦ δὲ καὶ ἄστρων οὐσίαν μὲν αἰθέρα καλοῦ-

---

¹ εἰς codd. Lor. : ἧς P Bekk.
² πᾶς ὄγκος κύκλῳ στρέφεται Stob. Lor. : πᾶς κόσμος κινεῖται.
ὁ μὲν οὖν κόσμος ἐν κύκλῳ περιστρέφεται codd. Bekk.

the cosmos, which is unmoved and fixed, is occupied by " life-bearing earth," [a] the home and mother of living beings of all kinds. The region above it, a single whole with a finite upper limit everywhere, the dwelling of the gods, is called *heaven*. It is full of divine bodies which we call *stars* ; it moves eternally, and revolves in solemn choral dance [b] with all the stars in the same circular orbit unceasingly for all time. The whole of the heaven, the whole cosmos,[c] is spherical, and moves continuously, as I have said ; but there are necessarily two points which are unmoved, opposite one another, just as in the case of a ball being turned in a lathe ; they remain fixed, holding the sphere in position, and the whole mass revolves in a circle round them ; these points are called *poles*. If we think of a straight line joining these two together (some call this the *axis*), it will be a diameter of the cosmos, having the earth at its centre and the two poles at its extremities. One of these two stationary poles is always visible, above our heads in the North : it is called the *Arctic* [d] pole. The other is always hidden under the earth, in the South : it is called the *Antarctic* pole.

The substance of the heaven and the stars we call

---

[a] Cf. Hesiod, *Theog.* 693.

[b] Ps.-Aristotle seems to recall Euripides, *Ion* 1079 ὅτε καὶ Διὸς ἀστερωπὸς ἀνεχόρευσεν αἰθήρ, χορεύει δὲ σελάνα. Cf. also Soph. *Ant.* 1146 f. He develops the same image below, 399 a 14.

[c] Ps.-Aristotle here uses κόσμος in a third sense, as a synonym for οὐρανός. This sense is quite common from Plato onwards.

[d] The terms Arctic and Antarctic do not appear in extant literature before Hipparchus (2nd cent. B.C.).

---

[3] μέσον TWZ Lor. : μέσην codd. cet. Bekk.

μεν, οὐχ, ὥς τινες, διὰ τὸ πυρώδη οὖσαν αἴθεσθαι,
πλημμελοῦντες περὶ τὴν πλεῖστον πυρὸς ἀπηλλαγ-
μένην δύναμιν, ἀλλὰ διὰ τὸ ἀεὶ θεῖν κυκλοφορου-
μένην, στοιχεῖον οὖσαν ἕτερον τῶν τεττάρων,
ἀκήρατόν τε καὶ θεῖον. τῶν γε μὴν ἐμπεριεχομένων
10 ἄστρων τὰ μὲν ἀπλανῆ τῷ σύμπαντι οὐρανῷ συμ-
περιστρέφεται, τὰς αὐτὰς ἔχοντα ἕδρας, ὧν μέσος
ὁ ζῳοφόρος καλούμενος κύκλος ἐγκάρσιος διὰ τῶν
τροπικῶν διέζωσται, κατὰ μέρος διῃρημένος εἰς
δώδεκα ζῳδίων χώρας, τὰ δέ, πλανητὰ ὄντα, οὔτε
15 τοῖς προτέροις ὁμοταχῶς κινεῖσθαι πέφυκεν οὔτε
ἀλλήλοις, ἀλλ' ἐν ἑτέροις καὶ ἑτέροις κύκλοις, ὥστε
αὐτῶν τὸ[1] μὲν προσγειότερον εἶναι, τὸ[1] δὲ ἀνώτερον.
τὸ μὲν οὖν τῶν ἀπλανῶν πλῆθός ἐστιν ἀνεξεύρετον
ἀνθρώποις, καίπερ ἐπὶ μιᾶς κινουμένων ἐπιφανείας
τῆς τοῦ σύμπαντος οὐρανοῦ· τὸ δὲ τῶν πλανήτων,
20 εἰς ἑπτὰ μέρη κεφαλαιούμενον, ἐν τοσούτοις ἐστὶ
κύκλοις ἐφεξῆς κειμένοις, ὥστε ἀεὶ τὸν ἀνωτέρω
μείζω τοῦ ὑποκάτω εἶναι, τούς τε ἑπτὰ ἐν ἀλλήλοις ἐμπεριέχεσθαι, πάντας γε μὴν ὑπὸ τῆς τῶν
ἀπλανῶν σφαίρας περιειλῆφθαι. συνεχῆ δὲ ἔχει ἀεὶ
τὴν θέσιν ταύτῃ ὁ τοῦ Φαίνοντος ἅμα καὶ Κρόνου
25 καλούμενος κύκλος, ἐφεξῆς δὲ ὁ τοῦ Φαέθοντος
καὶ[2] Διὸς λεγόμενος, εἶθ' ὁ Πυρόεις, Ἡρακλέους
τε καὶ Ἄρεος προσαγορευόμενος, ἑξῆς δὲ ὁ Στίλ-
βων, ὃν ἱερὸν Ἑρμοῦ καλοῦσιν ἔνιοι, τινὲς δὲ

---

[1] τὸ . . . τὸ Lor. : τὸν . . . τὸν Bekk.
[2] καὶ Lor. : ὁ καὶ BD : om. cett.

---

[a] The author follows Aristotle in making aether a fifth

aether,[a] not, as some think, because it is fiery in nature and so burns (they fall into error about its function, which is quite different from that of fire), but because it always moves in its circular orbit ; it is an element different from the four elements,[b] pure and divine. Now, of the stars which are encompassed in it, some are *fixed* and move in concert with the whole heaven always keeping the same position in it ; in the middle of these the *circle of the zodiac*, as it is called, set obliquely through the tropics, passes round like a girdle, divided into the twelve regions of the zodiac. The others, the *planets*, move, according to their nature, at speeds different from the fixed stars and from each other, each in a different circle, in such a way that one is nearer the earth, another higher in the heavens. The number of the fixed stars is not to be known by men, although they all move on one visible surface, namely that of the whole heaven : but the class of planets contains seven units, arranged in the same number of circles in a series, so that the higher is always greater than the lower, and all the seven, though contained one within another, are nevertheless encompassed by the sphere of the fixed stars. The circle which is always in the position next to this sphere is that which is called the circle of Phaenon (the Bright one) or Cronus (Saturn) ; then comes the circle of Phaëthon (the Shiner) or Zeus (Jupiter) ; next Pyroeis (the Fiery one), named after Heracles or Ares (Mars) ; next Stilbon (the Glittering one) which some dedicate to Hermes (Mercury), some

---

element : the Stoics identified it with fire. He rejects the derivation of the word from αἴθεσθαι (to burn) and relates it to ἀεὶ θεῖν (move always), as Plato and Aristotle did (*cf.* Plato, *Crat.* 410 B, Aristot. *De Caelo* 270 b 22).

[b] Earth, air, fire and water.

392 a

Ἀπόλλωνος· μεθ' ὃν ὁ τοῦ Φωσφόρου, ὃν Ἀφρο-
δίτης, οἱ δὲ Ἥρας προσαγορεύουσιν, εἶτα ὁ ἡλίου,
καὶ τελευταῖος ὁ τῆς σελήνης μέχρι γῆς ὁρίζεται.
30 ὁ δὲ αἰθὴρ τά τε θεῖα ἐμπεριέχει σώματα καὶ τὴν
τῆς κινήσεως τάξιν.

Μετὰ δὲ τὴν αἰθέριον καὶ θείαν φύσιν, ἥντινα
τεταγμένην ἀποφαίνομεν, ἔτι δὲ ἄτρεπτον καὶ ἀν-
ετεροίωτον καὶ ἀπαθῆ, συνεχής ἐστιν ἡ δι' ὅλων
παθητή τε καὶ τρεπτή, καί, τὸ σύμπαν εἰπεῖν,
35 φθαρτή τε καὶ ἐπίκηρος. ταύτης δὲ αὐτῆς πρώτη
392 b μέν ἐστιν ἡ λεπτομερὴς καὶ φλογώδης οὐσία, ὑπὸ
τῆς αἰθερίου φύσεως πυρουμένη διὰ τὸ μέγεθος
αὐτῆς καὶ τὴν ὀξύτητα τῆς κινήσεως· ἐν δὲ τῇ
πυρώδει καὶ ἀτάκτῳ λεγομένῃ τά τε σέλα διάττει
καὶ φλόγες ἀκοντίζονται καὶ δοκίδες τε καὶ βόθυνοι
5 καὶ κομῆται λεγόμενοι στηρίζονται καὶ σβέννυνται
πολλάκις.

Ἐξῆς δὲ ταύτης ὁ ἀὴρ ὑποκέχυται, ζοφώδης
ὢν καὶ παγετώδης τὴν φύσιν· ὑπὸ δὲ κινήσεως[1]
λαμπόμενος ἅμα καὶ διακαιόμενος λαμπρός[2] τε
γίνεται καὶ ἀλεεινός. ἐν δὲ τούτῳ, τῆς παθητῆς
ὄντι καὶ αὐτῷ δυνάμεως καὶ παντοδαπῶς ἀλ-
10 λοιουμένῳ, νέφη τε συνίσταται καὶ ὄμβροι κατ-
αράσσουσι, χιόνες τε καὶ πάχναι καὶ χάλαζαι
πνοαί τε ἀνέμων καὶ τυφώνων, ἔτι τε βρονταὶ καὶ

---

[1] ἐκείνης BCWZ Stob. Ap. Lor. : κινήσεως codd. cet. Bekk.
[2] λαμπρός Lor. : λαμπρότερός Bekk.

---

[a] This is the " Pythagorean " order of the planets, adopted
by Aristotle, Eudoxus, Eratosthenes, and probably the early
Stoics. The other order commonly given by ancient writers,
the " Chaldean," puts Venus and Mercury below the sun ;
this order was adopted by Panaetius, and probably also by

to Apollo ; after this is the circle of Phosphorus (the Light-bearer), which some call after Aphroditê (Venus) and others after Hera ; then the circle of the sun [a] ; and the last, the circle of the moon, is bounded by the terrestrial sphere.[b] The aether, then, contains the divine bodies and their ordered orbits.

After the aetherial and divine element, which is arranged in a fixed order, as we have declared, and is also unchangeable, unalterable and impassive, there comes next the element that is through the whole of its extent liable to change and alteration, and is, in short, destructible and perishable. The first part of this is the fine and fiery substance that is set aflame by the aether because of the latter's great size and the swiftness of its motion. In this *fiery and disorderly element*, as it is called, meteors and flames shoot across, and often *planks* and *pits* and *comets*, as they are called, stand motionless and then expire.[c]

Next under this is spread the air, opaque and icy by nature, but when it is brightened and heated by movement, it becomes bright and warm.[d] In the air, which itself also has the power to change, and alters in every kind of way, clouds are formed and rain falls in torrents ; there is snow, frost and hail, and gales and whirlwinds ; thunder and lightning,

Posidonius. Lorimer writes (*Notes*, p. 51) that there were few upholders of the " Pythagorean " order after 200 B.C., though it appears in an unknown astronomer in Rhodes of about 100 B.C. (*I.G.Ins.* i. 913).

[b] γῆ here must refer to the whole " sublunary " sphere, not to the earth proper.

[c] This is inconsistent with 395 a 29 ff. where these phenomena are put in the air.

[d] The coldness of the air is a Stoic doctrine ; Aristotle said it was warm and capable of being inflamed by motion (*Meteor.* 341 a 18).

353

ἀστραπαὶ καὶ πτώσεις κεραυνῶν μυρίων τε γνόφων
συμπληγάδες.

3. Ἑξῆς δὲ τῆς ἀερίου φύσεως γῆ καὶ θάλασσα
ἐρήρεισται, φυτοῖς βρύουσα καὶ ζῴοις πηγαῖς τε καὶ
ποταμοῖς, τοῖς μὲν ἀνὰ γῆν ἑλιττομένοις, τοῖς δὲ
ἀνερευγομένοις εἰς θάλασσαν. πεποίκιλται δὲ καὶ
χλόαις μυρίαις ὄρεσί τε ὑψηλοῖς καὶ βαθυξύλοις
δρυμοῖς καὶ πόλεσιν, ἃς τὸ σοφὸν ζῷον, ὁ ἄνθρωπος,
ἱδρύσατο, νήσοις τε ἐναλίοις καὶ ἠπείροις. τὴν μὲν
οὖν οἰκουμένην ὁ πολὺς λόγος εἴς τε νήσους καὶ
ἠπείρους διεῖλεν, ἀγνοῶν ὅτι καὶ ἡ σύμπασα μία
νῆσός ἐστιν, ὑπὸ τῆς Ἀτλαντικῆς καλουμένης θαλάσσης περιρρεομένη. πολλὰς δὲ καὶ ἄλλας εἰκὸς
τῆσδε ἀντιπόρθμους ἄπωθεν κεῖσθαι, τὰς μὲν μείζους αὐτῆς, τὰς δὲ ἐλάττους, ἡμῖν δὲ πάσας πλὴν
τῆσδε ἀοράτους· ὅπερ γὰρ αἱ παρ' ἡμῖν νῆσοι
πρὸς ταυτὶ τὰ πελάγη πεπόνθασι, τοῦτο ἥδε ἡ
οἰκουμένη πρὸς τὴν Ἀτλαντικὴν θάλασσαν πολλαί
τε ἕτεραι πρὸς σύμπασαν τὴν θάλασσαν· καὶ γὰρ
αὗται μεγάλαι τινές εἰσι νῆσοι μεγάλοις περικλυ-
ζόμεναι πελάγεσιν. ἡ δὲ σύμπασα τοῦ ὑγροῦ
φύσις ἐπιπολάζουσα, κατά τινας τῆς γῆς σπίλους
τὰς καλουμένας ἀναπεφαγκυῖα[1] οἰκουμένας, ἑξῆς
ἂν εἴη τῆς ἀερίου μάλιστα φύσεως. μετὰ δὲ ταύτην
ἐν τοῖς βυθοῖς κατὰ τὸ μεσαίτατον τοῦ κόσμου
συνερηρεισμένη γῆ πᾶσα καὶ πεπιεσμένη συνέστηκεν, ἀκίνητος καὶ ἀσάλευτος· καὶ τοῦτ' ἔστι τοῦ

---

[1] ἀναπεφαγκυῖα coni. Usener Lor.: ἀναπεφυκυῖα codd. Bekk.

---

[a] Aristotle apparently thought nothing but sea lay from
Gibraltar westwards to India (*Meteor.* 362 b 28). Strabo (i.
4. 6 = 65 c) notices the possibility of other inhabited worlds
in his discussion of Eratosthenes.

too, and falling thunderbolts, and the clash of innumerable storm-clouds.

3. Next to the element of air comes the fixed mass of earth and sea, full of plants and animals, and streams and rivers, some winding about the surface of the earth, others discharging themselves into the sea. This region is adorned with innumerable green plants, high mountains, deep-shaded woodland, and cities established by the wise creature, man ; and with islands in the sea, and continents. The *inhabited world* is divided by the usual account into islands and continents, since it is not recognized that the whole of it is really one island, surrounded by the sea which is called *Atlantic*. Far away from this one, on the opposite side of the intervening seas, there are probably many other inhabited worlds,[a] some greater than this, some smaller, though none is visible to us except this one ; for the islands we know stand in the same relation to our seas as the whole inhabited world to the Atlantic Ocean, and many other inhabited worlds to the whole ocean ; for these are great islands washed round by great seas. The whole mass of the wet element lies on the surface of the earth, allowing the so-called inhabited worlds to show through where there are projections of the earth ; it is this element that would properly [b] be next in order to the air. After this, set in the depths at the centre of the cosmos, densely packed and compressed, is the whole mass of the earth, unmoved and unshaken. And this is the whole of that part of the

[b] Taking μάλιστα with the verb ; it is probably postponed for rhythmic effect. The meaning is that water is in theory next to air, but earth sometimes protrudes through the water. σπίλους (properly " stains " or " marks ") in the previous line seems to be used in the sense of σπιλάδας (" projections ").

κόσμου τὸ πᾶν ὃ καλοῦμεν κάτω. πέντε δὴ στοι-
393 a χεῖα ταῦτα ἐν πέντε χώραις σφαιρικῶς ἐγκείμενα,
περιεχομένης ἀεὶ τῆς ἐλάττονος τῇ μείζονι—λέγω
δὲ γῆς μὲν ἐν ὕδατι, ὕδατος δὲ ἐν ἀέρι, ἀέρος δὲ
ἐν πυρί, πυρὸς δὲ ἐν αἰθέρι— τὸν ὅλον κόσμον συνεστήσατο, καὶ τὸ μὲν ἄνω πᾶν θεῶν ἀπέδειξεν
5 οἰκητήριον, τὸ κάτω δὲ ἐφημέρων ζῴων. αὐτοῦ
γε μὴν τούτου τὸ μὲν ὑγρόν ἐστιν, ὃ καλεῖν ποτα-
μοὺς καὶ νάματα καὶ θαλάσσας εἰθίσμεθα, τὸ δὲ
ξηρόν, ὃ γῆν τε καὶ ἠπείρους καὶ νήσους ὀνομά-
ζομεν.

Τῶν δὲ νήσων αἱ μὲν εἰσι μεγάλαι, καθάπερ ἡ
10 σύμπασα ἥδε οἰκουμένη λέλεκται πολλαί τε ἕτεραι
μεγάλοις περιρρεόμεναι πελάγεσιν, αἱ δὲ ἐλάττους,
φανεραί τε ἡμῖν καὶ ἐντὸς οὖσαι. καὶ τούτων αἱ
μὲν ἀξιόλογοι, Σικελία καὶ Σαρδὼ καὶ Κύρνος
Κρήτη τε καὶ Εὔβοια καὶ Κύπρος καὶ Λέσβος, αἱ
15 δὲ ὑποδεέστεραι, ὧν αἱ μὲν Σποράδες, αἱ δὲ Κυ-
κλάδες, αἱ δὲ ἄλλως ὀνομάζονται.

Πέλαγος δὲ τὸ μὲν ἔξω τῆς οἰκουμένης Ἀτλαν-
τικόν τε καὶ Ὠκεανὸς καλεῖται, περιρρέων ἡμᾶς.
ἐν δὲ τῷ πρὸς δύσεις στενοπόρῳ διανεωγὼς[1]
στόματι, κατὰ τὰς Ἡρακλείους λεγομένας στήλας
20 τὸν εἴσρουν εἰς τὴν ἔσω θάλασσαν ὡς ἂν εἰς λιμένα
ποιεῖται, κατὰ μικρὸν δὲ ἐπιπλατυνόμενος ἀνα-
χεῖται, μεγάλους περιλαμβάνων κόλπους ἀλλήλοις
συναφεῖς, πῆ μὲν κατὰ στενοπόρους αὐχένας ἀν-
εστομωμένος, πῆ δὲ πάλιν πλατυνόμενος. πρῶτον
μὲν οὖν λέγεται ἐγκεκολπῶσθαι ἐν δεξιᾷ εἰσπλέοντι
25 τὰς Ἡρακλείους στήλας, διχῶς, εἰς τὰς καλουμένας Σύρτεις, ὧν τὴν μὲν Μεγάλην, τὴν δὲ Μικράν,
καλοῦσιν· ἐπὶ θάτερα δὲ οὐκέτι ὁμοίως ἀποκολπού-

cosmos that we call the lower part. So these five elements, occupying five spherical regions, the larger sphere always embracing the smaller—earth in water, water in air, air in fire, fire in aether—make up the whole cosmos ; the upper part as a whole is distinguished as the abode of the gods, and the lower part as that of mortal creatures. Of the latter, some is wet, and this part we call *rivers* and *springs* and *seas* ; the rest is dry, and this part we name *land* and *continents* and *islands*.

There are various kinds of island : some are large, like this whole inhabited world of ours, as I have said, and many others which are surrounded by great oceans ; others are smaller, visible to us and within the Mediterranean. Some of these are quite considerable—Sicily, Sardinia, Corsica, Crete, Euboea, Cyprus and Lesbos ; some are smaller, like the Sporades, the Cyclades, and others with various names.

The ocean that is outside the inhabited world is called the *Atlantic*, or *Ocean*, and surrounds us. To the West of the inhabited world, this ocean makes a passage through a narrow strait called the *Pillars of Heracles*, and so makes an entry into the interior sea, as if into a harbour ; gradually it broadens and spreads out, embracing large bays joined up to each other, here contracting into narrow necks of water, there broadening out again. They say that the first of these bays that the sea forms, to starboard, if you sail in through the Pillars of Heracles, are two, called the Syrtes, of which one is called the Major, the other the Minor ; on the other side it does not form gulfs

---

[1] διανεωγὼς Lor. : διανεωγὸς Bekk.

μενος τρία ποιεῖ πελάγη, τό τε Σαρδόνιον καὶ τὸ
Γαλατικὸν καλούμενον καὶ ᾿Αδρίαν, ἑξῆς δὲ τούτων
ἐγκάρσιον τὸ Σικελικόν, μετὰ δὲ τοῦτο τὸ Κρητικόν,
30 συνεχὲς δὲ αὐτοῦ, τῇ μὲν τὸ Αἰγύπτιόν τε καὶ
Παμφύλιον καὶ Σύριον, τῇ δὲ τὸ Αἰγαῖόν τε καὶ
Μυρτῷον. ἀντιπαρήκει δὲ τοῖς εἰρημένοις πολυ-
μερέστατος ὢν ὁ Πόντος, οὗ τὸ μὲν μυχαίτατον
393 b Μαιῶτις καλεῖται, τὸ δὲ ἔξω πρὸς τὸν Ἑλλήσ-
ποντον συνανεστόμωται τῇ καλουμένῃ Προποντίδι.

Πρός γε μὴν ταῖς ἀνασχέσεσι τοῦ ἡλίου πάλιν
εἰσρέων ὁ ᾿Ωκεανός, τὸν ᾿Ινδικόν τε καὶ Περσικὸν
διανοίξας κόλπον, ἀναφαίνει συνεχῆ τὴν ᾿Ερυθρὰν
5 θάλασσαν διειληφώς. ἐπὶ θάτερον δὲ κέρας κατὰ
στενόν τε καὶ ἐπιμήκη διήκων αὐχένα, πάλιν
ἀνευρύνεται, τὴν ῾Υρκανίαν τε καὶ Κασπίαν ὁρίζων·
τὸ δὲ ὑπὲρ ταύτην βαθὺν ἔχει τὸν ὑπὲρ τὴν Μαιῶτιν
λίμνην τόπον. εἶτα κατ᾽ ὀλίγον ὑπὲρ τοὺς Σκύθας
τε καὶ Κελτικὴν σφίγγει τὴν οἰκουμένην πρός
10 τε τὸν Γαλατικὸν κόλπον καὶ τὰς προειρημένας
῾Ηρακλείους στήλας, ὧν ἔξω περιρρέει τὴν γῆν ὁ

---

[a] The Ocean makes three separate incursions into the inhabited world—the Mediterranean, the Indian Ocean and the
Caspian (see n. c below). Festugière (*op. cit.* p. 465) thinks
these Eastern seas are spoken of as prolongations of the
Mediterranean ; but πάλιν εἰσρέων here is parallel to τὸν
εἰσροῦν . . . ποιεῖται at 393 a 19.

[b] Are these two gulfs or one ? If two, they are respectively
the Gulf of Cutch (or the Gulf of Cambay) and the Persian
Gulf ; if one, probably the Persian Gulf is meant. The Greek
could be interpreted either way.

[c] By ᾿Ερυθρά (red) the author probably means what was

at first in the same way, but makes three seas, the Sardinian, Galatian and Adriatic ; next to these, and across the line of them, is the Sicilian sea ; after this, the Cretan ; and continuing this on one side are the Egyptian and Pamphylian and Syrian seas, on the other the Aegean and Myrtoan. Lying opposite these that I have described, in another direction, is the Pontus, and this has very many parts : the innermost part is called Maeotis, and the outermost part, towards the Hellespont, is joined by a strait to the sea called Propontis.

In the East, the Ocean again penetrates ⟨the inhabited world⟩ [a] ; it opens out the gulf of India and Persia [b] and without a break reveals the Red Sea, [c] embracing these as parts of itself. Towards the other promontory ⟨of Asia⟩, [d] passing through a long narrow strait and then broadening out again, it makes the Hyrcanian or Caspian sea [e] ; beyond this, it occupies a deep hollow beyond Lake Maeotis. Then little by little, beyond the land of the Scythians and Celts, it confines the inhabited world as it passes towards the Galatian Gulf and the Pillars of Heracles, already described, on the farther side of which the Ocean

generally called the Erythraean Sea, which might include our Red Sea (called the Arabian Gulf at 393 b 28).

[d] Lorimer (*Notes*, p. 80, n. 3) quotes Mela i. 2 (9) to confirm this interpretation. In Mela, the two promontories are the land between the Nile and the Red Sea, and that between the Tanaïs and the Caspian.

[e] Or " bounding the Hyrcanian and Caspian country " (Forster). But θάλασσαν is easier to understand here than γῆν ; admittedly ὁρίζων has an odd sense (perhaps " marking out "), but the author is running short of synonyms for " forming " seas. At all events, he means the Caspian Sea, which was thought of as a gulf of the Northern Ocean from the time of Alexander to Ptolemy.

Ὠκεανός. ἐν τούτῳ γε μὴν νῆσοι μέγισται[1] τυγ-
χάνουσιν οὖσαι δύο, Βρεττανικαί[2] λεγόμεναι, Ἀλβίων[3] καὶ Ἰέρνη, τῶν προϊστορημένων μείζους, ὑπὲρ
τοὺς Κελτοὺς κείμεναι. τούτων δὲ οὐκ ἐλάττους
15 ἥ τε Ταπροβάνη πέραν Ἰνδῶν, λοξὴ πρὸς τὴν
οἰκουμένην, καὶ ἡ Φεβὸλ καλουμένη, κατὰ τὸν
Ἀραβικὸν κειμένη κόλπον. οὐκ ὀλίγαι δὲ μικραὶ
περὶ τὰς Βρεττανικὰς καὶ τὴν Ἰβηρίαν κύκλῳ
περιεστεφάνωνται τὴν οἰκουμένην ταύτην, ἣν δὴ
νῆσον εἰρήκαμεν· ἧς πλάτος μέν ἐστι κατὰ τὸ βαθύ-
20 τατον τῆς ἠπείρου βραχὺ ἀποδέον τετρακισμυρίων
σταδίων, ὥς φασιν οἱ εὖ γεωγραφήσαντες, μῆκος
δὲ περὶ ἑπτακισμυρίους μάλιστα. διαιρεῖται δὲ
εἴς τε Εὐρώπην καὶ Ἀσίαν καὶ Λιβύην.

Εὐρώπη μὲν οὖν ἐστιν ἧς ὅροι κύκλῳ στῆλαί
τε Ἡρακλέους καὶ μυχοὶ Πόντου θάλαττά τε Ὑρ-
25 κανία, καθ' ἣν στενότατος ἰσθμὸς εἰς τὸν Πόντον
διήκει· τινὲς δὲ ἀντὶ[4] τοῦ ἰσθμοῦ Τάναϊν ποταμὸν
εἰρήκασιν. Ἀσία δέ ἐστι τὸ ἀπὸ τοῦ εἰρημένου
ἰσθμοῦ τοῦ τε Πόντου καὶ τῆς Ὑρκανίας θαλάσσης
μέχρι θατέρου ἰσθμοῦ, ὃς μεταξὺ κεῖται τοῦ τε
Ἀραβικοῦ κόλπου καὶ τῆς ἔσω θαλάσσης, περι-

---

[1] post μέγισται add. τε Bekk.
[2] Βρεττανικαὶ Lor. : Βρετανικαὶ Bekk.
[3] Ἀλβίων Lor. : Ἄλβιον Bekk.
[4] ἀντὶ Stob. Lor. : ἀπὸ codd. Bekk.

---

[a] Very mysterious. It might well be Socotra, as Bochert
suggests (*Arist. Erdkunde*, p. 93) ; Capelle (*op. cit.* p. 539)
suggests Madagascar ; Müllenhoff (*Deutsche Altertums-
kunde*, pp. 322 f.), quoted with approval by Lorimer (*Notes*,
p. 37, n. 1), suggests it is the island in Lake Tana (*Psebo* in
Strabo) in Abyssinia, magnified and transplanted.

flows round the earth. There are two very large islands in it, called the British Isles, Albion and Ierne ; they are larger than those already mentioned, and lie beyond the land of the Celts. No smaller than these are Taprobane (Ceylon) beyond the Indians, which lies obliquely to the inhabited world, and the island known as Phebol,[a] by the Arabian Gulf. There is quite a number of other small islands round the British Isles and Spain, set in a ring round this inhabited world, which as we have said is itself an island ; its breadth, at the deepest point of the continent, is a little short of 40,000 stades, in the opinion of good geographers,[b] and its length is approximately 70,000 stades. It is divided into Europe, Asia and Libya.

Europe is the area which is bounded in a circle by the Pillars of Heracles and the inner parts of the Pontus and the Hyrcanian Sea, where a very narrow [c] isthmus passes between it and the Pontus ; but some have said the river Tanaïs, instead of this isthmus.[d] Asia is the region from this isthmus of the Pontus and the Hyrcanian Sea to another isthmus, which lies between the Arabian Gulf and the Mediterranean ;

---

[b] Posidonius put the length of the οἰκουμένη at 70,000 stades, but no one reports his figure for the width ; since he thought the Ocean was quite close to Maeotis in the North, his figure would presumably be under 30,000 stades " in agreement with the view then current " (Thomson, *History of Ancient Geography*, p. 213). Eratosthenes estimated the length at 70,800 stades (with the addition of 7,000 for bulges and possible islands), and the width at 38,000.

[c] Strabo reports (xi. i. 5 = 491 c) that Clitarchus and others made this isthmus absurdly narrow, while Posidonius thought it was 1500 stades.

[d] These variant opinions are noted by Eratosthenes *ap.* Strabo i. 4. 7 (65 c).

393 b

30 ἐχόμενος ὑπό τε ταύτης καὶ τοῦ πέριξ Ὠκεανοῦ·
τινὲς δὲ¹ ἀπὸ Τανάιδος μέχρι Νείλου στομάτων
τὸν τῆς Ἀσίας τίθενται ὅρον. Λιβύη δὲ τὸ ἀπὸ
τοῦ Ἀραβικοῦ ἰσθμοῦ ἕως Ἡρακλέους στηλῶν.
394 a οἱ δὲ ἀπὸ τοῦ Νείλου φασὶν ἕως ἐκείνων. τὴν δὲ
Αἴγυπτον, ὑπὸ τῶν τοῦ Νείλου στομάτων περιρρεο-
μένην, οἱ μὲν τῇ Ἀσίᾳ, οἱ δὲ τῇ Λιβύῃ προσ-
άπτουσι, καὶ τὰς νήσους οἱ μὲν ἐξαιρέτους ποιοῦσιν,
οἱ δὲ προσνέμουσι ταῖς γείτοσιν ἀεὶ μοίραις.

5 Γῆς μὲν δὴ καὶ θαλάττης φύσιν καὶ θέσιν, ἥντινα
καλεῖν εἰώθαμεν οἰκουμένην, τοιάνδε τινὰ ἱστορή-
καμεν.

4. Περὶ δὲ τῶν ἀξιολογωτάτων ἐν αὐτῇ καὶ περὶ
αὐτὴν παθῶν νῦν λέγωμεν, αὐτὰ τὰ ἀναγκαῖα κεφα-
λαιούμενοι.

Δύο γὰρ δή τινες ἀπ' αὐτῆς ἀναθυμιάσεις ἀνα-
10 φέρονται συνεχῶς εἰς τὸν ὑπὲρ ἡμᾶς ἀέρα, λεπτο-
μερεῖς καὶ ἀόρατοι παντάπασιν, εἰ [τι]² μὴ κατὰ
τὰς ἑώας ἔστιν αἷ [τε] διὰ³ ποταμῶν τε καὶ ναμάτων ἀναφερόμεναι θεωροῦνται. τούτων δὲ ἡ μέν
ἐστι ξηρὰ καὶ καπνώδης, ἀπὸ τῆς γῆς ἀπορρέουσα,
ἡ δὲ νοτερὰ καὶ ἀτμώδης, ἀπὸ τῆς ὑγρᾶς ἀναθυ-
15 μιωμένη φύσεως. γίνονται δὲ ἀπὸ μὲν ταύτης
ὁμίχλαι καὶ δρόσοι καὶ πάγων ἰδέαι νέφη τε καὶ
ὄμβροι καὶ χιόνες καὶ χάλαζαι, ἀπὸ δὲ τῆς ξηρᾶς
ἄνεμοί τε καὶ πνευμάτων διαφοραὶ βρονταί τε καὶ
ἀστραπαὶ καὶ πρηστῆρες καὶ κεραυνοὶ καὶ τὰ ἄλλα

¹ post δὲ add. τὸ CGZ Bekk.   ² τι secl. Lor.

it is surrounded by the Mediterranean and the encircling stream of the Ocean ; but some say that Asia stretches from the Tanaïs to the mouths of the Nile. Libya lies between the Arabian isthmus and the Pillars of Heracles (but some say from the Nile to the Pillars). Egypt, which is encompassed by the mouths of the Nile, is attached by some to Asia, and by others to Libya, and some make the islands separate, others attribute them to their nearest region of mainland.

We have now given some account of the nature and situation of the land and sea which we call " the inhabited world."

4. Now let us turn to the most notable phenomena in and about the inhabited world, summarizing only the most essential points.

There are two exhalations [a] from it, which pass continually into the air above us, composed of small particles and entirely invisible, except that in the early mornings some can be observed rising along rivers and streams. One of these is dry and like smoke, since it emanates from the earth ; the other is damp and vaporous, since it is exhaled from the wet element. From the latter come mists, dews, the various kinds of frost, clouds, rain, snow and hail ; from the dry exhalation come the winds and various breezes, thunder and lightning, fiery bolts ($\pi\rho\eta\sigma\tau\hat{\eta}\rho\epsilon\varsigma$) [b] and thunderbolts and all the other things of the same

---

[a] For the two exhalations and their products *cf.* Aristot. *Meteor.* i. 4-12. Much of this chapter derives, ultimately, from Aristotle ; the proximate sources are discussed by Maguire (*op. cit.* pp. 128-133).   [b] *Cf.* 395 a 10 and note.

---

[3] αἱ [τε] διὰ scripsi : αἵ τε διὰ vel αἵ τε ἐκ codd. : ὅτε ἀπὸ Lor. (*De Mundo*) : αἱ [τε] ἀπὸ Lor. (*Notes*).

394 a

ἃ δὴ τούτοις ἐστὶ σύμφυλα. ἔστι δὲ ὁμίχλη μὲν
20 ἀτμώδης ἀναθυμίασις ἄγονος ὕδατος, ἀέρος μὲν
παχυτέρα, νέφους δὲ ἀραιοτέρα· γίνεται δὲ ἤτοι ἐξ
ἀρχῆς νέφους ἢ ἐξ ὑπολείμματος. ἀντίπαλος δὲ
αὐτῇ λέγεταί τε καὶ ἔστιν αἰθρία, οὐδὲν ἄλλο οὖσα
πλὴν ἀὴρ ἀνέφελος καὶ ἀνόμιχλος. δρόσος δέ ἐστιν
ὑγρὸν ἐξ αἰθρίας κατὰ σύστασιν λεπτὴν φερόμενον,
25 κρύσταλλος δὲ ἀθρόον ὕδωρ ἐξ αἰθρίας πεπηγός,
πάχνη δὲ δρόσος πεπηγυῖα, δροσοπάχνη δὲ ἡμι-
παγὴς δρόσος. νέφος δέ ἐστι πάχος ἀτμῶδες
συνεστραμμένον, γόνιμον ὕδατος· ὄμβρος δὲ γίνεται
μὲν κατ' ἐκπιεσμὸν νέφους εὖ μάλα πεπαχυσμένου,
διαφορὰς δὲ ἴσχει τοσάσδε ὅσας καὶ ἡ τοῦ νέφους
30 θλῖψις· ἠπία μὲν γὰρ οὖσα μαλακὰς ψακάδας δια-
σπείρει, σφοδρὰ δὲ ἁδροτέρας· καὶ τοῦτο καλοῦμεν
ὑετόν, ὄμβρου μείζω καὶ συνεχῆ συστρέμματα ἐπὶ
γῆς φερόμενον.[1] χιὼν δὲ γίνεται κατὰ νεφῶν πε-
πυκνωμένων ἀπόθραυσιν πρὸ τῆς εἰς ὕδωρ μετα-
35 βολῆς ἀνακοπέντων· ἐργάζεται δὲ ἡ μὲν κοπὴ τὸ
ἀφρῶδες καὶ ἔκλευκον, ἡ δὲ σύμπηξις τοῦ ἐνόντος
ὑγροῦ τὴν ψυχρότητα οὔπω χυθέντος οὐδὲ ἡραιω-
394 b μένου. σφοδρὰ δὲ αὕτη καὶ ἀθρόα καταφερομένη
νιφετὸς ὠνόμασται. χάλαζα δὲ γίνεται νιφετοῦ
συστραφέντος καὶ βρῖθος ἐκ πιλήματος εἰς κατα-
φορὰν ταχυτέραν λαβόντος· παρὰ δὲ τὰ μεγέθη τῶν
ἀπορρηγνυμένων θραυσμάτων οἵ τε ὄγκοι μείζους
5 αἵ τε φοραὶ γίνονται βιαιότεραι. ταῦτα μὲν οὖν
ἐκ τῆς ὑγρᾶς ἀναθυμιάσεως πέφυκε συμπίπτειν.

Ἐκ δὲ τῆς ξηρᾶς ὑπὸ ψύχους μὲν ὠσθείσης ὥστε
ῥεῖν ἄνεμος ἐγένετο· οὐδὲν γάρ ἐστιν οὗτος πλὴν
364

class. Mist is a vaporous exhalation which does not produce water, denser than air but less dense than cloud ; it comes into being either from a cloud in the first stage of formation or from the remnant of a cloud. The condition contrary to this is rightly called a *clear sky*, for it is simply air, with no cloud or mist. Dew is moisture that falls out of a clear sky in a light condensation ; ice is solidified water, frozen in a clear sky : hoar-frost is frozen dew, and dew-frost is half-frozen dew. Cloud is a dense, vaporous formation, productive of water : rain comes from the compression of a well-compacted cloud, and varies in character according to the pressure on the cloud : if the pressure is light it scatters gentle drops of rain, but if it is heavy the drops are fuller : and we call this latter condition a *downpour*, for it is larger than a shower of rain and pours continuous drops of rain upon the earth. Snow occurs when well-condensed clouds break up and split before the formation of water : the split causes the foamy and brilliantly white condition of the snow, and its coldness is caused by the coagulation of the moisture contained in it, which has not had time to be either fused or rarefied. If there is a thick and heavy fall of snow, we call it a *snow-storm*. Hail occurs when a snow-storm is solidified and gathers weight because of its increased density so as to fall more rapidly ; the hailstones increase in size and their movement increases in violence according to the size of the fragments that are broken off the cloud. These then are the natural products of the wet exhalation.

From the dry exhalation, when it is forced to flow by the cold, wind is produced : for this is nothing but

---

[1] φερόμενον Lor. : φερόμενα Bekk.

ἀὴρ πολὺς ῥέων καὶ ἀθρόος· ὅστις ἅμα καὶ πνεῦμα
10 λέγεται. λέγεται δὲ καὶ ἑτέρως πνεῦμα ἥ τε ἐν
φυτοῖς καὶ ζῴοις καὶ διὰ πάντων διήκουσα ἔμψυχός
τε καὶ γόνιμος οὐσία, περὶ ἧς νῦν λέγειν οὐκ ἀναγκαῖον. τὰ δὲ ἐν ἀέρι πνέοντα πνεύματα καλοῦμεν
ἀνέμους, αὔρας δὲ τὰς ἐξ ὑγροῦ φερομένας ἐκπνοάς.
τῶν δὲ ἀνέμων οἱ μὲν ἐκ νενοτισμένης γῆς πνέοντες
15 ἀπόγειοι λέγονται, οἱ δὲ ἐκ κόλπων διεξάττοντες
ἐγκολπίαι· τούτοις δὲ ἀνάλογόν τι ἔχουσιν οἱ ἐκ
ποταμῶν καὶ λιμνῶν. οἱ δὲ κατὰ ῥῆξιν νέφους
γινόμενοι καὶ ἀνάλυσιν τοῦ πάχους πρὸς ἑαυτοὺς
ποιούμενοι ἐκνεφίαι καλοῦνται· μεθ' ὕδατος δὲ
ἀθρόως ῥαγέντες[1] ἐξυδρίαι λέγονται. καὶ οἱ μὲν
20 ἀπὸ ἀνατολῆς συνεχεῖς εὗροι κέκληνται, βορέαι δὲ
οἱ ἀπὸ ἄρκτου, ζέφυροι δὲ οἱ ἀπὸ δύσεως, νότοι
δὲ οἱ ἀπὸ μεσημβρίας. τῶν γε μὴν εὔρων καικίας
μὲν λέγεται ὁ ἀπὸ τοῦ περὶ τὰς θερινὰς ἀνατολὰς
τόπου πνέων ἄνεμος, ἀπηλιώτης δὲ ὁ ἀπὸ τοῦ περὶ
τὰς ἰσημερινάς, εὗρος δὲ ὁ ἀπὸ τοῦ περὶ τὰς χει-
25 μερινάς. καὶ τῶν ἐναντίων ζεφύρων ἀργέστης μὲν
ὁ ἀπὸ τῆς θερινῆς δύσεως, ὅν τινες καλοῦσιν ὀλυμ-
πίαν, οἱ δὲ ἰάπυγα· ζέφυρος δὲ ὁ ἀπὸ τῆς ἰση-
μερινῆς, λὶψ δὲ ὁ ἀπὸ τῆς χειμερινῆς. καὶ τῶν
βορεῶν ἰδίως ὁ μὲν ἑξῆς τῷ καικίᾳ καλεῖται βορέας,
ἀπαρκτίας δὲ ὁ ἐφεξῆς ἀπὸ τοῦ πόλου κατὰ τὸ
30 μεσημβρινὸν πνέων, θρασκίας δὲ ὁ ἑξῆς πνέων τῷ

---

[1] ῥαγέντες B Lor. : ῥαγέντος codd. cet. Bekk.

---

[a] This is a common Greek way of describing points of
the compass. They divided each quarter by three; so their

air moving in quantity and in a mass. It is also called *breath*. In another sense " breath " means that substance found in plants and animals and pervading everything, that brings life and generation ; but about that there is no need to speak now. The breath that breathes in the air we call *wind*, and the breath that comes from moisture we call *breeze*. Of the winds, some blow from the earth when it is wet and are called *land-winds* ; some arise from gulfs of the sea and are called *gulf-winds*. There is a similarity between these winds and those which come from rivers and lakes. Those which arise at the breaking up of a cloud and resolve its density against themselves are called *cloud-winds* : those which burst out all at once accompanied by water are called *rain-winds*. Eurus is the name of the winds that blow steadily from the East, Boreas is the name of the North winds, Zephyrus of the West winds, and Notus of the South winds. One of the Euri is called Caecias : this is the one that blows from from the direction of the summer sunrise.[a] Apeliotes is the one that comes from the direction of the equinoctial sunrise, and Eurus proper the one that comes from the direction of the winter sunrise. Of the Zephyri, which blow in the opposite direction, Argestes comes from the direction of the summer sunset ; some call this Olympias, and some Iapyx. Zephyrus proper comes from the direction of the equinoctial sunset, Lips from the direction of the winter sunset. Of the winds called Boreas, the one properly so-called is next to Caecias ; next to it is Aparctias, which blows from the North pole to the South ; Thrascias is the one

minor points cannot be translated simply into modern terms. Equinoctial sunrise and sunset can be taken as E. and W.

394 b

ἀργέστῃ, ὃν ἔνιοι κιρκίαν¹ καλοῦσιν. καὶ τῶν
νότων ὁ μὲν ἀπὸ τοῦ ἀφανοῦς πόλου φερόμενος
ἀντίπαλος τῷ ἀπαρκτίᾳ καλεῖται νότος, εὐρόνοτος
δὲ ὁ μεταξὺ νότου καὶ εὔρου· τὸν δὲ ἐπὶ θάτερα
μεταξὺ λιβὸς καὶ νότου οἱ μὲν λιβόνοτον, οἱ δὲ
35 λιβοφοίνικα, καλοῦσιν.

Τῶν δὲ ἀνέμων οἱ μέν εἰσιν εὐθύπνοοι, ὁπόσοι
διεκπνέουσι πρόσω κατ' εὐθεῖαν, οἱ δὲ ἀνακαμψί-
395 a πνοοι, καθάπερ ὁ καικίας λεγόμενος, καὶ οἱ μὲν
χειμῶνος, ὥσπερ οἱ νότοι, δυναστεύοντες, οἱ δὲ
θέρους, ὡς οἱ ἐτησίαι λεγόμενοι, μῖξιν ἔχοντες τῶν
τε ἀπὸ τῆς ἄρκτου φερομένων καὶ ζεφύρων· οἱ δὲ
ὀρνιθίαι καλούμενοι, ἐαρινοί τινες ὄντες ἄνεμοι,
5 βορέαι εἰσὶ τῷ γένει.

Τῶν γε μὴν βιαίων πνευμάτων καταιγὶς μέν ἐστι
πνεῦμα ἄνωθεν τύπτον ἐξαίφνης, θύελλα δὲ πνεῦμα
βίαιον καὶ ἄφνω προσαλλόμενον, λαῖλαψ δὲ καὶ
στρόβιλος πνεῦμα εἰλούμενον κάτωθεν ἄνω, ἀναφύσημα δὲ γῆς πνεῦμα ἄνω φερόμενον κατὰ τὴν
10 ἐκ βυθοῦ τινος ἢ ῥήγματος ἀνάδοσιν· ὅταν δὲ
εἰλούμενον πολὺ φέρηται, πρηστὴρ χθόνιός ἐστιν.
εἰληθὲν δὲ πνεῦμα ἐν νέφει παχεῖ τε καὶ νοτερῷ,
καὶ ἐξωσθὲν δι' αὐτοῦ, βιαίως ῥηγνύον τὰ συνεχῆ
πιλήματα τοῦ νέφους, βρόμον καὶ πάταγον μέγαν
ἀπειργάσατο, βροντὴν λεγόμενον, ὥσπερ ἐν ὕδατι

---

¹ κιρκίαν Forster : καικίαν codd. Bekk.

a Phenomena connected with wind and those connected
with thunder and lightning are not clearly distinguished in
Greek, and translation is difficult. Here πρηστήρ seems to

next Argestes, though some call this Circias. Of the winds called Notus, the one that comes from the invisible pole, opposite to Aparctias, is properly called Notus, and Euronotus is the one between Notus and Eurus. The one on the other side, between Notus and Lips, is sometimes called Libonotus, sometimes Libophoenix.

The current of some winds is direct—that is, they blow straight ahead ; the current of others varies in direction, as in the case of Caecias. Some of them prevail in the winter, like the Noti ; some prevail in the summer, like those called Etesian winds, which are a mixture of North winds and Zephyri. Those which are called Ornithian winds, which occur in the spring, belong to the class Boreas.

Of the violent types of wind, a squall is a wind that strikes suddenly from above ; a gust is a violent wind that suddenly jumps up at you ; a whirlwind, or cyclone, is a wind that whirls upwards in a spiral. A blast of wind from the earth is a gust caused by the expulsion of wind from some pit or chasm ; when it moves with a fierce whirling motion, it is an earth-hurricane ($\pi\rho\eta\sigma\tau\dot\eta\rho$).[a] When the wind whirls round in a thick cloud full of water and is pushed out through it and forcibly breaks up the closely packed material of the cloud, it makes a great din and crash, which is called *thunder*—as air does when it is passed violently

---

mean some kind of whirlwind, but in 394 a 18 and 395 a 24 it is a sort of thunderbolt. Aristotle says (*Meteor.* 371 a 15): " When it (*i.e.* the cloud pulled down by a descending whirlwind) is inflamed as it is pulled downwards . . . it is called a $\pi\rho\eta\sigma\tau\dot\eta\rho$; for it inflames ($\sigma\upsilon\nu\epsilon\kappa\pi\dot\iota\mu\pi\rho\eta\sigma\iota$) the neighbouring air and colours it with its fire." The name implies a connexion with fire and perhaps here the $\pi\rho\eta\sigma\tau\dot\eta\rho$ comes up from a fiery chasm (*cf.* 395 b 20).

15 πνεῦμα σφοδρῶς ἐλαυνόμενον. κατὰ δὲ τὴν τοῦ
νέφους ἔκρηξιν πυρωθὲν τὸ πνεῦμα καὶ λάμψαν
ἀστραπὴ λέγεται· ὃ δὴ πρότερον τῆς βροντῆς
προσέπεσεν, ὕστερον γενόμενον, ἐπεὶ τὸ ἀκουστὸν
ὑπὸ τοῦ ὁρατοῦ πέφυκε φθάνεσθαι, τοῦ μὲν καὶ
πόρρωθεν ὁρωμένου, τοῦ δὲ ἐπειδὰν ἐμπελάσῃ τῇ
20 ἀκοῇ, καὶ μάλιστα ὅταν τὸ μὲν τάχιστον ᾖ τῶν
ὄντων, λέγω δὲ τὸ πυρῶδες, τὸ δὲ ἧττον ταχύ,
ἀερῶδες ὄν, ἐν τῇ πλήξει πρὸς ἀκοὴν ἀφικνούμενον.
τὸ δὲ ἀστράψαν ἀναπυρωθέν, βιαίως ἄχρι τῆς γῆς
διεκθέον, κεραυνὸς καλεῖται, ἐὰν δὲ ἡμίπυρον ᾖ,
σφοδρὸν δὲ ἄλλως καὶ ἀθρόον, πρηστήρ, ἐὰν δὲ
25 ἄπυρον παντελῶς, τυφών· ἕκαστον δὲ τούτων κατα-
σκῆψαν εἰς τὴν γῆν σκηπτὸς ὀνομάζεται. τῶν δὲ
κεραυνῶν οἱ μὲν αἰθαλώδεις ψολόεντες λέγονται,
οἱ δὲ ταχέως διᾴττοντες ἀργῆτες, ἑλικίαι δὲ οἱ
γραμμοειδῶς φερόμενοι, σκηπτοὶ δὲ ὅσοι κατα-
σκήπτουσιν εἴς τι.

Συλλήβδην δὲ τῶν ἐν ἀέρι φαντασμάτων τὰ μέν
30 ἐστι κατ᾽ ἔμφασιν, τὰ δὲ καθ᾽ ὑπόστασιν—κατ᾽
ἔμφασιν μὲν ἴριδες καὶ ῥάβδοι καὶ τὰ τοιαῦτα, καθ᾽
ὑπόστασιν δὲ σέλα τε καὶ διᾴττοντες καὶ κομῆται
καὶ τὰ τούτοις παραπλήσια. ἶρις μὲν οὖν ἐστιν
ἔμφασις ἡλίου τμήματος ἢ σελήνης, ἐν νέφει νοτερῷ καὶ κοίλῳ καὶ συνεχεῖ πρὸς φαντασίαν, ὡς ἐν
35 κατόπτρῳ, θεωρουμένη κατὰ κύκλου περιφέρειαν.
ῥάβδος δέ ἐστιν ἴριδος ἔμφασις εὐθεῖα. ἄλως δέ
395 b ἐστιν ἔμφασις λαμπρότητος ἄστρου περίαυγος·

ᵃ See p. 368, n. a.

ᵇ τυφών is often a typhoon or hurricane (cf. 400 a 29), but
here it is connected with lightning. In mythology Typhon

370

through water. Because of the breaking up of the cloud the wind is set on fire, and flashes : this is called *lightning*. This lightning falls upon our senses before the thunder, though it occurs later, because what is heard is by nature slower than what is seen : for the latter is seen a great way off, the former only when it approaches the ears ; particularly when one is that swiftest thing of all, the element of Fire, while the other is less swift, since it is of the nature of air and impinges upon the hearing by physical contact. When the flashing bolt is aflame and hurtles violently to the ground it is called a *thunderbolt*; if it is half alight, but in other respects strong and dense, it is called a *fiery bolt* [a] ; if it is altogether fireless it is called a *smoking bolt* [b] ; but each one of these when it falls upon the ground is called a *falling-bolt*. Lightning [c] is called *smoky* when it looks dark, like smoke ; *vivid*, when it moves very rapidly ; and *forked*, when it moves along jagged lines ; but when it falls on to something it is called a *falling-bolt*.

Briefly, the phenomena of the air are divided into those which are mere appearances and those which are realities : the appearances are rainbows and streaks in the sky and so on ; the realities are lights and shooting stars and comets and other such things. A rainbow is the appearance in reflection of a portion of the sun or moon, seen, like an image in a mirror, in a cloud that is wet and hollow and presents an unbroken surface, and shaped like an arc of a circle. A streak is a straight rainbow. A halo is an appearance of brightness shedding its light round a star ;

is the son of Typhos, the giant, who causes the eruption of Etna ; hence the connexion with fire.

[c] κεραυνός is used for " lightning " and " thunderbolt."

διαφέρει δὲ ἴριδος ὅτι ἡ μὲν Ἶρις ἐξ ἐναντίας φαίνεται ἡλίου καὶ σελήνης, ἡ δὲ ἄλως κύκλῳ παντὸς
ἄστρου. σέλας δέ ἐστι πυρὸς ἀθρόου ἔξαψις ἐν
ἀέρι. τῶν δὲ σελάων ἃ μὲν ἀκοντίζεται, ἃ δὲ
5 στηρίζεται. ὁ μὲν οὖν ἐξακοντισμός ἐστι πυρὸς
γένεσις ἐκ παρατρίψεως ἐν ἀέρι φερομένου ταχέως
καὶ φαντασίαν μήκους ἐμφαίνοντος διὰ τὸ τάχος,
ὁ δὲ στηριγμός ἐστι χωρὶς φορᾶς προμήκης ἔκ-
τασις καὶ οἷον ἄστρου ῥύσις· πλατυνομένη δὲ
κατὰ θάτερον κομήτης καλεῖται. πολλάκις δὲ τῶν
10 σελάων τὰ μὲν ἐπιμένει πλείονα χρόνον, τὰ δὲ
παραχρῆμα σβέννυται. πολλαὶ δὲ καὶ ἄλλαι φαντασμάτων ἰδέαι θεωροῦνται, λαμπάδες τε καλού-
μεναι καὶ δοκίδες καὶ πίθοι καὶ βόθυνοι, κατὰ τὴν
πρὸς ταῦτα ὁμοιότητα ὧδε προσαγορευθεῖσαι. καὶ
τὰ μὲν τούτων ἑσπέρια, τὰ δὲ ἑῷα, τὰ δὲ ἀμφιφαῆ
15 θεωρεῖται, σπανίως δὲ βόρεια καὶ νότια. πάντα
δὲ ἀβέβαια· οὐδέποτε γάρ τι τούτων ἀεὶ φανερὸν
ἱστόρηται κατεστηριγμένον. τὰ μὲν τοίνυν ἀέρια
τοιαῦτα.

Ἐμπεριέχει δὲ καὶ ἡ γῆ πολλὰς ἐν αὑτῇ, καθάπερ
ὕδατος, οὕτως καὶ πνεύματος καὶ πυρὸς πηγάς.
20 τούτων δὲ αἱ μὲν ὑπὸ γῆν εἰσιν ἀόρατοι, πολλαὶ δὲ
ἀναπνοὰς ἔχουσι καὶ ἀναφυσήσεις, ὥσπερ Λιπάρα
τε καὶ Αἴτνη καὶ τὰ ἐν Αἰόλου νήσοις· αἳ δὴ[1] καὶ
ῥέουσι πολλάκις ποταμοῦ δίκην, καὶ μύδρους ἀναρ-
ριπτοῦσι διαπύρους. ἔνιαι δὲ ὑπὸ γῆν οὖσαι πλησίον πηγαίων ὑδάτων θερμαίνουσι ταῦτα, καὶ τὰ
25 μὲν χλιαρὰ τῶν ναμάτων ἀνιᾶσι, τὰ δὲ ὑπέρζεστα,
τὰ δὲ εὖ ἔχοντα κράσεως.

it differs from a rainbow in that the rainbow appears opposite the sun or moon, but the halo is in a circle round the whole of the star. A light is the kindling of a mass of fire in the air. Some lights shoot like javelins, others are set in one position in the sky. The shooting is a generation of fire by friction in the air ; the fire moves rapidly, giving the impression of length because of its rapidity. The latter, the stationary light, is extended and lengthy but keeps the same position, as if it were an elongated star ; if it spreads out towards one end it is called a *comet*. Often there is a variation in the duration of the light, some lasting a long time, some being extinguished at once. There are also many phenomena of different kinds to be seen, called *torches* and *planks* and *jars* and *pits*, taking their names from their likeness to these objects. Some of these can be seen in the West and some in the East, and some in both ; they rarely appear in the North and South. All of them are unstable ; for none of them has ever been described as always visible in the same place. So much, then, for the things of the air.

The earth contains in itself many sources, not only of water, but also of wind and fire. Some of these are subterranean and invisible, but many have vents and blow-holes, like Lipara and Etna and the volcanoes in the Aeolian islands. These often flow like rivers and throw up fiery, red-hot lumps. Some of the subterranean sources, which are near springs of water, impart heat to these : some of the streams they make merely lukewarm, some boiling, and some moderately and pleasantly hot.

---

[1] αἱ δή codd. Lor. : αἱ δὲ Bekk.

395 b

Ὁμοίως δὲ καὶ τῶν πνευμάτων πολλὰ πολλαχοῦ
γῆς στόμια ἀνέῳκται· ὧν τὰ μὲν ἐνθουσιᾶν ποιεῖ
τοὺς ἐμπελάζοντας, τὰ δὲ ἀτροφεῖν, τὰ δὲ χρη-
σμῳδεῖν, ὥσπερ τὰ ἐν Δελφοῖς καὶ Λεβαδείᾳ, τὰ
30 δὲ καὶ παντάπασιν ἀναιρεῖ, καθάπερ τὸ ἐν Φρυ-
γίᾳ. πολλάκις δὲ καὶ συγγενὲς πνεῦμα εὔκρατον
ἐν γῇ παρεξωσθὲν εἰς μυχίους σήραγγας αὐτῆς,
ἔξεδρον γενόμενον ἐκ τῶν οἰκείων τόπων, πολλὰ
μέρη συνεκράδανεν. πολλάκις δὲ πολὺ γενόμενον
ἔξωθεν ἐγκατειλήθη τοῖς ταύτης κοιλώμασι καὶ
35 ἀποκλεισθὲν ἐξόδου μετὰ βίας αὐτὴν συνετίναξε,
ζητοῦν ἔξοδον ἑαυτῷ, καὶ ἀπειργάσατο πάθος
396 a τοῦτο ὃ καλεῖν εἰώθαμεν σεισμόν. τῶν δὲ σεισμῶν
οἱ μὲν εἰς πλάγια σείοντες κατ' ὀξείας γωνίας ἐπι-
κλίνται καλοῦνται, οἱ δὲ ἄνω ῥιπτοῦντες καὶ κάτω
κατ' ὀρθὰς γωνίας βράσται, οἱ δὲ συνιζήσεις ποιοῦντες εἰς τὰ κοῖλα ἱζηματίαι[1]· οἱ δὲ χάσματα ἀνοί-
5 γοντες καὶ τὴν γῆν ἀναρρηγνύντες ῥῆκται καλοῦνται.
τούτων δὲ οἱ μὲν καὶ πνεῦμα προσαναβάλλουσιν,
οἱ δὲ πέτρας, οἱ δὲ πηλόν, οἱ δὲ πηγὰς φαίνουσι τὰς
πρότερον οὐκ οὔσας. τινὲς δὲ ἀνατρέπουσι[2] κατὰ
μίαν πρόωσιν, οὓς καλοῦσιν ὤστας. οἱ δὲ ἀνταποπάλλοντες[3] καὶ ταῖς εἰς ἑκάτερον ἐγκλίσεσι καὶ
10 ἀποπάλσεσι διορθοῦντες ἀεὶ τὸ σειόμενον παλματίαι
λέγονται, τρόμῳ πάθος ὅμοιον ἀπεργαζόμενοι. γίνονται δὲ καὶ μυκηταὶ σεισμοί, σείοντες τὴν γῆν
μετὰ βρόμου. πολλάκις δὲ καὶ χωρὶς σεισμοῦ
γίνεται μύκημα γῆς, ὅταν τὸ πνεῦμα σείειν μὲν μὴ
αὔταρκες ᾖ, ἐνειλούμενον δὲ ἐν αὐτῇ κόπτηται μετὰ

---

[1] ἱζηματίαι Z Lor. (cf. Johann. Lyd. *De Ost.* 54): χωματίαι
Stob. : χασματίαι codd, cet, Bekk,

Similarly, too, there are in many places on the earth's surface open vents for the winds, which have various effects on those who approach them, causing ecstatic inspiration, or wasting sickness, or in some cases prophecy, like those at Delphi and Lebadeia, or even complete destruction, like the one in Phrygia. Often, too, a moderate earth-born wind, forced into deep, hollow caves in the earth and becoming dislodged from its home, causes shocks in many places. Often when a large quantity from outside is confined within the hollows of the earth and cut off from exit, it shakes the earth violently, seeking an exit for itself, and produces the effect that we call an *earthquake*. Earthquakes which shake the earth obliquely at a very acute angle we call *horizontal*; those which blast upwards and downwards perpendicularly are called *heaving* earthquakes; those which cause a settlement of the earth into hollows are called *sinking* earthquakes; and those which open up chasms and split the earth are called *splitting* earthquakes. Some of them stir up a wind, or rocks, or mud; and some reveal springs that were not there before. Some, called *thrusting* earthquakes, overturn things with a single heave. Others cause recoil this way and that, and in the process of lurching to one side and rebounding again the things that are shaken are held upright: these are called *oscillating* earthquakes, and their effect is a sort of trembling. There are also *roaring* earthquakes, which shake the earth with a great din. There is often, also, a roaring of the earth without an earthquake, when the wind is not sufficient to shake the earth but lashes about enveloped in the

---

[2] ἀνατρέπουσι Lor. : ἀνατρέποντες Bekk.
[3] ἀνταποπάλλοντες Lor. : ἀναπάλλοντες Bekk.

15 ῥοθίου βίας. συσσωματοποιεῖται δὲ τὰ εἰσιόντα
πνεύματα καὶ ὑπὸ τῶν ἐν τῇ γῇ ὑγρῶν κεκρυμ-
μένων.

Τὰ δὲ ἀνάλογον συμπίπτει τούτοις καὶ ἐν θα-
λάσσῃ· χάσματά τε γὰρ γίνεται θαλάσσης καὶ ἀνα-
χωρήματα πολλάκις καὶ κυμάτων ἐπιδρομαί, ποτὲ
20 μὲν ἀντανακοπὴν ἔχουσαι, ποτὲ δὲ πρόωσιν μόνον,
ὥσπερ ἱστορεῖται περὶ Ἑλίκην τε καὶ Βοῦραν.
πολλάκις δὲ καὶ ἀναφυσήματα γίνεται πυρὸς ἐν τῇ
θαλάσσῃ καὶ πηγῶν ἀναβλύσεις καὶ ποταμῶν ἐκ-
βολαὶ καὶ δένδρων ἐκφύσεις ῥοαί τε καὶ δῖναι ταῖς
τῶν πνευμάτων ἀνάλογον, αἱ μὲν ἐν μέσοις πε-
25 λάγεσιν, αἱ δὲ κατὰ τοὺς εὐρίπους τε καὶ πορθμούς.
πολλαί τε ἀμπώτεις λέγονται καὶ κυμάτων ἄρσεις
συμπεριοδεύειν ἀεὶ τῇ σελήνῃ κατά τινας ὡρισμέ-
νους καιρούς.

Ὡς δὲ τὸ πᾶν εἰπεῖν, τῶν στοιχείων ἐγκεκρα-
μένων ἀλλήλοις ἐν ἀέρι τε καὶ γῇ καὶ θαλάσσῃ
30 κατὰ τὸ εἰκὸς αἱ τῶν παθῶν ὁμοιότητες συνίσταν-
ται, τοῖς μὲν ἐπὶ μέρους φθορὰς καὶ γενέσεις
φέρουσαι, τὸ δὲ σύμπαν ἀνώλεθρόν τε καὶ ἀγένητον
φυλάττουσαι.

5. Καίτοι γέ τις ἐθαύμασε πῶς ποτε, εἰ ἐκ τῶν
ἐναντίων ἀρχῶν συνέστηκεν ὁ κόσμος, λέγω δὲ
35 ξηρῶν τε καὶ ὑγρῶν, ψυχρῶν τε καὶ θερμῶν, οὐ
πάλαι διέφθαρται καὶ ἀπόλωλεν, ὡς κἂν εἰ πό-
λιν τινὲς θαυμάζοιεν, ὅπως διαμένει συνεστηκυῖα
ἐκ τῶν ἐναντιωτάτων¹ ἐθνῶν, πενήτων λέγω καὶ
πλουσίων, νέων γερόντων, ἀσθενῶν ἰσχυρῶν, πονη-
ρῶν χρηστῶν. ἀγνοοῦσι δὲ ὅτι τοῦτ᾽ ἦν πολιτι-

---

¹ ἐναντιωτάτων codd. pler. Lor. : ἐναντίων codd. cet. Bekk.

earth with tumultuous force. The blasts of wind that enter the earth are recondensed also by the moisture that is hidden in the earth.[a]

There are also analogous happenings in the sea : chasms occur in the sea, and its waves often withdraw ; and there are incursions of waves, sometimes with a recoil, sometimes with a forward rush only, as they say was the case at Helice and Bura.[b] Often too there are exhalations of fire in the sea and eruptions of fountains, and rivers are shot forth, and trees grow, and there are currents and vortices like those of the winds, some in the middle of the oceans, some in the narrows and straits. There are many tides and tidal waves too, which are said to occur in concert with the moon at certain definite times.

To sum up, since the elements are mingled one with another, it is natural that phenomena in the air and land and sea should show these similarities, which involve destruction and generation for the individual parts of nature, but preserve the whole free from corruption and generation.

5. Some people, however, have wondered how the cosmos, if it is composed of the " opposite " principles (I mean dry and wet, cold and hot), has not long ago been destroyed and perished ; it is as if men should wonder how a city survives, composed as it is of the most opposite classes (I mean poor and rich, young and old, weak and strong, bad and good). They do not recognize that the most wonderful thing of all about

[a] i.e., wind entering the earth may (a) cause an earthquake, (b) cause a roar only, or (c) be recondensed and so cause neither.

[b] Cf. Strabo viii. 7. 2 (384 c), i. 3. 10 (54 c), Aristot. Meteor. 343 b 1, etc., on the destruction of these two cities in Achaia. The date was 373/2 B.C.

5 κῆς ὁμονοίας τὸ θαυμασιώτατον, λέγω δὲ τὸ[1] ἐκ
πολλῶν μίαν καὶ ὁμοίαν ἐξ ἀνομοίων ἀποτελεῖν[1]
διάθεσιν, ὑποδεχομένην[2] πᾶσαν καὶ φύσιν καὶ τύχην.
ἴσως δὲ καὶ τῶν ἐναντίων ἡ φύσις γλίχεται καὶ ἐκ
τούτων ἀποτελεῖ τὸ σύμφωνον, οὐκ ἐκ τῶν ὁμοίων,
ὥσπερ ἀμέλει τὸ ἄρρεν συνήγαγε πρὸς τὸ θῆλυ καὶ
10 οὐχ ἑκάτερον πρὸς τὸ ὁμόφυλον, καὶ τὴν πρώτην
ὁμόνοιαν διὰ τῶν ἐναντίων σηνῆψεν, οὐ διὰ τῶν
ὁμοίων. ἔοικε δὲ καὶ ἡ τέχνη τὴν φύσιν μιμουμένη
τοῦτο ποιεῖν. ζωγραφία μὲν γὰρ λευκῶν τε καὶ
μελάνων, ὠχρῶν τε καὶ ἐρυθρῶν, χρωμάτων ἐγ-
κερασαμένη φύσεις τὰς εἰκόνας τοῖς προηγου-
15 μένοις ἀπετέλεσε συμφώνους, μουσικὴ δὲ ὀξεῖς
ἅμα καὶ βαρεῖς, μακρούς τε καὶ βραχεῖς φθόγγους
μίξασα ἐν διαφόροις φωναῖς μίαν ἀπετέλεσεν ἁρμονίαν, γραμματικὴ δὲ ἐκ φωνηέντων καὶ ἀφώνων
γραμμάτων κρᾶσιν ποιησαμένη τὴν ὅλην τέχνην
ἀπ' αὐτῶν συνεστήσατο. ταὐτὸ δὲ τοῦτο ἦν καὶ
20 τὸ παρὰ τῷ σκοτεινῷ λεγόμενον Ἡρακλείτῳ·
" συνάψιες ὅλα καὶ οὐχ ὅλα, συμφερόμενον διαφερό-
μενον, συνᾶδον διᾷδον· καὶ ἐκ πάντων ἓν καὶ ἐξ
ἑνὸς πάντα."[3] οὕτως οὖν καὶ τὴν τῶν ὅλων σύστασιν, οὐρανοῦ λέγω καὶ γῆς τοῦ τε σύμπαντος
25 κόσμου, διὰ τῆς τῶν ἐναντιωτάτων κράσεως ἀρχῶν

---

[1] τὸ . . . ἀποτελεῖν Lor. : ὅτι . . . ἀποτελεῖ Bekk.
[2] ὑποδεχομένην Lor. : ὑποδεχομένη Bekk.
[3] sic Diels (*Vorsokr.*[6] 22 B 10) : v. Lor. ad loc.

---

[a] The idea that art imitates nature occurs in Aristotle's
Protrepticus (see Jaeger, *Aristotle*, pp. 74 f.), and in *Phys.*
B 199 a 15, *Meteor.* 381 b 5, *De Part. Anim.* 639 b 15 ff. But
in Aristotle the point of comparison concerns teleology, not

the harmonious working of a city-community is this :
that out of plurality and diversity it achieves a homo-
geneous unity capable of admitting every variation
of nature and degree. But perhaps nature actually
has a liking for opposites ; perhaps it is from them
that she creates harmony, and not from similar things,
in just the same way as she has joined the male to
the female, and not each of them to another of the
same sex, thus making the first harmonious com-
munity not of similar but of opposite things. It seems,
too, that art does this, in imitation of nature [a] : for
painting mixes its whites and blacks, its yellows and
reds, to create images that are concordant with their
originals ; music mixes high and low notes, and longs
and shorts, and makes a single tune of different
sounds ; by making a mixture of vowels and con-
sonants, grammar composes out of them the whole of
its art. This is precisely what Heracleitus the Dark [b]
meant when he said " Junctions are wholes and not-
wholes, concord and discord, consonance and disso-
nance. One out of All ; All out of One." So in the
same way the complex of the Universe, I mean heaven
and earth and the whole cosmos, by means of the
mixture of the most opposite elements has been

the harmony of opposites. The four colours mentioned by
Pseudo-Aristotle are the colours of the restricted palette used
by the Four Colour Painters, of whom the earliest recorded
is Polygnotus and the latest Aëtion in the age of Alexander
the Great. *Cf.* Pliny, *N.H.* xxxv. 50, and A. Rumpf, *JHS*
lxvii (1947), p. 16. It has been suggested that Empedocles'
comparison of painting and creation (Diels, *Vorsokr.*[6] 31
B 23) was inspired by Four Colour Painting.

[b] It is not likely that the author read Heracleitus in the
original, or that the whole context is to be attached too
closely to Heracleitus. Maguire (*op. cit.* pp. 134 ff.) finds the
closest parallels to this passage in the Neo-Pythagoreans.

μία διεκόσμησεν ἁρμονία· ξηρὸν γὰρ ὑγρῷ, θερμὸν
δὲ ψυχρῷ, βαρεῖ τε κοῦφον μιγέν, καὶ ὀρθὸν περι-
φερεῖ, γῆν τε πᾶσαν καὶ θάλασσαν αἰθέρα τε καὶ
ἥλιον καὶ σελήνην καὶ τὸν ὅλον οὐρανὸν διεκόσμησε
μία ἡ διὰ πάντων διήκουσα δύναμις, ἐκ τῶν ἀμίκ-
30 των καὶ ἑτεροίων, ἀέρος τε καὶ γῆς καὶ πυρὸς καὶ
ὕδατος, τὸν σύμπαντα κόσμον δημιουργήσασα καὶ
μιᾷ διαλαβοῦσα σφαίρας ἐπιφανείᾳ τάς τε ἐναντιω-
τάτας ἐν αὐτῷ φύσεις ἀλλήλαις ἀναγκάσασα ὁμο-
λογῆσαι καὶ ἐκ τούτων μηχανησαμένη τῷ παντὶ
σωτηρίαν. αἰτία δὲ ταύτης μὲν ἡ τῶν στοιχείων
35 ὁμολογία, τῆς δὲ ὁμολογίας ἡ ἰσομοιρία καὶ τὸ
397 a μηδὲν αὐτῶν πλέον ἕτερον ἑτέρου δύνασθαι· τὴν
γὰρ ἴσην ἀντίστασιν ἔχει τὰ βαρέα πρὸς τὰ κοῦφα
καὶ τὰ θερμὰ πρὸς θάτερα,[1] τῆς φύσεως ἐπὶ τῶν
μειζόνων διδασκούσης ὅτι τὸ ἴσον σωστικόν πώς
ἐστιν ὁμονοίας, ἡ δὲ ὁμόνοια τοῦ πάντων γενετῆρος
5 καὶ περικαλλεστάτου κόσμου. τίς γὰρ ἂν εἴη φύσις
τοῦδε κρείττων; ἣν γὰρ ἂν εἴπῃ[2] τις, μέρος ἐστὶν
αὐτοῦ. τό τε καλὸν πᾶν ἐπώνυμόν ἐστι τούτου καὶ
τὸ τεταγμένον, ἀπὸ τοῦ κόσμου λεγόμενον κεκοσμῆσθαι. τί[3] δὲ τῶν ἐπὶ μέρους δύναιτ' ἂν ἐξισω-
θῆναι τῇ κατ' οὐρανὸν τάξει τε καὶ φορᾷ τῶν
10 ἄστρων ἡλίου τε καὶ σελήνης, κινουμένων ἐν ἀκρι-
βεστάτοις μέτροις ἐξ αἰῶνος εἰς ἕτερον αἰῶνα; τίς
δὲ γένοιτ' ἂν ἀψεύδεια τοιάδε, ἥντινα φυλάττουσιν
αἱ καλαὶ καὶ γόνιμοι τῶν ὅλων ὧραι, θέρη τε καὶ
χειμῶνας ἐπάγουσαι τεταγμένως ἡμέρας τε καὶ

---

[1] θάτερα ETZ Lor. : τὰ θάτερα codd. cet. Bekk.

organized by a single harmony : dry mixed with
wet, hot with cold, light with heavy, straight with
curved—the whole of earth and sea, the aether, the
sun, the moon and the whole heaven have been set
in order by the single power which interpenetrates
all things : from things unmixed and diverse, air and
earth and fire and water, it has fashioned the whole
cosmos and embraced it all in the surface of a single
sphere, forcing the most opposite elements in the
cosmos to come to terms, and from them achieving
preservation for the whole. The cause of its preservation is the agreement of the elements, and the
cause of the agreement is the principle of equal shares
and the fact that no one of them has more power than
each of the others : for the heavy is in equipoise with
the light, and the hot with its opposite. In these
greater matters nature teaches us that equality is the
preserver of concord, and concord is the preserver of
the cosmos, which is the parent of all things and the
most beautiful of all. For what being could be better
than this ? Anything that might be suggested is a
part of it. And everything that is beautiful takes its
name from this, and all that is well-arranged ; for
it is called " well-ordered " (κεκοσμῆσθαι) after this
" universal order " (κόσμος). What particular detail
could be compared to the arrangement of the heavens
and the movement of the stars and the sun and moon,
moving as they do from one age to another in the
most accurate measures of time ? What constancy
could rival that maintained by the hours and seasons,
the beautiful creators of all things, that bring summers
and winters in due order, and days and nights to make

---

² εἴπῃ EP Lor. : εἴποι codd. cet. Bekk.
³ τί Lor. : τίς Bekk.

397 a

νύκτας εἰς μηνὸς ἀποτέλεσμα καὶ ἐνιαυτοῦ; καὶ
15 μὴν μεγέθει μὲν οὗτος¹ πανυπέρτατος, κινήσει δὲ
ὀξύτατος, λαμπρότητι δὲ εὐαυγέστατος, δυνάμει δὲ
ἀγήρως τε καὶ ἄφθαρτος. οὗτος ἐναλίων ζῴων
καὶ πεζῶν καὶ ἀερίων φύσεις ἐχώρισε καὶ βίους
ἐμέτρησε ταῖς ἑαυτοῦ κινήσεσιν. ἐκ τούτου πάντα
ἐμπνεῖ τε καὶ ψυχὴν ἴσχει τὰ ζῷα. τούτου καὶ αἱ
20 παράδοξοι νεοχμώσεις τεταγμένως ἀποτελοῦνται,
συναραττόντων μὲν ἀνέμων παντοίων, πιπτόντων
δὲ ἐξ οὐρανοῦ κεραυνῶν, ῥηγνυμένων δὲ χειμώνων
ἐξαισίων. διὰ δὲ τούτων τὸ νοτερὸν ἐκπιεζόμενον
τό τε πυρῶδες διαπνεόμενον εἰς ὁμόνοιαν ἄγει τὸ
πᾶν καὶ καθίστησιν. ἥ τε γῆ φυτοῖς κομῶσα παντο-
25 δαποῖς νάμασί τε περιβλύζουσα καὶ περιοχουμένη
ζῴοις, κατὰ καιρὸν ἐκφύουσά τε πάντα καὶ τρέ-
φουσα καὶ δεχομένη, μυρίας τε φέρουσα ἰδέας καὶ
πάθη, τὴν ἀγήρω φύσιν ὁμοίως τηρεῖ, καίτοι καὶ
σεισμοῖς τινασσομένη καὶ πλημμύρισιν ἐπικλυζομένη
30 πυρκαϊαῖς τε κατὰ μέρος φλογιζομένη. ταῦτα δὲ
πάντα ἔοικεν αὐτῇ πρὸς ἀγαθοῦ γινόμενα τὴν δι᾽
αἰῶνος σωτηρίαν παρέχειν· σειομένης τε γὰρ δι-
εξάττουσιν αἱ τῶν πνευμάτων παρεμπτώσεις κατὰ
τὰ ῥήγματα τὰς ἀναπνοὰς ἴσχουσαι, καθὼς ἄνω
λέλεκται, καθαιρομένη τε ὄμβροις ἀποκλύζεται
35 πάντα τὰ νοσώδη, περιπνεομένη δὲ αὔραις τά τε
ὑπ᾽ αὐτὴν καὶ τὰ ὑπὲρ αὐτὴν εἰλικρινεῖται. καὶ
397 b μὴν αἱ φλόγες μὲν τὸ παγετῶδες ἠπιαίνουσιν,² οἱ
πάγοι δὲ τὰς φλόγας ἀνιᾶσιν. καὶ τῶν ἐπὶ μέρους
τὰ μὲν γίνεται, τὰ δὲ ἀκμάζει, τὰ δὲ φθείρεται.

¹ οὗτος Lor. : ὁ αὐτὸς Bekk.
² ἠπιαίνουσι(ν) BCFG Lor. : πιαίνουσιν codd. cet. Bekk.

382

up the number of a month or a year ? In size too the
cosmos is mightiest, in motion swiftest, in brightness
most brilliant, in power never-aging and indestructible. It is this that has given a different nature to
the creatures of the sea, the land and the air, and
measured their lives in terms of its own movements.
From this all creatures breathe and take their life.
Of this even the unexpected changes are accom-
plished in due order—the winds of all kinds that dash
together, thunderbolts falling from the heavens, and
storms that violently burst out. Through these the
moisture is squeezed out and the fire is dispersed by
currents of air ; in this way the whole is brought into
harmony and so established. The earth, too, that
is crowned with plants of every kind and bubbles with
springs and teems with living creatures everywhere,
that brings forth everything in season and nurtures
it and receives it back again, that produces a myriad
shapes and conditions—this earth still keeps its never-
aging nature unchanged, though it is racked by
earthquakes, swamped by floods, and burnt in part by
fires. All these things, it seems, happen for the good
of the earth and give it preservation from age to age :
for when it is shaken by an earthquake, there is an
upsurge of the winds transfused within it, which find
vent-holes through the chasms, as I have already
said [a] ; when it is washed by rain it is cleansed of all
noxious things ; and when the breezes blow round
about it the things below and above it are purified.
Furthermore the fires soften things that are frozen,
and frost abates the force of the fires. And of the
particular things on the earth some come into being
while some are in their prime and others are perishing :

[a] 395 b 26.

καὶ αἱ μὲν γενέσεις ἐπαναστέλλουσι τὰς φθοράς,
5 αἱ δὲ φθοραὶ κουφίζουσι τὰς γενέσεις. μία δὲ ἐκ
πάντων περαινομένη σωτηρία διὰ τέλους ἀντιπερι-
ισταμένων ἀλλήλοις καὶ τοτὲ μὲν κρατούντων, τοτὲ
δὲ κρατουμένων, φυλάττει τὸ σύμπαν ἄφθαρτον δι'
αἰῶνος.

6. Λοιπὸν δὲ δὴ περὶ τῆς τῶν ὅλων συνεκτικῆς
10 αἰτίας κεφαλαιωδῶς εἰπεῖν, ὃν τρόπον καὶ περὶ τῶν
ἄλλων· πλημμελὲς γὰρ περὶ κόσμου λέγοντας, εἰ
καὶ μὴ δι' ἀκριβείας, ἀλλ' οὖν γε ὡς εἰς τυπώδη
μάθησιν, τὸ τοῦ κόσμου κυριώτατον παραλιπεῖν.
ἀρχαῖος μὲν οὖν τις λόγος καὶ πάτριός ἐστι πᾶσιν
ἀνθρώποις ὡς ἐκ θεοῦ πάντα καὶ διὰ θεοῦ ἡμῖν
15 συνέστηκεν, οὐδεμία δὲ φύσις αὐτὴ καθ' ἑαυτήν
ἐστιν αὐτάρκης, ἐρημωθεῖσα τῆς ἐκ τούτου σωτηρίας. διὸ καὶ τῶν παλαιῶν εἰπεῖν τινες προήχθη-
σαν ὅτι πάντα ταῦτά ἐστι θεῶν πλέα τὰ καὶ δι'
ὀφθαλμῶν ἰνδαλλόμενα ἡμῖν καὶ δι' ἀκοῆς καὶ
πάσης αἰσθήσεως, τῇ μὲν θείᾳ δυνάμει πρέποντα
20 καταβαλλόμενοι λόγον, οὐ μὴν τῇ γε οὐσίᾳ. σωτὴρ
μὲν γὰρ ὄντως ἁπάντων ἐστὶ καὶ γενέτωρ τῶν
ὁπωσδήποτε κατὰ τόνδε τὸν κόσμον συντελου-
μένων ὁ θεός, οὐ μὴν αὐτουργοῦ καὶ ἐπιπόνου
ζῴου κάματον ὑπομένων, ἀλλὰ δυνάμει χρώμενος
ἀτρύτῳ, δι' ἧς καὶ τῶν πόρρω δοκούντων εἶναι
25 περιγίνεται. τὴν μὲν οὖν ἀνωτάτω καὶ πρώτην
ἕδραν αὐτὸς ἔλαχεν, ὕπατός τε διὰ τοῦτο ὠνόμασται, [καὶ]¹ κατὰ τὸν ποιητὴν '' ἀκροτάτῃ κο-

¹ καὶ om. BCG Lor.

and generation is set in the balance against destruction, and destruction lightens the weight of generation. There is one single principle of preservation, maintained without interruption among all these things that interchange with one another, ascending to power and declining in turn, and this keeps the whole system safe, eternally indestructible.

6. It remains now to discuss summarily, as the rest has been discussed, the cause that holds the world together ; for in describing the cosmos, if not in detail, at least sufficiently to convey an outline, it would be wrong for us to omit altogether that which is supreme in the cosmos. It is indeed an ancient idea, traditional among all mankind, that all things are from God and are constituted for us by God, and nothing is self-sufficient if deprived of his preserving influence. So some of the ancients were led to say that all the things of this world are full of gods,[a] all that are presented to us through our eyes and hearing and all the senses ; but in saying this they used terms suitable to the power of God but not to his essence. For God is indeed the preserver of all things and the creator of everything in this cosmos however it is brought to fruition ; but he does not take upon himself the toil of a creature that works and labours for itself,[b] but uses an indefatigable power, by means of which he controls even things that seem a great way off. God has his home in the highest and first place, and is called Supreme for this reason, since according to the poet [c] it is on " the loftiest crest "

[a] Cf. the saying attributed to Thales (Diels, Vorsokr.[6] 11 A 22 = Aristot. De Anima 411 a 7).

[b] The αὐτουργός (cf. 398 a 5, b 4) is the man who works his own land without a slave, e.g. Electra's husband in Euripides' Electra. [c] Hom. Il. i. 499.

397 b

ρυφῇ'' τοῦ σύμπαντος ἐγκαθιδρυμένος οὐρανοῦ·
μάλιστα δέ πως αὐτοῦ τῆς δυνάμεως ἀπολαύει τὸ
πλησίον αὐτοῦ σῶμα, καὶ ἔπειτα τὸ μετ' ἐκεῖνο,
30 καὶ ἐφεξῆς οὕτως ἄχρι τῶν καθ' ἡμᾶς τόπων. διὸ
γῆ τε καὶ τὰ ἐπὶ γῆς ἔοικεν, ἐν ἀποστάσει πλείστῃ
τῆς ἐκ θεοῦ ὄντα ὠφελείας, ἀσθενῆ καὶ ἀκατάλληλα
εἶναι καὶ πολλῆς μεστὰ ταραχῆς· οὐ μὴν ἀλλὰ
[καὶ]¹ καθ' ὅσον ἐπὶ πᾶν δικνεῖσθαι πέφυκε τὸ
θεῖον, καὶ τὰ καθ' ἡμᾶς ὁμοίως συμβαίνει τά τε
35 ὑπὲρ ἡμᾶς, κατὰ τὸ ἔγγιόν τε καὶ πορρωτέρω θεοῦ
398 a εἶναι μᾶλλόν τε καὶ ἧττον ὠφελείας μεταλαμβά-
νοντα. κρεῖττον οὖν ὑπολαβεῖν, ὃ καὶ πρέπον ἐστὶ
καὶ θεῷ μάλιστα ἁρμόζον, ὡς ἡ ἐν οὐρανῷ δύναμις
ἱδρυμένη καὶ τοῖς πλεῖστον ἀφεστηκόσιν, ὡς ἔνι
γε εἰπεῖν, καὶ σύμπασιν αἰτία γίνεται σωτηρίας,
5 μᾶλλον ἢ ὡς διήκουσα καὶ φοιτῶσα ἔνθα μὴ καλὸν
μηδὲ εὔσχημον αὐτουργεῖ τὰ ἐπὶ γῆς. τοῦτο μὲν
γὰρ οὐδὲ ἀνθρώπων ἡγεμόνιν ἁρμόττει, παντὶ καὶ
τῷ τυχόντι ἐφίστασθαι ἔργῳ, οἶον στρατιᾶς ἄρχοντι
ἢ πόλεως ἢ οἴκου, [καὶ]² εἰ χρεὼν στρωματό-
δεσμον εἴη δῆσαι καὶ εἴ τι φαυλότερον ἀποτελεῖν
10 ἔργον, ὃ³ κἂν τὸ τυχὸν ἀνδράποδον ποιήσειεν, ἀλλ'
οἶον ἐπὶ τοῦ μεγάλου βασιλέως. ἱστορεῖται. τὸ
⟨γὰρ⟩ Καμβύσου³ Ξέρξου τε καὶ Δαρείου πρό-

---

¹ καὶ om. CGZ Lor.
² καὶ del. Wendland et Wilamowitz.
³ ὃ . . . Καμβύσου sic Lor. : ὃ ἐπὶ τοῦ μεγάλου βασιλέως οὐκ
ἂν τὸ τυχὸν ἀνδράποδον ποιήσειεν· ἀλλ' οἶον ἱστορεῖτο Καμβύσου
κτλ. Bekk. : v. Lor. ad loc.

of the whole heaven that he dwells : his power is experienced most of all by the body that is closest to him, less by the next, and so on down to the regions inhabited by us. So earth and the things that are on earth, being at the farthest remove from the help of God, seem to be feeble and discordant and full of confusion and diversity ; but nevertheless, in that it is the nature of the Divine to penetrate to every-thing, even the things around us occur in the same way as the things above us, each having a greater or smaller share of God's help in proportion to its distance from him. So it is better to suppose, what is also fitting and most appropriate to God, that the power which is based on the heavens is also the cause of preservation in the most remote things, as we may say, and indeed in everything, rather than that of itself it carries out its tasks on earth by penetrating and being present where it is not honourable or fitting that it should.[a] For it is not fitting even among men for princes to superintend each and every action that may have to be done—for example, the com-mander of an army or leader of a city or head of a household, if it were necessary to pack up bedding or perform some other menial task which could be done by any slave—but rather it is fitting that they should act in the manner which was adopted, according to the records, under the Great King.[b] The pomp of Cambyses and Xerxes and Darius was ordered on a

[a] The " power " has here become identified with god ; this is literally inconsistent with 397 b 19 above.
[b] Pseudo-Aristotle describes the King of Persia in his glory in the 6th/5th century B.C. He accords well with Herodotus's (i. 98) account of Deïoces' palace and régime at Ecbatana. This is a description of a fabulous past such as Aristotle would hardly have given.

398 a

σχῆμα εἰς σεμνότητος καὶ ὑπεροχῆς ὕψος μεγα-
λοπρεπῶς διεκεκόσμητο· αὐτὸς μὲν γάρ, ὡς λόγος,
ἵδρυτο ἐν Σούσοις ἢ Ἐκβατάνοις, παντὶ ἀόρατος,
15 θαυμαστὸν ἐπέχων βασίλειον οἶκον καὶ περίβολον
χρυσῷ καὶ ἠλέκτρῳ καὶ ἐλέφαντι ἀστράπτοντα·
πυλῶνες δὲ πολλοὶ καὶ συνεχεῖς πρόθυρά τε σύχνοις
εἰργόμενα σταδίοις ἀπ' ἀλλήλων θύραις τε χαλκαῖς
καὶ τείχεσι μεγάλοις ᾠχύρωτο· ἔξω δὲ τούτων
ἄνδρες οἱ πρῶτοι καὶ δοκιμώτατοι διεκεκόσμηντο,
20 οἱ μὲν ἀμφ' αὐτὸν τὸν βασιλέα δορυφόροι τε καὶ
θεράποντες, οἱ δὲ ἑκάστου περιβόλου φύλακες,
πυλωροί τε καὶ ὠτακουσταὶ λεγόμενοι, ὡς ἂν ὁ
βασιλεὺς αὐτός, δεσπότης καὶ θεὸς ὀνομαζόμενος,
πάντα μὲν βλέποι, πάντα δὲ ἀκούοι. χωρὶς δὲ
τούτων ἄλλοι καθειστήκεσαν προσόδων ταμίαι καὶ
25 στρατηγοὶ πολέμων καὶ κυνηγεσίων δώρων τε
ἀποδεκτῆρες τῶν τε λοιπῶν ἔργων ἕκαστοι κατὰ
τὰς χρείας ἐπιμεληταί. τὴν δὲ σύμπασαν ἀρχὴν τῆς
Ἀσίας, περατουμένην Ἑλλησπόντῳ μὲν ἐκ τῶν
πρὸς ἑσπέραν μερῶν, Ἰνδῷ δὲ ἐκ τῶν πρὸς ἔω,
διειλήφεσαν κατὰ ἔθνη στρατηγοὶ καὶ σατράπαι
30 καὶ βασιλεῖς, δοῦλοι τοῦ μεγάλου βασιλέως, ἡμε-
ροδρόμοι τε καὶ σκοποὶ καὶ ἀγγελιαφόροι φρυκτωρίων[1] τε ἐπόπτηρες. τοσοῦτος δὲ ἦν ὁ κόσμος,
καὶ μάλιστα τῶν φρυκτωρίων,[1] κατὰ διαδοχὰς
πυρσευόντων ἀλλήλοις[2] ἐκ περάτων τῆς ἀρχῆς
μέχρι Σούσων καὶ Ἐκβατάνων, ὥστε τὸν βασι-
35 λέα γινώσκειν αὐθημερὸν πάντα τὰ ἐν τῇ Ἀσίᾳ
398 b καινουργούμενα. νομιστέον δὴ τὴν τοῦ μεγάλου βασιλέως ὑπεροχὴν πρὸς τὴν τοῦ τὸν κόσμον

---

[1] φρυκτωρίων . . . φρυκτωρίων scripsi : φρυκτωριῶν . . .
φρυκτωριῶν Bekk.

grand scale and touched the heights of majesty and magnificence : the King himself, they say, lived in Susa or Ecbatana, invisible to all, in a marvellous palace with a surrounding wall flashing with gold, electrum and ivory ; it had a succession of many gate-towers, and the gateways, separated by many stades from one another, were fortified with brazen doors and high walls ; outside these the leaders and most eminent men were drawn up in order, some as personal bodyguards and attendants to the King himself, some as guardians of each outer wall, called Guards and the Listening-Watch, so that the King himself, who had the name of Master and God, might see everything and hear everything. Apart from these there were others appointed as revenue officials, leaders in war and in the hunt, receivers of gifts to the King, and others, each responsible for administering a particular task, as they were necessary. The whole Empire of Asia, bounded by the Hellespont in the West and the Indus in the East, was divided into nations under generals and satraps and kings, slaves of the Great King, with couriers and scouts and messengers and signals-officers. And such was the orderly arrangement of this, and particularly of the system of signal-beacons which were ready to burn in succession from the uttermost limits of the Empire to Susa and Ecbatana, that the King knew the same day all that was news in Asia. Now we must suppose that the majesty of the Great King falls short of the majesty of the god who rules the cosmos by as much

---

² πυρσευόντων ἀλλήλοις Lor. : πυρσευουσῶν ἀλλήλαις Bekk.

ἐπέχοντος θεοῦ τοσοῦτον καταδεεστέραν ὅσον τῆς
ἐκείνου τὴν τοῦ φαυλοτάτου τε καὶ ἀσθενεστά-
του ζῴου, ὥστε, εἴπερ ἄσεμνον ἦν αὐτὸν αὑτῷ
5 δοκεῖν Ξέρξην αὐτουργεῖν ἅπαντα καὶ ἐπιτελεῖν ἃ
βούλοιτο καὶ ἐφιστάμενον διοικεῖν, πολὺ μᾶλλον
ἀπρεπὲς ἂν εἴη θεῷ. σεμνότερον δὲ καὶ πρε-
πωδέστερον αὐτὸν μὲν ἐπὶ τῆς ἀνωτάτω χώρας
ἱδρῦσθαι, τὴν δὲ δύναμιν διὰ τοῦ σύμπαντος κόσμου διήκουσαν ἥλιόν τε κινεῖν καὶ σελήνην καὶ τὸν
10 πάντα οὐρανὸν περιάγειν αἴτιόν τε γίνεσθαι τοῖς
ἐπὶ τῆς γῆς σωτηρίας. οὐδὲν γὰρ ἐπιτεχνήσεως
αὐτῷ δεῖ καὶ ὑπηρεσίας τῆς παρ' ἑτέρων, ὥσπερ
τοῖς παρ' ἡμῖν ἄρχουσι τῆς πολυχειρίας διὰ τὴν
ἀσθένειαν, ἀλλὰ τοῦτο ἦν τὸ θειότατον, τὸ μετὰ
ῥαστώνης καὶ ἁπλῆς κινήσεως παντοδαπὰς ἀπο-
15 τελεῖν ἰδέας, ὥσπερ ἀμέλει δρῶσιν οἱ μηχανοποιοί,[1]
διὰ μιᾶς ὀργάνου σχαστηρίας πολλὰς καὶ ποικίλας
ἐνεργείας ἀποτελοῦντες. ὁμοίως δὲ καὶ οἱ νευρο-
σπάσται μίαν μήρινθον ἐπισπασάμενοι ποιοῦσι καὶ
αὐχένα κινεῖσθαι καὶ χεῖρα τοῦ ζῴου καὶ ὦμον καὶ
ὀφθαλμόν, ἔστι δὲ ὅτε πάντα τὰ μέρη, μετά τινος
20 εὐρυθμίας. οὕτως οὖν καὶ ἡ θεία φύσις ἀπό τινος

---

[1] μηχανοποιοί Z Lor. (*Notes*): μηχανοτέχναι Lor. (*De
Mundo*): μεγαλότεχνοι codd. pler. Bekk.

---

[a] It is not clear what kind of machine is meant; the

as the difference between the King and the poorest and weakest creature in the world, so that if it was beneath the dignity of Xerxes to appear himself to be the actual executor of all things, to carry out his wishes himself and to administer the Empire by personal supervision, it would be still more unbecoming for God. It is more noble, more becoming, for him to reside in the highest place, while his power, penetrating the whole of the cosmos, moves the sun and moon and turns the whole of the heavens and is the cause of preservation for the things upon the earth. He has no need of the contrivance and support of others, as rulers among us men need a multitude of workers because of their weakness; the most divine thing of all is to produce all kinds of result easily by means of a single motion, just like the operators of machines, who produce many varied activities by means of the machine's single release-mechanism.[a] In the same way too the men who run puppet-shows,[b] by pulling a single string, make the creature's neck move, and his hand and shoulder and eye, and sometimes every part of his body, according to a rhythmical pattern. So also the divine being,

" varied activities " probably refer to the various parts of the machine, and do not imply multi-purpose machines. *Mechanopoios* is most frequently used of military engineers. *Schasteria* is used of the release mechanism of catapults and ballistae. It is also used of the release-mechanism of automatic machines (such as Hero's machine for providing holy water); but in conjunction with *mechanopoios* and *organon* a reference to catapults, etc., seems more likely.

[b] Plato twice refers to puppets in the *Laws* (644 D, 804 B) as well as in the shadow-theatre of the *Republic* (514); in the *Laws* the puppets are worked by wires. Aristotle uses the example of puppets to illustrate a scientific theory in *De Gen. An.* 734 b 10 ff.

ἁπλῆς κινήσεως τοῦ πρώτου τὴν δύναμιν εἰς τὰ
συνεχῆ δίδωσι καὶ ἀπ' ἐκείνων πάλιν εἰς τὰ πορρωτέρω, μέχρις ἂν διὰ τοῦ παντὸς διεξέλθῃ· κι-
νηθὲν γὰρ ἕτερον ὑφ' ἑτέρου καὶ αὐτὸ πάλιν ἐκίνησεν
ἄλλο σὺν κόσμῳ, δρώντων μὲν πάντων οἰκείως ταῖς
25 σφετέραις κατασκευαῖς, οὐ τῆς αὐτῆς δὲ ὁδοῦ πᾶσιν
οὔσης, ἀλλὰ διαφόρου καὶ ἑτεροίας, ἔστι δὲ οἷς καὶ
ἐναντίας, καίτοι τῆς πρώτης οἷον ἐνδόσεως εἰς
κίνησιν μιᾶς[1] γενομένης· ὥσπερ ἂν εἴ τις ἐξ αἴπους[2]
ὁμοῦ ῥίψειε σφαῖραν καὶ κύβον καὶ κῶνον καὶ κύ-
λινδρον—ἕκαστον γὰρ αὐτῶν κατὰ τὸ ἴδιον κινη-
30 θήσεται σχῆμα—ἢ εἴ τις ὁμοῦ ζῷον ἔνυδρόν τε καὶ
χερσαῖον καὶ πτηνὸν ἐν τοῖς κόλποις ἔχων ἐκβάλοι·
δῆλον γὰρ ὅτι τὸ μὲν νηκτὸν ἁλόμενον εἰς τὴν
ἑαυτοῦ δίαιταν ἐκνήξεται, τὸ δὲ χερσαῖον εἰς τὰ
σφέτερα ἤθη καὶ νομοὺς διεξερπύσει, τὸ δὲ ἀέριον
ἐξαρθὲν ἐκ γῆς μετάρσιον οἰχήσεται πετόμενον,
35 μιᾶς τῆς πρώτης αἰτίας πᾶσιν ἀποδούσης τὴν
399 a οἰκείαν εὐμάρειαν. οὕτως ἔχει καὶ ἐπὶ κόσμου·
διὰ γὰρ ἁπλῆς τοῦ σύμπαντος οὐρανοῦ περιαγωγῆς
ἡμέρᾳ καὶ νυκτὶ περατουμένης ἀλλοῖαι πάντων δι-
έξοδοι γίνονται, καίτοι ὑπὸ μιᾶς σφαίρας περιεχομένων, τῶν μὲν θᾶττον, τῶν δὲ σχολαιότερον
5 κινουμένων παρά τε τὰ τῶν διαστημάτων μήκη
καὶ τὰς ἰδίας ἑκάστων κατασκευάς. σελήνη μὲν
γὰρ ἐν μηνὶ τὸν ἑαυτῆς διαπεραίνεται κύκλον αὐξο-
μένη τε καὶ μειουμένη καὶ φθίνουσα, ἥλιος δὲ ἐν
392

with a single movement of the nearest element distributes his power to the next part and then to the more remote parts until it permeates the whole. One thing is moved by another, and itself then moves a third in regular order, all things acting in the manner appropriate to their own constitution ; for the way is not the same for all things, but different and various, in some cases quite opposite, though the key of the whole movement, as it were, is set by a single opening note. For instance, a similar effect would be produced if one threw from a height a sphere, a cube, a cone and a cylinder, all together : each of them will move in the manner appropriate to its own shape ; or if one held in the folds of one's cloak an aquatic animal, a land animal and a winged animal, and then threw them out all together ; clearly the animal that swims will leap into its own habitat and swim away, the land animal will crawl off to its own customary pursuits and pastures, and the winged creature will rise from the ground and fly away high in the air ; a single cause has restored to all of them the freedom to move, each in the manner of its species. So too in the case of the cosmos : by means of a single revolution of the whole heaven completed in a night and a day, the various motions of all the heavenly bodies are initiated, and though all are embraced in one sphere, some move rapidly and others more slowly, according to their distances and their individual characters. For the moon completes its orbit in a month, waxing and waning and disappearing ; the sun and those which have an equal

---

[1] μιᾶς Lor. : μίαν codd. Bekk.
[2] αἴπους scripsi : ἄγγους codd. Lor. Bekk. : ὄρους Z : *per proclive* Ap.

ἐνιαυτῷ καὶ οἱ τούτου ἰσόδρομοι, ὅ τε Φωσφόρος
καὶ ὁ Ἑρμοῦ λεγόμενος, ὁ δὲ Πυρόεις ἐν διπλασίονι
10 τούτων χρόνῳ, ὁ δὲ Διὸς ἐν ἑξαπλασίονι τούτου,
καὶ τελευταῖος ὁ Κρόνου λεγόμενος ἐν διπλασίονι
καὶ ἡμίσει τοῦ ὑποκάτω. μία δὲ ἐκ πάντων ἁρ-
μονία συνᾳδόντων καὶ χορευόντων κατὰ τὸν οὐρανὸν
ἐξ ἑνός τε γίνεται καὶ εἰς ἓν ἀπολήγει, κόσμον
ἐτύμως τὸ σύμπαν ἀλλ' οὐκ ἀκοσμίαν ὀνομάσασα.
15 καθάπερ δὲ ἐν χορῷ κορυφαίου κατάρξαντος
συνεπηχεῖ πᾶς ὁ χορὸς ἀνδρῶν, ἔσθ' ὅτε καὶ γυ-
ναικῶν, ἐν διαφόροις φωναῖς ὀξυτέραις καὶ βαρυ-
τέραις μίαν ἁρμονίαν ἐμμελῆ κεραννύντων, οὕτως
ἔχει καὶ ἐπὶ τοῦ τὸ σύμπαν διέποντος θεοῦ· κατὰ
γὰρ τὸ ἄνωθεν ἐνδόσιμον ὑπὸ τοῦ φερωνύμως ἂν
20 κορυφαίου προσαγορευθέντος κινεῖται μὲν τὰ ἄστρα
ἀεὶ καὶ ὁ σύμπας οὐρανός, πορεύεται δὲ διττὰς
πορείας ὁ παμφαὴς ἥλιος, τῇ μὲν ἡμέραν καὶ
νύκτα διορίζων ἀνατολῇ καὶ δύσει, τῇ δὲ τὰς τέσ-
σαρας ὥρας ἄγων τοῦ ἔτους, πρόσω τε βόρειος καὶ
ὀπίσω νότιος διεξέρπων. γίνονται δὲ ὑετοὶ κατὰ
25 καιρὸν καὶ ἄνεμοι καὶ δρόσοι τά τε πάθη τὰ ἐν τῷ
περιέχοντι συμβαίνοντα διὰ τὴν πρώτην καὶ ἀρχέγονον[1] αἰτίαν. ἕπονται δὲ τούτοις ποταμῶν ἐκροαί,
θαλάσσης ἀνοιδήσεις, δένδρων ἐκφύσεις, καρπῶν
πεπάνσεις, γοναὶ ζώων, ἐκτροφαί τε πάντων καὶ
ἀκμαὶ καὶ φθίσεις, συμβαλλομένης πρὸς ταῦτα καὶ
30 τῆς ἑκάστου κατασκευῆς, ὡς ἔφην. ὅταν οὖν ὁ
πάντων ἡγεμών τε καὶ γενέτωρ, ἀόρατος ὢν ἄλλῳ

---

[1] ἀρχέγονον Wendland et Wilamowitz, Lor.: ἀρχαιόγονον
codd. Bekk.

course with it, namely Phosphorus (Venus) and Hermes (Mercury), complete their course in a year, Pyroeis (Mars) in twice this time, Zeus (Jupiter) in twelve years, and lastly the star called after Cronus (Saturn) in two and a half times the period of the one below it.[a] The single harmony that is produced by all these as they sing and dance in concert round the heavens has one and the same beginning and one and the same end, in a true sense giving to the whole the name of " order " (κόσμος) and not " disorder " (ἀκοσμία). Just as in a chorus at the direction of the leader all the chorus of men, sometimes of women too, join in singing together, creating a single pleasing harmony with their varied mixture of high and low notes, so also in the case of the god who controls the universe : the note is sounded from on high by him who might well be called the chorusmaster ; then the stars and the whole heavens move continually, and the all-shining sun makes his double journey, dividing night from day by his rising and setting, and bringing the four seasons of the year as he moves forwards to the North and back to the South. There are rains in due season, and winds, and falls of dew, and all the phenomena that occur in the atmosphere—all are the results of the first, original cause. These are followed by the springing up of rivers, the swelling of the sea, the growth of trees, the ripening of fruit, the birth of animals, the nurture, the prime and the decay of all things ; and the individual constitution of each thing contributes to the process, as I have said. So when the leader and author of all things, unseen except to the eye of

---

[a] *i.e.* thirty years. These periods correspond to those of Eudoxus (*ap.* Simplic. *In de Caelo* 495. 26 ff.).

399 a

πλὴν λογισμῷ, σημήνῃ πάσῃ φύσει μεταξὺ οὐρανοῦ
τε καὶ γῆς φερομένη, κινεῖται πᾶσα ἐνδελεχῶς ἐν
κύκλοις καὶ πέρασιν ἰδίοις, ποτὲ μὲν ἀφανιζομένη,
35 ποτὲ δὲ φαινομένη, μυρίας ἰδέας ἀναφαίνουσά τε
καὶ πάλιν ἀποκρύπτουσα ἐκ μιᾶς ἀρχῆς. ἔοικε
399 b δὲ κομιδῇ τὸ δρώμενον τοῖς ἐν πολέμου καιροῖς
μάλιστα γινομένοις, ἐπειδὰν ἡ σάλπιγξ σημήνῃ τῷ
στρατοπέδῳ· τότε γὰρ τῆς φωνῆς ἕκαστος ἀκού-
σας ὁ μὲν ἀσπίδα ἀναιρεῖται, ὁ δὲ θώρακα ἐνδύεται,
5 ὁ δὲ κνημῖδας ἢ κράνος ἢ ζωστῆρα περιτίθεται·
καὶ ὁ μὲν ἵππον χαλινοῖ, ὁ δὲ συνωρίδα ἀναβαίνει,
ὁ δὲ σύνθημα παρεγγυᾷ· καθίσταται δὲ εὐθέως ὁ
μὲν λοχαγὸς εἰς λόχον, ὁ δὲ ταξίαρχος εἰς τάξιν,
ὁ δὲ ἱππεὺς ἐπὶ κέρας, ὁ δὲ ψιλὸς εἰς τὴν ἰδίαν
ἐκτρέχει χώραν· πάντα δὲ ὑφ' ἕνα σημάντορα δο-
10 νεῖται κατὰ προστάξιν τοῦ τὸ κράτος ἔχοντος ἡγε-
μόνος. οὕτω χρὴ καὶ περὶ τοῦ σύμπαντος φρονεῖν·
ὑπὸ γὰρ μιᾶς ῥοπῆς ὀτρυνομένων ἁπάντων γίνεται
τὰ οἰκεῖα, καὶ ταύτης ἀοράτου καὶ ἀφανοῦς. ὅπερ
οὐδαμῶς ἐστιν ἐμπόδιον οὔτε ἐκείνῃ πρὸς τὸ δρᾶν
οὔτε ἡμῖν πρὸς τὸ πιστεῦσαι· καὶ γὰρ ἡ ψυχή, δι'
15 ἣν ζῶμέν τε καὶ οἴκους καὶ πόλεις ἔχομεν, ἀόρατος
οὖσα τοῖς ἔργοις αὐτῆς[1] ὁρᾶται· πᾶς γὰρ ὁ τοῦ βίου
διάκοσμος ὑπὸ ταύτης εὕρηται καὶ διατέτακται καὶ
συνέχεται, γῆς ἀρόσεις καὶ φυτεύσεις, τέχνης ἐπί-
νοιαι, χρήσεις νόμων, κόσμος πολιτείας, ἔνδημοι
πράξεις, ὑπερόριος πόλεμος, εἰρήνη. ταῦτα χρὴ
20 καὶ περὶ θεοῦ διανοεῖσθαι, δυνάμει μὲν ὄντος ἰσχυ-
ροτάτου, κάλλει δὲ εὐπρεπεστάτου, ζωῇ δὲ ἀθανά-
του, ἀρετῇ δὲ κρατίστου, διότι πάσῃ θνητῇ φύσει

reason, gives the sign to every moving thing between heaven and earth, everything is moved continually in its orbit and within its peculiar limits, now disappearing, now appearing, revealing innumerable different forms and concealing them again, all from a single beginning. The process is very like what happens, particularly at moments in a war, when the trumpet gives a signal in a military camp ; then each man hears the sound, and one picks up his shield, another puts on his breast-plate, and a third his greaves or helmet or belt ; one harnesses his horse, one mounts his chariot, one passes on the watchword ; the company-commander goes at once to his company, the brigadier to his brigade, the cavalryman to his squadron, and the infantryman runs to his own station ; all is stirred by a single trumpeter to a flurry of motion according to the orders of the supreme commander. It is a similar idea that we must have of the universe : by a single inclination all things are spurred to action and perform their peculiar functions—and this single agent is unseen and invisible. Its invisibility is no impediment either to its own action or to our belief in it ; for the soul, whereby we live and build households and cities, though it is invisible is perceived through its deeds : for all the conduct of life is discovered, arranged and maintained by the soul—the ploughing and sowing of land, the inventions of art, the use of laws, the order of a city's government, the activities of people in their own country, and war and peace with foreign nations. This is what we must also believe about God, who is mightiest in power, outstanding in beauty, immortal in life, and supreme in excellence, because

---

[1] αὐτῆς codd. Lor. : αὐτοῖς codd. al. Bekk.

399 b

γενόμενος ἀθεώρητος ἀπ' αὐτῶν τῶν ἔργων θεωρεῖται. τὰ γὰρ πάθη, καὶ τὰ δι' ἀέρος ἅπαντα καὶ
τὰ ἐπὶ γῆς καὶ τὰ ἐν ὕδατι, θεοῦ λέγοιτ' ἂν ὄντως
25 ἔργα εἶναι τοῦ τὸν κόσμον ἐπέχοντος· ἐξ οὗ, κατὰ
τὸν φυσικὸν Ἐμπεδοκλέα,

πάνθ' ὅσα τ' ἦν ὅσα τ' ἔσθ' ὅσα τ' ἔσται ὀπίσσω,
δένδρεά τ' ἐβλάστησε καὶ ἀνέρες ἠδὲ γυναῖκες
θῆρές τ' οἰωνοί τε καὶ ὑδατοθρέμμονες ἰχθῦς.

ἔοικε δὲ ὄντως, εἰ καὶ μικρότερον παραβαλεῖν,[1]
30 τοῖς ὀμφαλοῖς λεγομένοις τοῖς ἐν ταῖς ψαλίσιν
[λίθοις],[2] οἳ μέσοι κείμενοι κατὰ τὴν εἰς ἑκάτερον
μέρος ἔνδεσιν ἐν ἁρμονίᾳ τηροῦσι καὶ ἐν τάξει τὸ
πᾶν σχῆμα τῆς ψαλίδος καὶ ἀκίνητον. φασὶ δὲ καὶ
τὸν ἀγαλματοποιὸν Φειδίαν κατασκευάζοντα[3] τὴν ἐν
35 ἀκροπόλει Ἀθηνᾶν ἐν μέσῃ τῇ ταύτης ἀσπίδι τὸ
ἑαυτοῦ πρόσωπον ἐντυπώσασθαι, καὶ συνδῆσαι τῷ
100 a ἀγάλματι διά τινος ἀφανοῦς δημιουργίας, ὥστε ἐξ
ἀνάγκης, εἴ τις βούλοιτο αὐτὸ περιαιρεῖν, τὸ σύμπαν
ἄγαλμα λύειν τε καὶ συγχεῖν. τοῦτον οὖν ἔχει τὸν
λόγον ὁ θεὸς ἐν κόσμῳ, συνέχων τὴν τῶν ὅλων
5 ἁρμονίαν τε καὶ σωτηρίαν, πλὴν οὔτε μέσος ὤν,
ἔνθα ἡ γῆ τε καὶ ὁ θολερὸς τόπος οὗτος, ἀλλ' ἄνω
καθαρὸς ἐν καθαρῷ χωρῷ βεβηκώς, ὃν ἐτύμως καλοῦμεν οὐρανὸν μὲν ἀπὸ τοῦ ὅρον εἶναι τὸν ἄνω,
Ὄλυμπον δὲ οἷον ὁλολαμπῆ τε καὶ παντὸς ζόφου καὶ

---

[1] μικρότερον παραβαλεῖν Lor.: μικρότερον, παραβάλλειν τὸν
κόσμον Bekk.

[2] λίθοις del. Wendland et Wilamowitz.

[3] κατασκευάζοντα BDZ; [Arist.] *De Mir. Ausc.* 155; Lor.:
κατασκευαζόμενον Bekk.

though he is invisible to every mortal thing he is seen through his deeds. For it would be true to say that all the phenomena of the air, the land and the water are the works of the God who rules the cosmos; from whom, according to Empedocles [a] the natural philosopher,

> grows all that is and was and is yet to come,
> the trees and the whole race of men and women,
> beasts, birds and water-nurtured fish.

Though it is rather a humble comparison, he is truly like the so-called " keystones " of vaults, which lie in the middle and by their junction with each side ensure the proper fit of the whole structure of the vault and preserve its arrangement and stability. They say too that the sculptor Pheidias, when he was making the Athena on the Acropolis, carved his own face into the middle of her shield, and by some hidden trick of craftsmanship attached it to the statue in such a way that if anyone tried to remove it he inevitably destroyed and demolished the whole statue.[b] And this is the position held in the cosmos by God, who maintains the orderliness and preservation of the whole : except that he is not in the centre— for here lies the earth, this turbulent, troubled place —but high aloft, pure in a pure region, which we rightly call " heaven " (οὐρανός) because it forms the uppermost boundary (ὅρος . . . ἄνω) or " Olympus " because it shines brightly all over (ὁλολαμπής) and is

[a] Diels, *Vorsokr.*[6] 31 B 21.
[b] *Cf.* Ps.-Aristot. *De Mir. Ausc.* 846 a 19 ff.; Plut. *Pericles* 31 ; Cic. *Tusc. Disp.* i. 15. 34 ; Val. Max. viii. 14. 6. Cicero and Plutarch only mention the portrait. The statue was the gold and ivory Athena in the Parthenon. In several economic crises the gold was removed and melted down and later restored.

400 a

ἀτάκτου κινήματος κεχωρισμένον, οἷα γίνεται παρ'
10 ἡμῖν διὰ χειμῶνος καὶ ἀνέμων βίας, ὥσπερ ἔφη
καὶ ὁ ποιητὴς ["Ομηρος]¹

Οὔλυμπόνδ', ὅθι φασὶ θεῶν ἕδος ἀσφαλὲς αἰεὶ
ἔμμεναι· οὔτ' ἀνέμοισι τινάσσεται οὔτε ποτ'
ὄμβρῳ
δεύεται, οὔτε χιὼν ἐπιπίλναται, ἀλλὰ μάλ' αἴθρη
πέπταται ἀνέφελος, λευκὴ δ' ἐπιδέδρομεν αἴγλη.

15 συνεπιμαρτυρεῖ δὲ καὶ ὁ βίος ἅπας, τὴν ἄνω χώραν
ἀποδοὺς θεῷ· καὶ γὰρ πάντες ἄνθρωποι ἀνατείνομεν
τὰς χεῖρας εἰς τὸν οὐρανὸν εὐχὰς ποιούμενοι. καθ'
ὃν λόγον οὐ κακῶς κἀκεῖνο ἀναπεφώνηται

Ζεὺς δ' ἔλαχ' οὐρανὸν εὐρὺν ἐν αἰθέρι καὶ νεφέλησι.

20 διὸ καὶ τῶν αἰσθητῶν τὰ τιμιώτατα τὸν αὐτὸν
ἐπέχει τόπον, ἄστρα τε καὶ ἥλιος καὶ σελήνη·
μόνα τε τὰ οὐράνια διὰ τοῦτο ἀεὶ τὴν αὐτὴν σώ-
ζοντα τάξιν διακεκόσμηται, καὶ οὔποτε ἀλλοιω-
θέντα μετεκινήθη, καθάπερ τὰ ἐπὶ γῆς εὔτρεπτα
ὄντα πολλὰς ἑτεροιώσεις καὶ πάθη ἀναδέδεκται·
25 σεισμοί τε γὰρ ἤδη βίαιοι πολλὰ μέρη τῆς γῆς
ἀνέρρηξαν, ὄμβροι τε κατέκλυσαν ἐξιιίοι καταρ-
ραγέντες, ἐπιδρομαί τε κυμάτων καὶ ἀναχωρήσεις
πολλάκις καὶ ἠπείρους ἐθαλάττωσαν καὶ θαλάττας
ἠπείρωσαν, βιαί τε πνευμάτων καὶ τυφώνων ἔστιν
30 ὅτε πόλεις ὅλας ἀνέτρεψαν, πυρκαϊαί τε καὶ φλόγες
αἱ μὲν ἐξ οὐρανοῦ γενόμεναι πρότερον, ὥσπερ
φασίν, ἐπὶ Φαέθοντος τὰ πρὸς ἕω μέρη κατέφλεξαν,
αἱ δὲ πρὸς ἑσπέραν ἐκ γῆς ἀναβλύσασαι καὶ ἐκφυ-
σήσασαι, καθάπερ τῶν ἐν Αἴτνῃ κρατήρων ἀναρ-
ραγέντων καὶ ἀνὰ τὴν γῆν φερομένων χειμάρρου
400 b δίκην. ἔνθα καὶ τὸ τῶν εὐσεβῶν γένος ἐξόχως

400

removed from all darkness and disorderly motion such as occurs among us when there is a storm or a violent wind ; as the poet says,[a]

> To Olympus, where they say the gods' dwelling stands always safe ; it is not shaken by winds, nor drenched
> by showers of rain, nor does snow come near it ; always unclouded
> the air spreads out, and a white radiance lies upon it.

And all ages bear witness to this fact, and allot the upper region to God : all of us men stretch out our hands to the heavens when we pray. According to this reasoning, the following also has been well said [b] :

> To Zeus belongs the wide heaven in the clouds and the aether.

So also the same place is occupied by the most honoured of perceptible things, the stars and the sun and the moon ; and for this reason only the heavenly bodies always keep the same order and arrangement, and are never changed or altered ; while the transient things on earth admit many alterations and conditions. For violent earthquakes before now have torn up many parts of the earth, monstrous storms of rain have burst out and overwhelmed it, incursions and withdrawals of the waves have often made seas of dry land and dry land of seas ; sometimes whole cities have been over-turned by the violence of gales and typhoons ; flaming fires from the heavens once burnt up the Eastern parts, they say, in the time of Phaëthon, and others gushed and spouted from the earth, in the West, as when the craters of Etna erupted and spread over the earth like a mountain-torrent. Here, too, the race of pious

---

[a] Hom. *Od.* vi. 42-45.   [b] Hom. *Il.* xv. 192.

[1] Ὅμηρος om. Z Lor.

400 b

ἐτίμησε τὸ δαιμόνιον, περικαταληφθέντων ὑπὸ
τοῦ ῥεύματος διὰ τὸ βαστάζειν γέροντας ἐπὶ τῶν
ὤμων γονεῖς καὶ σώζειν· πλησίον γενόμενος ὁ τοῦ
πυρὸς ποταμὸς ἐξεσχίσθη παρέτρεψέ τε τοῦ φλογ-
5 μοῦ τὸ μὲν ἔνθα, τὸ δὲ ἔνθα, καὶ ἐτήρησεν ἀβλα-
βεῖς ἅμα τοῖς γονεῦσι τοὺς νεανίσκους.

Καθόλου δὲ ὅπερ ἐν νηὶ μὲν κυβερνήτης, ἐν
ἄρματι δὲ ἡνίοχος, ἐν χορῷ δὲ κορυφαῖος, ἐν πόλει
δὲ νομο⟨θέτη⟩ς,[1] ἐν στρατοπέδῳ δὲ ἡγεμών, τοῦτο
θεὸς ἐν κόσμῳ, πλὴν καθ' ὅσον τοῖς μὲν καματη-
10 ρὸν τὸ ἄρχειν πολυκίνητόν τε καὶ πολυμέριμνον, τῷ
δὲ ἄλυπον ἄπονόν τε καὶ πάσης κεχωρισμένον
σωματικῆς ἀσθενείας· ἐν ἀκινήτῳ γὰρ ἱδρυμένος
πάντα κινεῖ καὶ περιάγει, ὅπου βούλεται καὶ ὅπως,
ἐν διαφόροις ἰδέαις τε καὶ φύσεσιν, ὥσπερ ἀμέλει
καὶ ὁ τῆς πόλεως νόμος ἀκίνητος ὢν ἐν ταῖς τῶν
15 χρωμένων ψυχαῖς πάντα οἰκονομεῖ τὰ κατὰ τὴν
πολιτείαν· ἐφεπόμενοι γὰρ αὐτῷ δηλονότι ἐξίασιν
ἄρχοντες μὲν ἐπὶ τὰ ἀρχεῖα, θεσμοθέται δὲ εἰς τὰ
οἰκεῖα δικαστήρια, βουλευταὶ δὲ καὶ ἐκκλησιασ-
ταὶ εἰς συνέδρια τὰ προσήκοντα, καὶ ὁ μέν τις εἰς
τὸ πρυτανεῖον βαδίζει σιτησόμενος, ὁ δὲ πρὸς τοὺς
20 δικαστὰς ἀπολογησόμενος, ὁ δὲ εἰς τὸ δεσμωτή-
ριον ἀποθανούμενος. γίνονται δὲ καὶ δημοθοινίαι
νόμιμοι καὶ πανηγύρεις ἐνιαύσιοι θεῶν τε θυσίαι
καὶ ἡρώων θεραπεῖαι καὶ χοαὶ κεκμηκότων· ἄλλα
δὲ ἄλλως ἐνεργούμενα κατὰ μίαν πρόσταξιν ἢ νό-
μιμον ἐξουσίαν σώζει τὸ τοῦ ποιήσαντος ὄντως ὅτι

25 πόλις δ' ὁμοῦ μὲν θυμιαμάτων γέμει,
ὁμοῦ δὲ παιάνων τε καὶ στεναγμάτων,

---

[1] νομο⟨θέτη⟩ς coni. Lor. : νόμος codd. Bekk.

men was especially honoured by the divinity,[a] when they were overtaken by the stream of lava, because they were carrying their old parents on their shoulders to keep them safe ; for when the river of fire drew near them it was split in two and turned one part to this side and the other to that, and preserved unharmed both the young men and their parents.

In a word then, as the helmsman in his ship, as the charioteer in his chariot, as the leader in a chorus, as the lawgiver in a city, as the commander in a military camp, so is God in the cosmos, except that their command is wearisome and fraught with many movements and cares, while God rules without pain and toil, free from all bodily weakness : for he is established in the immovable, and moves and directs all things as and where he wishes, among the varieties of form and nature ; just as the law of the city, itself immovably established within the minds of those who observe it, disposes all the activities of the state : for in obedience to the law the magistrates go to their offices, the judges to their appropriate courts, the councillors and members of the assembly to their appointed meeting-places ; and one man goes to the prytaneum for his meals, another to the law-courts to defend himself, a third to prison to die. The law also ordains public feasts and annual festivals, sacrifices to the gods, cults of heroes and libations to the dead : and other varied activities, all arising from a single ordinance or authority of the law, accord well with these words of the poet [b] :

> The city is full of heavy incense-fumes,
> with crying for deliverance, and laments.

[a] The story is told of Amphion and his brother by the poet of the *Aetna* (625 f.)   [b] Soph. *O.T.* 4-5.

400 b

οὕτως ὑποληπτέον καὶ ἐπὶ τῆς μείζονος πόλεως,
λέγω δὲ τοῦ κόσμου· νόμος γὰρ ἡμῖν ἰσοκλινὴς ὁ
θεός, οὐδεμίαν ἐπιδεχόμενος διόρθωσιν ἢ μετά-
30 θεσιν, κρείττων δέ, οἶμαι, καὶ βεβαιότερος τῶν ἐν
ταῖς κύρβεσιν ἀναγεγραμμένων. ἡγουμένου δὲ
ἀκινήτως[1] αὐτοῦ καὶ ἐμμελῶς ὁ σύμπας οἰκονο-
μεῖται διάκοσμος οὐρανοῦ καὶ γῆς, μεμερισμένος
κατὰ τὰς φύσεις πάσας διὰ τῶν οἰκείων σπερμάτων
εἴς τε φυτὰ καὶ ζῷα κατὰ γένη τε καὶ εἴδη· καὶ γὰρ
401 a ἄμπελοι καὶ φοίνικες καὶ περσέαι

συκέαι τε γλυκεραὶ καὶ ἐλαῖαι,

ὥς φησιν ὁ ποιητής, τά τε ἄκαρπα μέν, ἄλλας δὲ
παρεχόμενα χρείας, πλάτανοι καὶ πίτυες καὶ πύξοι

κλήθρη τ' αἴγειρός τε καὶ εὐώδης κυπάρισσος,

5 αἵ τε καρπὸν ὀπώρας ἡδὺν ἄλλως δὲ δυσθησαύ-
ριστον φέρουσαι,

ὄχναι καὶ ῥοιαὶ καὶ μηλέαι ἀγλαόκαρποι,

τῶν τε ζῴων τά τε ἄγρια καὶ ἥμερα, τά τε ἐν ἀέρι
καὶ ἐπὶ γῆς καὶ ἐν ὕδατι βοσκόμενα, γίνεται καὶ
10 ἀκμάζει καὶ φθείρεται τοῖς τοῦ θεοῦ πειθόμενα
θεσμοῖς· "πᾶν γὰρ ἑρπετὸν πληγῇ νέμεται," ὥς
φησιν Ἡράκλειτος.

7. Εἷς δὲ ὢν πολυώνυμός ἐστι, κατονομαζόμενος
τοῖς πάθεσι πᾶσιν ἅπερ αὐτὸς νεοχμοῖ. καλοῦμεν
δὲ αὐτὸν καὶ Ζῆνα καὶ Δία, παραλλήλως χρώμενοι
15 τοῖς ὀνόμασιν, ὡς κἂν εἰ λέγοιμεν δι' ὃν ζῶμεν.
Κρόνου δὲ παῖς καὶ χρόνου λέγεται, διήκων ἐξ
αἰῶνος ἀτέρμονος εἰς ἕτερον αἰῶνα· ἀστραπαῖός
τε καὶ βρονταῖος καὶ αἴθριος καὶ αἰθέριος κεραύνιός

---

[1] ἀκινήτως Stob. Lor. : ἀεικινήτως codd. Bekk.

So it is, we must suppose, with that greater city, the cosmos : God is a law to us, impartial and admitting no correction or change ; he is surely a stronger and more stable law than those inscribed on tablets.[a] Under his motionless and harmonious guidance all the orderly arrangement of heaven and earth is administered, extending over all things through the seed proper to their kind, to plants and animals by genus and species ; vines, palms and *perseae*, " sweet figs and olives," [b] as the poet says, and those that bear no fruit but serve some other purpose, planes and pines and box-trees, " the alder, the poplar and the sweet-scented cypress-tree " [c] ; and those which in the autumn bring forth a harvest that is sweet but hard to store, " pears and pomegranates and apples with shining fruit " [d] ; and animals, some wild, some tame, that live in the air and on the earth and in the water,—all these come into being and grow strong and perish, obedient to the laws of god. " For every creature that crawls is driven to pasture by his goad," [e] as Heracleitus says.

7. Though he is one, he has many names, according to the many effects he himself produces. We call him both Zena and Dia, using the names interchangeably,[f] as if we were to say " Him through whom (διὰ ὅν) we live (ζῆν)." He is called the Son of Cronus and of time (Chronos), because he lives from endless age to another age ; God of Lightning and of Thunder, God of the Air and Aether, God of the Thunderbolt

---

[a] At Athens, tablets on which the early laws were written.
[b] Hom. *Od.* xi. 590.   [c] Hom. *Od.* v. 64.
[d] Hom. *Od.* xi. 589.
[e] Diels, *Vorsokr.*[6] 22 B 11.
[f] Ζῆνα and Δία are used interchangeably as accusatives of Zeus.

401 a

τε καὶ ὑέτιος ἀπὸ τῶν ὑετῶν καὶ κεραυνῶν καὶ τῶν
ἄλλων καλεῖται. καὶ μὴν ἐπικάρπιος μὲν ἀπὸ τῶν
20 καρπῶν, πολιεὺς δὲ ἀπὸ τῶν πόλεων ὀνομάζεται,
γενέθλιός τε καὶ ἑρκεῖος καὶ ὁμόγνιος καὶ πατρῷος[1]
ἀπὸ τῆς πρὸς ταῦτα κοινωνίας, ἑταιρεῖός τε καὶ
φίλιος καὶ ξένιος καὶ στράτιος καὶ τροπαιοῦχος,
καθάρσιός τε καὶ παλαμναῖος καὶ ἱκέσιος καὶ μειλί-
χιος, ὥσπερ οἱ ποιηταὶ λέγουσι, σωτήρ τε καὶ
25 ἐλευθέριος ἐτύμως, ὡς δὲ τὸ πᾶν εἰπεῖν, οὐράνιός
τε καὶ χθόνιος, πάσης ἐπώνυμος φύσεως ὢν καὶ
τύχης, ἅτε πάντων αὐτὸς αἴτιος ὤν. διὸ καὶ ἐν
τοῖς Ὀρφικοῖς οὐ κακῶς λέγεται

Ζεὺς πρῶτος γένετο, Ζεὺς ὕστατος ἀρχικέραυνος[2]·
Ζεὺς κεφαλή, Ζεὺς μέσσα, Διὸς δ' ἐκ πάντα
τέτυκται·

401 b
Ζεὺς πυθμὴν γαίης τε καὶ οὐρανοῦ ἀστερόεντος·
Ζεὺς ἄρσην γένετο, Ζεὺς ἄμβροτος ἔπλετο νύμφη·
Ζεὺς πνοιὴ πάντων, Ζεὺς ἀκαμάτου πυρὸς ὁρμή·
Ζεὺς πόντου ῥίζα, Ζεὺς ἥλιος ἠδὲ σελήνη·
5 Ζεὺς βασιλεύς, Ζεὺς ἀρχὸς ἁπάντων ἀρχικέραυ-
νος[3]·

πάντας γὰρ κρύψας αὖθις φάος ἐς πολυγηθὲς
ἐξ ἱερῆς κραδίης ἀνενέγκατο, μέρμερα ῥέζων.

Οἶμαι δὲ καὶ τὴν Ἀνάγκην οὐκ ἄλλο τι λέγεσθαι
πλὴν τοῦτον, οἱονεὶ ἀνίκητον αἰτίαν[4] ὄντα, Εἱμαρ-
10 μένην δὲ διὰ τὸ εἴρειν τε καὶ χωρεῖν ἀκωλύτως,

[1] πατρῷος Wendland et Wilamowitz, Lor.: πάτριος codd.
Bekk.

[2] ἀρχικέραυνος P Lor.: ἀργικέραυνος codd. cet. Bekk. (et
401 b 5).

and the Rain—he takes his name from all these things. He is called Harvest-God and City-God, God of the Family and the Household, God of Kinsmen and Ancestral God, because of his connexion with these things; God of Fellowship and Friendship and Hospitality, of War and Victory, of Purification and Vengeance, of Supplication and Grace, as the poets say, and in a true sense Saviour and Liberator. To sum up all, he is a God of Heaven and God of Earth,[a] and takes his name from every kind of nature and estate; for he himself is the cause of all. So it is rightly written in the Orphic books [b]:

Zeus is the first-born, Zeus is last, the lord of the lightning ;
Zeus is the head, Zeus the centre ; from Zeus comes all that is ;
Zeus is the foundation of the earth and the starry heavens ;
Zeus is a man, Zeus an immortal maid ;
Zeus is the breath of all things, Zeus is the spring of tireless fire ;
Zeus is the root of ocean, Zeus is the sun and moon ;
Zeus is king, Zeus is the master of all, the lord of the lightning.
For he hid all men away, and has brought them again to the lovely light
from the holiness of his heart, working great marvels.

I think too that Necessity ('Aνάγκη), is nothing but another name for him, as being a cause that cannot be defeated (ἀνίκητος) ; and Destiny (Εἱμαρμένη), because he binds things together (εἴρειν) and moves

---

[a] Χθόνιος usually implies the Underworld ; but Pseudo-Aristotle is probably stretching the meaning slightly to suit his own cosmology.

[b] Kern, *Fragm. Orph.* 21 a.

---

[3] vid. 401 a 28.

[4] αἰτίαν CG Lor. : οὐσίαν codd. al. Bekk.

Πεπρωμένην δὲ διὰ τὸ πεπερατῶσθαι πάντα καὶ
μηδὲν ἐν τοῖς οὖσιν ἄπειρον εἶναι, καὶ Μοῖραν μὲν
ἀπὸ τοῦ μεμερίσθαι, Νέμεσιν δὲ ἀπὸ τῆς ἑκάστῳ
διανεμήσεως, 'Αδράστειαν δὲ ἀναπόδραστον αἰτίαν
οὖσαν κατὰ φύσιν, Αἶσαν δὲ ἀεὶ οὖσαν. τά τε περὶ
15 τὰς Μοίρας καὶ τὸν ἄτρακτον εἰς ταυτό πως νεύει·
τρεῖς μὲν γὰρ αἱ Μοῖραι, κατὰ τοὺς χρόνους με-
μερισμέναι, νῆμα δὲ ἀτράκτου τὸ μὲν ἐξειργα-
σμένον, τὸ δὲ μέλλον, τὸ δὲ περιστρεφόμενον·
τέτακται δὲ κατὰ μὲν τὸ γεγονὸς μία τῶν Μοιρῶν,
"Ατροπος, ἐπεὶ τὰ παρελθόντα πάντα ἄτρεπτά ἐστι,
20 κατὰ δὲ τὸ μέλλον Λάχεσις—[εἰς]¹ πάντα γὰρ ἡ
κατὰ φύσιν μένει λῆξις—κατὰ δὲ τὸ ἐνεστὸς
Κλωθώ, συμπεραίνουσά τε καὶ κλώθουσα ἑκάστῳ
τὰ οἰκεῖα. περαίνεται δὲ καὶ ὁ μῦθος οὐκ ἀτάκτως.

Ταῦτα δὲ πάντα ἐστὶν οὐκ ἄλλο τι πλὴν ὁ θεός,
καθάπερ καὶ ὁ γενναῖος Πλάτων φησίν· '' ὁ μὲν δὴ
25 θεός, ὥσπερ ὁ παλαιὸς λόγος, ἀρχήν τε καὶ τελευτὴν
καὶ μέσα τῶν ὄντων ἁπάντων ἔχων, εὐθείᾳ περαίνει
κατὰ φύσιν πορευόμενος· τῷ δὲ ἀεὶ ξυνέπεται δίκη,
τῶν ἀπολειπομένων τοῦ θείου νόμου τιμωρός—ἧς
ὁ γενήσεσθαι² μέλλων μακάριός τε καὶ εὐδαίμων
ἐξ ἀρχῆς εὐθὺς μέτοχος εἴη.''

---

¹ εἰς del. Wendland et Wilamowitz.
² γενήσεσθαι Bücheler : εὐδαιμονήσειν vel εὐδαιμονῆσαι codd.
(cf. Plato, Laws 716 A).

without hindrance ; Fate (Πεπρωμένη), because all things are finite (πεπερατῶσθαι) and nothing in the world is infinite ; Moira, from the division of things (μερίζειν) ; Nemesis, from the allocation of a share to each (διανέμησις) ; Adrasteia—a cause whose nature is to be inescapable (ἀναπόδραστος αἰτία) ; and Aisa— a cause that exists for ever (ἀεὶ οὖσα). The story of the Fates (Μοῖραι) and the spindle also has much the same tendency : there are three Fates, corresponding to different times, and part of the yarn on their spindles is already completed, part is still to be spun, and part is now being worked. The past is the concern of one of the Fates, called Atropos, because all past things are irreversible (ἄτρεπτα) ; the future belongs to Lachesis, for a fortune allotted (λῆξις) by nature awaits all things ; the present is Clotho's province, who settles each man's own destiny and spins (κλώθειν) his thread. So the story ends, and it is well said.

All these things are no other than God, as the great Plato tells us [a] : " God, as the ancient story says, holding the beginning and the end and the middle of all things that are, moves by a straight path in the course of nature, bringing them to fulfilment ; and behind him, taking vengeance on all that fall short of the divine law, follows Justice—let no man be without this, even from his earliest years, if he is to live in blessed happiness."

[a] ὁ μέν . . . τιμωρός Laws 715 E—716 A ; ἧς . . . εἴη Laws 730 c. The antecedent of ἧς in Plato is ἀλήθεια. Pseudo-Aristotle runs the two passages together, making δίκη the antecedent of ἧς.

INDICES

ON SOPHISTICAL REFUTATIONS

References are given according to page, column and line of Bekker's Berlin edition, reproduced in this edition in the left-hand margin; otherwise references are to chapters (Roman figures).

I. GREEK INDEX

411

INDICES

ὁμωνυμία 165 b 26, 29 ff., 169 a
  23 ff., 170 a 14
ὄνομα (dist. πρᾶγμα) 165 a 7 ff.,
  b 29, 167 a 24 ; (dist. διά-
  νοια) 170 b 13 ff.
ὀργή 174 a 21

πειραστικός 165 b 1 ff., 169 b
  25 ff., 171 b 5 ff. See examination
προσῳδία 165 b 27, 166 b 1, 168
  a 27, 169 a 29, 177 b 3, 35 ff.,
  179 a 15

σημεῖον (ἀπόδειξις κατὰ τὸ σ.)
  167 b 10
σολοικισμός 165 b 15. See
  solecism
σοφιστικός 169 b 21, 171 b 7 ff.
  and passim ; σ. τέχνη=def.
  165 a 22

συκοφάντημα 174 b 9
συλλογισμός passim ; def. 165
  a 1
συμβεβηκός 166 b 22, 28 ff.,
  168 a 34 ff., b 27 ff., 169
  b 3 ff., 179 a 27
σύνθεσις 165 b 27, 166 a 22 ff.,
  168 a 27, 169 a 26, 177 a
  33 ff., 179 a 13

τετραγωνισμός, τετραγωνίζειν
  171 b 15 ff., 172 a 3 ff.

φιλονεικία 174 a 21
φιλοσοφία 175 a 5
φύσις (opp. νόμος) 173 a 7 ff.

ψευδογράφημα, ψευδογράφος,
  ψευδογραφεῖν 171 b 14 ff.,
  36 ff.

II. INDEX OF NAMES AND SUBJECTS

absolute (opp. qualified) use
  of expressions 166 b 23,
  37 ff., 168 b 11 ff., 169 b
  11 ff., 180 a 23
accent 165 b 27, 166 b 1,
  168 a 27, 169 a 29, XXI,
  179 a 15 ; written 177 b 3
accident (συμβεβηκός) 166 b
  22, 28 ff., 168 a 34 ff., b
  27 ff., 169 b 3 ff., 179 a 27
Achilles 166 a 38
ambiguity (ἀμφιβολία) 165 b
  26, 166 a 7 ff., XVII, 177
  a 16 ff., 179 a 20
Antiphon 172 a 7

babbling, see ἀδολεσχεῖν
breathings, written 177 b 4

Callias 176 a 1, 7
Callicles 173 a 8
Calliope 173 b 31
case-forms 173 b 26 ff., 182 a
  12 ff.
category-mistakes 168 a 26,
  169 a 35, 178 a 6 ff., b
  24 ff.
cause, fallacy of mistaken
  166 b 26, 167 b 21 ff.,
  169 b 14
Cleon 182 a 32
Cleophon 174 b 28
consequent (τὸ ἑπόμενον),
  fallacy of 166 b 25, 167 b
  1 ff., 168 b 28 ff., 169 b
  7 ff., XXVIII
contentious argument 165 b

INDICES

COMING-TO-BE AND PASSING-AWAY

For a Greek index see the edition by H. H. Joachim (*Aristotle on Coming-to-be and Passing-away*, Oxford, 1922), pp. 278-296.

INDEX OF NAMES AND SUBJECTS

References are given according to page, column and line of Bekker's Berlin edition, reproduced in this edition in the left-hand margin; otherwise references are to chapters (Roman figures for book, followed by Arabic figures for chapter).

ON THE COSMOS

References are given according to page, column and line of Bekker's Berlin Edition, reproduced in this edition in the left-hand margin.

I. GREEK INDEX

ἄγαλμα 400 a 1
ἀγαλματοποιός 399 b 33
ἀγγελιαφόρος 398 a 31
ἄγονος 394 a 20
ἀδράστεια 401 b 13
αἰθέριος 392 a 31, b 1, 401 a 17
αἰθήρ 392 a 5, 30, 393 a 3, 396 b 27
αἰθρία 394 a 22 ff.
αἴθριος 401 a 17
αἶπος 398 b 27
αἶσα 401 b 14
αἰτία 397 b 9, 398 a 4, b 35, 399 a 26, 401 b 9
αἰών 391 b 19, 397 a 10, 11, 31, b 8, 401 a 16
ἀκήρατος 392 a 9
ἀκμή 399 a 29
ἀκοντίζεσθαι 392 b 3, 395 b 4
ἀκοσμία 399 a 14
ἀκρόπολις 399 b 34
ἀλεεινός 392 b 8
ἀλήθεια 391 a 4
ἀλλοιοῦσθαι 392 b 9, 400 a 22
ἅλως 395 a 36 ff.
ἄμπωτις 396 a 26
ἀμφιφαής 395 b 14
ἀνάβλυσις 396 a 22

ἀνάγκη 391 b 21, 400 a 1, 401 b 8
ἀνάδοσις 395 a 9
ἀναθυμίασις 394 a 9, 19, b 6
ἀνακαμψίπνοος 394 b 36
ἀνάλυσις 394 b 17
ἀναπνοή 395 b 20, 397 a 32
ἀνάσχεσις 393 b 2
ἀνατολή 394 b 19, 23, 399 a 22
ἀναφύσημα 395 a 8, 396 a 21
ἀναφύσησις 395 b 21
ἀναχώρημα 396 a 18
ἀναχώρησις 400 a 27
ἀνδράποδον 398 a 10
ἀνήρ 399 a 16
ἄνθρωπος 392 a 17, b 19, 397 b 14, 398 a 6, 400 a 16
ἀνοίδησις 399 a 27
ἀντανακοπή 396 a 19
ἀνταρκτικός 392 a 3
ἀντίπαλος 394 a 22
ἀντίπορθμος 392 b 23
ἀντίστασις 397 a 1
ἄντρον 391 a 21
ἄξων 391 b 26
ἀπαρκτίας 394 b 29, 32
ἀπηλιώτης 394 b 23

419

INDICES

INDICES

393 a 5, 394 b 10, 397 a 17 ff.,
b 23, 398 b 3, 18, 30, 399 a
28, 400 b 34, 401 a 7
ζωοφόρος 392 a 11
ζωστήρ 399 b 4

ἡγεμών 391 b 6, 398 a 6, 399 a
30, 400 b 8
ἦθος 398 b 33
ἤλεκτρον 398 a 15
ἥλιος 392 a 29, 393 b 2, 395 a
33, b 2, 396 b 27, 397 a 9, 398
b 8, 399 a 8, 21, 400 a 21
ἡμέρα 397 a 13, 399 a 2, 22
ἡμεροδρόμος 398 a 30
ἡνίοχος 400 b 7
ἤπειρος 392 b 19, 21, 393 a 7,
b 19, 400 a 27
ἥρως 400 b 22

θαυμάζειν 391 b 1
θεῖος 391 a 1, 15, b 16, 392 a 9,
30 f., 397 b 19, 33, 398 b 13,
20
θεολογεῖν 391 b 4
θεός 391 b 10 ff., 393 a 4, 397 b
14 ff., 398 a 22, b 2, 6, 399 a
18, b 19, 400 a 3, 16, b 8, 22,
28, 401 a 10, b 23
θεραπείυ 400 b 22
θερινός 394 b 22 ff.
θέρος 395 a 2, 397 a 12
θέσις 391 a 5, 392 a 23, 394 b 5
θεσμοθέτης 400 b 16
θεσμός 401 a 10
θεωρία 391 a 24
θῆλυ, τό 396 b 9
θλῖψις 394 a 30
θρασκίας 394 b 30
θραῦσμα 394 b 4
θύελλα 395 a 6
θύρα 398 a 18

θυσία 400 b 22
θώραξ 399 b 4

ἶαπυξ 394 b 26
ἰδέα 394 a 16, 395 b 11, 397 a
27, 398 b 14, 399 a 34, 400
b 13
ἱερός 392 a 26
ἱζηματία 396 a 4
ἱκέσιος 401 a 23
ἱππεύς 399 b 7
ἵππος 399 b 5
ἶρις 395 a 30, 32 ff.
ἰσημερινός 394 b 24 ff.
ἰσθμός 393 b 25 ff.
ἰσομοιρία 396 b 35
ἱστορία 391 b 6

καθάρσιος 401 a 23
καικίας 394 b 22, 28, 395 a 1
καινουργούμενα, τά 398 a 35
καιρός 396 a 27, 397 a 26, 399 a
24, b 1
καπνώδης 394 a 13
καρπός 399 a 28, 401 a 19
καταιγίς 395 a 5
κατασκευή 398 b 24, 399 a 6, 30
κάτοπτρον 395 a 34
κέρας 393 b 5, 399 b 8
κεραύνιος 401 a 17
κεραυνός 392 b 12, 394 a 18, 395
a 22 ff., 397 a 21, 401 a 18
κίνησις 391 b 5, 16, 392 a 30,
b 2, 7, 398 b 13 ff.
κιρκίας 394 b 31
κλίμα 392 a 3
κνημίς 399 b 4
κοίλωμα 395 b 34
κόλπος 393 a 21, b 3 ff., 394 b
15, 398 b 31
κομήτης 392 b 4, 395 a 32,
b 9

ON THE COSMOS

INDICES

II. ENGLISH INDEX

427

INDICES

earth (element) 392 b 14, 33, 396 b 30

earth, the 391 b 13, 397 a 24, b 30

earthquakes 395 b 36, 397 a 28 ff., 400 a 25

Ecbatana 398 a 10 n., 14, 34

Egypt 394 a 1

Egyptian Sea 393 a 29

elements 392 a 8, b 35, 396 b 34

Empedocles 396 b 12 n., 399 b 25

England 393 b 12

Ephialtes, see Giants

Erythraean Sea 393 b 4 n.

Etesian winds 395 a 2

Etna 395 a 24 n., b 21, 400 a 33 and n.

Euboea 393 a 13

Euronotus (wind) 394 b 33

Europe 393 b 22 ff.

Eurus 394 b 20, 24

exhalations 394 a 9 and n.

Fate (πεπρωμένη) 401 b 10

Fates, the 401 b 15

fire (element) 392 b 2, 395 a 20, 396 b 30

fire, subterranean 395 b 19 ff.

flames 392 b 3

floods 397 a 28

frost 392 b 10, 394 a 16, 26, 397 b 1

Galatian Gulf 393 b 9

Galatian Sea 393 a 27

gales 392 b 11

Giants 391 a 11 n., 395 a 24 n.

Gibraltar 392 b 23 n.

God 391 b 11, 397 b 14 ff., 398 a 22

gods 391 b 15, 397 b 17

gods, abode of the 391 b 16, 393 a 4

hail 392 b 11, 394 a 16, b 1

halo 395 a 36

harmony 396 b 8 ff., 25

heavens (οὐρανός), 391 b 16 ff., 400 a 7

Helice, Achaia 396 a 21 and n.

Hellespont 393 b 1, 398 a 27

Hera 392 a 28

Heracleitus 396 b 20, 401 a 11

Heracles, Pillars of 393 a 24, b 10, 23, 32

Hermes (planet), see Mercury

Hero 398 b 15 n.

Herodotus 398 a 10 n.

Hyrcanian Sea, see Caspian Sea

Iapyx (wind) 394 b 26

ice 394 a 25

Ierne, see Ireland

India 392 b 23 n.

India, Gulf of 393 b 3

Indians 393 b 14

Indus 398 a 28

inhabited world (oikoumene) 392 b 20 ff.; dimensions of 393 b 18

inhabited worlds, plurality of 392 b 23 ff.

Ireland 393 b 13

islands 392 b 20, 393 a 8 ff.

ON THE COSMOS

INDICES

D0914231